LEADERSHIP IN AN INTERDEPENDENT WORLD:
THE STATESMANSHIP OF ADENAUER,
DE GAULLE, THATCHER, REAGAN
AND GORBACHEV

# Leadership in an Interdependent World: The Statemanship of Adenauer, De Gaulle, Thatcher, Reagan and Gorbachev

*Ghiţa Ionescu*

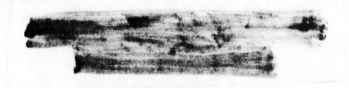

Westview Press
BOULDER & SAN FRANCISCO

**Longman Group UK Limited,**
Longman House, Burnt Mill, Harlow,
Essex CM20 2JE, England
*and Associated Companies throughout the world.*

Published in 1991 in the United States by Westview Press
5500 Central Avenue, Boulder, Colorado 80301, USA

ISBN 0–582–07852–0 (Longman USA)
ISBN 0–582–05302–1 (Longman ppr)
ISBN 0–8133–1398–8 (Westview HC)
ISBN 0–8133–1399–6 (Westview PB)

First published 1991

**British Library Cataloguing in Publication Data**
Ionescu, Ghita
  Leadership in an interdependent world:
  Adenauer, De Gaulle, Thatcher, Reagan and Gorbachev.
  1. Government
  I. Title
  350

  ISBN 0–582–07852–0 csd
  0–582–053021 ppr

**Library of Congress Cataloging in Publication Data**

CIP data available upon request

Set in 10/12 pt Bembo
  Produced by Longman Singapore Publishers (Pte) Ltd.
  Printed in Singapore

# Contents

# Contents

# Preface

We are living in an age when people and peoples with an interest in politics are particularly concerned by the question whether their states are losing their absolute sovereignty and are being constrained to submit to transnational, indeed now global interdependence. This book may have the calming effect of showing them with examples of contemporary statesmanship, that there is nothing either new, or wrong, with this change in ultimate political responsibility. At least since the second world war, and the subsequent information revolution, political leaders reputed to be staunch defenders of their states' sovereignty, such as Adenauer, de Gaulle, Mrs Thatcher, Reagan, and Gorbachev, have practised the politics of interdependence. As the book attempts to explain, sovereignty has been increasingly relativized and interdependence is the dominant fact of life of modern politics.

The calming effect of such a revelation, if it is one, can be compared with what happens to a patient, told by his physician that what seems to him to be a new and critical condition in his health is in fact a chronic and even hereditary condition which has helped him all his life; or it can be compared with the shock to an old football spectator when he sees that methods of tackling which were considered a 'foul' in his youth have now been incorporated into the rules of the game. But the classic and most appropriate comparison is with Molière's hero, Monsieur Jourdain who, eager to learn the art of literature, was told that while certain rules had to be observed in order to write poetry, prose was something which even he spoke whenever he opened his mouth. The realization and acceptance of such surprising facts requires of course a mental double-take, hence the insistence, in each of the essays on each of the five leaders, on the conflicts between tendencies within their own statesmanship, and on modern statesmanship and political judgment in general.

This also explains the many years this book took to write, and the imperfections which it still shows: critics who like to point out textual mistakes will have plenty of opportunities. And this also explains my haste to urge that my friends who so generously helped me to correct as many errors as possible, and who warned me of the dangers inherent in trying to compress into one volume what could well take up whole shelves of books, should be exonerated from all share of responsibility. The errors are all mine.

The list of those who helped me with this book is long and best broken down into different groups. The first comprises those who read most of, or the whole of, the manuscript: Professor Isabel de Madariaga, M. Émile Noël, Sir Ian Gilmour, Professor Benjamin Barber, Mr Chris Harrison, and last but certainly not least, my wife, Valence. The second group comprises those friends who helped me with specific parts of the book: Mr. Nicholas Bayne, the OECD and Foreign Office expert on economic problems; Professor Susan Strange on the new philosophy of international political economy; Mr John Campbell, of the Council on Foreign Relations, on the chapter on Reagan and Mr G. E. Llewelyn, Director at the OECD in Paris and author of studies on interdependence. The third group is composed of friends and colleagues with whom I discussed my work in general terms at its inception, and as it progressed: Professors Roger Williams, David Marquand, Geraint Parry, and John Pinder.

I must also express my gratitude to the International Political Science Association, in which, for the last twenty years I have been chairman of the Research Committee on European Unification, and for, and with which, I edited the book *Sovereignty and Integration*; to the European Commission, for and with which I undertook many research projects and edited the book *The European Alternatives*; to the European Parliament, where I conducted in 1989, with the help of a great number of Euro-MPs and EP experts, an inquiry into the transition from the national to the European political judgement; and to the OECD in Paris.

In a different way, I have great pleasure in expressing my gratitude to the Leverhulme Foundation for a very generous grant at the very beginning of this work – and I apologize for producing it after so long a time.

For more technical reasons I am grateful to my colleague on *Government and Opposition*, Mrs Rosalind Jones, and to Joy Cash, from

Longmans, who have all shown such patience and kind attention during the long and painful gestation. And I also thank the staffs of the libraries of the Royal Institute of International Affairs, the London School of Economics, the University of Manchester, and the London Library for their help in many ways.

G.I.
Manchester, December 1990

# Acknowledgements

The publishers are grateful to Faber and Faber Ltd for granting their permission to use copyright material from "Choruses from 'The Rock' – 1934" from *Collected Poems 1909–1962* by T. S. Eliot.

# Introduction

> *Where is the wisdom we have lost in knowledge?*
> *Where is the knowledge we have lost in information?*
>
> T. S. Eliot

In both form and substance this book is an inquiry into modern statesmanship or into statesmanship in the age of interdependence.

In form, it consists of an examination, even if brief, of the statesmanship of five people, namely Konrad Adenauer, Charles de Gaulle, Mrs Margaret Thatcher, Ronald Reagan and Mikhail Gorbachev, with special reference to the way in which they adapted themselves to the new policies of interdependence. These five personalities deserve to be called statesmen because they fulfilled the conditions which, ever since Plato first compared the two, distinguished them from mere politicians. Thus they all stayed in power for a long time – an average of a decade for the first four, while in his first five years Gorbachev has moved at breath-taking speed; during their period in government they have all frequently proved their courage and decisiveness, as well as the consistency of their political aims; and because of their achievements they have succeeded in leaving a mark on the history of their respective states, as well as on world history, commensurate with the importance of their states during the period of some forty-five years (1944–90) of 'cold war' in which they were active. All these qualities are essential to statesmanship.

But what they also had in common, and what makes the point of this inquiry, is that they all had to exert their statesmanship in the new circumstances of *interdependence* – one of the concepts to be explained in this introduction – and to adapt their *political cognition* – another such concept – to the changed conditions of the sovereignty of the state, and in general to the new processes of policy-making. By comparing the different performances of the five in the conclusions of the book it will be easier to extrapolate the similarities between them and to answer such overall questions as: how successfully did each one

1

adjust his or her statesmanship to the new techniques, mentalities and perspectives? Or, conversely, how much were they, like M. Jourdain who was surprised to learn that when he spoke it was in prose, simply acting in conformity with the laws of interdependence without knowing it, while publicly arguing that they were only fighting for the sovereignty of their respective states?

For, in substance, this inquiry is directed at the examination, with the help of these historical cases, of the more general problem of the changes imposed by interdependence on the processes of policy-making and therefore on the very concepts of state, statesman and statesmanship. The three notions are linked by etymological as well as by chronological filiations. The root concept, 'state' itself, is conditioned by history. It came into full and legitimate existence only in the nineteenth century. (In order not to encumber these introductory pages with a survey of the controversies on the date of birth of the 'state', let us remember that even the *Encyclopaedia Britannica*, in the classic edition of 1911, the repository of scholarly knowledge at the time, stressed that: 'In England we may say that the notion of state, from the constitutional point of view, is still inchoate . . .') But by the twentieth century, interdependence was already visibly conditioning the state and restricting sovereignty in the industrialized society, and through it in the world as a whole. By the middle of the century the winds of the information revolution were blowing through the formally state-centred economic and political structures. Obviously what was required was an adjustment of political cognition to the new conditions of interdependence, the two concepts to the explanation of which we now turn.

Political cognition[1] like all forms of cognition, consists of judgement and knowledge, Neurophysiologists explain that the *functions* of the brain remain the same – although it does adapt to cultural changes – and that the breadth of comprehension and the capacity of human mental storage cannot be endlessly amplified. This puts political judgement – and indeed all kinds of judgement – at an obvious disadvantage, and leads it to lag behind the other element of political cognition, political knowledge. For, in the meantime, political knowledge has grown, and continues to grow in quantity and quality, rapidly accumulating in artificial intelligence masses of information too complex to be digested by normal political judgement. What, as a result, is now necessary is that political judgement should catch up with the ever advancing waves of interdisciplinary political knowledge. This is now tentatively achieved by using artificial intelligence to put some synoptical order into the expanding quantities of information, but this is not to say that the human brain masters it all.

Without anticipating the conclusions which will be drawn from the studies in this book, one may nevertheless sketch in the most evident change to be expected in the exercise of political judgement and in political practice, which is that it should be more deductive than inductive. 'Theorists of international relations distinguish two approaches to understanding foreign policy. "Inside-out" explanations emphasize domestic factors, such as political coalitions, whereas "outside-in" explanations focus on systematic forces, such as the international power structures,' write Putnam and Bayne in their excellent book *Hanging Together*[2].

But that cannot be properly discussed before examining how interdependence affects the old political judgement and, obviously, what interdependence is.

## THE CONCEPT OF INTERDEPENDENCE

Because of the natural tendency of the human mind and of human speech to use new expressions anachronistically for old, analogous concepts (as, for instance, polis d state) interdependence, too, seems to have a familiar, even legendary, ring. There was a prescience, one might almost call it a prefiguration of what we now call 'interdependence' from the very earliest days when, in Greek mythology, Hermes was the god of communication, of trade *and* of the art of politics notably international policy; and, later, when the Christian Church proclaimed the universal human *confraternity* summed up in John Donne's warning that 'the bell tolls for thee'. All the universalistic, pacifistic and federalistic ideas sprang like hope from those aspirations. But they were all normative, indeed, idealistic, whereas interdependence, as we see it today, is pragmatic, empirical and may be 'nasty and brutish', according to how it is played.

Historically, too, one is rightly reminded that Greece and Rome, the Church and the Empire, feudal English and French lords, the kingdoms of France, Spain, England and their conflicting territorial ambitions, and above all the worldwide trade and colonization which led to the conflicts between the nineteenth-century European powers, were 'interdependent' in practice; while the thought of the

3

French Revolution and of the Napoleonic Empire which unsettled the European mind, and conversely the thinking at the Congress of Vienna which tried to steady Europe again, foretold to a certain extent what was to become the theory of interdependence. But in reality these were still partial and parallel developments, lacking in real correspondence and in cultural cohesion.

What is submitted here is that interdependence is such a new, modern and general political phenomenon that not only could it not have been established before technology had created the conditions for its appearance, i.e. in the last 50 years or so, but also that because of its rapidity and its universal power, its meaning was and is not easy for traditional human cognition to assimilate, generally and completely.

The definition of interdependence is particularly complex and it might be useful to precede it by outlining its principal specific features. Thus:

- interdependence is the outcome of the micro-electric and the communication information revolutions of the twentieth century. These technological revolutions have in turn inexorably generated the phenomenon of 'globalization', that is the linkage of common human interests over the whole planet, and now also over outer space, explored and exploited by human interest. Interdependence is fully achieved only when globalization is completed; and, conversely, once globalization has been achieved, interdependence becomes a new dimension of human interest. After interdependence human activities which still preserve some of the old historical parallelisms and geographical separations increasingly converge into an overall and continuous relation of causality.

- that universal relation of causality is the sum total of all the principal political, social, cultural and, last but not least, economic, human activities linked in a perpetual motion of chain-reactions of all parts of the world accessible to 'information'. But what is characteristic is that this sum total is less than, and different from, its synergic result. This becomes a superior factor in itself, what I prefer to call a circumambience of all those human activities which, chasing each other in a *perpetuum mobile*, alters them by its very mobility. The decision by the USSR, after a long period of 'stagnation', to dissolve its 'anti-capitalist' autarchy in order to revivify itself in the stream of cultural and economic interdependence, is one of the most recent examples of how ineluctable interdependence is. The unprecedented quasi-unanimity of the

United Nations against Iraq's old-fashioned invasion of Kuwait is an even more recent example.

– finally, the ubiquity of interdependence cannot but flatten and relativize such proud concepts as state, sovereignty and, yes, power itself. Neither their institutions nor their functions risk being abolished but, to use a modern expression, they are flexibilized so as to be manageable under the cover and in the speedy rhythm of the circumambient interdependence. Theorists and practitioners of such concepts – and notably the statesmen – inclined as they are to keep the absolute significance of these concepts, find these exercises in relativization and interconnection difficult to understand, let alone accept. This is not, though, the first time that statesmen found that the 'time was out of joint' for them. Other historical 'breaks' have caught statesmen unaware. Marcus Aurelius, the philosopher–emperor, meditated, very intelligently, on everything with the sole exception of the advent of Christianity, which was undermining his empire, under his very throne. Conversely, Richelieu, still considered as 'the statesman par excellence', was incapable of dissociating his belief in 'raison d'état' from his belief in the divine origin of the monarchy. And Neville Chamberlain, a most lucid statesman, promised 'peace in our time' when Fascist and Axis aggression was already in full swing in Europe and in the Far East. It so happens, as we shall see, that the 'qualitative jump' made by scientific revolutions in our time is putting political judgement to a severe test now too.

The brief definition of interdependence is therefore: Interdependence is the effect of the scientific information revolution of the mid twentieth century on the conduct of human, domestic and international affairs, which links those affairs so closely that they become, by synergy, a circumambiance superior to, and different from, their sum total.

The definition itself must be situated in its double context. For, first, it must be recognized to be a compilation of the definitions made by earlier theorists. And second, it has already ingested as *faits accomplis* the great technological, political and cultural changes which established interdependence, and which will be described here as 'the mutations' of the 1970s.

In its more modern sense the word appeared sometime during and after the First World War (itself one of the most dramatic embodiments of interdependence), and according to bibliographical researchers, it was 'coined' by Norman Angell the by now almost forgotten author of *The Great Illusion* (1916) and *The Conditions of Allied Success* (1918). Angell also defined interdependence as 'the linkage of fates'. In official terminology it was first used in the 1957 Kennedy–Macmillan Declaration of Common Purpose, 'which Harold Macmillan wanted to entitle "Declaration of Inter-dependence"',[3] and which contained the ringing sentence: 'The countries of the free world are interdependent.'

The contradiction between sovereignty and interdependence has particularly struck national and world public opinion. Sovereignty, as we know, has two aspects, epitomized since the days of the Romans in the two faces of Janus. They are external and internal sovereignty. Interdependence curbs each of them separately and both of them together. It challenges the external sovereignty of the state, whatever its size and location, by constraining it on the one hand to co-ordinate its policies and policy-making processes with other states, and thus to *share* power with them; and on the other hand by interpenetrating the national societies, constitutionally under the jurisdiction of the relevant states, through economic, cultural (knowledge and technology), and political *transnationalization*, which is the motor of interdependence. If examples are still needed, the European Community illustrates inter-statal power-sharing to a sufficient extent already; and the second case is illustrated by the multi-national corporations, by transnational mergers, and even more by the international dimension of any major event happening in any state. More easily perceived perhaps by the general public are the sovereignty-defying fumes of Chernobyl, the domino-like worldwide fall on all stock exchanges in October 1987, the conflict between European and Muslim countries around a novel published in Britain, the capitulation of the USSR to capitalism, and the worldwide anti-Iraq stance.

But interdependence also curbs the national internal sovereignty of modern states, although in a quite different way. The representative system of government, the only form of democracy which has proved practicable in the genuine meaning of government of and by the people, makes parliament into the incontestable seat of sovereignty. Parliament, the legislative power, issues the laws, which are applied by the executive power, in a manner supervised by the judiciary. These are the sole instruments of order and stability in any constitutional state. But the developed constitutional states have now passed through three successive industrial revolutions, and as a result a new form of representation, the functional or corporate representation, has made its political impact. One can take as an example of this development any local strike, which then takes on the proportions of a national and sometimes an international crisis in a given branch of industry; or the uncontrollable 'marketing' of multinational enterprises which defy all sovereignties; or the influence of 'wage-push' pressure on national and international financial and economic conditions, etc.

Gradually, this led to the establishment of the welfare society, and of its 'states' in which the elaboration of policies and the actual processes of policy-making constrain the representative political government to 'share power' with the corporate institutions. A more direct, tripartite, system of 'concerted' policy-making process: government–enterprises–socio-economic and pressure groups is in operation in states like the Federal Republic of Germany, or Sweden, or in the French Plan. The corporate pressure has thus displaced some of the powers of the sovereign state towards civil society. On the other hand, privatization and deregulation first extensively practised in Britain and later in most European industrial states is, in reality, and in spite of its motivations being quite opposed to those of neo-corporativism, yet another way of transferring sovereignty from state to society in conditions of private property and private initiative.

R. O. Keohane and J. S. Nye described 'interdependence' as *mutual* 'vulnerability' in a strategic sense, and 'sensitivity', in the socio-economic sense, of all units of rule in the contemporary world. But they completed their theory with that of 'complex interdependence', which they describe as presenting three main characteristics: (1) multiple channels, which can be inter-state, transgovernmental, and transnational ('when we relax the assumption that states are the only units'); (2) absence of hierarchy among issues which 'means among other things, that military security does not consistently dominate the agenda' and, in some ways repeating the second point, (3) the minor role of military force, 'force being often not an appropriate way of achieving other goals (such as economic or ecological welfare)'.[4] Described in this way, 'complex interdependence' comprises such narrower notions of subordinate categories as *interdependencies*, 'linkages', 'interactions', *dependencia*, 'interconnectedness' and even 'integration' as long as processes of integration remain regional and not worldwide.

Yet Keohane and Nye's basic description needed completion in two major respects. It needed a clearer distinction between mutual dependence between states and interdependence as a system of chain reactions and relations of causality, a system which is more than the sum of all these relations, and which functions as a synergic system over and above all component actors: states and other organizations. And it needed a clearer and more complete description of its relation with power in general. In this respect, in spite of the competition among important authors[5] who have discussed this issue, I shall concentrate on two theories which seem to me most relevant to complete the definition of interdependence.

Peter Willetts[6] insists that a clearer distinction should be drawn between 'mutual dependence' as a relation between given actors (more often than not states and on issues of interest to them) and interdependence as a synergic system (or what I prefer to call a circum-ambiency) superior to all such interdependencies, in the plural, and acting as a self-propelling system above all of them. He expresses this felicitously when he writes, for instance:

Actor interdependence exists for a set of actors, to each of which the same policy question is salient when each of the actors is dependent for that question upon one or more of the other members of the set . . . Interdependence as defined above rules out purely hierarchical relationships . . . The formal definition of dependence and interdependence makes plain a level of analysis question. *Dependence is a property of a single actor, while interdependence is a property of a system* . . . Individual actors may be vulnerable, but the system is not vulnerable when particular actors are constrained.

This is also why one can have phases of negative or positive, hostile or co-operative, orderly or chaotic interdependencies which can pass without interrupting or hindering the *perpetuum mobile* of the global process of interdependence.

Interdependence is, by its own logic, opposed to either historical or economic determinism. Its fundamental logic is to comprehend historically the myriad autonomous, even accidental, human actions. In economics its logic is to subsume in one world market all the hazardous activities of all the markets in the world, market being a notion which Marx considered as the source of all evils and therefore bound to be eliminated. If anything is determining in the theory of interdependence it is human action.

It was here that Professor Susan Strange[7] insisted most rewardingly on the evident primacy of the element of 'knowledge' in the development of interdependence. Already aware of how the theories of pluralism, the backbone of democratic politics, have relativized the old concept of power, Strange casts further doubts on the existence of such a concept *per se*. Looking at it from the point of view of interdependence and of the interdisciplinary International Political Economy, Strange describes power anatomically – especially the Leviathan-like power of the state which old schools of political theory (Hobbes), and new schools too, like to consider as predominant. She then dissects it into four interrelated and mutually conditioned structures. These are, according to her, the structure of security (or international order); of production (the foundation of almost all political economies); of finance (the new, revolutionary 'credit and monetary systems'), and last but not least, as singled out in the first pages of this introduction, of knowledge ('what is believed, what is known and perceived as understood and the channels by which beliefs, ideas and knowledge are communicated').

Of these four structures, as Strange shows, knowledge is the first and foremost not only because it was recognized, ever since Socrates, as the principal and undetermined activity of the free human mind (even if that was denied by Freudian and Marxist determinisms); but also because now it is almost synonymous with the principal cause of change in modern society, the information and scientific revolution. As Strange does, it is essential to lay the accent on knowledge, as the foremost condition of power in the modern world, and in consequence on political judgement as the one means by which 'power' could be won or lost in the age of interdependence.

## THE MUTATIONS OF THE 1970s

At this point it is useful to question two assumptions which underlie our argument, and which have been taken for granted. The first is: why is it asserted that the seemingly unprecedented difficulties from which the average political judgement suffers when attempting to interpret the quality and quantity of new political knowledge appeared so suddenly in the second part of the twentieth century? And the second question, which derives from the first is: which were the historical events and developments or what is called here the 'mutations' of the 1970s, which speeded up the process of interdependence so much that they blinded the traditionally state-centred political judgement?

To be sure, not everyone agrees that it is possible to pinpoint exactly the period usually indicated as the decade 1965–75. Yet more than one contemporary thinker asserts, if not for exactly the same reasons, that the decade will go down in history not only as a decade of transition, but as a decade of transformation. In a chapter of his brilliant book, *The Modern Social Conflict*, Ralf Dahrendorf, that astute observer of the modern political and social world, not only answers this question under the title of 'The crisis in the 1970s' but frees me from the burden of repeating the abundant bibliography of works on this theme.

Principally a sociologist Dahrendorf sees the decade – which in my context should rather be extended to include the twenty years from 1960 to 1980 – as societal crises which he finds, after a brief, but magisterial examination, to have seriously affected, indeed changed the previous economic, moral and intellectual bases of the industrial society.[8]

When I first conceived this book, some five years ago, I had already decided on the term *mutations* rather than *crises* for the conceptual description of the conglomerate of developments which interdependence brought together in the years 1960–80. This was because while a crisis is an ongoing process which may or may not leave marks, *mutations* are the evident, indeed manifest, results of the change effected in the human world (beings, institutions and values) by a coincidental development of different crises, and which make the human world look and feel different from that which preceded it. Hence also the strong *generational* aspect of this change, which both Dahrendorf and myself consider to be of special importance. But, otherwise, I think that the society which Dahrendorf so well explores from within, that is in terms of values, occupations, incomes, classes, groups, statuses and indeed generations has been 'mutated' from without by five synergic and therefore parapolitical and parasocial human developments.

These are: interdependence (which we have already discussed); the information or, to give it its original name, the technological and especially the micro-electronic revolution which is, as I shall explain, the essential historical cause of interdependence; the terminal illness of Marxism-Leninism-Stalinism; the Vietnam war, and the creation of the European Community.

## The micro-electronic, information revolution

After the revolution in travel and telecommunications had already shrunk the world so as to make it universally accessible and intercommunicating, the information technology revolution and notably the micro-electronic or information revolution was fully achieved in the 1970s. In 1976 INTEL was the first enterprise to possess an 'integrated circuit' (computer–television–telephone), while in the 1980s no important enterprise in the developed society could survive without one. The 'integrated circuit' and the micro-processing revolution not only foster interdependence, they are interdependence.

The original factor of most other changes was, and continues to be the computer. Computer technology is not only the third and most effective 'industrial revolution', given its endlessly ramified applicability; it is also, because it replaces wealth and power by knowledge, a more powerful social revolution than even Saint-Simon had dared to imagine. Because of it, the old scale of values is replaced. In a very popular American science book John Naisbit[9] hits the right note when he exclaims, almost in passing that: 'We need to create a knowledge theory of values to replace Marx's theory of value.' And with the coming of the information society we have for the first time an economy based on a key resource that is not only renewable but 'self-generating'; or as Daniel Bell prophetically described it: the 'strategic resource'.

The influence of the revolutionary process of micro-electronics was overwhelming both as a 'generic' technology, i.e. in its own sphere of 'computer' production, but also in the determining part it played in the development of other sciences (even as different and life-challenging ones as bio-genetics) and in the transformation of human daily life in the developed societies. Indeed, we are now reaching the stage, so often predicted in science fiction, of letting human science go beyond the interest and the survival of the human race, with robots replacing multitudes of workers, computers proving unbeatable at chess as well as electronic guided human procreation, while the electro-magnetic spectrum and the geo-stationary orbit create such dangers as the depletion of the ozone layers, the greenhouse effect, acid rain and the poisoning of the marine and river ecosystems. 'It is the burden of contemporary science and technology to produce change at a rate, and of a scale and character which are genuinely without precedent,' writes Roger Williams.[10] 'Science and technology have between them made the world a smaller and inescapably interdependent place, and as instruments of change they are far from finished yet. It is a benchmark to which political systems, and above all the international system have still fully to accommodate themselves.'

Last, but not least, the information revolution, again because it is based on knowledge, led to another system hierarchy of the comparative power of nations, or indeed continents. When hierarchy was based on military power, the list of powers was headed by two, the super-powers, followed by Britain, France, etc. But once hierarchy came to depend on knowledge and its application to technology, while the United States still remained top of the list, other powers came to the fore, notably one only recently re-militarized, namely the Federal Republic of Germany and one still virtually demilitarized,

Japan. The other former super-power, the USSR, fell behind badly in the new order of valuation (with the exception, again, of military and space technology). The inherent incapacity of a totalitarian regime to produce true and basic scientific knowledge and innovation, in its anti-cultural conditions, was the principal reason why even within the regime the diagnosis of its apparent stagnation was death by suffocation.

## The terminal illness of Marxism-Leninism-Stalinism

The disintegration of the Leninist-Stalinist ideology, structures and system became increasingly evident after the 'de-Stalinization' Twentieth Congress of the CPSU in 1956. This was followed by the 'polycentrism' of the Communist parties of the world, shaken by the revelations of that Congress, and by the 1966–69 Chinese 'cultural revolution', which was another fatal blow to the integrity of Marxism-Leninism-Stalinism. The collapse of the international 'centre' of the CPSU disorientated the whole communist world, one of the strengths of which was the solidarity and discipline of its worldwide ideological and organizational network. Once 'polycentrism' had cracked the monolithic ideological mould of Soviet communism, the Chinese party moving to the left and the Italian and most European parties moving to the right, the whole legitimacy of the Communist movement as directed until then from Moscow was brought into question. Khrushchev's 'de-Stalinization' speech proclaimed the falsity of the whole system. From then on, the USSR and the CPSU fought a losing battle with the modern requirements of interdependence, a concept which contradicted the Stalinist idea of socialism in one country, or even socialism in one (Soviet) bloc. From then on, and until Gorbachev, Soviet policy became an adventurism of science fiction and of military sabre-rattling, unjustified and especially unsustainable by the miserable economic, political and cultural conditions of the USSR itself.

Khrushchev was the last leader of the USSR and of the CPSU who tried to seize and use the advantages which scientific and geopolitical interdependence might still have offered during his leadership if he could have taken the initiative, as he tried to do. Even before he assumed full leadership he was operative in launching the first space-satellite, the *Sputnik* in 1957, thus stunning the world with the advance of Soviet science; and, indeed, it prompted the United States, especially after the election of John F. Kennedy as President in 1960, to intensify its own space-research and explorations. But soon, given the technical spread and economic robustness of its basis, American industry, including now that of 'spacecrafts' and 'satellites' competed successfully with the overstrained Soviet economy. The only men ever to land on the moon remain Americans. Concomitantly the contrast between the nuclear extravagance of the USSR, while its people and those of Eastern Europe suffocated in economic poverty and mismanagement, and the really homogeneous development in every way of Western economy, science, and technology became increasingly evident during the years of Khrushchev's bluff: the 1956 Polish and Hungarian revolutions, the latter crushed by the Soviet military, were the writing on the wall. Later, under Brezhnev, the Czechoslovak revolution of 1968, which coincided almost day for day with the revolt of the Paris students (of which more later), was also crushed by Soviet tanks. This Soviet invasion unmasked the clear reality that the final basis and refuge of Soviet power lay only in its military strength and preparedness.

Indeed, the second attempt by Khrushchev to regain the initiative in the bi-polar world competition as established after the Second World War consisted in using the newly-installed pro-Soviet Castro regime in Cuba as a strategic basis against the cities of the United States. The 'jaw-jaw' lasted for thirteen days, 16–29 October 1962. On the last day Khrushchev had to give way and order the withdrawal of the Soviet installations from Cuba. Kennedy, the victor, (who, after the drama of October 1962, said himself that he thought that 'the odds on war had been between one out of three and even') showed both diplomatic finesse and magnanimity towards Khrushchev, confirming the decision already taken to close some US bases in Turkey as a kind of compensation.

After Khrushchev, it took another twenty-odd years for the 'mutation' of the Communist world to be completed, to bring Gorbachev and his generation really to sign the death warrant of the Marxist-Leninist-Stalinist system and to try to save the peoples of the USSR by opening windows towards interdependence and the forcible co-operation which it imposes. But during those twenty years interdependence was operating other 'mutations' as we shall see.

## The Vietnam war

The US military intervention began in 1963, under John F. Kennedy's presidency. The local cause was the dissolution of the South–Vietnamese government under the weak and corrupt leadership of Ngo Dinh Diem, a government which was both incapable of resisting the mounting Vietcong terrorist attacks and disliked by the population. 'Three weeks before JFK died some Vietnamese military officers unseated Diem. They acted with the knowledge and consent of Americans in Saigon and Washington. To Kennedy's horror, they killed Diem too, which was not in the script as most Americans had understood it' write Neustadt and May.[11] Lyndon Johnson, who was preparing his election, i.e. his transformation from successor-President to full President, obtained (after some hesitation and procrastination) in 1964 a unanimous Congressional resolution, with only two dissenting votes in the Senate, authorizing him to 'take all necessary measures . . . to prevent further aggression'. By 1965 he had 'Americanized' the war, bombing North Vietnam and sending increasing numbers of US troops. The 'hostile interdependence' between the USA-led democratic camp and the Soviet-led communist camp caused a new, but much graver 'hot war'.

The origin of 'hostile interdependence' had a long history. As the authors[12] of *Wise Men* show in great detail after Roosevelt's death, once the illusion that a new international order, based on the United Nations and on the collaboration within it between the USA and the USSR, was dispelled by Stalin's evident aggressiveness, a group of 'Wise Men' was formed almost instinctively around the State Department and later around President Harry Truman. The story of American foreign policy during the cold war is recounted in that and many other books.

Yet it is still useful to mention here that the manifesto and the text-book of the new doctrine of 'containment' was George Kennan's 'Long Telegram' from Moscow of 5 March 1946, which was afterwards published in *Foreign Affairs* under the pseudonym XXX. In this telegram he asserted that the Soviets were intent on 'destroying our traditional way of life', from without by embarking on further territorial expansion and from within by undermining Western resolve, by 'penetrating labor unions, youth leagues, women's organizations, racial societies, liberal magazines, publishing houses, etc.'. Although Kennan insisted on many occasions that containment did not have an exclusively or even necessarily military connotation, 'defence' was the predominant element in its interpretation by the political and military leaders. This, combined with the still burning memories of the mistakes made by the Western democracies in Hitler's case and with the new geo-political reality of the two super-powers facing each other, like two chess-players, on every point of the globe, gave birth to the Truman doctrine of the 'defence of freedom everywhere' where free peoples were attacked by dictatorial conquering powers.

14

As Stalin's USSR and its 'allies' sought to extend Soviet communism all over the world by military and revolutionary means, so the US and its allies were now sworn to fight by all means for democracy and freedom all over the world. Truman's decision to begin the North Korean war on Friday, 30 June 1950, was the first implementation of the Truman doctrine. Acheson was the hero of the action. On 19 July Truman cabled to him: 'Your actions on Korea show that you are a great Secretary of State.'[13]

Acheson, therefore, encouraged by what could be called 'doctrinal deformation' and by political instinct, encouraged Johnson to go on with the war in Vietnam, which was not even, incidentally, what in International Law could be called a 'war'. But he soon realized that the situation was entirely different in 1965 from what it had been in 1950. The US did not have the backing of the United Nations; on the contrary, the United Nations' Assembly which now comprised a majority of nations from the Third and the Communist Worlds, repeatedly condemned the action of the United States; the Western allies of the USA did not help or follow them; television and the media in general gave a horrifying presentation of American military actions to American and world public opinion; the new generation which provided, through a questionable system of drafting, most of the 50,000 dead had a new mentality; and the financial cost ($150 billion) destabilized the American balance of payments, and ultimately the credibility of the American dollar, which was already shaken for other reasons. After Lyndon Johnson's humiliating attempts to negotiate a peace with the Vietcong in the last weeks of his presidency, it fell to the new President, Richard Nixon, to complete the total withdrawal of the US forces from Vietnam.

The 'mutation' caused by the Vietnam war was especially significant with regard to the position of the US as the unchallenged super-power of the West. The lost military prestige, the new racial movement within the US population itself, the generational division between parents and children and, last but not least, as we shall see, the devaluation of the dollar, once the world's leading currency, led to a great change in the American position, and through it to all relations of interdependence in the world.

## The monetary, financial and social disorders following the Vietnam war

The problem of national monetary disorder and insufficient international order since the collapse of the Bretton Woods system (1944–76) and even while it was in force, is one of the best examples of the theory of interdependence, as this disorder continues to be of daily concern to the guardians of the monetary sovereignty of European states faced with the demands of monetary integration. It was therefore of interest to the high theories of monetary transnationality[14] as well as in practice to the agitated stock-exchanges, and to normal tradesmen, tourists and travellers. As such, it cannot be expected that within a few pages this particular author could do more than provide a brief summary of the dollar crisis.

Although the Bretton Woods agreement, signed in 1944 in the American locality of that name, and the system this agreement set up, fell into two phases, 1944–58 and 1958–76, in reality it formed a continuum of thirty years during which the dollar was the fixed currency of the exchange rate. The difference between the two phases was that in the first phase the dollar was actually convertible at one ounce of gold for thirty-five dollars, while in the second phase the dollar imposed itself mostly as the currency of the free world through its omnipresence in all monetary, financial, commercial and military activities of that world. In both phases the principle agreed upon by the Western welfare societies was the establishment of an international monetary framework, while respecting the sovereignty of the signatory-states, which still considered their national currency as an element in, and a symbol of, their sovereignty. But the Bretton Woods agreement nevertheless situated them all in a framework of economic and monetary order, based on free trade, but with fixed exchange rates. It tried especially to avoid such domino-disasters for the capitalist world as the economic crisis of the 1930s, which was one of the principal causes of the advent of Hitler and of the war he launched. Moreover, a new credit institution was created, the International Monetary Fund, whose role was both to monitor the working of the new system and to provide medium-term loans to member states, whose currencies suffered, for one reason or another, from severe external fluctuations. But the gold-exchange standard system really came into full force only after the arduous years of European reconstruction, during and with the help of the Marshall Plan.

Liberal economic theorists found the Bretton Woods system as satisfactory as any system can be which is designed to reconcile such contradictory propositions as the encouragement of the mercantile and growth-pursuing economic policies of each of the associated states; and also to maintain a certain co-ordination between their activities. Sovereignty and interdependence still seemed to be able to co-exist harmoniously.

But interdependence soon raised its head in its ugliest form, namely the conflict between dependence and hegemony. Robert Gilpin[15] encapsulated the whole story of American hegemony in a few words. 'The classical Bretton Woods system,' he wrote, 'lasted only from 1958 to 1964 when it was replaced by what the French call the hegemony of the dollar.' And he added:

American hegemony had been based on the role of the dollar in the international monetary system and on the extension of its nuclear deterrent to include its allies . . . the United States must have the foreign exchange to finance its global position . . . The economic burdens of global hegemony have been achieved in large part through taking advantage of the international position of the dollar. The price paid for America's exploitation of its role as the world's banker was the destruction of the Bretton Woods system, the transformation of the United States from a creditor into a debtor nation and growing dependence on Japanese capital.

The dollar had in fact lost its value and its credibility as a gold exchange standard. This had happened because, on the one hand, the Western European economies – and especially those of the countries of the European Community – and of Japan had asserted their own new strength against the erstwhile overall American domination; and on the other hand America's gold reserves were being drained away by the increasingly costly war in Vietnam (which coincided with President Johnson's also very costly social programme known as 'The Great Society'). This led to mounting inflation in America which, again, given economic interdependence, produced a painful inflationary infection all over the Western world, with even more painful effects in the Third World.

After a long and not particularly rewarding period of 'benign neglect' the new American President, Richard Nixon, suspended the convertibility of the dollar into gold on 15 August 1971, and through the Smithsonian agreement of December 1971 carried out a drastic devaluation of the dollar. The events of the early 1970s not only removed the dollar from the centre of the system, but replaced the regime of fixed parities by one of floating exchange rates. This is one more clear example, if needed, of the increased power of the private sector, that is the market operators, at the expense of governments and monetary authorities. It is also a very clear example of worldwide interdependence, since all major financial markets are linked and trends move from one market to the other without interruption, helped of course by IT and the telephone. But by then already Japan and the European Community, and especially Western Germany, possessed greater holdings of dollars than they would normally use.

From being the greatest creditor nation, the US had become the greatest debtor of the OECD world. The great monetary 'mutation', caused by the change in the position of the dollar, has continued to unbalance world markets ever since.

Another development linked with the Vietnam war is the generational mutation. The essentially psychological generational mutation (Raymond Aron coined the expression *psychodrama* to describe the student movement in Paris in 1968) started long before and continued long after what is historically considered as the very precise date of the students' revolt: 1968. Like all the other mutations singled out here its original causes preceded the 'event' by years and even decades. But unlike all the others observed until now, those causes were imperceptibly, but ineluctably, linked with the changes in human nature itself, which in turn was being influenced by the new stability of the 'cold war' and by the way of life of the consumerist society; the fact that once installed in peace and in a stable democracy, the parents of what was going to be the 'new generation', relaxed in a comfortable, even hedonistic way of life, affected their judgement of their own behaviour and of the behaviour and education of their children. So the 'new young' of the developed societies differed from their parents and from their ancestors. They had been born more precocious and therefore more blasé; in better material conditions and therefore more spoilt; earlier in their lives directly and indirectly, consciously and subconsciously, more aware by visual and auditive means of communication, and therefore more sensitive and anxious; and earlier satiated with carnal and other pleasures and therefore pursuing 'new', often violent, pleasures as spectators or actors, or indulging in drugs or terrorism or both.

The concept of *generation*, which is notoriously vague in sociological terms, was fashionable in France and in Germany even before the Second World War, and indeed was a proto-fascist rallying cry. But the break between the generations of parents and children of the 1960s was particularly striking. The 'young generation' of that decade was, as I have said elsewhere, one of the most 'prefigurative generations' in the history of the world, to use Margaret Mead's expression for the generation of young people who impose their conceptions and ways of life on their elders. For a while 'the young' seemed to dominate even the political debate – indeed they brought down both Lyndon Johnson and de Gaulle – and they effected a revolution in mores and styles, notably in sartorial style. Of course, the 'young movement' left indelible social, political and ideological marks on Western society. Ralf Dahrendorf expresses very candidly the extent to which the historian remains puzzled by this movement:

> To the present day 1968 divides peoples in many countries of the OECD world. What did it really mean? Was it the revolt of the spoilt children of a new prosperous class produced by the economic miracle? Was it the rise of the citizens against governments which had not realized that the time of subjects was over? Was it the first assertion of value changes which were soon to envelop Western societies? Was it simply a stage in the reform of modern society with institutions which were overdue for change at the centre?'[16]

But there were also two historical causes which aroused in young people a need for the destructive action of 'contestation'. These were, in general, the crisis of Marxism-Leninism-Stalinism and, more locally, yet rapidly reverberating everywhere, the Vietnam war.

The impact of the Soviet agony on the 'ideology' – if it can even be called that – of the young was twofold: it was first of all a terrible confirmation of the end of the Promethean (Marxist and Nietzschean) dreams of elitist dictatorships which had excited their imagination; but one of the principal consequences of that agony, the Chinese cultural revolution, was regarded as a model of how to rescue revolution from the dead hand of communism. The fact that Herbert Marcuse, who had first written the bitter *Soviet Marxism* and only afterwards his *One-Dimensional Man* was the inspirer of the popular slogans, and of the simple theories, of the 'movement', proves that what underlay it was the despair that the *Great Alternative*, the Communist Revolution, had been abandoned for good. If communism meant only bureaucracy, authoritarianism, and state terror, then at least 'Revolution' should be saved. 'Revolution for revolution's sake' was also the purpose of the Chinese cultural 'revolution', a mixture of sheer 'contestation' and disgust with Leninism-Stalinism, which was finally brought to an end by the Chinese army. Trotskyism *via* the Frankfurt School and Isaac Deutscher, Maoism and Castroism *via* Sartre, and vulgar hedonism and intoxication with drugs *via* Leary and Ginsberg,[17] made up the intoxicating anti-'communist' and anti-'capitalist' mixture of the movement, with much the same result as drinking mixed drinks on an empty stomach.

The anti-war movement was a movement which gathered more and more members when more people were 'drafted' as recruits to be sent to the Vietnam war, by methods and with criteria which became increasingly questionable. The front organization *Students for a Democratic Society* (SDS) which linked the American universities with each other, and increasingly with the European universities, had organized the public burning of draft cards ever since 1966. It is estimated that some 27,000 cards were burnt. The movement spread from the elite students, who were in any case in the most protected category, to young working-class men and to the blacks. In that sense therefore the 1968 students' movement was caused by the Vietnam war.

But the other properly academic claim of the movement – which was a general revolt against society – was its protest against the particularly old-fashioned and professor-ridden universities. This was true of the American universities, but was even truer of the European universities and notably of the German and French ones. The students' revolt in Paris was, for at least two reasons, the most important of all. The first reason was that, once, in Paris, the students succeeded in inciting and gathering around them, sometimes in the form of *groupuscules*, large numbers of the population in general and most significantly of the non-communist working class. (The French Communist Party and the Communist trade union stood aside, thus confirming the essentially Trotskyist atmosphere of the movement, which the soundly Stalinist French party abhorred.) The vast popular movement launched in this way shook the government, and after some delays and much high political intrigue, it led to the resignation of de Gaulle.

The second reason for the particular importance of the revolt in Paris was that French culture being what it is, it was in Paris that the movement revealed and asserted some authentic philosophical foundations and assertions. Marcuse's works, which had obviously influenced the American movement, together with Ginsberg's poems and tracts, were too thin and derivative when compared with the much deeper roots the movement had in France – or in Germany. The existentialist philosophy of the absurd, represented in the works of Albert Camus, Beckett, Merleau-Ponty and Ionesco, had been corrupted by Sartre, who had organized a team around his review, *Les Temps Modernes* which claimed to be, unlike the other four, faithful to communist ideals and principles. But Sartre already seemed old-fashioned to students in search of a more radical, more intoxicating and more total rejection of all values. In reality, Sartre *followed* the new spirit, limping along behind it, but he neither provided the ultimate inspiration, nor led it.

The ultimate inspiration came from the post-structuralists. (Structuralism itself, was in fashion for a while, but it had been found to offer insufficient ground for the total rejection of modern society and for the thirst for destruction of the 'young'.) In a passage of his *Mémoires*,[18] Raymond Aron explains the real causes: 'the student riots *which spread from one end of the non-communist world to the other* meant the weakening of the authority of adults, of leaders, and of the institutions themselves'. The passage is doubly important, first because in the phrase I have italicized, Aron distinguished clearly between the non-communist and the communist countries in which there were simultaneous student movements. Although they occurred at the same time (notably in May 1968 in Czechoslovakia and in France, but with such different results!) the Eastern European revolts had completely different motives, aspirations and indeed philosophies from those of the 'non-communist world'. While the latter's elitist theme was '*élections–trahisons*', the one thing that the students of Eastern Europe wanted was free elections, which they have at last succeeded in imposing on their regimes in 1990; they wanted constitutional pluralism and the rule of law, while the students in the West wanted the abolition of all laws, institutions, and norms.

This brings us to the second sense in which Aron's phrase is important. This is his feeling that at the bottom of the philosophical origins of the movement there was a quest for the *destruction* of all perennial human values – not only of 'bourgeois values', something even deeper than anarchy, and which Michel Foucault, the most celebrated leader of the post structuralist, *deconstructionist*, school called the 'death of man' (a not so original paraphrase of a phrase of one of Foucault's masters, Nietzsche, the 'death of God').

The bulk of Foucault's work was published after 1968, but he was already then an influential teacher and writer. Like the young 'in revolt', Foucault's themes were: the defence of madness (*Folie et déraison*, 1961), in which the reason of society was the real madness; the rejection of discipline (*Surveiller et punir*, 1975) in which he set the keystone of his philosophy, namely that all *norms* are *abnormal* because they are *imposed* as rules by society, that enormous prison, and that therefore only *abnormality* was normal, logically and biologically; and of course sexuality (*Histoire de la sexualité*, three vols, 1976, 1984, 1984), in which the Freudian themes of the repression of *normal* instincts by the *abnormal* morality of society were transformed into a theory of the primacy of sexual and notably homosexual pleasures. The conclusion of such a philosophy was, on the one hand, the negation of power, and on the other 'the death of man'. For if man destroys, deconstructs, all the norms which keep society viable, in the end he must destroy himself, and perish in an apotheosis of mental aberration.

*Leadership in an interdependent world*

The 'contestation' of normalcy remained for a full decade at least the main cultural heritage of 1968, as it spread into all layers of society. Indeed, it progressed proportionately faster as the information revolution advanced. The more the micro-electronic society was imposing its technological and economic rigidities, the more the weak and the young were withdrawing from it into communes, drugs and terrorism. A double marginalization eliminated them from the new society of interdependence, and from the search for ways of making society function more *normally*.

## The Creation of the European Community

The signature of the Treaty of Rome in 1957 which founded the European Economic Communities – to be unified afterwards into one *Community* – marked yet another mutation of the 1960s. Between an aggressively unpredictable USSR, and a USA showing some signs of economic unpredictability, France, Western Germany, Italy, The Netherlands, Belgium and Luxemburg, regenerated by American help after the war, proceeded to establish a new interdependent unity. By means of their union they sought to achieve the size and the quasi-continental pool of economic resources which would enable their economic and political association to attain viability in the fierce world of interdependence which each of them was now facing alone.

The story of the Community will be followed in each of the five essays in this book, at five different phases of its evolution, because it is one of the principal mutations of post-war politics. But such mutations are conceived long before they see the light of day – hence we should briefly recall the very early origins of the Community.

When for mysterious geological reasons, the sea-bed moves and forces the tips of mountain ranges to rise above sea-level, what first emerges, before the continents appear, are archipelagos of islands and islets of which some will disappear again, while others will join together. In a political institutional context this is what happened to the European Community which is still for the time being an institutional archipelago, although it manifests an obvious tendency towards institutional regrouping and unification. Its principal islands and islets are in the chronological order of their emergence: Benelux (January 1948), the Council of Europe (May 1949), NATO (1949), the European Iron and Steel Community (ECSC) (July 1952), the Western European Union (1955) and the OECD which in 1961 replaced the

OEEC, set up by the Marshall Plan, and which therefore, although born under the new name of Organization for Economic and Co-operation Development, nevertheless forms part of a chronological continuum.

When, therefore the archipelago of institutional European islands and islets emerged so rapidly in the first decade after the war, there was a growing feeling in European and world opinion that the fragmentation would soon cease and that a gradual unification would logically and functionally conclude the process. Moreover, that process had been set in motion in European public opinion long before the governments and the chanceries had started their institutional bargaining. It had originated in the early projects for a European Union which had arisen in the Resistance movements and in the Nazi concentration camps.

These first projects sprang from the genuine, idealistic, federalist inspiration of the early movement for European unification. Federalism is the twin of pacifism, the other idealistic doctrine which claims that the human race could and should establish universal peace. But in the case of Europe, it sprang also from the European historical heritage, in which these ideas had been born. The European mutation was *cultural* before it became *institutional*, economic, or political.

For centuries idealistic European political philosophers have pursued the ideal of perpetual European peace and have put forward detailed plans to achieve it. Yet Europe has been continuously devastated by wars, culminating in two world wars which were triggered off by European nation-states. The First World War was the most distressing of all, because it proved how easily all political ideologies – and, sad to say, even the inherently internationalist socialism, could collapse before the bloodthirsty instincts of nationalism. The Second World War was at least fought and won on moral, anti-fascist grounds and therefore with strong popular support.

Indeed, even during the Second World War, the European Resistance had revealed its resolutely pacifist and anti-nationalist principles. To give only one example: in December 1943, *Combat*, the clandestine newspaper of the French Resistance, edited by Albert Camus, wrote:

France's place is in the Europe of the Resistance. There is her mission. . . . Not in the theoretical Europe, carved up on the green baize tables by the diplomats of the 'Great Powers', but in this Europe of sorrows, waking at dawn in anguish, in this underground Europe of the maquis and false papers, in this Europe of blood which has been wounded. *The European resistance will remake Europe. A free Europe, composed of free citizens, because we have all known slavery. A Europe politically and economically united because we have paid the full price of division.*

In Italy, Altiero Spinelli, who had drafted the Ventotene manifesto in 1941 which demanded 'the abolition of the division of Europe into national sovereign states', later reminded us that

those who dreamed of it were exiles on penal islands, or in concentration camps, or members of the Resistance in a number of countries – groups in each country which were unaware of the existence of similar groups elsewhere. As was to be revealed later, members of the French, Italian, Dutch, Czech, Yugoslav, Polish and German underground movements had here and there developed the same feelings and ideas.

In spring 1944, 'several militants of the Resistance movements of Denmark, France, Italy, Norway, The Netherlands, Poland, Czechoslovakia and Yugoslavia had already met in Geneva', according to a communiqué of 7 July 1944, and published a 'Draft Declaration of the European Resistance'. In this document, they declared that 'because within the span of a single generation Europe had been the epicentre of two world wars, the problem could only be solved by the creation of a federal union among the nation-states of Europe which should be endowed with supreme federal institutions'. In the light of this past history it is impossible to give credence to the popular impression, fed by politicians, that the EC was in fact only an economic annex of NATO, and that its original motivation was the defence of the West against Stalinist Russia. Just as unsubstantiated is also the impression that the politicians were the real founders of the European Community (for instance Churchill in his speech at Zurich, or the Conference at The Hague in 1948). In actual fact, in the first decade after the war, it was pressure from the peoples of Europe, especially of continental Europe, towards European unification which pushed politicians and governments to move ahead in that direction.

Thus the European Community could be viewed as the result of two different pressures: the pressure of world interdependence and the pressure of European public opinion on European governments. The build-up was very much the result of the purposeful activity of individuals and groups inspired by the idea of a European Union. There were two approaches to the feasibility of such a union: the federalistic-institutional, and the integrationist-functional.

The federalists suspected that the approaches of the integrationists were deterministic, even 'economic deterministic' (hence the conceptual telescoping by Denis de Rougemont when he referred to Jean Monnet and his team as *the economists*). The federalists did not believe that, once they were engaged together as partners in operations in which their national interests might achieve favourable results unattainable by each of them alone, the nation-states would then proceed on their own to enlarge their association into a loose union. They asserted that as long as the structures remained unchanged, and the new institutions were not properly and solidly built on the ruins of former national institutions, the expected 'spill-over' would never spill far enough to produce the complete change of structures required by federation.

On the other hand, the integrationists were convinced that European Union was such an historical necessity that it was bound to happen, indeed that it was happening in any case, bearing along states and peoples alike in its wake. They believed that any beginning or separate beginnings could only accelerate the inevitable developments. In a sense, they were more confident in the spill-over from any European developments than the pacifists–federalists. They believed that a two-pronged approach, by European public opinion urging the governments to proceed with integration, and by the governments agreeing to embark on separate integrative actions which most of the states considered to be justified from the point of view of their respective national interest, would inaugurate functional reactions which would inevitably lead to the necessity of adopting federal principles.

In the end, the two worked together with some mutual understanding, when public action really started, at the Congress of Europe of 1–10 May 1948 at The Hague, which was organized by a United International Committee of the Movements for European Unity, led by Jean Monnet.[19] The Congress called for political and economic union in Europe, a European Assembly and a European Court of Human Rights.

But soon Jean Monnet's functional-integrationist approach took the lead. He argued that European federation, which was the final goal and the inevitable conclusion, could and should be achieved piecemeal, by sectors of integration and by some common policies. Thus, in May 1950 he had already written that 'Europe must be organized on a federal basis. A Franco-German union is its essential element. Therefore the French government should propose to put the whole of the Franco-German production of coal and steel under an International Authority to be open to the participation of other European countries.' Robert Schuman, the Foreign Minister of France, soon adopted the idea, which became the Schuman Plan – which in turn became in April 1951 the formidable 'European Coal and Steel

Community' with Jean Monnet as its first President (see essays on Adenauer and de Gaulle). But after the collapse of the plan for a European Defence Community, European public opinion felt that more should be done. The Messina conference of 2 June 1955 called by the Benelux Ministers submitted the basic memorandum, inviting Italy, France and Germany to participate, Great Britain having refused to attend. The Messina conference decided that even if only on the basis of six countries, 'it is necessary to work for the establishment of a United Europe by the development of common institutions, the progressive fusion of national economies, the creation of a common market and the progressive harmonization of their social policy'.[20] The 'mutation' of the European Community was effected and greatly influenced world developments.

## The Oil Crisis: *a* crisis*, but not a* mutation

These examples of the 'mutations' which occurred in mid-twentieth century show, it is hoped, that while they were unfolding as historical developments of interdependence they were also modifying human political judgement in their direction. As they were installing themselves as *faits accomplis* of history, they were also signalling to political judgement, according to its degree of alertness, that each of them and all of them together, under the cover of interdependence, *had* already modified the givens or premisses of political judgement.

How slow, though, was that judgement in receiving and following the signals which had been emitted can be illustrated by the counter-example of what was rightly called the oil crisis. It ranks as a crisis and not as a mutation, because as all crises, it passed: soon after there was a glut of oil. Moreover the fact that it passed demonstrated that it could have been avoided had political judgement been readier to interpret and act upon it appropriately. Yet contemporary political rhetoric and history still consider the oil crisis as a historical threshold and Western governments and political circles continue to present it as the 'event' which turned their financial and economic policies upside down.

The oil problem, part of the energy problem as a whole, also exemplifies the relations of interdependence. Developed countries, and the USA, increasingly depended on imports from oil-producing countries and the latter depended on their exports. So evident was the conflictual relation between these two categories of 'sovereign states' that on one side the oil producers formed a cartel called OPEC in 1960, while on the other in December 1968, the Commission of the

EC produced its 'First Guidelines on Community Energy Policy'. Its three main points were: to work out a framework for joint action; to establish a common energy market; to ensure cheap and secure supplies.[20]

The two last points were the easiest to implement in so far as the decade 1960–70 went down in history as an era of plentiful and cheap energy. Yet the Council of Ministers of the six member-states of the EEC did nothing.

In the meantime, on the contrary, on the OPEC side, things were proceeding at a very fast pace. By the end of 1972, Algeria, Libya, Syria and Iraq had nationalized their oil industries. Both the European Commission and the USA had repeated since 1970 their warnings of an impending crisis. (Britain was already in consultation as a future member of the Community.) For a while the national 'champion' oil companies acted as the middlemen between the two sides (incidentally also making exceptionally high profits). But the governments of the nine countries now in the EC did nothing.

When, in October 1973, the Yom Kippur war broke out and OPEC unilaterally and very drastically raised oil prices, the Western European and US governments were, as it were, caught with their pants down. The harsh conditions imposed on them by OPEC found them still disunited, each of them trying to solve its instant needs by paying ever higher prices to their oil companies. In the exercise each of them dislocated its economic, financial and monetary policies, and then explained candidly to its people, punished in this way, that the sole cause of the new disasters was the 'unexpected' oil crisis. Seldom in history has political judgement failed in its duty as glaringly as in the case of that crisis.

## Re-introduction

These last lines bring us back to the subject of this book which, simplified in the extreme, is the change operated by modern knowledge in the realm of politics from the old political judgement and statesmanship to the new political judgement and statesmanship of interdependence. What we expect to find is whether and how that transition was achieved in the performance of the five statesmen during the period in which they governed their five countries, the half century which goes by the name of the 'cold war', but which in reality was the age of the advent of interdependence. For it was the increasing pressure of interdependence on the USSR which brought the 'cold war' to an end. The difficulties which the five statesmen met in adapting their statesmanship to the politics of interdependence will be examined in the five essays which follow, each of them divided into two sections. The historical antecedents and circumstances, and the policies of interdependence he or she actually practised, deliberately or not, consciously or not.

## NOTES AND REFERENCES

1.  See also G. Ionescu, 'Political Undercomprehension or the Overload of Political Cognition' in *Government and Opposition*, vol. 24, No. 4., Autumn 1989, pp. 413–27.

2.  Robert D. Putnam and Nicholas Bayne: *Hanging Together: The Seven-Power Summit*, Harvard, 1984, p. 208. Putnam and Bayne's book deals exclusively with the policy-making processes of 'summitry', that is with the meetings of the G-7, inaugurated by the Rambouillet meetings of 1975–76, and since then institutionalized as a regular and frequent occasion for the seven, and often only five monetary and economic powers in need of consultation and co-ordination of their national policies. As such, 'summitry' is also a clear proof of the domination of interdependence over sovereignty, as explained in this book. Where, however, their interpretation differs from the more general explanation offered here is that rightly the authors find that these frequent *personal* contacts between the leaders instead of increasing 'animosity', to use our expression, facilitate their communications and as such the ultimate common decisions. Moreover, rightly so, the authors underline that the 'summits' produce a certain common view and approach, according to their different and successive protagonists: the summits which comprised Carter–Callaghan–Giscard d'Estaing and Helmut Schmidt had a different affinity from that of those comprising Reagan, Thatcher and Kohl. Moreover, from our point of view, it can even be added that this kind of collegial atmosphere develops also at the European Community, OECD, meetings of the governors of Central Banks and any other such institutionalized forms of consultation of the developed market-states – not to speak of NATO. But regular and personalized as these consultative processes may be, the problems which they have to face and try to solve are not of their making, but of that of the circumambient and ultimately collective and anonymous interdependence which covers all continents, and in which small and episodic causes set in motion processes of concern to the whole world, and notably to the developed world.

3.  William Wallace, 'What Price Independence? Sovereignty and Interdependence in British Politics' in *International Affairs*, Summer, 1986, p. 369.

4.  Robert O. Keohane and Joseph S. Nye, *Power and Interdependence*, Harvard University Press, 1977, pp. 25–7.

5.  To give a selective and heterogeneous list: Robert Cox, R. Gilpin, Pierre Lalouche, N. J. Rosenau, Joan Spero, William Wallace, Edmund Dell, Thierry de Montbrial, John Vasquez, and of course Susan Strange, of whom more later.

6.  Peter Willetts, 'Interdependence: New Wine in Old Bottles', in Rosenau and Tromp, eds. *Interdependence and Conflict in World Politics*, Gower, 1988, p. 203 (italics added).

7. Susan Strange's principal works are: *States and Markets*, London, 1988; *Casino Capitalism*, London, 1986 (ed.); *Paths to International Political Economy*, London, 1984; *International Monetary Relations, vol. 2 of International Economic Relations in the Western World, 1959–71*, (ed. A. Shonfield, Oxford, 1975); and 'The Persistent Myth of Lost Hegemony', in *International Organization*, Autumn, 1987; 'The Future of the American Empire', in *Journal of International Affairs*, Fall, 1988.

8. Ralf Dahrendorf: *The Modern Social Conflict*, London, 1986, pp. 118–41.

9. John Naisbit: *Megatrends*, London, 1984.

10. Roger Williams: 'Political Decisions where the Technical Component is Substantial' in *Government and Opposition*, vol. 24, No. 4, Autumn 1989, pp. 458–9.

11. Richard E. Neustadt and Ernest R. May, *Thinking in Time*, New York, 1988, p. 77.

12. Walter Isaacson & Evan Thomas, *The Wise Men*, New York, 1986, p. 652.

13. Dean Acheson: *Present at the Creation*, New York, 1969.

14. But see, among many others, Fred E. Block, *The Origins of Economic Disorder*, Berkeley, 1977; Robert Gilpin, *The Political Economy of International Relations*, Princeton, 1987; Albert Hirschmann, *Essays in Trespassing*, Cambridge 1981; Robert Keohane and S. Nye, Jr., *Peace and Interdependence*; Charles Kindelberger, *Peace and Money*; Joan Spero, *The Politics of International Economic Relations*, New York, 1977; Susan Strange, see footnote 7; John Williamson, *The Open Economy and the World Economy*, London, 1983.

15. Gilpin, op. cit., p. 134.

16. Ralf Dahrendorf, *The Modern Social Conflict*, p. 114.

17. 'He [Ginsberg] was also a passionate advocate of the drug culture. Monogamous sex and anti-drug laws were all part of the repressed system's big jealous arrangement . . . Much of his poetry was written when very high'. David Caute, *Sixty-Eight, the Year of the Barricades*, London, 1988, pp. 279–81.

18. R. Aron, *Mémoires*, Paris, 1983, p. 482, my italics.

19. See J. Monnet, *Mémoires*, Paris, 1976, and Richard Mayne, *The Recovery of Europe*. Monnet had been the co-ordinator of American–British equipment during the war, then the initiator of the French Economic Plan (see below, essay on de Gaulle) but was now devoting all his energy to the task of organizing Europe, functionally, sector by sector, counting on the inevitable spill-over of economic co-operation onto other activities. See also the works of E. Haas.

20. Official journal of the EC No. C 123, 25 November 1968. Quoted in Robert de Bauw: 'Oil policy before the Yom Kippur War' in G. Ionescu (ed.): *The European Alternatives*, The Hague, 1979, pp. 79–95.

# CHAPTER ONE
# *Konrad Adenauer*

*Im Anfang war Adenauer – so lässt sich der Beginn der Bundesrepublik kürz kennzeichnen.* (In the beginning there was Adenauer. This is how the beginning of the German Federal Republic can be briefly described.) Indeed, Arnulf Baring, a not particularly hagiographic historian of 'Foreign Policy in Adenauer's Chancellor Democracy' begins his book with this striking description of a man alone in a desert of ruins and guilt.[1] Baring stresses that after the crashing collapse of Hitler's Third Reich, the Germans who had no constitution, no elected parliament, no employers' or trade union organizations, no capital city, let alone a Supreme Court of Justice, had only Adenauer – as if implying that one man alone was going to give the kiss of life to his inanimate people.

There are two coinciding reasons why the case studies in this inquiry into the diffusion of sovereign policy-making processes in the sea of interdependence should begin with the case study of Adenauer. The first is the chronological one. It is true that of the five leaders studied here, two, de Gaulle and Adenauer, embarked at the same time in 1944 on the task of reconstructing their respective countries, tasks which were to converge in their ultimate common understanding. But there is first this difference, that while de Gaulle came back from afar in as it were the first year of the new France, Adenauer was in his own country, which he had never left, already from what German historians have rightly called the year zero of Germany. And there is the further difference that while de Gaulle's period of office was interrupted after two years of premiership in 1946, Adenauer's leadership continued uninterruptedly from 1949 to 1963, when he retired just in time to write his memoirs and then to die.

One might also argue that it is not really possible to compare in such miniatures the sheer magnitude of the tasks undertaken and achieved by the two different leaders. But the effort of transforming a country both ruined and universally hated into a most powerful and respected one, in less than twenty years and by one man alone, probably surpasses those of the other three Western statesmen, whose activity in the field of reconstruction had started from much more solid bases, and in much more normal circumstances.

Finally, another reason for starting our enquiry with the case study on Adenauer is that his case and that of his country provide the first evident case of the replacement of sovereignty by a political stability based on interdependent processes of policy-making. He used his political genius to combine, by the sheer necessity of the past, but also with a shrewd sense of the future, exclusive national goals with imposed and compulsory inter- and trans-national means of implementation. The 'state' which he had reconstructed with, and could not have reconstructed without, specific methods of interdependence, emerged then, as it is today, as one of the most integrated in all the concentric circles of interdependence of the developed society. Internally, it became one of the most decentralized and devolutive federations and internationally one of the most co-operative, thus linking national and transnational interdependence dialectically in a continuum of relations of causality. Yet at the time of writing, the Federal Republic of Germany is one of the most 'successful' countries in the world.

But, to repeat, this was not by accident. The constitutional structure of the Federal Republic of Germany and its external policy reflect Adenauer's early plan for the reconstruction of the state as much as a finished house reproduces the plans and sketches of an architect. This, for instance, is how he described his initial idea of integration in a letter of 31 October 1945, quoted in his memoirs[2]:

> The division of Europe into Eastern Europe, the Russian territory and Western Europe is a fact . . . the part of Germany not occupied by Russia is an integral part of Western Europe. It is in the real interests, not only of that part of Germany but also of Britain and France, the leading great powers in Western Europe to unite Europe under their leadership. In the long run, the French and Belgian demand for security can only be met by the economic integration of western Germany, France, Belgium, Luxemburg and Holland. If Britain, too, were to decide to participate in the economic integration, we would be much closer to the ultimate goal of a Union of the States of Western Europe. As for the constitution of the part of Germany not occupied by Russia . . . a constitutional structure must be found and restored. As the creation of a unitary and centralized state will be neither possible nor desirable, the constitutional cohesion can be looser than before; it might take the form of a federal relationship.

31

I

# PERSONAL CIRCUMSTANCES AND HISTORICAL ANTECEDENTS

Before examining Adenauer's long and arduous political action, and notably the statesman-like way in which he wove external necessities together with internal possibilities, it might be useful briefly to consider the personal circumstances and historical antecedents which presided over his activities and his success.

Several personal circumstances and theoretical inclinations, indeed beliefs, determined Adenauer's *predisposition* towards the modern – in his time almost futuristic – political conceptions. These circumstances and inclinations were disparate; but they all converged into the same predisposition, towards the same instinctive search for modern political stability. The most salient of these personal circumstances were:

## His age

Tall, stiff, soberly dressed, with a strangely Mongolian cast of countenance, he was already seventy years old in 1944, when he started what he himself described as his third life. The first life ran between his birth in 1875 and his appointment as Oberbürgermeister (Mayor) of Cologne in 1917 – an appointment which he held until he was dismissed by Hitler in 1933, when his second life began.

His second life consisted of a long fight for survival from Nazi persecution, of continuous hiding and underground activity, until his final arrest, from which he escaped only when the American troops surrounded the town. And his third life, which lasted from 1944 until his death and with which we are concerned here, is indistinguishable from his political efforts and achievements. But at the very advanced age at which he started and completed his colossal task, his strong sense of duty was a greater motivation than personal ambition, although they were always very closely interwoven; and that also helped others to trust and to follow him. Indeed, the nickname by which he was popularly known after the end of the Second World War and the beginning of his period of ascendancy was 'der Alte' (the old one): and as he advanced into the eighth and ninth decades of his life, the affectionate popular joke was that 'Death has forgotten him'.

## His anti-Nazi record

A member of the *Zentrum* (Centre) Party in his first life, Adenauer was as fundamentally opposed to Nazism as the Nazis believed him to be, which is why they persecuted him, politically and in every way. Yet luck, Machiavelli's *fortuna*, which the latter rightly considered to be a prerequisite of statesmanship, helped him to remain alive, while his enemies were finally destroyed. This was an extraordinary exception: most of the German anti-Nazis had been exterminated, others had fled the country, while others like his arch-rival Kurt Schumacher, the leader of the SDP, emerged after twelve years of concentration camps so mutilated and debilitated that he could live only a short time. Of the very few anti-Nazis who had survived inside Germany itself, Adenauer was also the most politically prominent. Indeed, at the end of his 'first life', some of the agonizing Weimar political parties had asked him to accept the chancellorship, an offer which he declined, thus proving his sound political perceptiveness, even at a much earlier age. His authority and popularity were thus twice enhanced, and so was his aplomb in assuming the leadership at each stage in the re-formation of Germany's political structure and stability.

## His solitary personal life

Adenauer was twice a widower. His first wife died in 1916, aged 36, after only fourteen years of marriage, leaving him with two sons and a daughter. In 1919, still mayor of Cologne, he married for a second time, a woman eighteen years younger than himself, who gave him another four children, lived with him, and helped him to survive the threats and terrors of Nazi persecution. She died exhausted by her efforts, in March 1948, when Adenauer was already seventy-two. Apart from his work, to which he gave more of his time, he only enjoyed being with his family, reading (Goethe, Shakespeare, St Augustine and thrillers), listening to music (and notably Schubert's *Lieder*), playing *boccia*, the Italian 'boules', talking, inventing (from his early youth till late in life, he collected innumerable patents) and, above all, gardening. There is no doubt that had he been free to choose his life's occupation, he would have been a gardener.

His loneliness, aggravated by his condition as a widower, showed also in his relations with people. He was, generally speaking, sceptical and while inclined towards idealism, was always prepared to be disappointed in human relations. This gave him a rather ironical, sometimes even sarcastic, way of speaking to people which, in turn, did not improve his sociability.

But he was also lonely in public affairs. Because he had taken such a solitary lead in the party which he founded, then with the help of that party in the political leadership and, indeed, in the formation of the new state – and possibly also because of his age, he developed an authoritarian style of government, which soon received the critical appellation 'Chancellor democracy'. 'For the first time', writes Karl Dietrich Bracher, 'the Germans were shown that parliamentary democracy can bring security and economic progress . . . (but) Adenauer's style perpetuated an unpolitical bureaucratic-authoritarian tradition which many critics felt was reminiscent of the Wilhelmian era.'

## His mature intellect

Adenauer had been a late developer, and indeed, had started his administrative career at a very low level, only after persevering in arduous, but inglorious, studies in law. But from these studies he acquired the greatest quality both of his intelligence and of his otherwise monotonous and dull oratory (someone once remarked that Adenauer's vocabulary comprised only a few words, but that each of these words was used most appropriately in each case). This reflects the natural advantage of a mature intellect; the power of concentrating on the essentials of a problem. This also went together with experience and with the capacity to persevere and to endure. The more life subjected him to contrasting joys and sorrows, hope and despair, rises and falls, the riper grew his mind, almost in illustration of Shakespeare's words, 'men must endure their going hence even as their coming hither: ripeness is all'.

*Stamina*, indeed longevity, was the quality which compensated for the lack of *brio* in his personality, as his moral authority compensated for his lack of charisma. He 'endured' in both senses of the word, i.e. remaining alive and undergoing pain and humiliation. To the longevity of his life must be added his exceptionally long leadership in power. He was elected Chancellor on 14 August 1949, and resigned (reluctantly) on 15 October 1963, so that his chancellorship lasted only four years less than Bismarck's – but then Bismarck resigned when he was only 75, while Adenauer was 87. Disraeli, too, was in his seventies during his last premiership, but it lasted only six years. Reagan's presidency began when he was 69 and lasted nine years, until 1989. Only Charles de Gaulle, his great partner, approached Adenauer's record with a presidency lasting eleven years between his 68th and 79th years. As for endurance, in the second sense of suffering, leaving aside the private dramas of his life, Adenauer's public career was punctuated by extraordinary setbacks – the last and most surprising of which was his abrupt dismissal by the British military authorities from his post as mayor of Cologne, to which he had naturally been reinstated by the Americans before Cologne was allocated to the British occupation zone. Six months later, in a letter dated 6 October 1945, Brigadier Sir John Barraclough, the new Commander of the North Rhine Province of the Military Government, informed him that 'he was not satisfied with the progress of clearance in Cologne' and ordered him 'as soon as possible and in any case not later than 14 October' to leave Cologne and to refrain from indulging 'either directly or indirectly in any political activity whatsoever', lest 'he be brought to trial by the Military Court'. This last provision, obviously of a party political nature, indicates that the measure had been adopted by the British Labour Government on the advice of the fraternal German Socialist Party in the Rhineland. When, years later, Barraclough asked Adenauer what he had thought of the letter, the latter replied with his usual scepticism that having just closed the file entitled 'Dismissed by the Nazis', he had opened a new one entitled 'Dismissed by the British'.

## His Christian education and philosophy

Adenauer's conceptual framework had a Christian foundation. Born into a staunchly Catholic family, in the deeply Catholic Rhineland, in the Catholic capital of Germany, Cologne, he was from the beginning to the end of his life a practising Catholic. This had both political and personal consequences for him. Politically, he acquired almost with his mother's milk, a deep-rooted distrust and dislike of Prussia, the Protestant, expansionist state from which Bismarck had launched a massive persecution of German Catholicism, which went by the name of the *Kulturkampf*. He also acquired and maintained the discipline of a communicant. The personal intransigence of his faith came to light when he was deeply in love with Gussi Zinsen, who was to become his second wife and was the young daughter of his Protestant neighbours and friends. While he was able to laugh off the considerable difference in age between them, he nevertheless insisted that she become a Catholic.

Thus deeply-rooted in the Christian logic of life, he could not but apply it to all problems, from the deeply personal to the general ones. In that logic politics derives from ethics and ethics from religion. His reading also consisted in great part of Christian theology and philosophy; he told his biographer, Paul Weimar that one of the maxims which had always guided his life was St Augustine's 'Thou has created us for Thyself and our hearts are restless till we find repose in Thee.'

The period of almost a year which he spent in hiding from Nazi persecution in the eleventh century Maria Laach monastery in the Eifel mountains proved to be a most profitable 'pause' for him, before fate entrusted him with further historical tasks. The seclusion offered him a welcome opportunity to read and meditate. The study in depth of the famous papal encyclicals on social questions, *Rerum Novarum* and *Quadragesimo Anno* gave to his almost instinctive social and political beliefs a new theoretical firmness and clarity. The ideas of a *Rechtssozialstaat,* of *Sozialwirtschaft,* of 'ordo-liberalism', *Mitbestimmung,* and expanding federalization, (i.e. national and international) which were to become the pillars and early slogans of the Federal Republic of Germany, were already engraved on his mind as the best foundations for the future Germany polity. The basis of this philosophy was the fundamental Christian belief in the sanctity of the individual, and therefore in the inviolability of his rights and his conscience by the state or any other organization which did not have the legitimacy of the free consent of the human beings comprised in it. Hence also the quest for effective decentralization for which federalization was the obvious prerequisite.

Furthermore, the Christian political conception inspires those who follow it with a wider vision, which goes beyond the frontiers of the nation-state. The ultimate aspiration towards the universality of the Church, associated in the German mind with the controversial concept of the *Reich* (of which more in the next section) and the spirit of human fraternity of the Christian faith runs counter to the very principle of the nation-state which historically was responsible for the break-up of the universal Church and tones down the visceral instinct of nationalism. This ultimate goal of Christian political philosophy catalysed the common action of the Christian Democratic statesmen: the French Robert Schuman, the Italian de Gasperi and the German Adenauer, by then heads of government. Arnolf Baring in a slightly gossipy manner investigates the ways in which Pope Pius XII's ideas of a (Catholic) European Union made their impact within these international Catholic manoeuvres through the hitherto unremarked Catholic prelate Wilhelm Böhler, whose travels between Rome, Paris and Bonn according to him prepared later negotiations.

In the countries which had suffered a great deal of destruction in the war, like France, Germany and Italy (and many others) and in peoples haunted by a sense of guilt, like the Italians and above all, the Germans, the Christian sense of life proved a powerful impulse of political psychology. It led many of those who had lived through years of torture, terror and betrayal, of the organized cruelty of a Fascist war, towards the Christian doctrine as the only consolation and source of forgiveness. As Adenauer wrote in his memoirs[3],

when I look back on those dark days, it seems to me almost a miracle that everywhere, all over Germany, groups were being formed to demand a new Christian party. They demanded it because of the experience of the National Socialist period . . . These groups wanted their name to include the word 'Christian'; they wanted to indicate their essential aims and opposition to National Socialism.

But in his interpretation, this popular return to the Christian faith and this quest for a new Christian *Weltanschauung* and organization had two further, but essential, qualifications.

On the one hand, Christianity meant, in a more general sense, idealism[4]:

A materialist ideology was bound to emphasize the importance of power and of the state which gathered and embodied this power, and to lead to the subordination of ethical values and of the dignity of the individual. Marxist materialism contributed a great deal to this development . . . That such a result is inevitable is shown by the history of the countries that regard Karl Marx as their Messiah and his teachings as Gospel. National Socialism was the most logical development – pushed to criminal lengths – of that worship of power and that scorn for the individual which naturally arise from a materialistic ideology . . . National Socialism found the strongest mental and moral opposition in those parts of Germany which, whether Catholic or Protestant, had been least affected by socialism and by the doctrine of Karl Marx . . . Materialistic ideology turns the individual into a small, anonymous cog in a huge machine. I regard this ideology as destructive.

Secondly, as is evident from a sentence quoted above, Adenauer wanted the German Christian Democrat Party, unlike the Italian Christian Democrat Party, whose membership was overwhelmingly Catholic, to comprise both German Catholics and German Protestants. He had devoted the first two years of his political activity to the formation of this party (at the beginning, clandestinely because of Brigadier Barraclough's prohibition of any political activity). For, in his view, they both shared the idealistic, or even more specifically, the anti-materialistic Christian belief. As he put it: 'Protestant and Catholic Germans, indeed all who know and value the importance of Christianity in Europe, should be able to join – and it goes without saying that this also applies to our Jewish fellow-citizens.'[5] In other words, he wanted to include in the new party all those whose belief in God and therefore whose idealism led them to abhor materialism and materialistic philosophies, and their ultimate pursuit of power, which is, according to them, the dispenser of happiness on earth.

The new Christian Democrat Party, the party he had set out to form, was open to all men of good will in the Christian sense of the words, and it was to enjoy a lightning popular success. Christian democracy caught the mood of the German people for redemption and benefited from a dramatic religious revival which swept across Germany in the early post-war period. In Bavaria, however, a different party, the Christian Social Union (CSU) was formed on the same basis: it was going to form a permanent joint parliamentary *Fraktion* within the CDU. In the 1949 elections, the CDU/CSU won 31 per cent of the votes, the Socialists (SDP) 29.2 per cent and in 1945, the CDU/CSU won 45.2 per cent as against the SPD's 28.8 per cent. The Adenauer era had begun.

## He was a Rhinelander

As already mentioned, one of the leitmotifs of German history has been the profound difference in political psychology and national character between some of its provinces, erstwhile independent kingdoms, principalities, bishoprics, free cities *et al.*, and most notably between the principal regions like the Rhineland or Westphalia and the southern provinces like Bavaria on the one hand, and the north-eastern region like Brandenburg-Prussia on the other, which in the nineteenth century had been the leader in the formation of the Second Reich. Possibly the original cause of these differences and indeed mutual antipathies lay in past history. For Prussia, that is the Mark of Brandenburg and East Prussia, had not formed part of the Roman Empire nor of Charlemagne's western empire nor even of the first German *Reich*, founded in 962, when Otto of Saxony was crowned emperor of a revived Roman empire of the West, known as the Holy Roman Empire of the German nation, but to the Germans always known as the *Deutsches Reich*.

By the eighteenth century Prussia had become, from a military and administrative point of view, the most powerful of the individual units of the Reich, qualities which were to help Bismarck in the nineteenth century to expel Austria from the Reich in 1866 and then to unite all the German regions into one single *Second Reich*, after the defeat of the French in 1870. Hitler's *Reich* was to be the *Third*, after he succeeded in dissolving the Weimar Republic. But even the latter, oddly enough, still considered itself to be a kind of *Reich*, as can be seen in the names of its principal institutions: *Reichstag*, *Reichspräsident*, *Reichsregierung*, *Reichsgericht*, etc. The Federal Republic of Germany is the first German state in which the word *Reich*, with all its implications, is not officially used.

As a Catholic and a Rhinelander, therefore geo-politically much closer to France and Western Europe than to Prussia, and as a man of robust democratic opinions, Adenauer had an instinctive dislike and fear of Prussia. These feelings affected his political activity in two ways: first in the political alternative with which he was faced in three different historical circumstances of the possibility of the creation of a Rhenish state or Rhenish independent unit of government; and, secondly, in the explicit logic of his permanent quest for a European Union.

The first time Adenauer was faced with this problem was in 1919, when he was still Mayor of Cologne. As his biographer, Paul Weymar puts it, he was alleged 'to have played a part in the Rhenish separatist movement, which early in 1919 endeavoured to detach the Rhineland from Prussia and establish it as a separate Rhenish state'. There were two schools of thought among the notables assembled by Adenauer, in his capacity as Mayor, in the City Hall of Cologne on 1 February 1919: the extremists who advocated 'a complete detachment of the Rhineland from the body of the German Reich and the establishment of an independent Rhenish state' and the moderates who 'were in favour of detaching the Rhineland from Prussia, but insisting that such a Federal Rhenish State must remain within the framework of the German Reich'.

In his speech, Adenauer objectively explained, as a true statesman, that it was natural from her point of view that France, now victorious, should wish to exact a safeguard against future German aggression, either by incorporating the Rhineland in her territory or by creating a further state between her and the Reich. Moreover, in his speech that day Adenauer also predicted that the more severe the treatment meted out by the Allies, the greater would be the spirit of revenge in Prussia, thus perpetuating the recurrent Franco–German wars over the frontier zones. Prussia was the crux of the matter.

In the opinion of our former enemies, he (Adenauer) said that it was Prussia who drove the world into this war . . . Public opinion abroad therefore demands: Prussia must be partitioned. Now if this were done, if the western provinces of Germany were joined together in a federal state, it would no longer be possible for Prussia, in the opinion of other countries, to dominate Germany. Owing to its size, and it must be larger to exercise adequate influence, and its economic importance, this West German Republic would be able to guide Germany's foreign policy along strong, peaceful and conciliatory lines. This could, and should satisfy France.

The text of the final resolution of the meeting was also significant:

We, the undersigned representatives of the Rhenish people in occupied Prussian territory, register our emphatic and solemn protest against all plans and efforts now discernible in the press of foreign countries, aiming at the detachment of the Rhine, or parts of it, from Germany . . . In view of the fact that the partition of Prussia is now being seriously considered, we charge a special committee, elected by ourselves, with the task of preparing plans for the establishment of a West German Republic within the constitutional framework of the German Reich.[6]

Adenauer was, surprisingly, elected chairman of that committee.

Nothing came of the resolution and Paul Weymar, like Clemenceau at the time, thinks Adenauer had taken the lead in order to be able to adopt delaying tactics. But it should not have been too surprising that, in the extraordinarily similar situation which prevailed after the Second World War, though for quite different reasons, Adenauer, who had previously played such an open role, would be attacked by the Opposition for his 'treacherous anti-Prussian' attitude after the First World War.

The second time that Adenauer was faced with the question of the separation of the Rhineland from the Reich was when, in quite different circumstances, he and other Rhineland officials were called to Berlin on 13 November 1923, by the then Reich Chancellor, Gustav Stresemann, to be told that, given the catastrophic financial and monetary situation of the country, the government 'was faced with the necessity of discontinuing its policy of subsidies for the occupied territories' (Rhineland and Westphalia). After his strong opposition to such a national 'sacrifice for purely financial reasons' and after the fall of the Stresemann government, ten days later, the matter was forgotten.[7]

And the third time occurred on 15 July 1946 when Adenauer and his great socialist opponent, Dr Kurt Schumacher, leader of the SDP, were urgently called to Berlin to be told by Lieutenant-Colonel Sir Brian Robertson, the British Deputy Military Governor, that the British Military Government had decided to create a new political unit, indeed a *Land*, in the British zone: the *Land* of North Rhine Westphalia. The creation of this *Land* also showed the clear intention to prevent Prussia being reconstituted as a *Land*. 'Foreign policy considerations played the chief role here' wisely remarked Adenauer in his memoirs.[8] When Robertson asked what they thought of the proposal, Schumacher after being told that the decision was final, rejected it and protested, but Adenauer recognized in his memoirs that he accepted, adding that 'it was necessary to interlock the former Rhine province as far as possible with other regions to the East and West in order to protect the left bank of the Rhine from France's demands.' And Adenauer comments further:

If the French demands for the detachment of the left bank of the Rhine from Germany had been met, it would, in my opinion, have meant the economic disintegration, not only of Germany, but also of Europe. Since economic decay is good soil for the growth of communism, communism and with it the Soviet Union would have eventually become master of the whole of Germany . . . In my view, such a West German *Land* was the surest guarantee against Germany, even after her recovery, initiating action that might lead to war. Such a territorial unit must in the nature of things, both because of the views of its inhabitants and because of its economic structure, aim at collaboration with Germany's Western neighbours, with Holland, Belgium, Luxemburg, France and Britain.[9]

But Adenauer's biographer, Paul Weymar adds to his version of the story a note of humour. Adenauer told him that when Robertson asked whether they were in agreement with this measure, Schumacher answered 'No, Herr General'. Adenauer replied 'Yes, Sir Brian'. That ended the interview. As they left the room, Adenauer with a slight movement of his head towards Schumacher murmured to his companion, 'He's a Prussian, after all.'[10]

The fact that Adenauer was a Rhinelander was significant also in another respect. 'I am a German, but I am also and have always felt like a European' is one of the opening phrases in his memoirs. It was also one of the leitmotivs of his important speeches or declarations.

But when Adenauer used the phrase 'I have always been a European' after the First World War, it had a quite different significance. First of all, it was very early. It is true that already in the 1920s, the League of Nations, and great statesmen like Briand and Stresemann (whom Adenauer disliked because he was a Prussian) were trying to find European policies in which the national policies, and the nationalism which fostered them, could be subsumed. But Adenauer did not join them. His name does not appear among early supporters of the League of Nations or among the early federalists. Therefore the sentence meant something else in his mouth.

As a Christian and a Rhinelander, his Europeanism conjured up the glory of Christian Europe, of a continent divided into small local and decentralized polities, but all united by the bond of faith and by the supreme authority of the Church. And as a Rhinelander, he knew very clearly that, for instance, his people were culturally and politically nearer to the French across the Rhine than to the Prussians from his own country. Together, these two subconscious sentiments emanated from the concept of *Reich*, not in the 'Nordic', Prussian sense Hegel or Fichte gave to it, but in the sense which Charlemagne gave to it of a religious–geopolitical community, locally administered by small, autonomous units and deliberately, to use the word in an anachronistic sense, *federated* in the ever-expanding Christian empire. But it so happened that both the concept and the expression of *Reich* were German – and in that sense there was a deeper meaning and sincerity in Adenauer's phrase than when it was used as a cliché. Moreover, the north eastern provinces had been converted to Christianity much later, and with specific tendencies which contributed to its becoming Protestant after the Reformation.

For, ultimately, the concept of *Reich* gave the German people who lived under its symbol the sense or even the feeling of belonging to a free association of different, and somehow autonomous, polities like kingdoms, principalities, duchies, prince-bishoprics, etc., but united by their people's natural inclination towards universality. Whereas a nation-state is an exercise in inner concentration on the people's own qualities and rights, the *Reich* required a spiritual association in a broader framework, and especially in a goal which must be universal. This tendency, in many respects synonymous with its 'idealism', is characteristic of German culture as a whole. The German genius is manifested above all in the two most abstract universal and idealistic activities of the human mind: music and philosophy. Lessing, Herder, Schiller, Goethe, Leibnitz, Kant, Hegel, Bach, Beethoven, Schumann or the Wagner of *Tristan und Isolde* or *Parsifal*, strive to reach that supreme level where the human soul, freed from the triviality of human life, can interrogate its fate and its God.

That the other side of the coin of the German pursuit of universalism is a dominating sense of authority is also true. Hegel's philosophy, as a more modern example, encloses the individual in a pre-established system in which his spirit must bend to the laws of the overall Spirit. This implies an act of submission and a recognition of the domination of supreme authority – which in political terms is the supreme authority of the nation state and of its consequential imperialism. But Goethe's message to the German people to avoid forming a nation until each of them had developed within himself the precondition of the independence of the soul, sounds in retrospect like a prophetic curse. Since that moment, soon after the French revolution, the ambition of German nationalism to build an organized *Staat* to rival that built by Napoleon, rapidly escalated and reached its apogee in Hitler's Third Reich. For what was missing in this political evolution, as Goethe had prophesied, was the strong sense of free will of the citizen. In spite of the attachment of the individual German to his local or regional homeland, the urge to create a united and powerful *Staat* prevailed, crushing the individual in the exercise.

Adenauer's *democratic*, *pluralistic* and *federal* political ideals, derived from Goethe who was one of his masters, enabled him to combine in his action the German and European aspirations.

## II

## ADENAUER'S POLITICS OF INTERDEPENDENCE

At the year zero, 1944, and for another couple of years, there was no politics in what had been Germany. There was no politics, partly because the Occupying Powers did not allow political parties to function. They were first permitted in 1945 by the USSR in its zone of occupation, but this was primarily in order to assert the priority of the Communist Party and to utilize it immediately as an administrative instrument of occupation. In the American and French zones, political parties were allowed to form in late 1945 and in the British zone in 1946. But could there be politics when there was no state, no constitution, no capital, no parliament and when the Germans were faced with so many pressing problems? Among these problems first came grinding poverty: the ration was about 1500 calories of food per person per day; there were hardly any habitable houses in towns; tuberculosis and hunger-induced oedema were widespread. Then they were faced with the clearing of the rubble and hasty reconstruction: with the invasion of these miserable abodes by some seven million expellees and refugees from the territories annexed by Russia, Poland and Czechoslovakia, six million others having died in the exercise; with the see-saw contradiction between the dismantling of German industry and the increasing demands for reparations. And, last but not least, there prevailed the same operation of denazification, the fear of which allowed few adult Germans to be certain of their personal future, as it culminated in the exemplary Götterdämmerung of the Nuremberg trials and its high gallows. In such conditions, politics could have been only a Utopian luxury.

When all mature Germans had undergone their moral examination, what emerged predominantly from the depths of the individual and collective conscience was shame: shame in the form of resentment at having been defeated in a great number of them, but more overwhelmingly, shame at having shared in the diabolic cruelty and monstrous crimes of a political regime and a leader for whom they and their parents had voted, and whom they had allowed to continue in his criminal war to the bitter end. Two alternative post- and anti-Nazi political attitudes resulted from this agonizing re-examination of the

German conscience – where it existed – and their common motive was *peace*.

One was the somewhat ready-made socialist response, with its natural assumptions of war-mongering capitalism and imperialism (but forgetting in the exercise the Nazi–Soviet Pact), its goals of social justice as the overall moral remedy, and its ready-made organization into which new wine could easily be poured. The Socialists also benefited from the active sympathy of the new British Labour Government, the French Socialist Party and, for a while, from Soviet duplicity towards the Socialist Party which was soon, however, forcibly merged in the Russian zone with the Communist Party.

The other attitude was that of the *new* Christian Democratic Party, as new a political phenomenon as its Italian and French (MRP) counterparts, whose moral roots of guilt, pursuit of redemption, human fraternity and hope have already been touched on here. This was Adenauer's new political inspiration around which he succeeded in rallying unexpectedly large numbers of members in the three Western zones. The meeting of the Zonal Committee of Neuheim-Pusten in late February 1946, where he was also elected chairman of the party, was ultimately to lead to its unexpected victory in the first, 1949, national elections in the three Western zones and to his chancellorship, which was to last for fifteen years.

## Sovereignty, by any other name

Adenauer's purpose was to reconstruct a new German state. He explicitly spoke of reconstruction as the reconquest of sovereignty. Not only in his speeches at the time, which might have been electorally motivated, but even in his memoirs the advance on the way to 'sovereignty' is marked as the most significant stage of the recovery. This is, of course, a most apposite method of assessing the fulfilment of a statesman's goals. Yet, most especially in Adenauer's case, the concept of sovereignty was already intrinsically relativized by the surrounding prerequisites of interdependence.

In his particular case, sovereignty had to be wrested from the Occupiers slowly and painfully, bit by bit – without full sovereignty being *formally* achieved. This had made Adenauer adopt a characteristic political style. For, long before his election as Chancellor on 15 September 1949, and the ensuing Petersberg agreements of 21 September 1949 (which were in reality a complete change in the Occupation-status, restoring to the Germans most political and administrative functions, apart from defence and foreign affairs, and were duly marked by Adenauer as a point of no return towards sovereignty) because of his position, and because of the fact that alone he had immediately to take joint decisions with the real organs of power, the Foreign High Commissioners, Adenauer became accustomed to a personal decision-making process which afterwards degenerated with age into 'Chancellor's democracy'. (The Petersberg agreements led to an historical, almost uninterrupted debate which lasted for 48 hours in the Bundestag: the Opposition reproached Adenauer for having committed the country to obligations which were not authorized by parliament. Dr Schumacher (leader of the SDP) had to be suspended by the Speaker for 21 days, when he refused to retract the insulting epithet of 'Allies' Chancellor', which he threw at Adenauer in his rage.)

Secondly, the alternative Socialist or Christian Democratic policies – the former aiming at the neutrality of a unified Germany, within a pacifist and planned Europe, while the latter aimed at the integration of West Germany into Western (Atlantic and European) democracy, with its welfare and social market economy – were directly dependent on the course external events were to take. After a couple of years of uncertainties, it became clear that the view Adenauer obtained from his periscope was a more adequate representation of external developments and a more appropriate prescription for the internal evolution of the new German polity. But at the same time it became clear that, to put it more cynically, many of the German initiatives derived from major predetermined and predetermining events. This does not exclude at all the part he and the evolution of his country under his leadership had in the external events themselves. But that spelled interdependence – within the impact of which the very concept of 'sovereignty', so eagerly sought, and fervently stimulated, had acquired a new and much more relative meaning.

What follows is an inevitably much too brief examination of the 'coincidence' of six major stages in the constant progress of Adenauer's policy in and for Germany with the two evolutionary stages of the double forms of Western co-operation: Atlantic and European.

## The North Rhine Westphalia Land and the change in East–West relations

One of the first major steps towards securing some German autonomy was the creation of the *Land* of North Rhine Westphalia in July

1947. The creation of this *Land* was to be followed in September by the establishment of the Anglo-American bi-zone, the French adding theirs in 1948. This move, hotly contested by the Socialist and Communist opposition as a direct attempt to dismember German territory for good, had been explicitly introduced by the British Deputy Military Governor as a consequence of the Soviet refusal to merge the four zones and the wish of the British and American governments to consolidate the parts of Germany occupied by them. 'Germany's salvation is in your hands to win or cast away', said Sir Brian Robertson when he introduced the plan.

Only have the courage and you will win it. Come forward determined to make the best of the largest part of your country, which is on the right side of the iron curtain . . . The time has come to realize that the interest of all Europeans is converging. Our needs and your needs cannot be dealt with separately for we all form part of Europe.[11]

As mentioned above, Adenauer approved immediately of this measure as a 'step of far-reaching political importance for us Germans and for Europe'. The view from his periscope was correct. But it was, nevertheless, periscopic.

For this was in reality one of the initial consequences of the fundamental change in the relations between the Allies, as well as in the political thinking of the government of the US and of British political circles, stirred from the opposition by Winston Churchill. Even Roosevelt and his *éminence grise*, Harry Hopkins, had begun to be 'disenchanted' by and suspicious of Stalin's behaviour. After Roosevelt's death, a new trend of thought began to impose itself from without and within the State Department by a number of professors, bankers and lawyers, sometimes seconded to the State Department, and it came to the fore especially under the new President, Harry Truman. A group of such intellectuals, all Ivy League colleagues and friends, among whom the principal were Dean Acheson, Averell Harriman, George F. Kennan, Charles (Chip) Bohlen, Robert A. Lovell and John McCloy, whose official leader was Acheson, at first Under Secretary and then Secretary of State and whose conceptual mentor was George Kennan, in 1947 Counsellor at the US embassy in Moscow, exerted first its informal and then official influence. They all engaged together in a thorough and, according to them overdue re-interpretation of Stalinist foreign policy, regardless of what had been Roosevelt's views and sentiments, or were at the time those of James F. Byrne or Henry L. Stimson, then Secretary of State and Secretary of War respectively, and they captured the attention of Harry Truman, the new President.[12]

One can retrace very briefly the initial and irreversible phase of that history-making process in the lightning succession of events in 1946. Truman was already concerned by Stalin's behaviour in Poland, Romania, Bulgaria and East Germany. And Churchill, in a telegram of May 1945 had already asked Truman 'What is going to happen about Russia? An iron curtain is drawn upon their front. We do not know what is going on behind it . . . Meanwhile the attention of our peoples will be occupied by inflicting severities upon Germany which is ruined and prostrate . . .' Yet Stalin's official rhetoric and behaviour maintained the façade of the old Alliance almost intact.

But on 9 February 1946, Stalin made a public speech during the electoral campaign for the Supreme Soviet, drawing the attention of the Soviet people for the first time openly to 'hostile' international surroundings, to 'capitalist encirclement', and to the inevitable incompatibility between communism and capitalism. The speech caused a sensation in Washington, and in the West in general. As the book *The Wise Men* shows, both the State Department and the US Treasury cabled the US embassy in Moscow. Harriman, the Ambassador, had just left for America, leaving George Kennan in charge. His pessimistic views about future relations with the USSR were so well known to Harriman and in great part shared by him, that when he left he told Kennan almost prophetically: 'Now you can send them all the telegrams you want'. On 5 March 1946, Kennan replied to the inquiries from Washington in what is now known as the 'Long Telegram' or the famous article signed XXX in *Foreign Affairs*, which the authors of *Wise Men* correctly described as 'the most influential cable in the history of the American Foreign Service'. The policy of 'containment' was born, the principle of which was that the USSR must be 'contained' by all means, including military means, and prevented from advancing further by any methods into the rest of the world, so that it would dissolve into its own basic contradictions. By sheer coincidence, on the same day, 5 March 1946, Winston Churchill delivered his Fulton speech about the 'Iron Curtain' and the new dangers of aggression. On 12 March 1946, upon the admission by the British government that it 'found it impossible to grant further assistance to Greece and to Turkey', President Truman delivered his speech, committing the United States to continuing help to Greece and Turkey, and to 'all free peoples to maintain their free institutions and their national integrity against aggressive movements that seek to impose upon them totalitarian regimes'. The Truman doctrine was born.

The reader will have ample opportunities in the rest of the book to establish the differences between the American policy of 'containment' of the Truman doctrine and later American policies of 'liberation'. Here it need only be noted that Adenauer grasped at once what they had in common: the breakdown of the Alliance and its replacement by the necessity of defending Europe against further Soviet military and political encroachment.

## *'Staatliche Fortexistenz', the Marshall Plan and the Berlin Blockade*

The year between 1948 and 1949 saw an accumulation of examples of interdependence. Starting with the bitter conclusions to be drawn from the total failure of the last conference of the Allied Foreign Ministers in the last days of December 1947, these years produced an amazing chain of actions and reactions. On the one hand, both the United States and the USSR proceeded to openly confrontational attitudes. On the other hand, the German problem came to the fore with dramatic topicality. Shortly afterwards, in June 1949, the Marshall Plan was announced. It, too, ran parallel to some extent with the policy of containment: it placed the emphasis on the necessity for the US to give massive assistance to the rehabilitation and strengthening of Western Europe in general, but bearing in mind the need to resist the expected aggression or subversion by Communist Russia.

The announcement of the Marshall Plan was immediately followed by the predictable refusal of the USSR to join, or to allow its satellites to join, although Poland and Czechoslovakia had originally welcomed the American proposal. Moreover, Stalin applied a strict policy control of the satellites by instituting the COMECON in 1948, a Russian controlled economic organization of the Soviet bloc, the follow-up to the COMINFORM, a political organization for eradicating national communism which had spread from Titoist Yugoslavia. The abyss between the two parts of Europe was further widened.

On the other hand, the three zones of Germany, now unified, benefited from the Marshall plan, as well as from the particular attention of American industrial firms. The latter were eager to invest in what rightly seemed to them to be the most industrious country, by comparison with the ideologically torn Italy, France and even Great Britain, and a country which responded with astonishing energy. An Economic Council, established in Frankfurt in February 1946 by the American and British authorities gave the first opportunity to a young professor, Ludwig Erhardt, himself a Christian Democrat, to launch the country on the road to the 'economic miracle' which was later attributed to him.

In the meantime, Adenauer was pressing the Military Commanders to allow the establishment of German constitutional institutions, and notably a Court of Justice and a 'Basic Law', if a constitution could not yet be envisaged. The Americans and the British would have proceeded faster had it not been for French opposition. France insisted that before any kind of German political entity could be re-established, the Ruhr should be placed permanently under international control, and the Saar should be separated from German territory as an independent unit of rule, and made other demands. On 29 December 1948, a Statute of the Ruhr was issued, setting up an authority of the Ruhr under the control of the three Western allies and of Benelux, with some German participation.

In the meantime, on both sides of the abyss, developments in the international sphere had been proceeding apace. In the West, the Marshall Plan showed immediate, startling results, although one of its aims, to act on Europe as a whole, was not so keenly observed by the national governments. But at the same time, the first intergovernmental European Congress was held from 7 to 10 May 1949 at The Hague. Until then, the movement for European Federation had been conducted mainly by groups from the former Resistance, by ex-prisoners of war and inmates of concentration camps of all nationalities, and led by intellectuals like Altiero Spinelli, Denis de Rougemont, Henri Brugmans, Albert Camus, Salvador de Madariaga, T. S. Eliot, André Malraux, etc. Adenauer attended the Congress as one of the 'German delegates', who were greeted by Churchill in his inaugural presidential address (though Jean Monnet, the actual organiser of the Congress mentioned his name in his *Mémoires* merely as 'and also some unknown persons: a German parliamentarian, Konrad Adenauer').

The Hague Congress resolved to ask for a United Europe, a Charter of Human Rights and a European Cultural Centre. It must be considered as the official starting point of European integration, although it is still stigmatized by federalists like Denis de Rougement as the turning point when the genuine European federal inspiration was stifled under the new official embrace of the intergovernmental as against the supranational idea by the national governments, their lawyers, economists and diplomats.

Stalin, on his side, was also doing his best to catalyse and concentrate the attention of the governments and public opinion by providing further proofs of his aggressiveness. Taking as a pretext the confusion created in Berlin, divided into four zones of occupation, by the monetary problems of the four different currencies, he decreed the

'Berlin Blockade', cutting all land and waterborne communications of the West with the city. Not only did this gesture give rise to an unprecedented reaction of fear and indignation in the West – and provide further arguments for those who like Adenauer thought that the only solution to the cold war was the military preparedness of the West, but it also resulted in a humiliation for the USSR, when it had to bring the blockade to an end in May 1949. For since technology was always on the side of the developed society of the West, the extraordinarily efficient airlift organized by the Western Powers kept the West Berliners fed, informed and in constant communication with the West.

But simultaneous important events had taken place in the West, possibly speeded up by the feeling of solidarity which developed during the Berlin blockade. The two most significant of these were the signing of the North Atlantic Treaty (NATO) on 4 April 1948 and the establishment of the Council of Europe on 28 May 1948. NATO, the perfect embodiment of the Truman doctrine, was a robust politico-military structure which was to prove its indispensability for keeping the peace over the next forty years. But its creation only sharpened more clearly the dilemma of the position of West Germany, the defence of which came to the forefront of the organization's military obligations. Yet, because of the fear and revulsion of Western, and especially French, public opinion, as well as of the Left in Germany, at the very thought of German rearmament, West Germany could not be allowed to take part in the new defence dispositions. The American government whose military and economic power were predominant in the organization, openly believed that, one way or another, a means should be found to facilitate Germany's contribution to its own and to the joint defence. And so did Adenauer, to whom, to quote Paul Weymar 'it seemed that the American demand was entirely justified, not only in material respects, but above all morally. If American soldiers were to defend the Ruhr territory, it would be the bounden duty of German soldiers to help them'.[13] Moreover, Adenauer used this argument to a great extent also to convince the three Western Powers to hasten their approval of the preparation for the reconstitution of a *sui generis* German 'political entity' (*staatliche Fortexistenz*), so that it could of its own volition also assume moral obligations in a common action. It is true to say that Adenauer's idea of 'sovereignty' was almost subconsciously connected with the right of a people to bear arms in its own defence. This was one of the reasons why the more progress was made in that field, the freer he felt to think and assert that Germany was reconquering its 'sovereignty'.

The Council of Europe, although at the beginning limited to only 11 members, and although by definition more of a consultative than a policy-making institution, created for Adenauer similar problems, but in a different context. The problem was that the Council was an interior concentric circle of the Atlantic Western circle, but nevertheless exclusively European. In continuation of the Western policy under Truman, the United States looked with a favourable eye on all Western European attempts to make their national efforts together in a continental perspective. This was the initial condition of the Marshall Plan (due to expire in 1952) and this was the reason for the encouragement which Washington constantly gave to the idea of a European union. But, again, a European organization without Germany went against the grain of Europeanism. Yet all Adenauer's questions about the admissibility of the future German *staatliche Fortexistenz* came up against deep-rooted French opposition. And later, once the 'political activity' had been finally set up, France only grudgingly accepted German participation in the Council of Europe under two conditions: that Germany should only be an associate member, and that it should be accepted only together with the Saar, for which France demanded an entirely independent status.

But, so as not to anticipate, for Adenauer the most important events of 1948–49 occurred in Germany itself. First, a Parliamentary Council, of which he had been elected chairman, was formed on 1 September 1948, with among other tasks that of preparing a 'Basic Law'. The 'Basic Law', which was not a constitution, was published with the approval of the Allies on 23 May 1949. On 14 August, elections were held and the CDU/CSU obtained the highest number of votes (31 per cent against 19 per cent for the SDP) and seats in the new Parliament (Bundestag). On 21 September, a coalition government was formed under his chancellorship.

The *staatliche Fortexistenz* thus established had from the beginning a clearly interdependent configuration: externally, because of its uncut umbilical cord with the still controlling Western powers, while from an internal point of view, its double character of a *Sozial Rechtstaat* gave it from the beginning a distinct modern character. As a modern federation, it observed a particularly strict separation of powers by which the judiciary, namely the Constitutional Court of Justice, could reject or amend the legislation. As a *Sozialstaat*, its economy was grounded in the new formula of the 'social market economy' (*Sozialmarktwirtschaft*), in which as its name indicates, the participation of the workers, farmers and all other producers is required, not only through the Keynesian market system as consumers, but also as decision-makers of production and in enterprises.

## The Soziale Marktwirtschaft

As already noted, even in his earliest vision of a future Germany, Adenauer was predisposed towards a new form of civic and economic solidarity, *Rechtsstaat*, but a '*Sozial*' *Rechtsstaat*. This was the model he had in mind and wished to be able to construct. But, in fact, he would not have been able to do so without the help of two men.

One, as old as Adenauer, was Hans Böckler, who was a pre-Hitler trade union leader, who had become again in 1949 chairman of the *Deutsche Gewerkschaften* (German Trade Union Confederation). Although he opposed many of the economic measures taken by the renascent German authorities and by the Frankfurt Economic Council, he kept his friendship with Adenauer and constantly advised him during the preparation of the Basic Law to give it a participatory character of social co-operation with all classes, and especially with the working class, whose role in the industrial technological society he visualized in a functional, quasi-corporatist light. *Mitbestimmung* (co-determination) was one of his principles and although Adenauer did not at the beginning accept the institutionalization of co-determination in factories, he found in Böckler's general philosophy a confirmation of his own ideas of societal solidarity. Böckler and his successor, von Hoff (for Böckler died in 1951) played a decisive role in the orientation of the Republic towards European integration, as well as in the problem of the admissibility of rearmament. The German trade unions, without the active co-operation of which the economic and social rehabilitation of the country could not have been achieved, although traditionally allied with the Socialist Party, had declared their political neutrality towards all parties and co-operativeness with all governments.

The second, much younger, man was the brilliant professor of economics, Ludwig Erhardt, who was to become Minister of Finance in the first Adenauer cabinet and finally Chancellor. Having worked closely with the Frankfurt Economic Council, he had the most valuable capacity of blending the American insistence on free trade, the 'planning' inclination of the representative of both the British and French governments, which were more 'dirigiste' and 'state-centred', and the trade unions' demand for social co-operation, into one socio-economic organization, the social market economy. 'Our business community is still the prisoner of protectionist economy', Erhardt is quoted as having told the Cabinet on 11 October 1949. 'We would have the opportunity of becoming the pace-makers of a European development towards a freer organization of economic relations in the spirit of America's economic policy.'

Many authors have described the new organization of the 'concerted' German economy as the 'Americanization' of West German industry, 1945–73, which is actually the title of a book by Volker R. Berghahn. It is true that on the one hand, the penetration or rather re-penetration of American capital into German industry, in which it played a considerable part before Hitler's nationalization, was and is massive. And it is also true that in the early formative years of the new German economy, the liberal and free-trade principles of American economic thinking prevailed over the more state-centred principles of the British and French governments of that time. The American authorities were especially adamant over the abolition of cartels – the erstwhile pivot of German industry – and over the orientation towards free enterprises, great or small. But at the end of the day, one may also ask whether the American economic principles of free trade and free market economy did not prevail in German economic thinking because in the meantime interdependence was the increasingly visible 'iron law' of the functioning of the modern economy and politics.

The structure of the new state was based on strict federal separation of powers. The relations between the executive and the legislative are also tighter because of the double control of two Chambers, the *Bundestag* and the *Bundesrat*, as well as the parliaments of the *Länder,* which can exert a final control on the central and local authorities.

The entire *representative government*, parliament and government together must, however, be seen as integrated and limited by the 'co-operative' federal system. Apart from the three levels of the Legislature, *Länder* parliaments, *Bundestag* and *Bundesrat*, there are at least three important institutions: the Federal Bank in Frankfurt, the Federal Constitutional Court in Karlsruhe and (complete innovation) the Federal Employment Institute in Nüremberg, as well as some 1000 'non-ministerial organization units or high federal authorities, among them the Statistical Office and the Federal Investigation Office in Wiesbaden, the Federal Environmental Office, which dominate certain policy areas'. Klaus von Beyme[14] adds the remark that 'the very distribution of important institutions in cities far from the capital is unheard of in other countries'.

As far as the power of the judiciary is concerned, the Constitutional Court controls the constitutionality of laws and policies. It has rejected so many important laws that there is now a strong tendency in German politics towards the judicialization of political problems, not only because of the post-factum rejection of laws by the Court, but also in anticipation of a judicial correction in the formulation of the law in parliament. In some cases, too, parliament abandoned the project of a law which it was anticipated would be rejected by the Constitutional Court. The FRG's Constitutional Court is stronger than the American Supreme Court or the French *Conseil Constitutionnel*. A law which it declares to be unconstitutional is invalidated forever and the judgment is binding on the courts as well as on political and administrative authorities. From 1951 to 1980, the Federal Constitutional Court had declared 107 laws invalid and 60 'incompatible with the Basic Law'. One of its most celebrated and controversial actions was its rejection in 1975 of the abortion law, which was replaced by another and very restricted law in 1976 – a verdict for which it has been increasingly criticized by the Left.

As for the 'Fourth Power', the media, its role in the policy-making processes was, at the foundation of the Republic and probably still is, particularly important in Germany. The reason for its growing importance was, of course, primarily the technological progress of audio-visual information and communication, so that every inhabitant receives, or could receive, instant information about important world news in his own home. But there was a reason more especially applicable to Germany. Since ultimately the media were controlled by the Military Authorities of the three foreign powers, the Press was encouraged to lead the critical campaigns in favour of the denazification and democratization of public life. Since that time, the Press has maintained this didactic (but in the case of the tabloids, muck-raking) role. But in the meantime, the concentration of capital in the hands of a few press magnates has led, as in other Western democracies, to the different problem of the oligopoly, if not monopoly, of the media in a few hands – a problem too well known now in other Western democracies.

## *The Schuman Plan*

Once the so-called 'Petersberg agreements', which were in reality a new and fundamentally changed occupation statute, were signed on 21 September 1949, the real 'national' problems began to face the first Adenauer government. The 'agreements' themselves were ratified by the Bundestag in the dramatic 48-hour long debate of 14–25 November 1949. The ratification was greatly helped by the telegram of approval and congratulations sent by Böckler that very night, on behalf of the German trade unions, to Adenauer, thus leaving the Socialist Party's opposition suspended in mid-air (from which point it only landed back into real political realism after the Godesberg Congress of 15 November 1959, where it freed itself from the rusty Marxism and the internal radical and external neutralistic attitudes it had preserved, even after Schumacher's death).

The embryonic German state had to grow further to reach its final stage of development, or in Adenauer's language its 'sovereignty'. In this it was again assisted by two developments of interdependence, one in the major area of East–West relations, the other in the narrower, but increasingly self-conscious Western European area.

To respect the chronological order, the European development must be given priority. The vexing question of the Saar and of the Ruhr had surfaced again. The British and American Allies had already acceded to the French demand for the economic integration of those regions in the French Republic in April 1947. As far as the Ruhr was concerned, France had obtained in 1949 a Ruhr Authority, with a membership of thirteen, including Germany, to regulate the entire coal, iron and steel production of the Ruhr. France's demands were justified on the grounds that both these territories were the source of German armament and the battlefields of the Franco-German wars.

The problem of re-armament for European defence gave to the question of the Ruhr a new topicality. But the advance of Germany in European co-operation, which would have started symbolically with its admission as an associate-member of the Council of Europe, was halted by the French demand that the Saar, as a quasi-sovereign entity, should also be admitted at the same time and in the same capacity. Socialist and nationalist opposition on the Left and on the Right and especially of their extremes were odd bedfellows, both in France and Germany, on this issue, as indeed everywhere else in Europe, forming one of the unholiest political and ideological alliances in the history of ideologies. Therefore, Adenauer was quite hesitant about asking the Bundestag for approval of the German government's demand to be accepted as an associate-member of the Council of Europe at the same time as the Saar, although the High Commissioners of the three occupying powers had assured him that the problem of the Saar could not be considered as really solved until a peace treaty with Germany had also been signed and that therefore whatever was done then was only temporary.

On Tuesday 9 May we held the Cabinet meeting on entry into the Council of Europe. A conference of the three Western Foreign Ministers was due to start in London on 11 May 1950 and it was to deal with the German question . . . I regarded our Cabinet decision of 9 May as of great importance and had therefore called a Press conference for 8 p.m.

wrote Adenauer in his memoirs.[15] And he continues:

While the Cabinet was conferring, I was informed that an emissary of the French Foreign Ministry, Schuman, had an urgent communication for me . . . in essence Robert Schuman proposed to place the entire French and German production of coal and steel under a common High Authority, within the framework of an organization that should be open to other European countries. Schuman explained that the pooling of iron and steel production would immediately provide for the first stage of a European federation . . . and that the purpose of his proposal was not economic, but eminently political. In France, there was fear that once Germany had recovered, she would attack France. Schuman's plan corresponded entirely with the ideas I had been advocating for a long time concerning the integration of the key industries of Europe. *I informed Robert Schuman at once that I accepted his proposal wholeheartedly.*

I italicized these last words because in their astonishing laconism they provide us with a perfect example of statesmanship, that is with the personal courage and authority to take such an important, indeed, historical, decision. Adenauer's style of government was rightly criticized as 'Chancellor's Democracy'. But, on the other hand, how can statesmanship be exerted in a democracy without such personal courage in decision?

Jean Monnet describes these events from his point of view in his *Mémoires*. He was still Commissar for the French Economic Plan and therefore hierarchically dependent only on the Prime Minister, who was then Georges Bidault. Reflecting on Schuman's mission to the London Conference on Germany of 10 May, for which France had no new proposal to make, he realized that 'the meeting of 11 May in London was an opportunity not to be missed . . . To achieve this purpose, an entirely new situation should have been created by transforming the Franco-German problem into a European problem'.[16] Together with a new member, Paul Reuter and an old one, Etienne Hirsch of his team, he had started on 15 April to work on a draft plan. The French 'team' of policy-making technocrats, of which also more later, differed from the American 'team' of 'Wise Men', with whom Monnet had been in close touch ever since his Washington days, in that in the former Jean Monnet was definitely the 'boss' and his brilliant team followed him from the French Plan to the European Community. It was initially composed of Hirsch, Marjolin, Pleven, Alphand, Felix Gaillard, Pierre Uri, Pierre Comert, Jean-Jacques Rabier, all by 1952 ministers or high dignitaries, as well as later and differently, two young Britons, Richard Mayne and

François Duchêne. Between 16 April and Saturday 6 May, Monnet's team had produced nine drafts of the plan which consisted of the creation of a High Common Authority for the production and marketing of the two products, ultimately the European Community for Steel and Coal (ECSC) 'whose decisions will be compulsory for France, Germany and the other countries which will adhere to it' and, therefore, 'will realise the first concrete foundations of a European Federation, indispensable to the preservation of peace'.

On 28 April, Monnet took the project to the office of Bidault, the Prime Minister to whom as Commissar of the Plan he was directly responsible. Soon after, Schuman's *chef de cabinet*, Clappier, asked him to send him a copy, too, which Monnet did. He gave him a copy which Clappier took at once to the station, whence Schuman was leaving for Metz, where he spent his weekends. Monnet writes:

Clappier found Schuman in his carriage; 'Could you read Monnet's paper? It is important.' On Monday morning, he came to the same place to meet him. As he was getting out of the train, Schuman said: 'I have read the paper. *Je marche.*' These few words were enough to link things: the idea had suddenly passed into the political realm – it had become the object of power and of its dangerous responsibility. It is the privilege of politicians to decide on the general interest. Insofar as I did not dispose of this privilege, I had to make my contribution through intermediaries.

Like fate, interdependence then moved to a third actor. Dean Acheson, who recounts this episode amusingly in his *At the Creation*, had stopped in Paris at the weekend of 8 January to meet Schuman before the May London Conference. Schuman decided to tell him of the Plan (called since then the Schuman Plan only because Bidault had neglected to read it when it was submitted to him. Otherwise it would have been called the Bidault plan). At first grudgingly, because he feared that it might conceal the creation of a giant 'cartel' of coal and steel, which would run counter both to the anti-trust legislation and the interest of the steel and coal industry of the United States. Acheson was quickly convinced of the Plan's historical importance by Monnet and by the US Ambassador in Paris, David Bruce, a close friend of his. The communiqué of the Foreign Ministers' Conference of 13 May 1949 struck Acheson as satisfactory for the Germans in every respect '. . . Germany would be liberated from the controls to which she was still subject and accorded her sovereignty to the maximum extent compatible with the basis of the occupation regime' he wrote in his *Memoirs*.[18] As for the Schuman Plan which, as McCloy puts it 'had the effect of a little atom bomb', although more coldly received

by Great Britain, it was decided to forge ahead with it at great speed
and set up the ECSC. Monnet was going to see to it.

## The Korean War, re-armament and the 'road to full sovereignty'

The second and major event which put Germany, as Adenauer said
himself in a chapter title of his book 'On the road to full sovereignty',
was the invasion of South Korea on 25 June 1950 by North Korean
troops. On Sunday 25 June, the opinion of all policy-makers in
Washington from Kennan to Acheson to Truman was that this was
a direct aggression by the USSR, its deliberate transformation of the
cold war into the hot war. Therefore, the invasion should be resisted
and only the US could do that, given the obvious weakness of the
South Korean forces.

It was particularly significant that this time Kennan himself advocated military intervention by the US because ever since the proclamation of the 'Truman doctrine' almost immediately after his presentation of the 'policy of containment', he had insisted on underlining
the difference between the two. He described the Truman doctrine as
an over-reaction to the, in his eyes, more balanced and less provocative policy of 'containment'. From that date onwards, he had deplored
the fatal escalation on both sides and feared the over-commitment
of the US to the military defence of any country threatened by a
Communist advance, predicting like a desolate Cassandra, an inevitable mishap as a result of such an undiscriminating attitude (as for
instance the Vietnam war). But this time he thought that the policy
of containment must draw upon the military alternative. Stung by
the fact that he had not been called as one of the innumerable experts
Acheson had summoned to the State Department, Kennan on his own
initiative went to see him and encouraged him to try to go ahead.

So did Truman at once, pursued as he was by the memory of the
fatal error made by the democracies threatened by the impending Nazi
aggression. And so did every military, political (Congress) and diplomatic adviser Truman consulted. Especially outspoken and influential
was the intervention of John McCloy, the US High Commissioner in
Germany, who stressed one particular aspect: the analogy between
North and South Korea and East and West Germany, the possibility
that the Soviet aggression in Asia through a puppet-proxy might be
a dress rehearsal for a similar performance in the West or even a
diversion for the real aggression in central Europe. In the curious
and still inexplicable absence of the Soviet Union from the urgently
called meeting of the Council of the United Nations, where it could

once more have used its habitual veto, the projected American action was endorsed by the UN, and it was with its formal approval and the military and economic support of its members that the American and other NATO troops engaged in the long Korean war, with its inevitable mixed fortune. The eventual result was that, by now, South Korea is one of the most prosperous and technologically advanced new industrializing countries in the world.

As in all relations of causality, in the politics of interdependence the influence and counter-influence between Adenauer and John McCloy, and generally speaking between American and German political circles is particularly difficult to disentangle. But the fact remains that it was Adenauer who was first 'firmly convinced that Stalin was planning the same strategy for Western Europe as had been used in Korea . . . using the Russian zone police for a so-called "liberation" of West German territory', as he himself wrote in his *Memoirs*.[19] And he continued:

The Federal Republic was in a very dangerous situation indeed. We were unarmed, we had no defence forces of our own. The forces of the Western Allies in Germany were not strong enough as far as I could judge. The Soviet zone, on the other hand, had its people's police and was strongly armed. The Federal Republic would be quite defenceless against an attack from the Russian zone.'[20]

At a conference with the High Commissioners on 17 August 1950, Adenauer asked the Allies first for some demonstration of military strength that might restore people's confidence and secondly that the Federal Government should be enabled to build up a defence force of volunteer units to a total strength of 150,000 men by the spring of 1951. Adenauer reported that McCloy's analysis of the situation was 'impressive and sombre'. The French High Commissioner, François Poncet, asked whether Adenauer could be sure that a West German police force would fight against the Soviet zone police. Sir Ivone Kirkpatrick, the British High Commissioner, thought that a reinforcement of Allied troops in Germany could contribute considerably to the raising of German morale. But the fundamental question was posed by McCloy, when he asked what the German government's attitude would be to Churchill's plan put forward on 11 August 1950 to the Council of Europe in Strasbourg for the creation of a European army with German participation, a plan warmly welcomed in the United States. Could Germany contribute a German contingent to this army? McCloy concluded by recalling that 'America had lost many battles, but won all its wars'. Re-armament was now proceeding at full speed. Europe would not be forgotten if it showed the courage to defend itself'.[21] In a memorandum of 29 August 1950, Adenauer stated that the German government was prepared, should an international army be formed, to contribute a German contingent, but only on condition that the relationship between Germany and the occupying powers should be put on a new basis, that is progressively replaced by a system of contractual agreements.

Adenauer's bold attitude on rearmament was to cost him something he had sought so much to obtain and preserve: the presence and collaboration in his government of the Protestant and especially Evangelical (Lutheran) Church, in one single Christian Democratic solidarity with the Catholics. The most important Evangelical Minister in the Cabinet was Dr Gustav Heineman, the Minister of the Interior. The quarrel between him and Adenauer was sparked off in an interview given at the very end of 1949 by the notorious pacifist leader and President of the Church, Dr Martin Niemöller, to the *New York Herald Tribune*, in which he not only opposed German rearmament, but called the new Federal Republic 'a child conceived in the Vatican and born in Washington'. But as Niemöller refused Adenauer's injunction to retract, or at least to produce the original text of his declaration, the basic differences of view between Protestants and Catholics materialized in a personal polemic between Adenauer and Heineman. The latter, strongly influenced by the philosopher Karl Barth, did not consider himself a pacifist, but he thought that German foreign policy should be aimed at the re-unification of all Germany and not at the integration of one part of it in the Atlantic fraternity. On 10 October 1950, Adenauer announced to a startled Cabinet that he was going to dismiss Heineman – another manifestation of his authoritarianism. But the government suffered ever afterwards from this breakdown of the ideological unity of German Christian Democracy.

But on the other hand, and coming back to the unfolding of the major trends of the politics of interdependence,

McCloy listened closely to Adenauer, so much so that some wags began calling the German Chancellor 'the real McCoy'. . . The Korean War hastened his sense of urgency. To McCloy, the challenge was to make Germany secure without arousing German bellicosity . . . The way to overcome old national hatreds McCloy believed was to nurture within Europe a sense of unity of common needs and purposes . . . McCloy was fortunate to have as his mentor and ally in the cause of European unity his old friend and law client, Jean Monnet 'the inspirer'.[22]

On 12 September 1950, Dean Acheson informed Schuman and Ernest Bevin, then British Foreign Secretary, that the US would send troops to Europe, but only when the Europeans themselves would have mobilized sixty divisions 'of which ten would be German'. 'This was the first time that the ghost of the German soldier was re-awakened' notes Jean Monnet in his memoirs.[23] Gathering his team around him again (Hirsch, Uri, Clappier, Reuter), he started to work on a plan. He hoped, instead of pursuing the absolutely negative attitude of the French government, to circumvent the problem of re-arming Europe with German troops by setting up a military organization similar in kind to the industrial organization of the Coal and Steel Community which, be it said in passing, was making extraordinary progress under his presidency. He proposed the formation of a European army, unified from the point of view of command, of its organization, and of its equipment and of its financing. Thus placed under the direction of a Supranational Authority the integration of the German units in its initial hard core could be progressively achieved.[24] He put his ideas to Schuman and to Pleven, his former secretary, now Defence Minister. Although they were sure that the Gaullists, the Right, the Communists, and even Mendès-France, leader of the MRP, would attack it, Pleven agreed to present such a plan but 'we have only one week in which to prepare it'. 'Here it is,' said Monnet. 'I have prepared an international declaration'.

The Pleven Plan for a European army was approved by the governments and ratified by the parliaments of Italy, Germany and Benelux. Meanwhile, on 10 March 1952, the Soviet government, obviously perturbed by the progress of the European idea, surprised its allies with a note addressed to the other three occupying powers in which it proposed considering a peace treaty for a 're-unified' Germany. In spite of the fact that the note touched the raw nerve of German public opinion about re-unification, and therefore strengthened the 'pacifist' opposition in Germany and in Europe as a whole, Adenauer asked the High Commissioners, who shared the same view, to treat it only as an obvious manoeuvre, meant to divert the efforts for the establishment of a European army. Much more important, however, was Stalin's death in 1953, and the subsequent peace offensive launched by his successors. How great a part these Soviet initiatives played in the evolution of French public opinion is still a moot point, but the fact is that on 30 August 1953, the French Parliament rejected the ratification of the EDC treaty again by the same unholy alliance of the Right and the Left oppositions, too strong for the hesitant Prime Minister Mendès-France, deeply absorbed in the defeat of France in the long and exhausting war in Indo-China.

But immediately after this setback, Anthony Eden, the Foreign Secretary of the then Churchill cabinet proposed that a conference be held in London to consider accepting the German Federal Republic at once as a sovereign state, with its own national army, into the North Atlantic Treaty Organization. The British and American reasoning was evidently based on the confidence that the new Federal Republic of Germany was able to inspire. For, on 6 September, new national elections were held in Germany, resulting in a massive victory for the CDU/CSU (45 per cent of the vote against 28.8 per cent for the SDP) which for the first time had an absolute majority, thus confirming German political stability and dispelling the fear that 'Bonn could be just another Weimar'. Meanwhile, the social market economy, under Ludwig Erhardt's direction, had achieved an 'economic miracle' which had brought Germany back to the head of the European economy and the standards of living of the West German people to heights unrivalled in Europe. And in the social field, the social market economy had also kept its pledges . . . The German political scientist, Klaus von Beyme, who cannot be suspected of bias towards Christian Democratic governments in Germany, says of the Adenauer era that the economy was largely left unregulated, but in social welfare policies Germany was in the lead and only later fell behind. Among secular achievements were welfare laws designed to achieve a sharing of burdens (1951) between native Germans and East German refugees, a law that guaranteed parity in workers' co-determination and the index linking of pensions. Some Christian Democrats even suspected that their own party went too far in a socialist direction in the field of social welfare. Adenauer used the economic growth to mobilize the poorer strata of the population, a calculation which proved successful. This was the only time in post-war German history that the party in power got an absolute majority of votes at the polls.[25] To be sure, the highly satisfactory functioning of the German political physiology could not escape its pathological consequences. Among the worst was the growth of violence and terrorism among the younger generation which led the government to adopt a particularly severe criminal law in 1951, which in turn was held by many to exacerbate the excesses of terrorism. Another negative aspect was the spread of corruption and the frequency of financial scandals – as well as the success of pornography, vice and drugs. But, altogether, German society was in a healthy and hard-working condition, and what is more significant in the context of these remarks, it showed a profound and tenacious attachment to the European idea.

In the light of this objective situation and under the pressure of the events, the Paris Agreements or Peace Treaty between Germany and the three Western Powers were signed on 5 May 1955, and on the same day, the Federal Republic of Germany became a member of NATO in which it participated with its own national army. Whether this was a more satisfactory result for the French and for those Europeans who feared German re-armament, even if Germany was prevented from producing or deploying nuclear weapons, ships, bombers and submarines, is a question which many people asked afterwards. Adenauer, although exhilarated by this achievement of 'full sovereignty' was one of them, for he himself had always feared Prussian militarism and had dreamt of a European Union. Happily enough, his by now great friend, Jean Monnet had surprisingly resigned his successful presidency of the ECSC to embark again alone on a 'relaunching' of the European idea. On 7 June 1955 a conference of six countries was held in Messina: France, Italy, the FRG and the Benelux, which was to lead to the formation of the Community of Six in 1957.

## External fulfilment

The last phase of Adenauer's politics of interdependence goes from the Peace Treaty and membership of NATO of 1955 to the signing of the Treaty of Rome for the European Economic Communities in 1957 and that of the Franco-German Treaty in 1963.

Having seen his principal goal fulfilled and his country restored to 'sovereignty', Adenauer was not drunk with success. His sceptical and cautious mind was still anxious. His concern in external policy lay still in relations with France not only because of the unsolved and vexing problem of the Saar, but also because he thought that relations with France could best be solved by the mutual sublimation of the two national interests into the European interest. He was happier when he thought that the European Defence Community – the history of which is treated in greater detail in the chapter on de Gaulle – would merge all West European national armed forces into one supranational one, than when faced with the re-formation of the German army on its own, albeit within NATO and albeit limited, and although he knew from old that national defence was the principal element of external sovereignty. At the time he had written:

At the heart of European unification, however, lay the problem of Franco-German understanding. In my opinion, the European nation-state had a past, but no future. This applied in the political and economic, as well as the social sphere. No single European country could guarantee a secure future for its people by its own strength. I regarded the Schuman Plan and the European Defence Community as preliminary steps to a political unification

63

of Europe . . . Thus I could not understand the *ohne-mich* attitude: it was irresponsible and in the last resort hopeless, yet it was widespread in the Federal Republic . . . There were those in Germany who thought that for us the choice was either a policy for Europe or a policy for German unity. I consider that 'either/or' a fatal error. Nobody could explain how German unity in freedom was to be achieved without a strong and united Europe'.[26]

Commenting on the effects of the failure of the EDC on Adenauer and on Germany in general Arnulf Baring remarks that it had discouraged and weakened him in his pursuit of integrating West Germany into Europe. The alignment of Germany into NATO did not have the character of a supranational amalgamation. At the same time in the Federal Republic itself, the European movements began to shrink. On the contrary, general German associations which looked eastwards came to the fore: in the very year 1954, when the EDC was already in doubt, the *Kuratorium Unteilbaren Deutschlands* (the guardianship of undivided Germany) was founded. 'Adenauer' states Baring 'became unsure, lost his orientation and felt, with his usual pragmatism, that there were political forces with which one had to reckon, which were being made use of by an increasingly strong national feeling. He himself therefore became more national in the traditional sense of the word.'[27]

Adenauer's thoughts returned to this almost instinctive feeling that the international agreement should be supplemented, indeed completed, by a Franco-German agreement. This seemed to him the best way of dealing with the unresolved problem of the Saar; but he also considered it advisable because of his feeling that as long as fear and antipathy of Germany in French political psychology was not replaced by a sense of trust and partnership between the two countries, no real progress could be made in Europe. This is the reason why he did not regard with *Schadenfreude* the tragic dilemma which stifled the politics of the French Fourth Republic, the war in Indo-China, soon to be followed by the Algerian war and the domestic ungovernability caused by the anti-constitutional opposition of both Gaullists and Communists, albeit for such different reasons.

As a matter of fact, he seems to have hoped already at that time that de Gaulle would seize the helm again, not only because of the stability that he alone might possibly restore to French politics, but also because he believed that both he and de Gaulle shared a common view of a Franco-German hard core in Europe. This belief had its early origin in the impression made on him by a statement by de Gaulle in a speech at Saarbrücken in 1945, to the effect that 'Frenchmen and Germans must let bygones be bygones and . . . they both must remember that they are West Europeans'; and was strengthened by the fact that when Adenauer had given an interview to the American journalist, Kinsbury-Smith, in which he had openly advocated the 'cross-fertilization between France and Germany' within the European Union, de Gaulle, surprisingly for him, had endorsed the idea of a Franco-German union.

What Adenauer did not seem to share with de Gaulle was the latter's personal and national reservations about American 'hegemony'. During his journey to America in April 1953, he frankly declared that 'it is rare in history that a victor has helped the vanquished in this way' and that 'the United States had become the most powerful nation on earth' and that 'America demands of us Europeans that we also use our might to preserve freedom. And this demand is justified.'[28]  The last point is a very sensitive one. It is true that the Marshall Plan and the particularly massive American private investments in Germany had been of prime importance in the rapid economic rehabilitation of Germany, that Europe and even the Korean war had helped the German economy in one respect, increasing the demand for steel and heavy industry and improving its exports. But after Germany's entry into NATO, the problem of the cost of re-armament and of what kind of re-armament, i.e. whether with Germany's own resources, fertilized by the rebirth of a German armament industry, or in collaboration with and again supplied by the US, came evidently to the fore. Now with a new Republican President, Eisenhower, a new Secretary of State, John Foster Dulles, who proclaimed a new foreign policy slogan of 'liberation' and 'roll-back' of the USSR from Eastern Europe, as against the 'containment' policy considered by contrast as cowardly, if not treasonable, the US was even more prepared to assist in European re-armament. The global cost of German re-armament and other military costs only came to 11 per cent of the German GNP. However, national capital was both insufficient and more inclined, because of the reminiscences of the Nazi period, towards private civil investment than towards military expenditure. But by deducting the payment of occupation costs now finished and by receiving American subsidies for military equipment through the NASH programme, the expenditure on the new *Bundeswehr* was held within the normal budgetary percentage.

Berghahn, interpreting Werner Abelshauser's important *Wirtschafts-geschichte der Bundesrepublik Deutschland* (Economic History of the FRG) believes that the 'question of how armaments were to be built into the national economy'. . . was triggered by a letter which McCloy sent to Adenauer on 6 March 1951. In it the US High Commissioner demanded that 'a significant modification' be made in existing economic policy. But Otto A. Friedrich, who was in charge of the co-ordination of raw materials of the federal government (*Rohstoffbeamtsträger der Bundesregierung*) concluded that

in fact we succeeded in maintaining *Soziale Marktwirtschaft*, even in the face of world-wide restrictions: apart from a few formal concessions to the Americans in the field of iron and steel, we also succeeded in initiating the march towards an even greater expansion of the economy, towards constantly growing employment and towards the abolition of the remaining chains imposed by the occupying Powers.[29]

So the more the relations of interdependence from within the Atlantic Alliance made every European state, Great Britain, France, Italy and now the Federal Republic of Germany face a bi-lateral relation with the 'hegemon' of the Alliance, the USA, the more Adenauer sought to encourage common European agreements, and especially within them a closer and more specific relation between France and Germany. To a great extent, the signing of the Treaty of Rome in 1957 founding the European Economic Community responded to many of his expectations. He himself and Professor Hallstein had worked in close collaboration with Jean Monnet for the setting up of this new Community, much more far-reaching than the Coal and Steel Community. But in the absence of Great Britain which had once more refused, after the Messina conference, to commit itself to join the Six, Adenauer felt that the EEC would have no reality if it were not based on an alliance between France and Germany, which was the principal aspiration of his foreign policy since his youth. But to achieve that he had to wait until 1963, his last and darkest year in power, when in a complex of circumstances to be explained in the chapter on de Gaulle, the latter and Adenauer finally signed the Franco-German treaty. (The signature of the Franco-German treaty is dealt with in the next chapter.) This final cementing of the alliance between the two countries was, from his personal point of view, the fulfilment of the goal he had set himself early in his life in the Rhineland battlefield.

## Internal decline and fall

But, in the meantime, things had greatly changed. The rude awakening for Adenauer came with the election of 1961, in which his party's share of the vote fell from 50.2 per cent in 1957 to 45.3 per cent, while the SDP's had climbed from 31.8 per cent to 36.2 per cent and the Liberals (Free Democratic Party) from 7.7 per cent to 12.8 per cent. This meant again a coalition with the Liberals, but in different conditions. What had gone wrong, just when he thought that he and his party had more than fulfilled their duty towards their country and their people?

Obvious as it might seem, one of the causes of the darkening of the horizon was not 'in the stars' but in himself, in his inevitable, albeit exceptionally well-carried ageing. There was less time for work: longer hours of sleep in the afternoons, longer weekends at home, longer pneumonias, longer holidays on the Lago Maggiore. There was also a growing weariness in his ideas, and in the public which was growing tired of listening to his somewhat repetitious speeches and formulas. The CD election slogans like *'keine Experiment'* (No experiment) or *'Sicher ist Sicher'* (What is sure is sure) showed this tendency towards immobilism of the leader. Moreover, when a statesman begins to say as quoted above that 'I cannot understand the *"ohne-mich"* mentality there is certainly something wrong. For statesmen need to understand the ideas and attitudes most abhorrent to them and must be able to combat them, not by sheer negation from outside, but by persuasion from inside. And yet the *ohne-mich* atmosphere was growing around him, in his own country, anti-war, anti-militarism, even anti-patriotic if need be.

The Korean war had in some respects ended positively for the US. South Korea was rescued and embarked on its astonishing path to industrial success. But in its wake a new policy described as liberation and fanatically argued by President Eisenhower's Secretary of State, John Foster Dulles, was advocated by the new American Establishment. Peoples from Eastern Europe were encouraged to fight for their freedom, indeed those who did so were called Freedom Fighters. Further encouraged also by Khrushchev's speech at the CPSU Congress, they did so in Poland in the spring and then especially in Hungary in the autumn of 1956. But the formidable Hungarian revolution was crushed by Soviet tanks, in the wake of the still incomprehensible aborted Israeli-Franco-British attack on Nasser's Egypt, just at the time of the Hungarian rising, when the 'liberating' West should, if its words meant anything, have defended the Freedom Fighters.

There followed a deep divergence between the USA and Britain and France. The Federal Republic of Germany profited from this to become the USA's 'most loyal' ally. Adenauer himself announced a new policy towards the East Germans, the Hallstein doctrine, whereby all countries having diplomatic relations with East Germany would endanger their relations with the FRG, already one of the most active economic powers in the world. He underlined this by accepting an invitation to go to Moscow, where he inaugurated new trade and diplomatic relations with the USSR and with the other East European countries, though he refused to have anything to do with Communist Germany.

Both the subordination to the new American offensive foreign policy and the arbitrary discrimination against East Germany were bound to indispose large sections of German public opinion of both extremes, the pacifist Left and the patriotic Right, the latter putting the ideal of 'German unification' above all. These discrepancies also appeared among the political parties of the coalition, the Liberals pressing for a policy of peace, the Christian Social Union, under Franz Joseph Strauss's bellicose leadership, asking for 'liberation'. To this was soon to be added, after his coming to power, de Gaulle's new 'independent' and overtly anti-American foreign policy, especially coupled with an overture to the East, both towards the USSR and separately towards each East European country. Adenauer had nothing new to add and his government was carrying on, successfully no doubt from an economic and social point of view, but monotonously and unimaginatively from the political aspect. The major justification for the self-assured continuity was the fact that for a while the principal opposition, the SDP, remained bogged down in the Marxist-nationalist philosophy of Schumacher, although he had died on 23 August 1952.

But this, too, was going to change. Under the new leadership of Willy Brandt the new generation of Social Democrats openly gave up the former Marxist tenets, and thus liberated from the obsolete ideology, embarked on new policies of modern socialism, able to comprehend in both senses of the word the fantastically rapid changing problems of interdependence and world-politics, among which was a particularly popular idea of a new *Ost-Politik*. This was in many respects a compliment to Adenauer, who had warned the SDP from the beginning that their Marxist policy was a cul-de-sac into which they were blindly pushing themselves for good. But, on the other hand, the change soon had the effect of drawing towards this rejuvenated and modern party great numbers of German voters, discontented with one or another aspect of Adenauer's policy. For that policy was not only stagnating in its conservatism – it was also becoming increasingly authoritarian in its internal behaviour or, as Ralf Dahrendorf has called it 'authoritarian without authority'. Just as de Gaulle was the obvious successor to Adenauer's previously uncontested leadership in European politics, so the SDP was rapidly becoming a credible successor to replace the tired and increasingly severe Christian Democrat government in power.

The government's rigidity was apparent in all fields, in the social field in its relations with the trade unions, for the new German managerial generation had learnt the American style of industrial leadership: in the constitutional field, where the Supreme Court of Justice had to amend the severities of new penal laws and to be critical of the measures of repression; and in the youth, as the Federal Republic of Germany had the sad privilege of being one of the European countries from which the specific terrorism of a young generation in revolt sprang. Rudi Dutschke, one of the first 'heroes' of the student movement was the leader in Germany and Cohn-Bendit, a German student, became the leader of a students' revolt in Paris, though it is true to say that both were active after Adenauer's departure from office. But violence and repression push each other in an ever escalating reciprocity and the inclination of the last Adenauer Cabinet towards repression stirred the rebellious youth.

Finally, two events which occurred in 1961 and 1962 shook the political situation even more and isolated Adenauer even further in the loneliness of old age. The first was the building of the Berlin Wall on 15 August 1961. Given the constant haemorrhage of intellectuals, professionals and skilled workers from East Germany to the Federal Republic, the Ulbricht government in the GDR felt it necessary to introduce the quite extraordinary measure of building a monstrous wall of cement around East Berlin, crowned with barbed wire, fully illuminated at night and manned with armed sentries. They hoped that this monstrous and shameful construction would put an end to the migration, which it actually did to a great extent. To be sure, nothing could possibly demonstrate more dramatically and admit more openly the total failure of Marxism-Leninism-Stalinism than the construction of a grotesquely medieval wall across the centre of Europe in 1961 AD. But the resentment of the population of the Western areas of Berlin against the lack of reaction of the German government and the 'liberating' Allies was also understandable.

The second episode was the notorious *Der Spiegel* affair, in which the mercurial Minister of Defence, Franz Joseph Strauss angered by the 'leak' of military information in that influential weekly, ordered its offices to be searched by the police and its editor to be arrested. The Courts of Justice having condemned these actions, the Minister, harassed by the parliamentary and extra-parliamentary opposition and even more by the media, was constrained to resign. The result was to widen the gap between the Christian Democratic and Christian Social wings of the main party, thus further dislocating the structure of the initial government team, already shaken by the withdrawal of the Lutheran, Dr Heineman.

Adenauer went from bitterness to bitterness. The pressure on him to resign and to make room at the helm for the increasingly popular Minister of Finance, Ludwig Erhardt, the architect of the 'economic miracle' was increasing. Isolated between the narrowing circle of his private counsellors, notably Globke and Blankerhorn, he developed a tendency to resist and to cling to office. Most ageing statesmen, to mention for instance only Churchill, react with the fury and despair of Beethoven's Last Quartets, when they arrive at the moment of separation from their task. But, like Beethoven too, what makes the separation more dramatic is their incapacity to hear, or indeed to understand, other harmonies than those which they have created. For a man born in 1876, the world of 1960 must have sounded very strident. The more tired Adenauer felt by the cruel advance of age, the more demands seemed to be made on the man at the helm; and the more he concentrated on what he had known to be the essential purposes, the more distracted were the others by, to him, obscure developments. Moreover, like Churchill too, he came to despise and to see in an unexpectedly critical light the former heirs apparent: Eden and Erhardt, whose only superiority lay in their age. Adenauer's secretary tells us in her *Errinerungen* (Memoirs) how, while he was writing his own memoirs, he angrily exclaimed when she hazarded the remark that they read as well as a novel: 'A novel', he cried. 'It is not a novel. It is a terrible tragedy'; and she also describes how he spent more and more time listening to his favourite Schubert *Lieder*, among which especially *Der Leierman* (The Organ-grinder).

> *Drüben hinterm Dorfe*
> *Steht ein Leierman*
> *Und mit starren Fingern*
> *Dreht er was er kann*
>
> *Keiner mag ihn hören*
> *Keiner sieht ihn an*
> *Und die Hunde knurren*
> *Um den Alten Mann*

(There behind the village/stands the organ-grinder/ and with frozen fingers/ grinds out what he can./ Nobody can hear him/ nobody looks at him/ and the dogs are snarling/ around the poor old man.)

## CONCLUSION

It is obvious that both the special case of Germany, and the personal case of Adenauer himself blur the lines of demarcation between sovereignty and interdependence, and consequently those between a patriot and a practitioner of interdependence. The fact that for the first five years after the war, Germany had no sovereignty at all and that he had to embark on his 'statesmanship' in the harsh conditions of negotiations between the occupiers and the occupied, imprinted on his political style an international flexibility and a national authoritarianism very seldom encountered in normal studies of statesmanship,

This being said, however, some relevant aspects of the enquiry emerged clearly after his death.

– The viability and power of the state of the Federal German Republic, although it was not, formally, a fully sovereign state in the traditional sense of the word is ensured instead by the high position it holds in the contemporary world of interdependence.

– The state of the Federal Republic of Germany as constructed by Adenauer is a faithful image of his initial idea of how it should be constructed as an autonomous unit within a supranational context, and is itself a federation formed by autonomous units co-ordinated by a central authority;

– It was also seen that two para-governmental teams of experts, the Washington 'Wise Men' and the 'Monnet Equipe' were the architects of the 'Atlantic' and the 'European' policies, which sometimes together, sometimes in opposition to each other, determined the rebuilding of Germany.

Later though, or to be more precise, twenty-two years after his death, Adenauer's greatest dream and at the same time his most feared nightmare have come together in the real world after the extraordinary and extraordinarily rapid changes caused by the collapse of the Soviet empire in Eastern Europe in the autumn of 1989. This collapse, of which more will be said in the final chapters, occurred with startling rapidity in Poland, Hungary, and Czechoslovakia, and later, and perhaps less decisively, in Romania and Bulgaria. In Germany, though, it led also to a totally different result: that of the unification of the democratic, western Federal Republic with the Communist German Democratic Republic. Once the monstrous Berlin wall had been breached, the *de facto* integration of the two opposite sides of the former Reich took place irresistibly. Soon after, *de jure* integration was necessarily accepted by the Western allies of the Federal Republic, and confirmed in principle by the four powers which exercised the post-war control over Germany, the USA, Britain and France. The newly acquired political authority, the military importance, the diplomatic firmness and last but not least, the leading economic and technological position of the Federal Republic rendered this acceptance easier.

The assertion of the Federal Republic as a sovereign state was not only Adenauer's great dream but, as can be deduced from the previous summary of the way in which he had built up the Republic, it was the direct result of his foreign policy of interdependence with the West. Nevertheless, the question whether Adenauer would have proceeded to the unification of the FRG with the DDR as hastily as Chancellor Kohl, his fellow Rhinelander and Christian Democrat, remains a moot point.

## NOTES AND REFERENCES

1. A. Baring, *Aussenpolitik in Adenauers Kanzlerdemokratie*, Munich, 1989, p. 1.

2. Konrad Adenauer, *Memoirs*, London 1966, pp. 36–7.

3. Ibid., p. 46.

4. Ibid., p. 39.

5. Ibid., p. 45.

6. Paul Weymar, *Konrad Adenauer, the Authorized Biography*, London, 1987, pp. 45–6.

7. Ibid., pp. 55ff.

8. Adenauer, *Memoirs*, p. 81.

9. Ibid., p. 92.

10. Weymar, op. cit., p. 211.

11. Ibid., p. 109.

12. Walter Isaacson and Evan Thomas, *The Wise Men. Six Friends and the World they Made*, New York, pp. 517–8 retells this historical episode in a most absorbing way.

13. Weymar, op. cit., p.376.

14. K. von Beyme, 'Policy-making in the Federal Republic of Germany: a systematic introduction' in K. von Beyme & Manfred G. Schmidt, eds., *Policy and Politics in the Federal Republic of Germany*, London, 1985, p. 3.

15. Adenauer, op. cit., pp. 256–7.

16. Jean Monnet, *Mémoires*, Paris, 1976, p. 348 (my translation).

16. Jean Monnet, *Mémoires*, Paris, 1976, p. 348 (my translation).

17. Ibid., p. 354.

18. D. Acheson, *Memoirs*.

19. Adenauer, op. cit., p. 273.

20. Ibid.

21. Ibid., p. 278.

22. W. Isaacson and E. Thomas, op. cit., pp. 517–8.

23. Monnet, op. cit., p. 100.

24. Ibid., p. 405.

25. von Beyme, op. cit., p. 56.

26. Adenauer, op. cit., pp. 416–17.

27. A. Baring, *Aussenpolitik*, p. 334.

28. Adenauer, op. cit., pp. 439, 451–2.

29. V. Berghahn, *Modern Germany: Society, Economy and Politics in the Twentieth Century*, Cambridge, 1987, pp. 274–9.

# CHAPTER TWO
## *Charles de Gaulle*

After Churchill, with Churchill and in some respects more than Churchill, to whom he was personally linked by a bond of manly mutual respect, de Gaulle was the most statesmanlike of all contemporary statesmen (in Orwell's sense that some are more equal than others). One must stress *after* Churchill for two reasons. Chronologically, de Gaulle's public activity began after Churchill's. Indeed, not only did it follow Churchill's, it could not have been initiated or carried to its victorious conclusion without that of Churchill. And de Gaulle also came after Churchill politically, because France, which was both the object and the instrument of his statesmanship, was weaker than Britain. At the moment when they both were called on by history to act, or in other words when each assumed the personal duty of saving his country and speaking for her, France was falling into the depths of national humiliation, while Britain was rising towards her 'finest hour'. One of the most dramatic of all the sayings of de Gaulle, whose sense of drama was one of the hallmarks of his genius, was his remark to Churchill when the latter advised him to be more flexible: '*C'est trop lourd et je suis trop pauvre pour pouvoir me plier*' (It is too heavy and I am too poor to be able to bend).[1] This difference in the power-ranking of the two countries was later reflected in the achievements of the two men during the war.

De Gaulle came at the same time as Churchill because each was, knew himself to be, and also knew the other to be, a man of destiny, that is a man who was born with what Alexander the Great called his 'hope', Caesar his 'luck' and Napoleon his 'star'. Both were historical personalities waiting for their cue in history's drama. Churchill had waited long years for Britain to wake from her 'sleep', as he himself called it. As for de Gaulle, in 1905, at the age of fifteen, he had already written a short story describing how France, invaded once more by Germany in 1930, was saved by the military and political genius of someone already called General de Gaulle. This sense of premonition, given to them by their 'hope', 'luck' or 'star', and of which de Gaulle especially provides astonishingly frequent examples, showed also in their opposition to the lethargic and ill-advised policies of the governments of their countries between the two world wars and in their eloquent prophecies of doom. De Gaulle, in his pre-war books warned of the necessity for modern armed forces, based on the use of aeroplanes and tanks and not on the precarious Maginot line; but also in his very first book *Le fil de l'epée*, he clearly asserted the inseparability of political from military leadership. Churchill, in turn, also combined political and military gifts in his personality, but in the reverse order from de Gaulle. In the long years 'while Britain slept' he continued indefatigably with his Cassandra-like appeals to be forewarned and forearmed.

De Gaulle came *with* Churchill, too, in the sense of the masculine fraternity between men. The Cross of Lorraine may have been, as Churchill said, the heaviest cross he had to bear; and de Gaulle may often have complained about the inevitable perfidy of Albion as incarnated in Churchill. But the ultimate trust between the two men was not only founded on the similarity of their actions and motivations; it was founded above all on the greatness of their minds, on the fact that they met almost alone at a level of human intelligence and dignity reached by few.

I also used the words 'in some respects *more* than Churchill'. There is no doubt that de Gaulle was more intense, more absolute and more mystical than Churchill. But this might turn out to be a back-handed compliment, for when such qualities go beyond the dialectical threshold, they become defects rather than qualities in statesmen. To change the metaphor, the political physiology becomes political pathology. De Gaulle reached levels of peculiarity, while Churchill remained always on the human scale even when undertaking super-human tasks.

But in one respect alone, which in English plain speaking is more often viewed as a defect, de Gaulle was superior to Churchill. He was more of an intellectual than Churchill. This does not mean that he had a better intelligence. But the expression 'un intellectuel' in French, unlike 'a scholar' in English (Churchill was after all an historian), applies to everyone dedicated predominantly to the exercise of the intellect and this exclusive dedication is recognized as a specific status. One of de Gaulle's ambitions was to have the credentials of that status.

When one reads his correspondence,[2] his respect and admiration for novelists, poets and writers, his pleasure in their company, contrasts with his somewhat dry attitude to others and contrasts sharply with his disdain of politicians.

In fact, de Gaulle was an intellectual as of right by sheer talent, and by his efforts, in his youth, to define himself in his own philosophy of life. Although his early writings were directly concerned with military theory, they revealed themselves as an integral part of his philosophy. In it, he reconciled, above the differing finalities of their doctrines, classics like Aristotle and St Augustine and moderns like Bergson, Péguy and Nietzsche. He was irresistibly attracted by the ethic rigours of French classicism and notably by Corneille, and yet his mind had also been moulded by Shakespeare and Goethe. The foreword to *Le fil de l'epée* has as its epigraph a verse from *Hamlet* which happens also to characterize his whole personality: 'Rightly to be great is not to stir without great argument'; while the first chapter is placed under the equally significant line from Goethe's *Faust*: 'In the beginning was the Word? No! in the beginning was the Deed.' During his whole life, he tried to keep company above all with the princes of French intellect, whatever their political attitudes, from Paul Claudel to Paul Valéry, and from François Mauriac to André Malraux, the 'genius' he 'always had on his right at the Council of Ministers'. He wanted thus to earn his place in the essentially high world of the spirit, pursuing 'grandeur' in all its manifestations.

# I

# PERSONAL CIRCUMSTANCES AND HISTORICAL ANTECEDENTS

Like a good Bergsonian, de Gaulle himself accepted that both intuition and reason give to the human being the creative force of life, and that life itself is a constant motion, changing the action and the actors simultaneously. The complexity of his personality and the twists and turns of his career can be, and have often been, explained in the light of these parallel complexities. But the extraordinary continuity, one could say even tenacity, of his singular character, denotes a rock-like psychological foundation, in which, as in a geological formation, different layers have been superimposed in the formative years, and have since constituted a monolith. The *élan de vivre*, generated by the intuition and the reason of man (in this case of the man Charles de

Gaulle) led him to pursue his destiny, but in accordance with his pre-established character. 'Il faut être un homme de caractère' he wrote in his notebook in 1916.

The three layers of de Gaulle's character were in logical and chronological order: faith, courage, and political ambition.

## Faith

Charles de Gaulle was born on 22 November 1890, in Lille, a town on the Franco–Belgian border. His father was a Catholic, a teacher of history and literature at the Jesuit college of the Immaculate Conception. The origin of his family can be traced, according to the recent thorough biography by Jean Lacouture,[3] at least to the battle of Agincourt, where an ancestor, Jean de Gaulle, fought so valiantly against Henry V's English troops that 'when afterwards the resistance against the English was organized, the resistants of that time rallied under his name as the "compagnons de Gaulle"'. But there was also another, albeit symbolical resonance to this family name; it derived from the 'Gauls', from the original Gauls who fought so valiantly against Julius Caesar's Roman legions but were afterwards latinized and fused with their conquerors. Conquered afresh by the Franks by whom they were converted to Christianity, they all merged into the new *Francia*.

De Gaulle's mother was Jeanne Maillot, of a more diverse national origin in so far as her family had Irish, Scottish and even German blood. But her son said of her in his *Mémoires* that 'she dedicated to her fatherland a passion equal only to her religious piety'.[4] Both parents were militant Catholics and monarchists, supporters of *Action Française*. But Jean de Gaulle had the right feelings and judgement, and in the greatest confrontation between the traditional French Right and the traditional French Left, the Dreyfus affair, he sided with the Left supporters of Dreyfus.

Charles de Gaulle's education took place entirely in Catholic schools: the school of St Thomas Aquinas, the Jesuit college of the Immaculate Conception where, with Georges Bernanos, he was his father's pupil, then after the closure of that college in France, the Jesuit college of Saint Antoine in Belgium and finally the Stanislas college in Paris, formerly also a Jesuit college, but later laicized. It can therefore be assumed that since religion was the dominant factor in his education – or to continue the metaphor – the bottom layer of the foundation of his personality, the initial *Weltanschauung* of the young Charles de Gaulle had a religious framework. Moreover, and what is more intriguing, it can also be assumed that his vocation for faith, or in other words the mystical pursuit of an object of adoration, had also evidently started at an early age. But this did not mean that such a mystical pursuit of faith could not be directed towards, or also towards, some secular objects of adoration.

André Malraux, unlike other analysts of de Gaulle's personality, is the only one who, in his book *Les chênes qu'on abat*, has dared to ask the otherwise fundamental question of the nature of de Gaulle's faith.

To be sure, de Gaulle and his wife were practising Catholics. Even, or perhaps especially, when he was in Moscow on official visits, de Gaulle received Communion as he did every Sunday. But in his *Le fil de l'epée*, he clearly surprised his fellow Catholics by writing in a purely Machiavellian vein that: 'It is essential that the plane on which the leader must concentrate all his faculties should bear the mark of grandeur. The question of virtue does not arise. The perfection preached by the Gospels never yet built an empire. Every man of action has a strong dose of egotism, pride, hardness and cunning.' More than many other leaders in history he proved to have used particularly large doses of these four qualities during his long public life, while remaining a deeply observant Catholic. If one adds to this, his vindictiveness, indeed, unforgivingness (it was only under great pressure from the government, the courts and public opinion that he agreed in some cases to commute the death-penalty on some of the French generals, who had rebelled in the Algerian war, into life-sentences), the image of a man of Christian charity fades away. But, generally speaking, de Gaulle preserved his Catholicism, and this in part explains his spontaneous trust in Adenauer. (Of all the innumerable pictures taken of the two leaders together, the most significant remains that of them both praying together on prie-dieux in Reims cathedral.) Indeed, each understood the other so easily and both felt estranged in Protestant surroundings. Hence also an often quoted reply, perceptive, if slightly incongruous which Macmillan made to de Gaulle one day in 1962: 'You want to rebuild the Holy Empire, we want the Roman one.' But there was something other and deeper that Malraux touched upon. Recalling the amusing incident when, during his audience with the Pope, de Gaulle said after a while: 'And now, Holy Father, could we speak of France?' Malraux writes: 'I am thinking of his own faith, which I cannot fully grasp. He seldom mentioned God, not even in his will. And never Christ.' 'I believe', opines Malraux in the same passage,

that his faith is so deep that he ignores the realms in which it could be challenged . . . His faith is not a question, it is a given, like France. He likes to speak of France, but he does not like to speak of his faith . . . God, Supreme Judge, his inspiration for his acts of Grace or for guessing the fate of France?[5]

Malraux had found there the most plausible interpretation of de Gaulle's faith: he had projected his need to believe on to his country. He believed that France had been the defender of Christianity throughout her history. His deification of France was, in part also, the result of the influence of Charles Péguy's writings. In Péguy, too, France is inseparable from Christianity, and Péguy's prophetic mysticism fused the two into one single devotion. Two of the profoundest assessments of de Gaulle and Gaullism were made, not surprisingly by Pompidou, his successor. The second will be discussed at the end of this essay, but the first, 'Gaullism is Péguyism', comes most appositely here. It is only if, and when, the mystical inspiration of de Gaulle's adoration of France is understood, that its absolute and passionate overtones can be accepted. 'La France vient de haut et de loin' he liked to say mysteriously.

For if they were not of mystical inspiration, sentences like those which follow would sound almost delirious or grossly demagogic. In the first volume of his *Mémoires de Guerre* he describes his 'certaine idée de la France' in which France appears as the 'princess of fairy tale' or the Madonna on the wall-frescos, destined to 'an eminent and exceptional destiny'. After France's defeat he wrote: 'It fell to me to assume the mantle of France.' At the end of the first paragraph comes this peroration: 'Now I hear France answering me. From the depths of the abyss, she now stands up, she walks, she climbs the slope. O! Mother, such as we are, we are here to serve you'[6] And in the last sentence of the first volume of his *Mémoires d'Espoir*[7] he writes:

My mission is always to take France higher on the slope she is now climbing, while all the voices from down below call her to go down again. Having chosen once more to follow me, she has put an end to the rot and has taken the way now toward rejuvenation. But again, like yesterday, I have no other goal to offer than the peak, no other path to it than the effort.

The very last sentence has echoes of Churchill's great 'blood, sweat, toil and tears' speech. But there are three differences, from this point of view, between the two masters of rhetoric. The first is that Churchill only seldom and on major occasions allowed his speeches to rise to climaxes of patriotic emotion – while in de Gaulle the mystical fervour is always at its highest pitch, thus greatly accentuating the traditional differences between French and British rhetoric. The second difference is that while Churchill never presented himself as the only son and saviour of a Madonna-like Britain, de Gaulle, perhaps because he was aware of the lack of legitimacy of his position in 1940 in relation to his defeated country, and apart from the mystical inspiration of his duty, openly stressed his personal historical role in the salvation of France.

And finally one can notice that whereas Churchill always spoke of the British people, and indeed of all peoples engaged in the war against the Nazis, de Gaulle, while calling to the people, 'Français et Françaises', was addressing the country, France, alone. While in Churchill's exhortations, people and country make one, de Gaulle focused his faith directly on the country, on *her* personified historical destiny, on *her* personified glorious past and future – above the vicissitudes of the present and of her present people. Without overstressing this observation, one can think of two reasons why Churchill's vision differed so much from that of de Gaulle. The first is the undeniable fact that Churchill believed more profoundly in democracy than did de Gaulle, who had an almost innate suspicion of the games of representative government. The second reason lies evidently in de Gaulle's despair after the rapid defeat of the French army, in his disgust with the political class which had so quickly abandoned hope and honour, hurrying to sign France's surrender, and in his bitter disappointment with the initially small number of French people who followed his first call, as well as with the quarrels and intrigues between French generals and politicians in exile. Malraux went so far as to suspect him of not having cared very much for the metropolitan resistance. 'Why, I asked him did your war speeches not give a greater role to the metropolitan resistance? Did you think that, sooner or later, the politicians would try to play it against you?' De Gaulle answered: 'The resistance had diverse motivations, even the noblest part of the resistance. I believe that France knows that my resistance was not that of one kind of politics in the name of another . . . not even in the name of Christendom.' (The allusion here is directed to the MRP, but in the background of this critique of the ideological and political aims of the resistance in France there obviously also loomed de Gaulle's suspicion of the revolutionary aims of the Communists.) And he continues: 'I was the resistance *de la France* (of France) . . . Some people criticize me for having claimed to assume the mantle of France; what else could I have done?'[8]

Whereas, therefore, the French people, with their historical ups and downs, and with their creative genius, but with a sense of individualism bordering on anarchism, had, in de Gaulle's eyes, an inevitable element of unpredictability, possibly even unreliability, France herself was above such accidents. In her continuous radiance, she never descended from her symbolic *grandeur*, to which her people acceded only when guided by the leader who had the courage and the power to help them to rise up to it. What Péguy had said in poems, de Gaulle was preparing himself to act in deeds. Only Unamuno's philosophical intransigence about the supremacy of Spain surpasses de Gaulle's theory and praxis of the supremacy of France. But then, while de Gaulle's symbol was Joan of Arc, Unamuno's was Don Quixote, with his compulsive chivalry, his transfiguring pursuit of ideals, and his inability to distinguish between them and reality.

More than in any other of our case studies, it is in the relationship between de Gaulle and the French people that one can find that typical relation of moral and political authority – of the statesman with his people. Here one obtains that initial impression that the statesman *could* reproach the French people for their share of the responsibility for the disaster which had befallen them, and from which the statesman has then to rescue them. The French people at the Liberation not only admired de Gaulle for his prowess – but had a 'certain sense' of guilt towards him. They had felt long before the Liberation transformed this feeling into a glorious fact and reality, that de Gaulle alone had preserved faith in France, and had resurrected France from the long agony which they had not, all, foreseen. When de Gaulle came twice to lead them, it was because twice the French people felt that only he could save France through his faith in her.

## Courage

De Gaulle's personal courage, was a by-product of his faith, and equal to it, both in military and in political terms.

In 1910 de Gaulle embarked on the military career to which he was irresistibly attracted by its functional prestige and elitism, and, nationally, as the one means to avenge the defeat of 1870. On 15 August 1914, when just 24 and already a lieutenant in Philippe Pétain's 33rd Regiment, he was wounded for the first time in Belgium; back at the front in October, he showed such prowess in battle that in January 1915 he was promoted captain and awarded the *Croix de Guerre*; in March he was again wounded; in 1916, at Verdun, his entire company was devastated. He was given out for dead. His commander, General Pétain, signed the following citation in the *Journal Officiel* of 7 May 1916:

Captain de Gaulle, head of his company, with a high reputation for his moral and intellectual valour, has led his men in a furious attack in ferocious hand-to-hand fighting, while his battalion was decimated under a frightening

81

bombardment and the Germans were surrounding them from all sides – the only solution he thought compatible with his sense of national honour. He has fallen in the fight. A peerless officer from all points of view.

Alas, for Pétain, de Gaulle had not been killed, but seriously wounded by a bayonet thrust. Captured, he spent three years as a prisoner of war, each marked by an unsuccessful, albeit heroic, attempt to escape, followed by long periods of solitary confinement. Freed at the end of the war, he was awarded the *Légion d'Honneur*, aged 28.

Although a career officer, (he had in the meantime taken his degree at the *École supérieure de guerre* and had been given a high position in the general secretariat of national defence) de Gaulle did not hesitate to publish four books, all imbued with a sense of prophetic realism. The first, *La discorde chez l'ennemi* (1924), argued that Germany had lost the war because the military command had the upper hand over the political institutions. The second, *Le fil de l'epée*, (1927) dedicated to Pétain, presents on the contrary a theory of the necessary fusion between military and political command, while the third, *L'armée de métier (1934)*, expounds a theory of the offensive and highly mechanized war of tomorrow, based on aircraft and tanks and entirely opposed to the idea of defensive war behind fortifications favoured by French governments and the Chiefs of Staff. The book is said to have inspired Hitler's ideas of rearmament; but it was ignored in France. The fourth book, *La France et son armée* (1938), by its advocacy of modern mobile warfare, led to an open quarrel with Pétain.

In 1937, already a colonel, de Gaulle took command of the 507th regiment of tanks; and in May 1940, after war had broken out, he was given command of all the tank regiments in Alsace. During the short *Blitz-krieg* a counter-offensive led by his tanks proved to be one of the few successful French military operations of the campaign. From May to June, now a General and Under-Secretary of State at the Ministry of Defence, he flew between Paris, London and Bordeaux, whither the French government had now withdrawn, trying to convince it to continue the fight, if necessary and above all from French North Africa. When the French government rejected the proposal, thought up by Jean Monnet and backed by de Gaulle, of a Franco-British union of confederal character, and decided to surrender to the Germans, he flew on 17 June to London and on 18 June 1940 'assumed the mantle of France', through the declaration he broadcast to the French People over the BBC.

After that extraordinary break in his life and fate, that is to say from the moment de Gaulle remained in London (where Madame Yvonne de Gaulle, née Ventoux, whom he had married in 1921 joined him with his son and two daughters), his courage was all concentrated on the political plane, to which, in his new capacity of national leader, the military plane was functionally subordinated. To be sure, his military courage had to be exerted also in that period of leadership in his life, during the many and often disastrous expeditions of the Free French Navy to the African and Middle Eastern ports where the French empire was at stake; during the Algerian Civil War, he undertook eight journeys to Algeria fraught with danger to his person, while in France itself he escaped the two attempts against his life, and in the second also against Madame de Gaulle, when both miraculously escaped from the well organized and well executed machine-gunning (the plot and action of which were used by F. Forsyth in his book *The Day of the Jackal*, and in the film based on it).

But from 18 June 1940 when he 'assumed the mantle of France' in his historic BBC speech, or indeed from 23 June when he was officially recognized by the British government as the Leader of Free France, he needed a different kind of courage, for which he was even better prepared. This was the moral and political courage finally to play the role of General Charles de Gaulle, the Liberator of martyred France, a role he had seen himself in since he was fifteen in the short story he then wrote. But it was also, to change the metaphor, the armour which he was going to wear until 1969. It is known that even in his childhood he signed his letters to his family and friends with his full name, Charles de Gaulle, and also that he often spoke or wrote about himself in the third person as 'de Gaulle'. This fusion of two identities, of a distinct Pirandellian character ('Henry IV' in reverse), was only too easy for him to operate. It was the very opposite of the case which will be considered later in this book, of the actor Ronald Reagan being called on by fate to play the part of governor of California and then of President of the United States. In the case of de Gaulle, the part he was called on to play was that of someone called de Gaulle, whose lonely and unusual role it was to become, in the play of history, the Liberator and then the Leader of France.

While Churchill and Eden believed in him, because Churchill himself was engaged in a supreme gamble which he believed he would win – even in that lonely and crucial year when Stalin was actively helping Hitler and Roosevelt could not yet break out of his country's neutrality – most people did not know of de Gaulle's existence, and many people in France and even in exile, in London, could not trust him, at any rate not at once. He himself describes this situation:

Even in London, with a few exceptions, the best known (notoires) Frenchmen . . . did not join Free France. Many chose to be sent home.

Others, remaining there, declared their loyalty to Vichy. While from those who opposed the surrender, some offered their services to the British or American governments . . . few were the 'able men' (capacités) who rallied to my standard.[9]

## A first aside on the relations between de Gaulle and Monnet

The second name which de Gaulle placed on the list of those who disappointed him was that of Jean Monnet – and for at least two reasons it is useful to ponder a while on Monnet's case. It was Jean Monnet's genius for planning the co-ordination and unification of collective national and especially international efforts which had made his name during the First World War with the Allied Maritime Transport Executive Committee (AMTE) which greatly helped American deliveries of war material to Britain and France. Since then he had established both an international reputation and a unique network of personal relations with the economic and political elites of Europe and America. Immediately after the First World War he helped to organize the League of Nations, which he conceived as the continuation for peaceful purposes of the international co-operation he had brought about during and after the war. Already in September 1918, he had written in a letter to Clemenceau and President Wilson: 'What is urgently needed now is to succeed in forming an economic union between the Western democracies which in turn will be the hard core of the economic union of all free peoples'.[10] One can already see here the basis of his future activity, leading to the establishment of the European Economic Community.

But when we meet Monnet in these pages, or rather when de Gaulle met him in London, it was in the very days of the fall of France. In order to keep France in the war, Monnet, in the hurry of events, had tried to convince Churchill to offer the French government, under the prime minister Reynaud, a Franco-British confederal union. Upon de Gaulle's arrival in London, and knowing that he was going to be received that morning by Churchill, Monnet went, with the then French Ambassador to see de Gaulle at dawn at his hotel to ask him to assist in convincing the hesitant British Prime Minister to make such a bold gesture. De Gaulle, in spite of his dislike of anything that could affect France's sovereignty, thought that if such a union could help to make the French government continue to fight, which was then his main aim, it was worth pursuing. He adopted the idea and indeed helped to persuade Churchill to launch the proposal on that same day. It was of no avail, however, because on that very night the

French government decided to surrender and Reynaud resigned.

It may therefore seem surprising that Monnet refused to join de Gaulle's National Committee. What were his reasons? One has already become transparently clear – and was to be the leitmotiv of the relations between these two great men, interwoven as they were going to be in the making of the fate of the new France and the new Europe in the next three decades. This was the fundamental difference between their two personalities and their personal philosophies. To begin with, de Gaulle was a man of war and independence and Monnet was a man of peace and interdependence. Secondly, de Gaulle believed that the goal came first, which could be achieved by will power, while Monnet thought that the 'means' came first. Thirdly, Monnet believed that those means could be secured by the co-ordination of international efforts, while de Gaulle concentrated exclusively on France.

Some of these differences emerge in a letter from Monnet to de Gaulle, which the former reproduces in its entirety in his *Mémoires*. De Gaulle only quotes two passages from this letter and oddly enough in a different version. 'You are wrong', de Gaulle quotes Jean Monnet as writing, 'to establish an organization which might appear in France to have been created under the protection of England'.[11] What Monnet actually wrote according to his *Mémoires* was: '*I consider that it would be a great mistake to try to establish in England an organization . . . etc.*')[12] And indeed, having gone to see de Gaulle and explained that he thought of going back to the US to foster the deliveries of the means of war to Britain, Monnet concluded in his *Mémoires*:

We could not understand each other. He reproached me with my choice which took me away from the nerve centre, where he had the intention to act so that France could have its share in the victory. But this victory, I remarked, could not come by heroism alone and by grandeur of character alone. Some men had the duty to take care of the indispensable material conditions, which were far from being fulfilled.[13]

Monnet's explicit objection to de Gaulle's self-appointment as the head of the Committee, lay in his considered view that the Committee should not be formed in Britain at all. As Monnet put it,

If the Resistance could be organized in North Africa, that is on French soil, under the authority of leaders appointed by a government which was not then under the enemy's control, I am sure that it would set up an immense echo in France and in all the French colonies. But it is not from London that the effort of resurrection can now be launched. In this form it will appear to the French as a movement protected by England, inspired by her interests, and because of that doomed to failure, which would make even more difficult the later efforts of recovery.[13]

Why did Monnet think that the liberation movement should not be launched from Britain? Most probably he thought, like de Gaulle himself, that it would be better to start the liberation movement on French soil, i.e. upon the soil of the French empire. He may also have believed that in those dramatic hours when everything was at stake, one could not be sure, especially if American armament and assistance did not reach her in time, that Britain herself would not also succumb to Nazi power. Was it perhaps also because he thought that the French post-Dunkirk resentment against Britain was still very strong in France?

Monnet may also have thought that if and when the United States, which for the moment still had diplomatic relations with France and an ambassador at Vichy, were to join in the war, it would be preferable for the resistance to be headed by some former legitimate official of the French government, already overseas (an admiral like Darlan or a general like Giraud). And Monnet was obviously aware of the reservations of the American administration and especially of Roosevelt himself, towards de Gaulle personally.[15] For, as will be seen later, American political circles, and Roosevelt's entourage in particular, were inclined to think of de Gaulle as a rather reactionary, authoritarian, representative of the old patriotic, possibly anti-Semitic and *revanchiste* France. Because he came to London they may also have suspected him of being under British influence, and therefore impervious to US influence if the two influences should differ. The Roosevelt administration therefore did everything in its power to prevent de Gaulle from becoming the leader of the French Liberation and of the Free French armed forces, once he had decided to make his base in Britain.

Yet it was in connection with the particular, and particularly significant problem of de Gaulle's relations with Roosevelt that Monnet twice tried to help him as much as he could. The first occasion occurred towards the end of the war when the problem of Allied recognition of the French Committee for National Liberation arose. The second problem arose in connection with the recognition of de Gaulle as leader of that Committee.

In his *Mémoires* Monnet described both phases: the first phase, which took place in June 1943 was that of the negotiations between de Gaulle, on the one side, and General Giraud (and to a lesser extent General Catroux) on the other for the formation of the Committee of National Liberation. General Eisenhower, the overall military commander, was authorized by Roosevelt to admit the Committee's right to administer those overseas French territories which recognized its authority, but only if it were headed by Giraud. Monnet succeeded in persuading de Gaulle to accept this solution for the time being in the pressing interests of France.

In the second phase, Monnet, now a member of the Committee, returned to Washington, where he did his utmost to convince Roosevelt to extend the authority of the Committee over those parts of French territory soon to be liberated by the Allied armies, and also to recognize de Gaulle, who was now the uncontested head of the resistance in France, as its natural leader. Monnet himself recounts the events in all their piquancy.

I exerted pressure on my friends to intervene with all their weight. Stimson, McCloy, Eisenhower, explained to Roosevelt how much the work which we were doing together and how far the authority which the Committee could be expected to exert in France so as to restore order in the liberated territories justified at least a *de facto* recognition. They convinced him. On Churchill's insistence de Gaulle undertook the journey to Washington. He came alone and asked me to go back to Algeria during his sojourn in the American capital, so that there would be no doubt that he had nothing to discuss with anyone else, that he owed nothing to anyone else. Roosevelt received him with courtesy, and gave him all the honours. But he granted him only a limited recognition. He had to wait until 23 October for the Provisional Government to be accepted for what it unequivocally was: the legitimate power in France.

But de Gaulle's trauma was, as we shall see, going to have long-lasting effects on his foreign policy (see below, pp. 119).

## Political ambitions

De Gaulle's conviction that he was predestined to save France as well as his military education, examined in the preceding two sections, helped to stimulate his ambition to achieve ultimate personal leadership, i.e. supreme leadership. The frequent irruptions in the modern politics of France, since the days of Napoleon, of generals determined to save the nation from political decomposition, combined with the deep national feeling that *L'Armée*, mute though it may be, is always ready to halt the country's decline, added to this determination. Hence already in his second book, *Le fil de l'épée*, he expressed firmly the conviction that military leadership and political leadership are indissolubly linked.

From the outset the book sounds three of the *leitmotivs* of de Gaulle's mental make-up. The first is the predominance of the 'will'; the second is the dignity of the character of a soldier, and the third and main one is the problem of the relations between political and military leaders. In the last chapter of *Le fil de l'épée* de Gaulle develops the theme of 'politics and the soldier'. 'In the theatre of peacetime, it is the statesman who plays the chief role . . . Then suddenly war calls another actor from the wings . . . the military chief appears.' His importance in history is primordial, given the inevitability of the recurrence of war in human history; *polemos pater pantom* (war is at the origin of all things) is a maxim inscribed in de Gaulle's earliest diaries and which he often repeated.[16]

From the beginning de Gaulle stressed the fundamental difference between the two professional characters: the political leader 'who must pose as the servant of the public in order to become its master' and 'comes and goes between power and powerlessness', and the soldier who 'must renounce his personal liberty' but for whom 'on the other hand, such authority as he may wield is absolute'. Hence the profound contrasts between the political leader and the soldier and their mutual lack of understanding. But this is all to the good. For 'in a nation where the soldiers make the law, it is almost certain that, sooner or later, the springs of power, stressed to excess, will break' whereas 'on the other hand, it is as well that politicians should not meddle with the army. All that is bred of a party system . . . cannot fail to corrupt a military order whose strength is drawn primarily from the soldierly virtues.'[17]

But, in spite of the harmony which, in his book, he so obviously recommends between the political and the military leader, there is also a third motivation. This third motivation is the presumption that if they really succeed in being 'leaders', each in his own realm, what they must have in common and what drives the political and the military leader equally is the ambition to play a part in history.

What is important is that those who are ambitious, more especially should be filled with the spirit of enthusiasm, and be obsessed by the necessity of finding in life an opportunity to leave their mark upon events . . . There is no soldier who, by winning fame for himself, has not served the hopes and aims of high policy, nor any statesman who, by the greatness (*grandeur*) of his achievements, has not won a still greater glory by contributing to the defence of his country.

These are the concluding lines of his book. De Gaulle therefore believed that, as proved by the most outstanding example of 'glory' in history, there are men whose exceptional 'enthusiasm' and 'ambition' enable them to be both a military leader and a political leader in the different circumstances of war and peace, and acting in a different manner in each of these situations. Hence, later, his unfailing admiration for Churchill, a great statesman who was a great military leader in wartime and his confidence in de Gaulle, a great military leader who became in peace time, a statesman and a political philosopher. The young de Gaulle did not say as much in *Le fil de l'épée*, but he very probably envisaged the probability.

As a soldier, de Gaulle obviously did not admire or even like the ambiguities of French political life, of parliament and political parties and above all of professional politicians. During the First World War, while he was fighting so bravely in the trenches he exclaimed 'We are governed by grocers!' and he wrote a direct criticism of the parliamentary regime in his diary:

The Parliament is becoming increasingly odious and stupid. The Ministers have literally all their days taken up by the meetings of the Chamber . . . We shall only win once we have got rid of that rabble, and there is not a single Frenchman who will not then rejoice. The men in arms (*les combattants*) above all. Actually, the idea is already spreading and I shall be very surprised if this regime will survive after the war.[17]

Although such criticisms by a military leader were to re-appear in full light after the shock the politicians ('les politiques') first gave him during the defeat in 1940 by their shortsightedness and their coward-ice, and secondly, soon after the Liberation, by their ideological and professional narrowness – such views never really amounted to the idea that the military should eliminate the politicians and govern in their stead. On the contrary, in his first book, *Discorde chez l'ennemi*, de Gaulle had already put forward as the main explanation of the defeat of Germany in the First World War the fact that the military had taken possession of political power, which led to the downfall of the German state in 1918.

To be sure, the inherent incompatibility between the logical and ethical nature of a soldier and that of a politician was aggravated in de Gaulle's case by his absolute, almost mystical, sense of ser-vice to France, of honour and of 'grandeur'. But this did not prevent him from exhibiting in himself most of the instincts of a politician: ambition, appetite for power, perseverance in pur-pose, theoretical versatility, cunning and an inborn reflex of hos-tility, the source of what is called adversarial politics. What he abhorred was the professionalization of the sacred duty, the sub-ordination of the national interest to ulterior ideological motives and, even worse, to vile electoral purposes. He felt that he had been 'elected' by France above the bargaining for power between political parties and groups, which prevented them from achieving any real national unity, political continuity and constructiveness.

De Gaulle's attitude towards the political reconstruction of France during and immediately after the war, that is at the beginning of the Provisional Government installed immediately after the Liberation in 1944, was surprisingly positive and open-minded. Even before, putting the salvation of France above any other consideration, he had insisted that the Resistance be opened to all French patriots – and when the Communist Party joined a year or so later, on the orders of Moscow, he welcomed them into the national fraternity. He only remarked to the French Communist leader, Maurice Thorez, when the latter finally came back from Moscow after the Liberation, with a supreme irony worthy of Pascal, that: 'You chose. I had no choice.' And he was constantly and completely aware that if he did not master the Communists with his authority and his means of supervision, they would, using Titoist techniques, try to transform the national liberation into a communist revolution. But he was sure of himself and of France and he knew that together they would make all her sons, whatever their political creeds, rally round her and the French state.

The primacy of the 'French state' is the main tenet in de Gaulle's political logic. In his theory as well as in his practice France means the French state and the French state means France. It was because the state was weak that France had lost its erstwhile superiority. He gave an almost subconscious primacy to the state in his 'certaine idée de la France'. Thus in his *Mémoires de Guerre*, he describes how, having arrived in liberated Paris, he went straight, and how significantly, to the building of the Ministry of Defence which, for him, was the centre of the state. Startled to see that, after all the tragic changes, the building, the furniture, the curtains, the tapestries, were all the same as when he had left them four years before, his first spontaneous thought was: 'Nothing is missing apart from the state. It is incumbent on me to reinstate it.'[19]

De Gaulle's theory of the state is as simple and as direct as his theory of the nation.

France comes from the depth of ages. She lives. The centuries call her . . . This is why the state which is responsible for France has the task of her past heritage, of her interests of today and of her hopes for tomorrow, an altogether vital necessity, which in case of public danger will fall again on the collectivity! This is why for a state (*pour un pouvoir*) its legitimacy consists of the sentiment which it inspires and on the basis of which it embodies the national unity and continuity when the motherland is in danger . . . '

And after describing how the Merovingians, the Carolingians, the Capets, the Bourbons, the Bonapartes and the Third Republic had used war for those supreme purposes, he adds that he, de Gaulle, too, has been able to lead the country to her salvation. As she arose out of her abyss, she was seen re-appearing as a victorious and independent state . . . But for the State to be as it should be, the instrument of French unity, of the superior interest of the state, of the continuity of national action, I considered it necessary that government should proceed (que le gouvernement procédât) not from Parliament or in other words from the parties, but above them, from a head directly mandated by the whole of the nation and enabled to will, to decide and to act.'[20]

Also, when on 31 July 1943, he was finally recognized by the Allies as head of the *Comité Français de libération nationale*, for him already a government, he wrote in his *Mémoires de Guerre*: 'It is the state which is now reappearing.' Finally, when in opposition in 1946, he made the same point in his Bayeux speech of 16 June 1946, which is one of the fundamental statements of his political philosophy:

This is why, once the state is saved in the victory thus achieved and the national unity is thus maintained, the most urgent and important task is to establish the new French institutions . . . so as to preserve the credibility of the laws, the cohesion of the government, the efficacy of the administration and the prestige of the authority of the State. For, in fact, if the State does not work well, the consequence is that the citizens do not respect the institutions. Then the slightest occasion could bring about the threat of dictatorship.

Upon which he describes with classic clarity the reasons why dictatorship should be avoided at any cost.[21]

But on the other hand, in spite of the fact that de Gaulle's perhaps inborn contempt for French parliamentarism had been greatly increased by the political collapse of 1940, when the moment came to begin to think of the kind of 'state' France would become after the Liberation, he recommended the re-formation of political parties within the Resistance. Influenced by a letter he had received from Léon Blum, then in prison at Riom, who advised him to do so, and who argued that 'there is no democratic state without parties . . . A democratic state is inevitably a federation of parties', he decided in February 1943 to 'approve of the formation within the country of a concrete organism grouping the representatives of the parties' under the sole sign of the struggle for the fatherland and for democracy. Moreover, when he instructed Jean Moulin (whom he had chosen as his chief of the Metropolitan Resistance, among many other qualities also because he had been a *préfet*, i.e. a high official) to apply this measure he opened up a serious split between Moulin and Pierre Brossolette – a young French socialist who was also prominent in the Resistance. However, the damage did not last too long in those terrible circumstances, which themselves soon solved the problem. Moulin was captured and shot by the Nazis, and Brossolette soon after, while under arrest, threw himself out of the window of the Gestapo prison in order not to give way under torture.

And it was still with the political parties that he accepted to form the Provisional Government in 1944 with himself as Prime Minister – a function obviously too narrow to give him sufficient freedom of action for his designs for France and for the French state. However, it was under that government and under the old constitution that such new institutions as the Plan, the Economic and Social Council, the ENA were founded, and that national unity began to be re-established in France. But when the French Communists to whom he had allotted only non-controversial portfolios in the Provisional Government began to agitate in France, as they were doing already in all European democracies, and the other 'parties' too soon manifested their parliamentary 'independence' which de Gaulle described as centrifugalism, he was quickly disgusted by the old game. 'To the fractional character of the parties, which afflicts them like an infirmity, there is now added their own decadence . . . they are declining to the point that each is becoming the representation of a category of interests', he wrote on this question.[22]

Thenceforward a new expression appeared in his vocabulary, 'les politiques', in inverted commas. French political scientists always envy the English language for having two expressions, 'policy' and 'politics', to express what they have to embrace in one word, *la politique*. But the French language in turn benefits from a distinction of gender: '*la* politique' differs from '*le* politique', which means both 'the realm of politics' and a 'statesman'. De Gaulle, for instance, described Churchill more often than not as *un* or '*le* grand politique'. But precisely because of that, when faced with the political parties and the professional politicians, his contempt expressed itself in the word 'les politiques' in inverted commas, an expression not unlike 'the politicos' in English.

The conflict between 'les politiques' and himself, 'un grand politique', as well as between 'his' government and representatives or alleged representatives of classes, socio-economic groups or even religions (MRP), inevitably grew more bitter. Already in his speech of 13 November 1945, when he accepted the premiership, he had warned the National Assembly that it ought to concentrate rigorously on its constitutional and legislative work and not allow itself to be diverted by adventitious (*adventices*) debates. His warning was clear: 'Let us not hide the truth! The representative regime will now undergo the decisive test.'

Soon, in his eyes, the regime had failed the test. In the eyes of history it would have been impossible to reconcile his high, if hazy, structural vistas and his historical ambitions for France with the hard daily grind of a provisional government faced with the enormous task of reconstruction, of national reconciliation, of liquidation of the colonial empire, and of economic hardship, alleviated only by American help which he abhorred. Moreover, his apprehension of transnational interdependence was aggravated by the fact that the 'Allies' were still keeping France out of their councils. The function of Prime Minister of the Provisional Government did not give de Gaulle sufficient authority and freedom of action to face the internal and external threats to France, caught as he felt himself to be between a factional Parliament and a mediocre President of the Republic. How could he face these threats with his hands tied by 'les politiques'?

As a statesman de Gaulle did not need to remain professionally in politics. If he could not achieve what he thought, rightly or wrongly, to be essential, he had better go. In his declaration of 1 January 1946 to the National Assembly he put the problem squarely: 'Is what is wanted a government which governs or an omnipotent Assembly only delegating its decisions to the government? If the Assembly does not give [to the government] all or part of the means it needs to fulfil the responsibility of the executive power, *eh! bien*, this government will resign' . . . On 20 January 1946 he wrote to the President of the Assembly that 'he dismissed himself', '*je me démets*', from the function of President of the Provisional Government of the Republic. Later he was to tell Claude Mauriac, his personal assistant: 'I have never played politics . . . I had to resign from power in order to continue not to play.'[23] He packed his bags, and withdrew to his country house at Colombey-les-deux-Eglises. His reasoning was the same: if France did not want him, if she did not want to renew his 'contract' with her, far be it from him to persist.

As far as his relations with France were concerned such an attitude can be compared with that of the devoted and faithful lover of a capricious mistress. He will always be there when she needs him and calls to him, but he will neither beg her to stay with him, nor force her to do so. This detached, albeit devoted attitude, is one of the psychological hallmarks of the statesman in contrast to the professional politician. *Mutatis mutandis*, (and bearing in mind that Churchill did really hold the British belief in the supreme legitimacy of parliament and in representative government), this was the same attitude of dignified withdrawal as that of Churchill after he lost the elections in 1945. Like Cato, they both went, the one to Chartwell, the other to Colombey, to build their houses and write their memoirs, yet knowing that they would be called on again.

## Grandeur

De Gaulle's political ambition and his philosophy had a name, which has since become famous. It was called '*grandeur*'. Although together with '*une certaine idée de la France*', '*grandeur*' is one of the principal concepts of de Gaulle's political vocabulary, it has never been precisely defined.

Most frequently the concept has been connected with de Gaulle's foreign policy. But for instance Philip Cerny, in the book (which won the praise of Michel Debré, in a special review for *The Times Literary Supplement*), entitled *The Politics of Grandeur: Ideological Aspects of de Gaulle's Foreign Policy*, recognized that

De Gaulle's foreign policy was not defined only by the structure of international relations or by his view of them in isolation. Rather it was part of a much wider view of man and his world, an ontological perspective of the nature of things which gave coherence to his political action and linked the various facets of his foreign and domestic policies when in power.[24]

Cerny, and the authors of the many other works on the same subject, consider that *grandeur*, in its basic political connotation, was both the idea which inspired de Gaulle's actions and the idea with which he inspired the French people and led them to rally around him. Or, to quote Cerny again,

grandeur refers primarily to the need to create a new and more profound sense of national consciousness capable of transcending the traditional divisions which have characterised the French polity, thus allowing and reinforcing the development of a consensus supportive of a firmly established and active state pursuing the general interest within a stable political system.[25]

But the political definition inevitably falls short of the complete definition of the concept and of its almost magical power of inspiration, both of the leader and of the led. Here the word still remains mysteriously veiled in its evocative, but elusive power. There are two principal reasons for this elusiveness.

One lies in the complexity of the concept itself. Its analogous, if not synonymous meanings are legion: greatness, height, power, rank, prestige, nobility, dignity, esteem, respect, authority, radiance, honour, magnanimity, generosity, charisma, perhaps even uniqueness. However different they may sound separately, most of them can be jumbled together into the patchwork of *grandeur*. Besides, popular language links all these eulogistic words with the opposing, sometimes even pejorative expressions of especially excessive *grandeur*, as in '*regarder du haut de sa grandeur*' which signifies an attitude of contempt, while '*la folie de grandeur*' or indeed '*le délire de grandeur*' belong to pathology.

But even de Gaulle himself never explained exactly what *grandeur* meant. When Malraux pressed him, he gave such metaphorical answers as '*La grandeur est un chemin vers quelquechose qu'on ne connaît pas*' (It is the way to an unknown objective); or more subjectively, '*Il s'agissait de l'espérance d'agir sur de grands évènements*'[26] (the hope of making an impact on great events); or more categorically, '*Ne marchandons pas sur la grandeur*' (one does not bargain about greatness).

What is accepted by the great majority of the authors who have tried to define the concept, is that *grandeur* is, and cannot but be, a spiritual quality. Pascal had already contrasted *les grandeurs d'établissement* (the established grandeurs) and *les grandeurs naturelles* (the natural grandeurs). The former are, according to Pascal, those 'which depend on the will of men who have thought it reasonable that certain positions (*états*) should be honoured and shown respect. But the natural grandeurs are those which are independent of man's imagination because they are inherent in the real and effective qualities of the soul.'

Malraux also arrived at the same essentially spiritual quality of *grandeur* by way of Chateaubriand's definition of intelligence which, he thought, best described the intelligence of de Gaulle. Says Malraux: 'Son intelligence [de Gaulle's] tient au *niveau* de sa réflexion, à ce que Chateaubriand appelait l'intelligence des grandes âmes.' (De Gaulle's intelligence was at the level of his thought, at what Chateaubriand called the intelligence of great souls.)[27] Chateaubriand's remark on great souls, or souls of a high level, is italicized by Malraux in the text, so as to stress that de Gaulle lived at such a high spiritual level, so different from, and so opposed to, mediocrity that from that level he could see only the continuity of France's *grandeur* in history past, present and future.

From a purely political point of view, the concept of 'greatness', to give *grandeur* its simpler English name, meant for de Gaulle, above all, *independence*, France's total independence. Therein lies an apparent contradiction, for absolute independence can be achieved only by total isolation, or by total domination: sovereignty in its most literal sense. But isolation was inconceivable for France, an integral part of European geography, and therefore history. Thus, though 'wing' countries, like Spain, or Sweden, or even Britain, could to a certain extent practise a policy either of quasi-neutrality or of balance of power, France could not withdraw to such an ambiguous position; and France's attempts at total domination had been brought to an end with the fall of Napoleon's empire. What had remained since then was the influence of France on the evolution of Europe, and consequently of the world, but through diplomacy, i.e. alliances and economic, commercial and cultural exchanges with other European powers. But this period had been punctuated by wars, which became world wars, in which France had to defend her independence against external attacks, mainly, of late, from Germany. Thus France's *grandeur* was kept intact in spite of the alternation between war and peace until the Second World War.

Or rather until the whole world was enmeshed in the global network of interdependence of which the Second World War was an obvious, if negative, proof. From then on, or rather from the moment when the information revolution established a *de facto* interdependence of all parts of the world, and facilitated the emergence of super-powers, or powers of continental size and of a military and technological predominance inaccessible to all other former powers, 'greatness' became an ambiguous notion. France's *grandeur* especially was dwarfed by the emergence of powers with higher stakes, as the Eiffel Tower has been dwarfed by the new skyscrapers built in Paris, and by the displacement of the centre of world policy-making from Europe, where France had exerted its millenary influence.

The double object of de Gaulle's dedication to the *grandeur* of France was only partially achieved. His straightforward military reactions and political decisions, both suitable for rapid implementation, were crowned with success in the pursuit of his first object, namely the rehabilitation of France's status. In the second, and much longer-term effort to give France back her total independence, his inability to adapt to the levelled and flattened perspectives of interdependence led to apparent successes which were soon to be belied by the ultimate realities.

## II

## DE GAULLE'S POLICIES OF INTERDEPENDENCE

This title, 'policies of interdependence' which is used for the second part of each of the essays on our five statesmen, sounds particularly inadequate, and even ironical, when applied to de Gaulle's policies. For certainly never was there a statesman in our time, and seldom in history, so obsessed by, and outspoken about the problem of national independence. It would therefore be a bitter irony if it were proved that in fact, and contrary to his claims, his foreign policy and some of his domestic policies, were in reality by-products of interdependence; and that in consequence, he, de Gaulle, too, had to suffer from the modern curbing of sovereignty, let alone *grandeur*.

Yet before embarking on the critical examination of de Gaulle's principal policies, those in which his aspiration to sovereignty was at its most intense, two caveats should be borne in mind. The first is that interdependence reduced the illusions of sovereignty not only of France, but of all former 'powers'. But de Gaulle dramatically accentuated the contrast between the rhetoric of his illusions and the reality. Secondly, although this might seem to be a contradiction of what has just been said, in spite of his illusions, and in spite of his negativism, de Gaulle ultimately possessed that sense of *mesure* which is characteristic of the true French mind. Hence his capacity to change, sometimes very abruptly, from stridently negative postures to flexible, common-sensical attitudes, as for instance, to anticipate, his notorious turnabout in the Algerian crisis, his unflinching support of Adenauer against the Soviet threat in the Berlin crisis of 1961, or his resolute support for President Kennedy in the Cuban crisis of 1962, the very year in which he had withdrawn France from NATO.

Thus, as in internal politics he was not and could not have been a dictator, so in his external policies he was not and did not want to be, an imperialist conqueror. Unlike Hitler, the man he loathed most, and even unlike Napoleon, whom he idealized, he did not aspire to, let alone plan a total domination of the world, under his leadership. What he wanted was that France should be an unchallenged member of the 'concert' (the term evoking here both the 'concert of Europe' and the French expression *concertation*, i.e. consultation into co-operation) of the powers of the world, with possibly the almost subconscious implication that given its clarity and radiance France's voice would be the one most distinctly heard at least in the continent of Europe. And, as a corollary, he wanted France's inviolability and immunity from German aggression to be established once and forever, whatever the political, diplomatic and, last but not least, military means. But his war-time allies subjected him from the outset to a trauma.

*The impact of war-time relations with the Allies on de Gaulle's foreign policy*

The concert of powers of which de Gaulle thought included a varying number of powers according to the rapidly changing history under his eyes. Initially there were only two powers: the first with which he wanted France to have an equal partnership was Britain, the one democracy at war with Hitler and to whom he had offered France's alliance. The misunderstandings which arose between him and the British government and military command (not to speak of the secret services) and even between him and Churchill, whose chivalrous sense of honour gave him a better insight into de Gaulle's mentality, form an endless tragi-comedy. He did not and could not see himself objectively as an exile from his defeated country, without an immediate contribution to make, and even without a clear national mandate to present to the country which had given him recognition and support, and which was engaged in a life-and-death struggle.

His susceptibility knew no limits whenever the British authorities took immediate decisions on any question which touched directly or indirectly on French sovereignty. Starting with the destruction of the French fleet by the British at Mers-el-kebir, on 3 July 1940, followed by the disastrous Dakar expedition in September 1941, by the arrest by mistake in London of the Free French Admiral Muselier by the British services in January 1941, by Roosevelt's and Churchill's failure to include 'France' in the Atlantic Charter in August 1941, all these incidents were more than sufficient to arouse his deepest resentment. The suspicion of Britain's innate perfidy which he acquired then, or the confirmation of his pre-instinctive French distrust of Britain, is known to have had lasting effects on the relations between the two countries during the war and even and most manifestly when he came to power after the war.

## Relations with the USSR

But it also had earlier diplomatic effects. During the second period, that is after the USSR and the US entered the war, on 21 June 1941 and 7 December 1941 respectively, he hoped to secure France's place on the same level as that of the two Western democratic Allies and her recognition as the third Western power in the new quartet of relations with the USSR. He tried to re-establish France in her place as the fourth power not only by claiming this place directly but also by playing the other three powers off against each other.

Thus the fact that Hitler, on 21 June 1941, had betrayed his erstwhile faithful ally and friend Stalin, and had invaded the USSR, was immediately perceived by de Gaulle as doubly propitious. Inside France this meant eventually the entry of the French Communist Party, even if as a separate organization, into the French National Committee of Liberation, formed and headed by de Gaulle in 1943. He always recognized, in all his writings, that once engaged in the battle, the contribution of the French Communist Party had a massive effect on the operations of the Resistance. But he always knew that the ultimate aim of the Communist Party, was to transform the liberation of France into the Communist revolution in France, like that of Tito in Yugoslavia, and he kept them under effective control.

From an external point of view, the entry of the USSR into the war revived in de Gaulle the hope of being able to break his exclusive dependence on Britain; he contemplated the possibility of a new collaboration between Free France and the new ally which could make Britain, the old and principal ally, aware of the objective importance of Free France. 'Furthermore', he wrote 'the presence [of Russia] in the camp of the Allies provided fighting France [*la France combattante*] with an element of equilibrium in its relations with the Anglo-Saxons which I was determined to turn to my advantage.'[28]

For it should be remembered that, after the Dakar fiasco, and de Gaulle's proclamation of a Council of the French Empire in Brazzaville (French Equatorial Africa) on 27 October 1940, relations between him and the British reached their lowest point. De Gaulle suspected that Britain shared the overt hopes of the American government, then in full diplomatic relations with Pétain's government in Vichy, that they would be able to loosen Vichy's links with Nazi Germany, or at least to find among the Pétainist hierarchy some military (Weygand) or naval (Darlan) leader, capable of effecting an about-turn from within France itself, with more power and legitimacy than de Gaulle could ever lay claim to. Hence de Gaulle's strange proposal on 5 June 1941 to offer the Americans free access to the French African naval bases which had rallied to the Free French. Yet, ominously, he never received an answer from the Americans to that offer; on the contrary, when Admiral Muselier won over the islands of Saint-Pierre-et-Miquelon, the Allies were displeased, because they considered that this was bound to stiffen the Vichy government's determination to fight alongside the Germans. Such deep misunderstandings and distrust explain up to a point de Gaulle's urge to establish good, basic relations with the USSR the moment she had been let down and treacherously attacked by her Nazi ally.

From the Middle East (Damascus and Beirut) where he was at that time, on 22 June 1941, de Gaulle cabled his headquarters in London on 24 June that 'without discussing now the vices and even the crimes of the Soviet regime we ought to proclaim, like Churchill, that we are on the side of the Russians in so far as they are fighting against the Germans'. It is of course true to say that in his own, traditional, French fear of Germany, de Gaulle considered the Franco-Russian

alliance as an obvious instrument of mutual security for both countries. In May 1935 he had approved of Laval's signature of 'the classic
Franco-Russian pact meant to counter-balance in the French tradition
the threats of the German neighbour' as Lacouture puts it. Lacouture
also quotes de Gaulle's letter to his mother of 1935: 'What do I think
of the Franco-Russian pact? My answer will be very simple. We are
rapidly moving towards a war with Germany and the moment things
will turn against us Italy will not fail to stab us in the back (*de nous
donner le coup de pied de l'âne*). It is a question of survival, the rest
is literature . . . We don't have the means to refuse the help of the
Russians, whatever the horror their regime inspires. It is the story of
Francis I allied to the Muslim Turks against Charles V.'[29]

Thus, on 2 August, after Hitler had forced the Vichy government
to break diplomatic relations with the USSR, de Gaulle cabled again
to ask his representatives to ask Maisky, the Soviet Ambassador in
London, 'to establish direct relations with us . . . and if the USSR
would consider making a declaration concerning her intention to
restore the independence and the grandeur (*sic*) of France and, if
possible, also her integrity'.[30] On 26 September, de Gaulle signed
an agreement with Maisky in which he was recognized as the head
of the Free French, and which laid down that the USSR would ensure
the full and entire restoration of the independence and grandeur (sic)
of France but, he adds, as in the 1940 agreement with Britain, it did
not promise to restore 'our integrity'.

Moreover he even tried to maximize Free France's 'special relations'
with the USSR by constantly reminding the Russians that if the
Anglo-Saxons, and notably the Americans, who were still maintaining diplomatic relations with Nazi Germany and with Vichy,
might one day find a compromise possible with Hitler, Free France
would fight at Russia's side to the end; and by dispatching French
troops to fight alongside the Soviet army in Russia, 'the regiment
Normandy-Nieman' which was going to serve magnificently and
was to be the only Western force to fight on the Eastern front.[31]

Finally, to anticipate, very soon after he came to power and before
the war had come to an end (the Ardennes offensive was still going
on) he went to Moscow to establish new relations between liberated
France and the USSR. After serious confrontation with Stalin, de
Gaulle, on 10 December 1944 signed a Franco-Soviet treaty of alliance
for twenty years. (It was suspended by the USSR in 1955 as a protest
against France's recognition of the new state of the Federal Republic
of Germany.) This did not give him the long delayed satisfaction he
hoped for. Only two months later, in February 1945, when the Yalta

conference was called, France, with Stalin's explicit assent, was not
invited to join the 'Three'.

## Relations with the Americans

But above and behind de Gaulle's unusually idiosyncratic and personalized approach to French relations with Britain and the USSR,
there lay the extraordinary mutual antipathy, one can say even allergy,
which separated him from F. D. Roosevelt, and as a result from the
USA. Why such a peculiar episode should afterwards have affected the
relations between two great Western democracies and, consequently,
Western foreign policies as a whole, has been examined at length by
historians and contemporary witnesses. To their honour it must also
be added that while most American historians lay the responsibility on
Roosevelt and his entourage, French historians do not clear de Gaulle
of all blame.

Lacouture, who has investigated the affair from all angles in a chapter entitled 'Ostracism', quotes Arthur Schlesinger, Roosevelt's dedicated historian, as attributing his hero's prejudice against de Gaulle
to three causes: the discrepancy observed by Roosevelt between de
Gaulle's *'amour propre'* and the objectives of the Allies; the unsavoury
reputation of the Gaullist secret services, passed on to the US by
the British services; and Roosevelt's firm conviction that France no
longer had a place among the great powers whom he would have
liked to entrust with the conduct of tomorrow's world. But, adds
Schlesinger, Roosevelt's convictions were fully shared by his Foreign
Secretary, Cordell Hull, and by the whole State Department.[32]

The last point is fully confirmed by Cordell Hull himself in a most
enlightening passage of his *The Memoirs of Cordell Hull*, in which he
confirms that

in 1942 de Gaulle wanted to be taken into the Anglo-American-Russian
military discussions, and he still sought some form of recognition in the
political sphere. Ambassador Winant reported [from London] to us in August
that the Free French wanted to be asked to sign the United Nations'
Declaration because they felt that such adherence would make them appear
as the French Provisional Government. He added that the British Foreign
Office supported this view with the thought that it would create greater
unity among the French. It was de Gaulle's insistence on political recognition,
however, that excited so much suspicion against him. If he, as an Army
general, had thrown himself wholeheartedly against the Axis in a military
sense, if he had actually led French troops against the enemy whenever
possible, instead of spending most of his time in London, he could have
rallied far more support to himself among the French and among the
United Nations. Instead, his own dictatorial attitude, coupled with his

adventures in the political field, inevitably inspired the thought that he was trying to develop a political standing that would make him the next ruler of France.[33]

Had this passage occurred in a diary written at the time its impatient attitude would have been justified in part by the mood of the day. But the fact that it is part of a record published in 1948, when de Gaulle's historical importance had been confirmed both in France and in the world at large, shows how deep-rooted was the personal hostility to de Gaulle among Roosevelt's personal and official counsellors with the honourable exceptions of Harry Hopkins, Judge Frankfurter and John McCloy. (A White House cabinet room pad of 1943 shows Harry Hopkin's doodles with a notation at the bottom: 'One more crack from McCloy to the boss about de Gaulle and McCloy is out.')[34]

Roosevelt's personal antipathy to de Gaulle was accentuated by the fact that de Gaulle was thought of as the 'Frenchman' manipulated by the British and by the fact that important Frenchmen living in Washington like Jacques Maritain, Alexis Léger, (the poet, St John Perse) former Secretary-General of the Quai d'Orsay and, last but not least, Jean Monnet, still had reservations about de Gaulle's present legitimacy and future political career. But this personal antipathy also concurred with two general political views about France which the President held at the time. The first was tactical. Influenced by General Pershing, a First World War hero and friend of Pétain, by Admiral Leahy, the new Ambassador to Vichy France and his two aides, Roosevelt would have preferred to wait until Pétain or a Pétainist personality was ready to revolt against Germany, from within the country itself. As Roosevelt explained to André Philip, an emissary of de Gaulle, since he, Roosevelt, was not an idealist, if Quisling were to hand him Oslo or Laval Paris he would be glad to accept them.[35]

The second view of France, strategic this time, was perhaps developed after the terrible shock Roosevelt suffered at the fall of France which, until then, he had apparently considered invincible. He now believed that France had fallen for good from her position as a world power. His idea of the post-war concert of powers consisted of a directorate of the USA, the USSR, China and possibly Great Britain. Thus, de Gaulle, who lacked qualification both for the present and for the future, gave him rather the impression of being a megalomaniac and an impostor. Until the end of the war, he and the American administration sought tenaciously to 'ostracize' de Gaulle. Only after the assassination of Admiral Darlan in December 1942, and the progressive abandonment of power over the French Committee for National Liberation by General Giraud (the Americans' choice) was the Committee grudgingly recognized on 26 August 1943 as 'representing the French interests', after its recognition by Britain and the USSR.

But nor did de Gaulle help to clear up this personal misunderstanding. Easily wounded in his pride as the representative of the true France, and of a vindictive nature, he allowed his resentment to grow into a general anti-American posture. While it is true to say, with de Tocqueville, that the French people have particularly great difficulty in understanding the Americans and their way of life, de Gaulle, during and after the war, transformed this sentiment into a geo-political theory. As we shall see later, with the exception of the period when Eisenhower was President, with whom he was linked in a soldierly friendship after the war, and of the presidency of Kennedy, whom he admired intellectually but with whom too he developed serious differences of views, de Gaulle entertained a permanent suspicion of American political methods and goals in the world and notably of American policies towards Europe and of the 'Atlantic' collaboration. As Raymond Aron noted, perhaps too severely: 'It is with General de Gaulle that the pejorative connotation of the term "Atlantic" originated and was dated.'[35]

But with this we leave behind the subconscious background of de Gaulle's aspirations towards the complete independence of France among the other powers to concentrate on the ultimate reality of interdependence built on his major policies.

## The dialectics of statesmanship

De Gaulle's premiership of the Provisional Government (the continuation of the Committee for National Liberation on French soil, 8 September 1944–20 January 1946) cannot be taken as a fair test of his statesmanship. His disciplined mind, his sense of command and his charisma were amply sufficient to put and to keep him at the head of affairs. But as long as he was still fighting the war with Germany, which ended officially on 8 May 1945, the tasks of reconstructing and reorganizing the liberated territories were too pressing and his position as Prime Minister too constricted by a mediocre government and selfish political parties to allow him to prepare and present his own programme of government. In spite of the enthusiasm of victory and of the fact that many of the institutions of which he approved were created under the provisional government, as far as he was concerned this was a period of political frustration.

But once free, that is in opposition, he soon used the opportunity, in his speech at Bayeux on 16 June 1946 to sound clearly and loudly his own theme, indeed his *leitmotiv*: that France needed a political revolution aimed at providing her with a state which was sufficiently strong to defend her independence in a world, notably in a Europe, already torn between two super-powers which, by their polarization, curbed and crushed the erstwhile autonomy of other states, and principally of the European states. The clue to the proposition was clearly constitutional reform, or rather the replacement of the constitution of the Fourth Republic, oriented towards the legislative by a constitution oriented towards the executive, as enacted afterwards in the constitution of the Fifth Republic.

But in the case of the politics of *grandeur* not only were the goals too high and therefore unattainable, they were deliberately set too high and unattainable by the leader. As in Hamlet 'the play's the thing', so in the politics of *grandeur* the effort was the thing. The effort itself could realize, almost by a miracle, unrealizable goals or, rather, try to transform the reality by fighting it for unreal purposes. This was later most dramatically expressed by de Gaulle, when he told Philippe de Saint Robert: '*C'est parce que nous ne sommes plus une grande puissance qu'il nous faut une grande politique, parce que si nous n'avons pas une grande politique comme nous ne sommes plus une grande puissance nous ne serons plus rien!*'[37] (It is because we are no longer a great power that we need a great political design, because if we do not have a great political design as we are no longer a great power we shall be nothing!)

His great and unrealistic political design was, as previously shown, France's independence. The reality, which he duly perceived but thought, or hoped, that France could master, by her own strength and efforts, was the interdependence of the developed world. These two contrary propositions formed, as in a dialectical triad, the thesis: independence, and the antithesis: interdependence. The synthesis could be only a mixture of positive achievements and negative obstructions, 'nuisance-value', for the others, and for himself, of initial satisfactions soon transformed into frustrations. In so far as de Gaulle's reign can be visualized as divided into two contrasting periods, one ascendant from 1958 to 1962, the second descendent from 1963 to 1969, the dialectical triad can be translated into the three distinct periods of his statesmanship. The thesis is the period of opposition (1948–58) when *la haute politique*, 'the great design', is presented: the achievement of

France's independence through the reconstruction of her strength and natural grandeur, directly, by endowing her with her own military (nuclear) strength and indirectly, that is by way of *grande politique*, by re-installing her on the commanding heights of international power occupied since the Second World War by three other powers.

The second period, or antithesis (1958–62) extends over the first four or five years of his reign, during which he did keep the promise of quickly equipping France, *within the framework of interdependence*, with a sufficiently modern (nuclear) defence-system, in spite of both the cost of the enterprise and of the almost prohibitive pressure brought by the Allies against this measure; and during which by applying the politics of *grandeur* he made France again into one of the centres of the polycentric world of today.

The third period or synthesis (1963–69) unfolded under the unforgiving pressure of life drawing to a close. Constrained by objective considerations to acknowledge the interdependent character of his otherwise considerable achievements in world affairs, he launched himself personally, indeed somewhat detached from his government, already in the hands of the shrewder Pompidou, into a last assault on *grandeur*. He tried to tear away the veil of interdependence; but it proved to be both too fluid and too universal to free France from under it. In his exasperation he became more and unnecessarily provocative, and he cast doubt through his contradictory attitudes even on his previous achievements, and in consequence, he harvested merely international hostility and national bewilderment. When he lost a referendum for the first time, he decided that this meant the end of his 'contract with France' and he retired on 27 April 1969 taking no further part in any political activity until his death on 9 November 1970.

In what follows we shall analyse in the light of the dialectical triad, as defined above, the internal and especially the external policies of his statesmanship, so as to get a closer and more precise view of the possibilities and impossibilities, hopes and despair of the pursuit of national independence in the age of interdependence.

But one more word should be added here about the choice of the year 1962 as the dividing line between the two periods of government. While the date of the change from opposition to the coming to power can be proved on the calendar, the date of the change in the policies and even in the fortunes of a political regime during its long existence is less easy to demonstrate. In such changes the trends usually start earlier and finish later than the year in which some climax occurs. While 1962 should really mean in this context the period 1961–63 the following are some of the landmarks which make it possible to discern the descending period already in 1962. One was the end of the Algerian crisis, which had frightened French public opinion more than anything else. With the proclamation of Algerian independence on 7 July 1962, French opinion felt much more relaxed than in 1958 when de Gaulle was brought to power, without any conditions, provided he could save the country from civil war. Another signal, this time on the European stage, was the rejection by the other five members of the European Community of de Gaulle's plan for a European Confederation, the so-called 'Plan Fouchet' of which more later. Later still, in the autumn of 1962, the government was for the first time defeated in the National Assembly – which de Gaulle dissolved forthwith. But in the new elections the Gaullists failed to re-obtain an absolute majority and had to share power with the 'Independent Republicans'.

De Gaulle himself gave a strong indication of the significance of 1962. The second, and unfinished volume of his *Mémoires d'Espoir*, with the subtitle *L'Effort 1962–1965* starts with the confident sentence: *'En l'an de grâce 1962, fleurit le renouveau de la France'* (The rejuvenation of France blossomed in the year of grace 1962). But towards the end of the volume, he tells us that *'Déjà en 1962 l'équilibre établi trois ans plus tôt commence à être ébranlé'* (By 1962 already, the [financial] balance established three years earlier began to be upset). Incidentally, the prime cause of the economic malaise which France was experiencing was even, in de Gaulle's view, the pressure of interdependence: the impact of the dollar crisis on the French economy. But surprisingly, when Malraux asked him when he thought that his 'contract' with France had begun to come to an end, in 1968 or possibly even in 1965 – de Gaulle answered cryptically: *'Bien avant. C'est pour ça que j'ai pris Pompidou.* ('Much earlier. This is why I brought in Pompidou').[38] Pompidou was appointed Prime Minister on 14 April 1962.

## The strong state and the 'stalled' society

De Gaulle's fundamental incapacity to reconcile himself to the patchy and competitive politics of the parties of the Fourth Republic has been studied in all its details in innumerable works, the most complete of which is Jean Charlot's *Le Gaullisme d'Opposition, 1946–1958,* (afterwards absorbed into his complete study *Gaullisme*).[39]

The theory that the decline of France could be arrested only by a strong state, strongly led by a strong president, and that therefore a new constitution was needed to establish these new features, was de Gaulle's repetitive, almost catechistic theme during his period in opposition; the negative theme was his criticism, indeed vilification of the inherent instability and corruption of the party political system of the 1946 constitution of the Fourth Republic. 'What is achieved by the party regime which now occupies [sic] the Republic?' he asked in one of the propaganda tracts he wrote in September 1951.

The public power, as formed by the parties, exhibits its impotence. Although the function of the state is to lead the country, it is events which lead us in our internal affairs. The re-awakened nation demands the profound reform of the regime. But the separatists [the new nickname he found for the Communists] do their utmost to prevent the reform. And how could the other parties give up a system which feeds them?'[40]

In 1951 de Gaulle was deeply critical of the Stalinist USSR which was then displaying violent aggressiveness and therefore also of its 'separatist agency' in France, the French Communist Party. He had publicly approved of the signature of the 1949 Atlantic Alliance. The conclusion of his tract was that, once clad in a strong constitutional armour, France would immediately master the 'events' and immunize herself against foreign infections.

Now, there is no doubt that the Fourth Republic suffered from the humiliating experience of a particularly maladroit decolonization (in 1951 the French army was trying to launch a new offensive in Indochina, but as the Korean war was drawing to its end, the Chinese were able to help Ho-Chi-Minh afresh). It suffered also from a grave budgetary and economic crisis as a result of the formidable expenditure on the war and on national reconstruction (the Marshall Plan whose hidden 'imperialistic' purposes de Gaulle feared, had just expired and the French people were reluctant to provide new national loans); and also from unprecedented governmental instability: weak coalition governments of the centre parties, from the catholic MRP to the socialists were rapidly toppled in a constant atmosphere of a crisis of ungovernability. And it is also true in general that French political culture is better suited by a firmer constitutional regime.

Yet, feeling in their bones that the 'de Gaulle alternative' might mean the end of their traditional and almost professional position in the governance of France, 'les politiques', the French political parties and 'politicos', organized a most effective 'ostracism' against him. The whole political class, most of the intelligentsia and the media, and all the political parties, ranging from the right-wing MRP to the Communists, were united in the effort to 'keep de Gaulle out'. His genuine hopes in 1945 when he resigned for the first time, that he would soon be recalled proved to be unfounded. What he called '*la traversée du désert*' (the march through the desert) lasted for more than twelve years, so strong was the deliberate attempt of the 'politiques'. In spite of their evidently growing incapacity to surmount the difficulties of their own government, and especially the acute problems of decolonization, with their direct effects on metropolitan politics, they had enough negative will to erect and keep intact their blockade against him. This organized unfairness made de Gaulle, too, react unfairly in some respects.

De Gaulle's opposition to the 'regime' was unfair in two main respects. Firstly, it was unfair in feigning to ignore the extent to which his very opposition exacerbated the political incapacity of the regime and the national morale. At the very beginning his own party (formed on 7 April 1947), though it went under the name of *Rassemblement du peuple français*, was to all intents and purposes an either/or electoral party – 'either' being the solution offered by the RPF, 'or' being total opposition. This inflexible stand helped to precipitate the opposing trends even further and led to the dangerous polarization between the Right RPF and the extreme Communist Left. Naturally, de Gaulle's demands or solutions were not all unreasonable or, especially, unpatriotic, like those of the Communists. As already mentioned, he had in 1949 agreed on the necessity of the Atlantic Alliance; in 1951 he had proposed a European confederation. With that confederation he countered the plan for a European Defence Community, then favourably viewed by the French, German, Belgian, Luxemburg, Italian and Dutch governments. He also showed a constant and positive interest in future relations with the former French empire, backed the French army efforts in Indochina and greatly blamed the US government for refusing the financial and technical assistance asked for. Above all, he was not entirely wrong in asking for constitutional reform. But all these positive attitudes were conditional: they could bear fruit *only* within his kind of political regime and under his leadership. As long as these two conditions were not fulfilled, his opposition remained intransigent.

But then, in terms of parliamentary efficacity this intransigence had the effect of reducing the policy-making elbow-room of the centre parties even more. In the 1951 elections, owing to the proportional representation of the electoral law of the Fourth Republic the centre returned 401 deputies (divided between at least five parties, in turn divided into innumerable factions) out of a total of 625. The 'Gaullists' had won the largest number, 118, followed by the Communists with 103 deputies. Fragile coalition governments were patched together and constantly dissolved by the inevitable conflicts of views and of interests between the governmental parties. And yet, although de Gaulle's parliamentary team had the greatest number of seats, it could not become more than what he himself called somewhat cynically *'une minorité de blocage'* a 'blocking minority'. The same 'blocking' effect was to be felt by public opinion in general which, under these political demonstrations of ungovernability developed an understandable mood of national impatience.

Secondly, de Gaulle's opposition was unfair, especially when seen in retrospect, because it did not recognize that in spite of the almost acrobatic conditions in which the ephemeral governments of the Fourth Republic had to govern, their policies showed a clearer line of continuity than he gave them credit for and laid many of the foundations of post-war French policies. Although criticized by him at the time, these French policies were rendered so logical, indeed inevitable, because of the prevailing interdependence, that in spite of all his efforts when in power, he failed to replace them or (as we shall see in the next sections in the case of Germany, the European Community and Algeria and even NATO). He shrewdly followed the lines laid down by the pre-1958 governments, while concealing their interdependent nature under his claims of independence and *grandeur*.

The second period, or anti-thesis (1958–62) started with an immediate confirmation of the success of the principle strong-state-strongly-led which de Gaulle had championed for twelve years in opposition. He had suffered yet another political disappointment with his own political party which he found he could not effectively control; its deputies often voted for the governments of the day either for reasons of national consciousness or for personal interest. In the end de Gaulle dissolved it and remained in his favourite position of splendid personal isolation. Nevertheless, the aggravation of the political and national crisis had played directly in his favour. The principal factor was the Algerian crisis, which threatened to become a civil war. The heads of the army in Africa might well try to imitate General Franco in 1936, by landing on metropolitan territory (de Gaulle thought that had they done so they could not have been opposed). For many reasons, both sides of the French nation deeply, almost irremediably, divided on this issue, began to look to him as the only man who could solve the problem, reassured perhaps by his ultimately reserved judgement on the line to be taken (the famous pledge he gave to the army in Algeria: *'Je vous ai compris!'* could mean anything). Both sides trusted him – most especially the army in Algeria and the *pieds noirs*, led by one of his most faithful collaborators, Jacques Soustelle;[41] both invited him to take the helm, regardless of his high constitutional conditions.

Recalling his feelings on 2 June 1958 when he had finally been restored to complete power, he wrote in his *Mémoires*: 'And here I find myself again committed as in the past by this contract which the France of the past, of the present and of the future imposed upon me eighteen years ago, to be saved from disaster. Here I am again, always constrained by the exceptional credit bestowed upon my by the French people.'[42]

And indeed, playing on the word 'credit', one of the signs of national reassurance was the enormous success of the 'loan' he persuaded the French people, on 12 June 1958, to give to the new state and the new leader – which was more than covered, both in cash and in gold, less than a month later, thus solving the problem of French international creditworthiness. Remarkable also was his statesman-like preparation to embark at once and simultaneously, in spite of events in Algeria, on the five main policies which, in his eyes, were interconnected: the reform of the constitution and of the institutions of the state; the remodelling of the former empire into a kind of commonwealth; the restoration of France to her place among the world powers, with special regard to NATO; the effective launching of the European Economic Community, but with a French finality; and the modernization of the French economy, giving a new start and orientation to French economic planning.[43]

The new constitution, which was rapidly introduced, also provided a new sense of stability. It did so by positive, as well as by negative means. The positive means were similar to, though more categorical than, those of any presidential type constitution in which, as American constitutional language stresses, the President 'reigns as well as rules'. To quote an American constitutional historian the French 'President is the head of state – in fact . . . the highest authority of the state', the guarantor of national independence . . . the 'arbiter' over political and institutional conflicts . . . and the commander-in-chief of the armed forces. He is also 'the guide of France and in charge of the destiny of France', and is the 'inspirer and mentor of national actions through the institution of referenda, revived and fully used by de Gaulle'.[44]

Although of a presidential nature, the French Fifth Republic preserved and consolidated all the principles of a constitutional-pluralistic state based on a market-economy and a welfare society. Thus the new constitution provided for the election of a President of the Republic, as well as of the deputies to the National Assembly, by direct universal suffrage. The President presides over the Council of Ministers and can send legislation of which he does not approve back to parliament. Moreover, he has the right to call a referendum on 'any bill' he disapproves of and to dissolve the National Assembly once in the course of a year if he wishes.

The power of the executive was thus greatly increased, while that of the National Assembly was greatly reduced. S. E. Finer has noticed that of the ninety-two articles of the constitution forty-six refer to the executive. 'We come pretty near the whole truth' wrote Finer 'when we say that apart from eleven articles concerned with the French Community and three transitional articles to bring the new instruments into effect, the Constitution is concerned with one matter alone: to redefine the powers of the executive and the legislative to the immense advantage of the former.'[45]

The electoral consultations were unfettered and their results binding on the government. But by abandoning the electoral system of proportional representation of the Fourth Republic and reverting to the electoral system of single-member districts with two ballots of the Third Republic, de Gaulle's electoral system favoured the party in power and reduced the previous advantage of multiple opposition parties – and of political parties in general.

De Gaulle won four referenda: in September 1959, January 1961, April 1962 and October 1962 and lost only one in April 1969, when he resigned and left politics for good. The Gaullist party itself was returned with great majorities and the 1962 elections already showed that the Communists had been reduced to only 44 deputies from 150 in the 1956 elections; the Socialists to 66 as against 94; the Republican (radical) 56 as against 58, while the *Groupe d'Union pour la Nouvelle République* (UNR) obtained 233 seats which together with the 118 of the Independents and Farmers of Social Action gave de Gaulle's government an all-too-easy majority.

Another consequence of the greater power of the executive in the Fifth Republic was the increased centralization of the highly centralized French decision-making processes and of the French bureaucracy. The already large number of civil servants grew even bigger, reaching more than one million people employed in the civil service alone in the 1970s. Within this powerful machine, the prefectorial service, which provided the central and traditional pivot of the administration of the country, was given even more power.

But the judiciary remained independent, even from the state. The *Conseil d'Etat*, during the first and most controversial phase of de Gaulle's administration, acted several times to prevent the government from taking anti-constitutional or indeed illegal measures. The

*Conseil Constitutionnel* which was founded by articles 546–63 of the new constitution, watches over the legality of the election of the President and of the deputies to the National Assembly and over the constitutionality of the organic laws. Much more rapidly than might have been expected this supreme instance has made a great impact on public life. It has quashed several presidential decisions, thus confirming the ultimate power of the judiciary over the other two powers in constitutional matters.

Thus the antithesis of the restoration of the power and authority of the state was confirmed.

But by the middle of 1962 the advantages of a stable and well-centralized state began to reflect, in the final synthesis, the disadvantages of what Michel Crozier has called a 'stalled society' *(la société bloquée)*[46] and the qualities of a strong leadership revealed the defects of a weakened opposition.

To take the latter first. One of de Gaulle's errors during his years of triumph was to believe that he had altered the traditional representative system for good. One of the most ominous sentences in this sense appears at the very end of the first volume of his *'Mémoires d'Espoir'* where he openly states that

Afterwards I am going to see to it *(je vais m'employer)* that the major reform of the representative system [which he undertook] could not be altered piecemeal and little by little, [a reform] which provides that, although the Parliament deliberates and votes on the laws and controls the government, it has ceased to be the source from which policies and the government proceed.[45]

This *sui generis* opinion on the representative system, which would make John Stuart Mill turn in his grave, was not only wrong in theory (i.e. the theory of representative government) but also illusory in fact.

For what de Gaulle overlooked was the fact that over and above his constitutional reforms, which had so effectively strengthened the hand of the executive and of its head, the electoral system which accompanied it gave a crushing majority to the new Gaullist party, the *Union pour la Nouvelle République* (UNR), and its associates in the first elections held in the Fifth Republic, leaving the Centre and the Left in a paralysing minority. The two conclusions which de Gaulle did not draw were – first, that in spite of his contempt for political parties, he had used his party-parliamentary majority for four years as a most useful instrument of policy-making; and secondly, that like nature, which abhors a vacuum, the lack of an effective parliamentary opposition has as a direct consequence the growth of *extra-* and more often than not also *anti*-parliamentary opposition. It was an extra- and anti-parliamentary majority which brought him down, even if with constitutional delays, in 1968–69.

But with this point we come back to the 'stalled society' – for however extremist, unrepresentative and, above all, irresponsible was the 'movement' of 1968, there is no denying that it was a symptom of the reaction of a developed society against a particularly strong, and therefore society-suffocating state. The more advanced was French society, technologically and culturally, nationally and internationally, the less effective because less justified its domination by the state; and the more dominating the French state, the less efficacious the society.

For French society had modernized very rapidly after the war, and one of the signs of the need to undertake that rapid modernization was the Plan itself and within its organization the *Commissions de Modernisation* (the Modernization Commissions) which were its principal and most significant organs. Further, modernization cannot be accomplished in this age of interdependence without transnationalization. Therefore, though we have not yet examined the effects of interdependence on de Gaulle's international economic policies it can nevertheless be assumed that gradually modern French *society* began to feel increasingly constricted within the rigidities of the Gaullist *state*.

This is not to say that, for instance, from the economic point of view, de Gaulle was opposed to technological modernization or to free trade. In the unfinished volume II of his *Mémoires d'Espoir*, he mentions explicitly 'the difficulty of adapting France to the conditions of a modern economy and international competition following the lifting of customs in the Common market and the liberalization of trade'.[48] It is undeniable that he pursued both as overt objectives of his policies. But he thought that those objectives were to be attained in a national union of the whole of French society under the generous auspices of the state; whereas, on the contrary, he had only contempt for the 'groups' which, in his eyes, pursued only sectorial interests. He failed to see that those 'groups' could not only communicate and collaborate, as it were internally, among themselves, through the grid of national socio-economic interdependence but also transnationally with foreign partners or, notably, multinationals, without necessarily having to be helped, let alone controlled by the state.

The tragedy was that, sheltering under his proclaimed cult of the state, the old, overpraised, bureaucratic French state had less opportunity, or indeed obligation to modernize itself too. It is true that de Gaulle, when he had founded the Plan in 1966, had endorsed

Jean Monnet's idea to set up an Economic and Social Council of a quasi-corporatist nature, in which the 'interests' of the society would have a role in the drafting of the Plan (some critics thought that this was yet another stick with which he could beat the political parties and the Parliament). But the Plan was only indicative, and the more interdependent the French economy became, the more flexible did the Plan have to become towards the European and the major world trends. But the old, almost unchanged, French bureaucracy, under strict ministerial control at the level of the state, and strict prefectorial control at the departmental level, was still too rigid to allow for the expansion of French developed society in all directions.

Nor can it be said that de Gaulle had 'stalled' French society culturally. During his reign, French culture reached particularly high levels of achievement and reputation in literature, the arts and the cinema, and he rejoiced in them, as he rejoiced in the successes of French sport during the same period, probably stimulated by the competitive spirit of *grandeur*. (*Allez la France* was the slogan with which, at the time, French crowds encouraged French teams in international competitions.) Neither was there any question of censorship of the press (radio and television were state-owned) or of publications. *L'Humanité*, the communist paper was then still widely read; Raymond Aron, an objective critic, but nevertheless a critic of de Gaulle was the chronicler most followed; the satirical *Le Canard Enchaîné*, which was never kind to him, was the most popular of the weeklies; Sartre's *Les Temps Modernes* the most popular monthly; while the *chansonniers*, those makers of modern folklore, found in him one of the most hilarious subjects of their anthology.

But, again, the bureaucracy of the stronger state weighed heavily on society in this realm too and especially on the younger generation. The universities had not been reformed, although the government was preparing a change. Seldom had de Gaulle written more apologetic pages than in the second volume of his *Mémoires d'Espoir* when he deals with the reform of education.

It was proved to me once more that unless one has the means of dictatorship or of revolution, no institution can be really reformed without the consent of its members. This is indeed the case with the teaching profession . . . This is why I propose to build one day a new National Education in which all those who will work in it: professors, administrators, students, parents of children, will take a direct part in its functioning, management order.[49]

But he was not going to fulfil this ideal. For in the meantime it was indeed from the universities that the revolt of the new society against the old state began.

Significantly, while the words: *France, state, Nation* and *people* are obsessively, catechistically repeated in de Gaulle's written and spoken vocabulary, the word *societé*, which is the central concept of modern social sciences today, since it was introduced by Saint-Simon and, later, by Auguste Comte, is only very seldom used by de Gaulle, and then with special connotations. Quantitative methods are not of course wholly relevant for the study of political psychology, but it is nevertheless significant that research carried out in France on the language of de Gaulle's 46 broadcasts in the years 1958–65 shows that while 'France' occurred 436 times, 'état' 144 times, and 'peuple' 109 times, 'société' figures only *three* times.[50] Obviously, in de Gaulle's subconscious the concept of 'society' was ignored or suppressed, because he perceived that unlike the other words, characterized by unity, society is complexity, diversity and interdependence, or nothing. Yet, it was the modern French *societé*, that spontaneous amalgam of complex activities, of unbounded competitions, associations and interdependencies which, from 1962 onwards became more and more estranged from the French state to the strengthening of which de Gaulle had devoted his most ardent efforts.

In his *La société bloquée*, Michel Crozier provided the correct diagnosis:

If it is really true that the acuity of the problems of French society derives first from the weakness of the organizational capacity and of the capacity of the entire French system, then the absolutely essential problem of French society is to increase those collective capacities, or in other words to render the French people more capable of organized and efficacious organization . . . to help gradually to develop a system of relationships and negotiations, ensembles of rules and customs and models of regulation, more open, more comprehensive and more effective.[51]

And an even more significant diagnosis was provided after de Gaulle's death by his successor, Georges Pompidou who, in his short book *Le noeud gordien*, wrote:

In truth what we need is a change of mind. And first in the state . . . Since the end of the war, generations of civil servants have been moulded in the idea that the general interest not only goes together with that of the state, which is natural, but with the interventionism of the state and the contempt for private enterprise. The institutes of politics, the *Ecole Nationale d'Administration*, the University as a whole have helped to maintain this mentality. The opening onto the external world, the revelation of foreign competition, now begin to cause a shock of recognition.

And in another chapter pointedly entitled *On the modern society* he asked rather anxiously 'What could France's place be in the future world and in modern society?' Pompidou proposed an interpretation of the events of May 1968 which runs counter to de Gaulle's interpretation of the same events; while critical of the concept of the 'strong state', he laid the accent on something quite different if not opposed, called *'the organization of society'*. Says Pompidou:

> However ridiculous the demonstrations, (*les exhibitions*) witnessed by the Sorbonne and the Odéon, however large the element of child's play in them, and of the pleasure of breaking their own toys, one is nevertheless right in detecting in the attitude of the young people in May, in that movement too widespread not to be to a great extent spontaneous, as well as in the feeling of guilt experienced by so many mature persons, a serious indication which does not allow us to pretend that it can be effaced and that we can start again from scratch . . . [according to] the findings of our research we shall have to concentrate on achieving more satisfactory relations between the needs of the individual and *the organization of society*.[52]

## LA FRANCE, THE WORLD AND EUROPE

The ultimate incompatibility between the grandiose politics of independence of the French nation-state and the politics of the national and international interdependent society is shown even more dramatically in de Gaulle's foreign policy to which we now turn. We shall examine that policy, like his domestic policy, in three dialectical phases: the thesis of enunciation, in the period of opposition, 1948–58; the antithesis of achievement, in the period of ascendant government, 1958–62; and their synthesis in the period of descendent government, 1963–69. But before that we should remember de Gaulle's general attitude in international affairs.

De Gaulle's internal and external policies were inseparable: the strong state is indispensable to international order and vice-versa. Therefore it is even more significant that when historians examined the origins and causes of his unexpected resignation from the premiership in 1946, they find that by accident, it was the principle of the emancipation of France from the self-imposed domination of the 'powers' over her which triggered off his resignation.

The historian, this time, again, Jean Charlot, in his *Le Gaullisme d'opposition, 1946–1958*[53] confirms that what started the march of events which brought down the provisional government under the leadership of de Gaulle was the difference of view between him and his government, and notably his Foreign Secretary, Georges Bidault.

The difference arose on the question of how to conduct France's relationships with the Allies. Two episodes seemed to convince him of the fundamental incompatibility between him and the government and may have precipitated the decision which he already considered to be inevitable in the end.

The first serious clash between de Gaulle and Bidault occurred immediately after the Yalta conference, when France as a whole was still smarting from the offence of her exclusion from participation in that conference at the special insistence of Roosevelt and Stalin. In order to attenuate that impression, the ailing Roosevelt invited de Gaulle to meet him on board his destroyer in the port of Algiers, whence he was to sail home after flying from Yalta. De Gaulle, to the consternation of some of his ministers, refused the invitation. He considered it as doubly offensive: first because since Algiers was French territory, it was for him to invite Roosevelt, should he wish to do so, and secondly, because the invitation was similar to that which Roosevelt had issued to the Presidents of the Syrian and Lebanese Republics. As he notes in his *Mémoires*, de Gaulle found '*la chose exagérée quel qu'en fût le rapport actuel des forces*' (an exaggeration, whatever the real level of forces between the two countries). Georges Bidault, on the contrary, thought that the encounter, despite formalities, might be useful. He remained seriously concerned by the consequences of de Gaulle's personal pique for the very difficult conduct of French foreign policy of which he was just then in charge. The conflict between the two men came visibly into the open at that time.

It flared up again on 28 December 1945, on the issue of the preparations of the peace treaty with Italy, Finland and the East European countries. As Charlot puts it, it was on that occasion 'that de Gaulle's conception of France's foreign policy clashed with that of his Minister for Foreign Affairs, supported by the Communists'.[54] The 'Three' had suggested that the conference of twenty-one states should be held in Paris. But given the fact, or the pretext, that only those countries which had been at war with each one of those states should be included in the peace negotiations, France herself could take part only in the preparation of the treaty with Italy. Bidault himself, on presenting the proposal to the Council of Ministers, recognized that the procedure was vexing; but, nevertheless, he thought that the offer to hold the preparatory talks in Paris should be accepted. He was backed by the Communist ministers, who insisted that after all it was the Three who had fought and won the war. But de Gaulle categorically rejected it. 'Without our participation in the preparation of the treaties, we cannot accept. We cannot accept our own humiliation.'

There followed an acrimonious personal discussion between de Gaulle and Bidault, which in spite of Bidault's insistence that the answer should be 'Yes', ended with de Gaulle's decision that the 'conference will not take place without France', followed by the pregnant phrase: 'If not no – or in any event without me'.[55] As it happens, de Gaulle was proved right because under pressure from France, it was decided on 17 January 1946 that all twenty-one countries should take part in the preparatory talks.

But three days later, de Gaulle resigned. That the decision had been maturing in him for a very long time was proved by the happiness he radiated after his resignation, like that of a man who had finally freed himself from a situation and a relationship which not only did not suit him but dishonoured him, because it contradicted his principles.

What were de Gaulle's convictions in the field of France's external policy? His general answer to the question was a ready-made and somewhat platitudinous formula: '*détente-entente-coopération*'. This formula could, and should, be universally applied; indeed, it did not make sense if it was not universal. In this light, if France, by her traditional radiance and influence in history, should succeed in applying his formula, it meant that she would make efforts first of all to establish normal and friendly relations with *all* countries, regardless of status and rank, regardless of geo-political situation and above all, regardless of ideological, or allegedly ideological, differences.

Writing in 1990, an optimist could wonder whether de Gaulle was not prophetic. For in the late 1980s, interdependence, has already flattened the relative heights and ambitions of national sovereignties; and the information revolution has imposed such a *rapprochement* (in the double, geographical and moral, sense of the French word) between all units of the world that the new international situation is characterized by an atmosphere of *détente*, except for a few local wars and by clear signs of *entente* between the powers. This *entente* could in turn be followed by co-operation of the kind required by interdependence.

But even seen from today's vistas (1990), so different from those of the 1950s, de Gaulle's formula was then a pious recommendation. In the 1960s and especially in the 1950s, when he first uttered it, it was definitely wrong. Besides, de Gaulle himself, in spite of his antipathy for the US had no hesitation whatsoever, at least until Stalin's death, in continuing the association of France with the Western camp and with the Atlantic Alliance. For, while the USSR was exerting direct *military* and indirect *political* pressure, as in France through the French

Communist Party and Trade Union, the US no matter what further motives de Gaulle suspected it of pursuing, proved to be indispensable to the reconstruction and defence of Europe, through its policy of 'containment'. This policy, launched in 1947 by President Truman and his 'Wise Men', enjoyed, with some fluctuations an uninterrupted continuity and success until 1990 when the 'cold war' came to an end.

One can even say that de Gaulle's formula *détente-entente-coopération* seemed utopian in the long years of the cold war. For the way to *détente* was far from being opened in the 1950s (Hungary, 1956) or in the 1960s (Cuba, 1962; Czechoslovakia, 1968) or even in the 1970s (Afghanistan 1979). De Gaulle knew this only too well and France played her part most loyally in the Atlantic Alliance in the Berlin and Cuban crises. Nevertheless, at the same time he succeeded in supplying France with her own nuclear *'force de frappe'* so that she, too, could 'contain', even if only for a short while, any attack, from any 'azimuth'.

The reasons he gave for his lack of confidence in the United States were in great part inspired, as we know, by his unfortunate personal relations with Roosevelt; but it made sense in several respects. One was his fear that one day the two super-powers might find sufficient common ground to achieve a *rapprochement*, in which case the future of Europe, especially that of a potential reunion of both its divided parts would be gravely compromised. Another reason was his fear that in the case of 'local' Soviet aggression against any part of Europe, the United States, whose strategic superiority lay in her nuclear armament, would not risk becoming involved in a global nuclear war, simply to honour her European obligations. And, finally, he distrusted the policies processes of the United States, especially those of its financial and monetary policies. His early criticism of the imposition of the dollar as a world currency allegedly based on gold, but in fact less and less 'covered', was almost prophetic. And so were his later, not always friendly, warnings against the danger for the US of getting bogged down in the Vietnam war.

What was less easy to understand was the discrepancy between the actual policy and the rhetoric of 'grandeur' in which both superpowers were described as equally pernicious when it came to the sovereignty and indeed 'grandeur' of France. Raymond Aron criticized this very point rather sharply.

The General placed the two great Powers together on the same plane, while in the same speech he called to mind both Soviet totalitarianism

119

and American friendship. He seemed to be putting forward as his aim the dislocation of the blocs and the *rapprochement* of the two sides of Europe as if the American hegemony were no different in substance from Soviet imperialism; by doing that he spread in the country a deceptive image of the world (*une image mensongère du monde*), he excited the latent anti-Americanism of the French people and made it forget that the Soviet Union, militarily established in the centre of Europe, was the one real threat to our national independence.[56]

But Aron himself afterwards directed his analysis to another point in de Gaulle's diplomatic theory which was the pivot of the entire 'strategy', even if subconscious or well-concealed. Says Aron: 'What seems to me most striking is (de Gaulle's) attitude towards Germany. An ambiguous attitude of which he might perhaps not even perceive the ambiguity.'[57]

Aron touches here on the first almost instinctive foundation of de Gaulle's foreign policy. As an officer who had fought in the First World War and been wounded and taken prisoner, and as the standard-bearer of free France in the Second World War, his concern about Franco-German relations in the future obviously lay behind all his interpretations of world politics. His eternal hope for France's 'grandeur' was the other side of the coin of his fear of Germany. France's domination of Germany in the future was for him a *sine qua non* of her security and of peace in Europe; it was the basis of all his diplomatic designs as well as of his projects. To achieve that prime goal any means, diplomatic or military, offensive or defensive, bilateral or multilateral or all of them, were good and should be used either separately or in subtle permutations.

Thus his belief that the nation-state was the only possible political organization made him, instinctively and logically abhor any idea or ideology which might be inspired by or even contaminated by the principles of super-nationality; his critical appreciation of the egoism of the British and his even more critical appreciation of the ever more dangerous imperialism of the Americans made him reject instinctively and logically any scheme of international organization which might lead to, or conceal within it, a direct or indirect 'Anglo-Saxon' domination; and his constant concern with Germany provided the framework for all his diplomatic thinking. That thinking also led to his vague theory of a European Confederation (of which more later) which could be free from the domination of her affairs by any non-continental power or super-power. Thus the three prerequisites of de Gaulle's foreign policy were: (1) an even stronger French state; (2) conducting a policy aimed at the formation of a '*Europe des patries*', which included Germany and (3) a Europe so strong in itself as to defend itself from any hostile intentions of any powers or super-powers. These three prerequisites remained together at the forefront in all the three phases of his statesmanship, opposition, ascendant government and descendent government, although they were differently formulated in each of the three phases. However, once he was in opposition, he could not see the politicians of the Fourth Republic and its ephemeral governments follow any of the lines which might lead to the implementation of this view of French foreign policy.

His overall criticism was summed up in one of the sharpest sentences he wrote in 1948: 'I would not have to change the foreign policy of France for the reason that France does not have a foreign policy. Its regime cannot allow it . . . It is chaos, that is the truth.'[58]

So consistent and general was de Gaulle's rejection of any French diplomatic or strategic initiative taken while he was in opposition that most international events in which France was involved at that time were indiscriminately devastated by his own and his party's criticisms.

Thus the Dunkirk treaty of alliance and mutual security of 4 March 1947 between France and Great Britain, extended on 17 March 1948 to include also the Benelux countries, was criticized by de Gaulle on the grounds that it centred on Britain rather than on France. Britain, being an island, could be of very little help to the Continent in case of war.

The Marshall Plan proclaimed on 5 June 1947 and finalized on 5 April 1948 was received by de Gaulle in a positive way. But he warned from the beginning against the dangers of American imperialism, hidden under the vague 'supra-national' integration conceived by the Plan, by which he believed the European states were weakened, helping the super-power to dominate them all. This warning was heard again and again, but was accentuated on the occasion of the signature on 16 April 1948 of the convention for establishing the Marshall Plan's subsequent institution, the OECD and the Economic Cooperation Administration by which the member countries abolished some of their reciprocal customs duties so as to facilitate exchanges between them. 'I do not believe' he declared on 1 October 1948 'that to proclaim a customs-union – which in any event will not be realized is enough to effect the Economic Union of Europe.'

The London agreements of 2 June 1948 by which the five signatories of the treaty of Dunkirk plus the United States agreed on the unification of the three zones of Western occupation in Germany

(which Adenauer considered as a great triumph) was directly criti
cized by de Gaulle in a special and personal communiqué because 'it
constrained France to accept conditions dangerous for her, for Europe
and for peace': because the provisions for the 'creation of a German
Constitutive Assembly amount to the creation of another Reich' (one
of his slogans was *Never again a Reich*),[59] because nothing would
thenceforward prevent the USSR from building up its own German
state and 'which of these states will effect German re-unification?'; and
because 'a new great Reich backed by the USSR would become such a
formidable power that the very fate of France would be endangered'.
This theme was repeated at the Frankfurt meeting of 10 October 1948.
On 17 November 1948 de Gaulle declared most unambiguously that
'what the British and the Americans want is the Reich. What is wanted
is the German Reich. For . . . if the unity of Germany is the goal to be
reached . . . this is virtually the Reich.'

He launched similar criticisms against the formation of the Council
of Europe, initiated by the Congress of the European Movement in
The Hague in May 1948. Here he had two reasons for his opposition.
On the one hand, he contested the idea of Germany becoming a
member-state of the Council on the grounds of his criticisms of
the 'absurd London agreement'. On the other, the Council itself
was mocked by him as 'a European institution without a European
mandate', as a possible 'study-group' or as a 'caricature'.

The signature of the North Atlantic Treaty on 4 April 1949 was
accepted by de Gaulle as an evident 'fact of life' – especially as in
the meantime the Soviet blockade of Berlin left no doubt about
Stalin's true intentions. But he and his party stridently denounced
the agreements on the Ruhr and on the Saar as almost treasonable
to France.

However the progress in three stages of a kind of supranational
European integration worried him most. The first and the last, the
formation of the European Coal and Steel Community (ECSC) and
of the European Economic Community (EEC) were crowned with
success; the second and middle stage, the attempt to agree on a
Treaty for a European Defence Community (EDC) failed. It was
not ratified by the French Parliament in great part because of the
violent opposition of de Gaulle and his followers. He recognized in all
three attempts the principle of supra-nationality which he abhorred.
(At least NATO was an inter-governmental organization of *states*.)
He suspected that behind all of them lay the power of the United
States. Thirdly, he believed that both the ECS and the EDC inclined
more in Germany's favour than in that of France. This is also how

it happened that he reopened, but this time publicly, his old quarrel with Jean Monnet whom he knew to be behind the new European offensive.

## A second aside on the relations between de Gaulle and Monnet

The story of the making of the ECSC has already been recounted in the chapter on Adenauer. But here a few more words must be said about the continuation and climax of the conflict of incompatible views and approaches between de Gaulle and Monnet. On 12 April 1953, during an exceptionally important press conference de Gaulle criticized publicly and with particular sarcasm both the 'supranational' steel and coal community with its High Authority (the head of which was then Jean Monnet) and the project of the European Defence Community, designed, as noted above, by Monnet, although called the 'Pleven Plan'. Ironically he called Monnet the 'inspirer' of all these plans.

In his answer, published in *Le Monde* on 17 November 1953,[60] Monnet not only accepted the qualification of 'inspirer' as honourable and recalled the direct help he had given to de Gaulle in London on his very arrival and in Algiers, when he reconciled him with Giraud, but described most clearly the differences between the respective conceptions of the European Union which both sought. In a short, but comprehensive, sentence he stated that 'General de Gaulle's propositions are founded on obsolete notions. They ignore the most recent lessons of history. They totally overlook the entire experience which has proved by a series of successive failures that it is impossible to solve (*de régler*) European problems between states which preserve their full sovereignty'.[61] The last words were the crux of the matter. Monnet believed that only *integration*, that is the process by which nation-states transfer increasingly larger parts of their sovereignty to the supranational, European, policy-making authority could lead to a European Union.

De Gaulle's ideas on Europe were old and vague. He mentioned for the first time in London in 1941 the need to 'reconstruct Europe'; then on 11 November 1942 in a celebrated speech in the Royal Albert Hall he expressed France's wish to make efforts after the war in Europe 'to link together' her interests and requirements with those of Europe; and, finally, on 18 March 1944, he revealed in Algiers his 'great design', according to which what should be created after the war was: 'a Western association, prolonged by Africa, whose main arteries were the Channel, the Rhône and the Mediterranean (and which could constitute a centre of capital importance in a global organization of production, of exchanges and of security.' Moreover, between 1944 and 1951, he often mentioned the project of a 'European federation' or more precisely of a 'European Confederation' to which the member-states could, he said in 1951, 'delegate parts of their sovereignty'. This was embodied soon in the 'Gaullist' project of Michel Debré of February 1953 for a kind of European Confederation. De Gaulle described it as a 'common organism to which the various states, without losing their bodies, their souls, their faces (*figures*) delegate a part of their sovereignty, in strategic, economic and cultural matters'.[62]

It was this approximate and deliberately vague notion of a European Confederation that de Gaulle and his followers proposed as a less pedestrian alternative to Monnet's functional organization, starting on a sectorial basis and hopefully progressing by 'spill-over'. Was the confederation of states a real solution in de Gaulle's mind which could then be extended 'from the Atlantic to the Urals'? Or was it again the tactic of offering something 'grander' and inaccessible against something mediocre, but at least practicable?

Be that as it may, it should also be noted that while he was vehemently opposed to the ECSC and the EDC, his opposition to the other two Communities, Euratom and the EEC was more reserved and muted. Indeed, towards Euratom he had an obviously favourable inclination, as he saw it as an opportunity for France to speed up its atomic research. The two French representatives at Euratom, Pierre Guillemot and Jean Wormser had been his own counsellors in atomic matters. But, generally speaking, the reasons for this were clear: by then (1957) the Federal Republic of Germany was already an independent state, an economic power and a member in its own right, that is with its own national army, of NATO, a situation which, ironically, was far more favourable than Germany would have achieved in the transnational European Defence Community. De Gaulle's thoughts of a Franco-German partnership in Europe had now a much more serious basis, provided he could convince the Germans of the necessity of a purely 'European Europe', progressively detaching itself from the previous Anglo-Saxon strategic and economic domination. And also, by then, it had become obvious that French agriculture, of which more later, could achieve its overdue modernization only by selling at profitable stable prices to a captive European Common Market, and especially to the agricultural-importing Federal Republic of Germany. De Gaulle's robust statesmanship could not ignore this reality.

Besides, two other reasons also explained his less vituperative opposition to Europe. The first was the sobering drama of the end of the war in Indo-China (Dien Bien Phu fell the same year as the French parliament rejected the European Defence Community) the dying embers of which were rekindled almost at once by the new flames of the Algerian war. The second, deriving in great part from the first, was the growing feeling in himself, as well as in the country at large, that the vessel of the French state had entered such terrible rapids that only a great and experienced pilot could still chart a course for her. Hence, his new attitude towards such important and already prepared projects as the French Economic Plan or the Treaty of Rome for the European Economic Community, which he shrewdly believed were doomed to remain unimplemented until and unless a stable and strong French government and a strong national leader should activate them in the interest of France.

This leads us to the antithesis, 1958–62, the most positive and glorious phase of his government.

We have called the first and positive part (1958–62) of de Gaulle's government the antithesis of the years of opposition. This is because, once he had come to power, he turned on their head some of the principal theses he had professed in opposition. The first, and for him most painful, was the necessity to act on the Algerian problem. In opposition he had maintained his general patriotic principles, but also a cautiously non-committal attitude. But now because of the responsibilities of statesmanship, he had to accept that there was no solution other than to allow Algeria to proclaim its independence. This meant that he had to fight with great severity, sometimes cruelty, against the French population in Algeria and, still worse, against the leaders of the Army which was protecting it. It must not be forgotten that the Algerian conflict, which also threatened civil war in metropolitan France, lasted for the entire four years of that period of government and was punctuated with most dramatic episodes. This also entailed another anti-thesis: de Gaulle was supported in his Algerian action more by the centre-left sectors of French public opinion, including the Communists and the Trade Unions than by his own political family of the centre-right.

To this must be added also the fact that, like Mrs Thatcher's first two governments, the Debré and the Pompidou governments benefited from the fact that there was no united opposition in Parliament which could inconvenience them. More than in any other European country, with the exception of Italy, did the left-wing opposition suffer in France from the terminal illness of Marxism-Leninism. The cumulative effects of the Stalinist years of horror and of Khrushchev's denunciation of those horrors in 1956, followed by the reaction in

Poland and Hungary, in turn followed by the Soviet invasion of that country in 1956, destroyed the possibility of uncritical enthusiasm and discipline which were unconditional for the strength of the European Communist Parties. But whereas, the Italian Communist Party took the way towards critical detachment from the erstwhile unique centre of ideological communism, the CPSU, the French Communist Party chose to remain faithful to that centre, indeed to the Stalinist interpretation of Marxism-Leninism. This caused frequent crises of conscience, not only in the French Communist Party itself, but in the French left altogether. It was the searchlight now turned on the unreality and deceit of Soviet Communism, and the consequent *Entzäuberung*, to use Weber's expression, which spread over all 'revolutionary' ideologies.

Debilitated for their own physiological and pathological reasons, the political parties in France were much more vulnerable to de Gaulle's own determined attack on them. What is more, he directed this attack against all parties. The MRP, the Christian Democratic Party, which at the Liberation was the newest and most promising political grouping of the young generation, dissolved under the pressure of de Gaulle's popularity and hold on the masses, including the Catholics who were the mainstay of the MRP. But before their demise, the centre parties, the MRP and the Socialists had nevertheless achieved the foundation of the European Community and the great *rapprochement* with Germany, both of which were endorsed, finalized and used by de Gaulle when he came to power.

Moreover, although in opposition, de Gaulle had sarcastically criticized the three main lines of foreign policy drawn up, in spite of their political and economic weaknesses, by the intermittent governments of the Fourth Republic had shown a remarkable continuity and a common solidarity of all parties, with the exception of the Communists. French foreign policy consisted of the Atlantic Alliance against the dangers of Soviet aggression, establishment of the European Community of Six and *rapprochement* with the former enemy, Germany. De Gaulle continued them and used the last two especially to implement some of his policies. As far as the Atlantic Alliance was concerned, he claimed on the one hand, that he did not want to withdraw France from the Alliance, but from NATO, a rather ambiguous proposition; and, on the other hand, that even this lesser objective could not be achieved immediately and completely. It is true to say, however, that one of his greatest achievements was the rapid restoration of the French armed forces; material restoration in the sense that the equipment was entirely modernized, and that since 1960 France had possessed her own, even if few, nuclear bombs; moral restoration because only he could achieve the feat of instilling a new and robust sense of patriotic confidence into an army so divided at the top in its loyalties.

What seemed to be two different orientations of his foreign policy were in reality the concentric circles of his alternative strategy towards Germany. The first concentric circle was a directorate *à trois*; the second circle, complementary to, but also replacing it, if the first failed, was a 'European Europe policy' and a third alternative was Franco-German *rapprochement*. For, by then, too the new West Germany possessed: (1) a respected international status in the West; (2) a federal structure which prevented her from falling into the centralistic, Reich-like, propensities; (3) a stable parliamentary democracy; (4) an industrial power already overtaking France and Britain; (5) a new generation particularly responsive to the ideal of a United Europe; (6) a military power in its own right, as a full and important member of NATO, to which it had been admitted after – and because of – the French opposition fostered also by de Gaulle, to the EDC; and (7) a stable Christian Democratic government, headed by an even older man than himself, who had an untarnished record of admiration for France and of detestation of Prussia and who had already begun, in collaboration with the French Christian Democratic leader, Robert Schuman to lay the foundations of the 'integrationist' European Communities, with in the background a Franco-German *rapprochement*.

Recognizing that his old anti-German stance was now quite untenable, he had invited Adenauer on 14–15 December to visit him in his home at Colombey-les-deux-Eglises, an honour never granted to any foreign statesman, because as he put it in his *Mémoires*, he wanted to give an exceptional character to the meeting at which an 'historical explanation' on behalf of their peoples was going to take place 'between this old Frenchman and this very old German'.[63]

His own account of what was achieved during that meeting is memorable. The two old men agreed on the need to replace the ancient hostility between their two peoples by an indestructible future friendship (indeed later during Adenauer's visit they went to Rheims Cathedral so that as he puts it 'the first Frenchman and the first German should unite their prayers that from now on the world of friendship should replace forever, on both sides of the Rhine the tragedies (*les malheurs*) of war').[64] They agreed on the principle of not attempting to unify (*confondre*) 'the respective policies of their two countries as the theorists of the ECSC, of Euratom and of the EDC had attempted, but, on the contrary, to recognize that the situations were very different and to build on this reality'.[65] This sounded like a surprising concession from Adenauer, who had always been a convinced federalist. However, in another passage of the account of the conversation, de Gaulle alleged that Adenauer had 'admitted that he had obtained great advantages for Germany from the mystique of integration and that, for that reason, he was grateful to the French protagonists (of that mystique) such as Jean Monnet and Robert Schuman for their gifts (*cadeaux*)'.[66] This was an unwarranted and most ungenerous misinterpretation by de Gaulle of what Adenauer must have really said.

Still in connection with the European Community the two men noted that some difficulties would arise from the 'problem of agriculture' which France needs to have solved and from the British candidacy which she (France) thinks should be refused 'as long as Great Britain remains economically and politically what she is'. And then there occurs in de Gaulle's account of that historical conversation a passage which puts in a nutshell the inherent contradictions of his policy of independence-through-interdependence. Writes de Gaulle:

On the subject of the Atlantic Pact I assured my interlocutor that we, the French, found it only too natural that the Federal Republic should adhere to it without restrictions. How, as a matter of fact could she do otherwise? In this age of atomic bombs and as long as the Soviets threaten her (the FRG), she obviously needed the protection of the United States. But in this respect as in others, France is not in the same situation.'[67]

Upon which de Gaulle summarily explained that 'while still adhering to the alliance in principle, as laid down (*prévue*) in a case of adverse aggression in the Washington Treaty, France intended to leave NATO, especially as she will provide herself one day with her own nuclear armament'.

The above-quoted passage is significant in many respects. As far as the main theme of this book is concerned, it would be difficult not only to find in his own writings, but even to paraphrase with words not his own, a passage which better illustrated de Gaulle's illusion of external independence and sovereignty. For, regardless of whether France was in or out of NATO and regardless of whether she had or did not have her necessarily limited nuclear armament, what scenario could be imagined in geo-political terms in which if the FRG were attacked and the United States were defending her with nuclear weapons France as (a) a member of the Alliance and (b) a country with a long common frontier with the FRG and, therefore, in the direct trajectory of the missiles of the two super-powers, could be considered as being in a 'different situation'? Or, vice-versa, could France be attacked without the FRG also being involved? In reality France, wisely committed by the politicians of the Fourth Republic to the Atlantic Alliance and to membership of NATO, was as dependent in case of nuclear war on the American nuclear arsenal as her geographic Siamese twin, the FRG. The negative interdependence of modern war is also even more strikingly evident than the positive – political, financial, commercial, economic, informative and technological – interdependence of peace.

The passage is also significant because it explains why and how once de Gaulle was convinced that Adenauer accepted the indispensability of a close association with France he came to believe that the original idea of keeping Germany under control by means of a directorate of three powers was bound to fail. He now thought he could achieve the purpose of limiting German aggressiveness through a combination of a bilateral alliance and a 'European Confederation'.

Almost the next day on 17 September, de Gaulle wrote the memorandum sent on 28 September to the 'Anglo-Saxons'. In it, according to the *Mémoires*, he demanded that France should

participate directly in the political and strategic decisions of the Alliance . . . I proposed therefore that the direction of the Alliance be exerted *à trois* and no longer *à deux*, whereas if not, France would no longer thenceforth take part in any development of NATO and would, by virtue of Article 12 of the treaty which instituted the system, either demand that it should be reformed or leave it.

And the passage continues at once: 'As I expected, the two recipients of my memorandum answered evasively.' In fact, Eisenhower was very categorical, enabling one to read between the lines the American intention of keeping exclusively the American finger on the nuclear trigger, which was also implicit in the Anglo-American 'special relation'. But, the passage continues further:

Nothing therefore should prevent us from acting. But everything requires us to act smoothly. We do not have bombs set. Algeria mortgages our army, our air-force and our fleet. We do not know what direction the Kremlin will ultimately want to take in its relations with us. We shall, therefore, take the appropriate measures towards Atlantic separation while maintaining our direct co-operation with the United States and with England.[65]

That co-operation was facilitated by several circumstances. One was that given the new authority and prestige of the Fifth Republic and of its leader, most foreign countries intensified their relations with France. Also, given his good relations with Khrushchev and

Eisenhower, de Gaulle succeeded in organizing a four-power conference in Paris for 14 May 1960, which in his view could open
up new avenues for a truly international *détente-entente-coopération*.
Unfortunately, on 1 May 1960 an American spy-plane was brought
down over the USSR which led to the collapse of de Gaulle's project. Secondly, the new American President, John F. Kennedy whose
wife was French in origin, had since his coming to power on 8
November 1960 established good relations with de Gaulle, whom
he admired and who in turn praised the youthful incisiveness of
Kennedy's mind. Although they disagreed in many basic respects,
Kennedy sought de Gaulle's advice on diplomatic relations at the start
of his presidency. De Gaulle advised him, for instance, to be firm and
strong at his meeting with Khrushchev in Vienna on 3 June 1961;
backed him unhesitatingly during the Cuban crisis of 22–29 October
1962, assuring him that France would be on the side of the US,
if there were to be armed confrontation; and prophetically warned
him as explicitly as possible, in 1962–63 against further American
involvement in Vietnam which, according to him, could only end
in a disaster similar to that of France in Indo-China or in Algeria.

At the same time, 'independent' France exerted a great attraction
on the small dependent countries of Latin America, Asia and Africa
as well as on the neutrals and, last but not least, on the East European
satellites and even on China.

But perhaps the most intriguing development in the eyes of the
rest of the world was the obvious success of the European Economic
Community of six countries which, although well-prepared, and especially with a strong Commission, presided over by Herr Hallstein,
had acquired a greater reality since de Gaulle gave it all the authority
of the stable France of the Fifth Republic, regardless at first of his
own motivations. For what de Gaulle had most positively achieved
was, to re-establish order in France's financial and economic situation.
The '*assainissement*' and rehabilitation of these two sectors were rightly
considered by him as a precondition of France's entry into a 'Common
Market' in which otherwise it would have been dominated by other
member states, and notably by Germany. That he wanted France's
economy, and especially France's agriculture to benefit directly from
the collaboration with the European Community is beyond doubt.
But, nevertheless, France had, first of all, to consolidate her own
economic and financial performance and the Fifth Republic under de
Gaulle's energetic leadership, was successful in this respect.

But after the painful proof he now had that the idea of a USA–UK–
France directorate was not a practical possibility, de Gaulle fell back on

the second alternative, or as Edmond Jouve called it in his monumental analysis of *Le Général de Gaulle et la construction de l'Europe* the *faute de mieux* (second-best) solution of giving new life and a new scope to the European Economic Community, although with the intention of transforming it into a political organization. Such an organization led by France might break the bi-polar stalemate of the two super-powers and might, in any event, prevent them from using European territory as their future battlefield. Moreover, in a ringing sentence of 1960 he gave an even more ambitious significance to the EEC by saying that: 'The cohesion of this great and powerful European Community could lead vast countries, which in other continents advance towards the conquest of power (*sont en marche vers la puissance*) themselves to take the path towards co-operation.'

But whereas such a sentence, often almost literally repeated, was good for the public at large, in his *Mémoires* de Gaulle explained, even if retrospectively, the real meaning for him and for France of the decision he took at the beginning of his reign, to make the Community into the instrument of his 'great design'. The following passage says almost everything that is to be said on this subject:

In fact, this led us to set in motion the Economic Community of the Six, to further their regular concertation in the political realm: to act in such a way that certain other countries, and above all Great Britain, could not drag the West towards an Atlantic System which could be incompatible with any possibility of a European Europe; in such a way that, on the contrary those centrifugal countries should themselves decide to become part and parcel of the continent by changing their orientations, habits and clients; finally, to give the example of *détente* and then of *entente* and co-operation with the countries of the East, with the idea that above the biases of the regimes and of their propaganda, it was peace and progress which answered best to the common need and wishes of human beings in both parts of Europe, accidentally torn asunder.

But, continues de Gaulle: 'At the heart of the problem and in the centre of the continent there is Germany.'[69] On this 'capital' subject, de Gaulle's ideas were firm. Provided that Germany accepted that her present frontiers, including the Oder–Neisse line, would never be contested and that she would never, at any price have the right to possess or to produce atomic armaments, she would have to be an integral part of the economic community and of the kind of political confederation he still intended to put in place of the 'Community'.

De Gaulle's support for the European Economic Community was also conditional in the sense that his effort to animate the Community was made only with the ultimate intention that it should (1) be transformed from an economic community into a *political* Community, like the Fouchet Plan, to be discussed later; (2) that it should be based on *states* and not on societal sectors of its member-countries integrating their policies in those sectors and pooling their resources; (3) that it should be able to gather enough strength by attracting Western and perhaps especially Eastern European 'centrifugal' states, so as to make of it a truly European Europe, or perhaps even a European Confederation, that is a totally independent and self-contained geo-political unit of the world and (4) that it should be under the natural guidance of France.

The difference between Monnet's integrationist conception and de Gaulle's 'confederal' conception of the Community is too obvious to need longer analyses. One of the reasons was that as Monnet conceived the Community – for the first period – in economic terms, it could allow the economic 'sectors' of the six countries forming it to intensify their reciprocal activities in a liberated and enlarged Common Market. Indeed, that 'Market' proved to be in a very short time such a success that it frightened even Great Britain who, after an unsuccessful attempt to set up a parallel organization (EFTA), applied as early as 4 August 1961 for membership; and, as Kissinger noted in his *Memoirs*, the success of the EEC at the same time antagonized American economic interests.[70]

The real secret of the success and the true *raison d'être* of Monnet's Community was that, if the metaphor is admissible, in its essentially functional way, it swam with the mainstream of modern technological interdependence, which united societies or some of their principal sectors rather than states. Or, in other words, as Karl Deutsch or Hass or Leon Lindberg perceived from the United States, the action of integration of the activities of national economic sectors into Common European and indeed transnational activities was stronger than that of the national *states*, which followed only grudgingly. (It must not be forgotten that in the meantime the information revolution had also produced the multi-national corporations which in many cases profited more, to J. S. Schreiber's righteous indignation, from the European Common Market than the European firms.)

For it was already evident that during the period of very 'negative integration', as John Pinder has called it (that is the long years between the inauguration of the Common Market and the major, if not complete, abolition of national customs barriers and tariffs within the Market) the European Community, although limited to sectoral activities, nevertheless developed a supra-national logic of its own. This supra-national logic was inevitably and increasingly frequently going to clash with the national logic of states and their national bureaucracies. The 'dialogue Council–Commission' to use Emile Noel's classic expression,[71] afterwards transformed into the tripartite debates Commission–Parliament on the one side and the Council of Ministers on the other, consisted over the years and continues to consist of variations on the irremediably opposing national-statist versus the trans- or even supranational societal themes and purposes.

From this point of view, then de Gaulle's idea of a *political confederation of states* clearly carried within it the germs of 'obsolescence' detected by Jean Monnet. For, while seemingly proposing a new institution of proper European 'grandeur', in reality it only strengthened the power of the nation-states. These should, on the one hand, secure more power in order to conduct and control by political means their societies and the interdependent society as a whole and, on the other hand, by shutting them hermetically into one unitary and isolated organization, would unavoidably lead to the supremacy of the stronger state or states over the weaker members in an unequal group. This approach was aggravated by de Gaulle's supplementary and overt aims such as the exclusion of Great Britain, by his illusory hope of achieving an opening to the East, and by the intention of forming a firm bilateral alliance between France and Germany, so that both together could, from within, guide the new European organization and, once it had gathered sufficient strength detach it from NATO.

But although the European *faute de mieux* (second-best) solution helped to raise Gaullist France and Europe to new unprecedented heights of international admiration and envy in the years 1958–62 it was in the end to prove as difficult to realize as the initially preferred solution of the three powers directorate. The difficulties began to appear when on 7 September 1961, the Commission of the Community of Six received only one complete proposal for a re-organization of the Community. This was the French proposal known ever since as the *Fouchet Plan*, after M. Christian Fouchet, the President of the Political Commission at the time.[72] The French Plan explained that it was for a *union of states* based on the mutual respect for the personalities (*personnalités*) of the peoples and the member-states and on the equality of rights and obligations. It was to have three organs: the Council, the Preliminary Assembly and the European Political Commission. The latter should be composed of high-ranking members of the respective Ministries of Foreign Affairs, with a President by rotation. The new plan would eliminate the supranational character of the existing Commission of the Community. The political Commission which the plan proposed can best be compared with what the COREPER (the

Committee of Permanent Representatives) is now in the European Commission. Also very characteristic was the absence of a Court of Justice. For by its very nature the judiciary in a federation is the supreme supranational institution or to be more precise the one institution which can control the actions of each state on behalf of the supranational whole. This condition could not be accepted by the states composing the union in the Fouchet plan because it would curb their respective *sovereignties*.

On behalf of and in defence of their own interests, Luxemburg and Belgium blocked the negotiations from the beginning by asking that Great Britain should be invited to take part in them. This was a natural reaction because as Professor Paul Reuter remarked in his book, *Organisations Européennes*, they were more afraid of direct domination by France and Germany than by that of the 'Anglo-Saxons'. Moreover, the Belgian Prime Minister, Paul-Henri Spaak also raised a conceptual objection: 'Europe will be supranational or it will not be anything.' From then on until 17 April 1962, the negotiations continued in the same acrimonious way between the Six around the same issues, namely the entry of Great Britain and supranationality.

A conference called by de Gaulle on 10 and 11 February 1962 in Paris failed to make Belgium and the Netherlands change their minds. As de Gaulle himself remarked afterwards in his *Mémoires*

clearly the Netherlands and Belgium, traditionally protected by the British Navy, now by the American one, dislike the idea of a system without the Anglo-Saxons. But it is obvious that if the Western (States) of the Old World remain subordinated to the New, never will Europe be European and never will it be able to bring together its two halves.[73]

With the Italians also making some reservations of the same kind, only Adenauer remained always on de Gaulle's side. On 17 April 1962, de Gaulle was confident that the 'Five' would approve the Fouchet Plan amended in the meantime. But he had on the contrary the unpleasant surprise of finding that with the exception of Adenauer's Germany, the other four all refused to sign. Spaak explained that Belgium would not sign until Great Britain had joined the Community. But as he later wrote to de Gaulle that he would be prepared to sign the Plan if the Council of States were to be changed into a body independent of the governments, de Gaulle ironically noted in his *Mémoires* that 'thus Spaak quite unashamedly advocated both theses which are opposed to each other, of the partisans of Anglo-Saxon hegemony and of the champions of supranationalism'. What is evident and somewhat melancholy in this exchange is to see that de Gaulle's genius, great as it was, was already too 'obsolescent' to be able to perceive, like the younger Spaak did, an increasingly open Europe in an increasingly open world. Spaak, and the integrationalists rightly thought that only a larger Community, that is including Great Britain and other free countries, forming a really supranational Europe, that is a Europe with common and unified policies, could become a self-supporting world unit, which in turn would be able to co-operate on equal terms with such quasi-continental units as the US, the USSR, China, etc.

When the 'second-best' solution also proved impracticable, de Gaulle concentrated on the last, in any event, inevitable proposition: the Franco-German alliance. The visits and counter-visits between him and Adenauer continued with increasing frequency and after de Gaulle's triumphal official visit to Germany on 4–9 September 1962, everything was ready for the signature on 14 January 1963 of the treaty. And so it was amid popular enthusiasm in both countries and great irritability and nervousness in both the United States and the United Kingdom that the signature took place with great solemnity on 22 January 1963. (After that date his relations with Kennedy, who was deeply offended by what he considered to be a deliberate attempt by de Gaulle to dislocate NATO from within, were never the same.)

Although initially the intention had been to sign an Agreement, what was signed on 22 January 1963 on the pressing demand of Chancellor Adenauer was a Treaty. Jouve quotes de Gaulle as telling a group of French deputies that 'Chancellor Adenauer preferred to conclude a treaty rather than a simple agreement so that it would have to be ratified by the parliaments.' In a solemn statement after the signature, de Gaulle stressed the 'capital importance of this act, not only because it turned the page (*il tourne la page après*) on such a long and bloody history of struggle and fights, but also because it opened the doors wide towards a new future for France, for Germany, for Europe and for the whole world'. This time his high rhetoric measured up to the significance of the event. After two world wars caused by conflicts between France and Germany which turned their countries into battlefields over which the rest of the world came to fight, the new friendship and the alliance between the two countries initiated during the Fourth Republic by Robert Schuman and Adenauer and finalized by the two elder statesmen at the very end of their careers, marked an achievement of supreme historic importance. Besides, as the treaty was framed within the context of a 'European Community', it did indeed mean that as far as Europe was concerned, there would no longer be wars in Western Europe and therefore also less risk of world wars altogether.

Yet, on one point which greatly interested de Gaulle and which had also made Kennedy so suspicious initially of the whole enterprise, namely the 'European' attitude to the Atlantic Alliance, a change in the Preamble of the Treaty, but not in the actual text, introduced during debates on the ratification in the Bundestag, did attenuate the exclusively European significance which de Gaulle wanted to give to this otherwise most satisfying document. The new text of the German Preamble, as modified by the Bundestag, and against Adenauer's wish, confirmed that the treaty would serve to 'maintain and consolidate the good relations between the free peoples with a particularly close co-operation between Europe and the United States of America. This principle was further explained in the Preamble by the statement of the obligation to respect 'the common defence within the North-Atlantic alliance' and the unification of Europe by following the way opened up by the creation of the European Community and including also Great Britain and other countries.[74] Although the preamble did not, and could not alter the substance of the text of the treaty, it did, especially as it was added by and in the German Parliament, remind de Gaulle that the time for European independence was not yet ripe. Atlantic interdependence still prevailed.

Nevertheless, the year 1962 was closing in an atmosphere of national and international triumph for de Gaulle, since it was also the year of the final proclamation of the independence of Algeria, with its corollary of the arrest and sentencing of the rebel French generals, of his already mentioned successful official visit to Germany, of his resolute support of the US in the 'jaw-jaw' Cuban confrontation, and of the new national elections in which the coalition UNR–UDT still won a majority of more than two-thirds of the votes, thus preparing a new start for de Gaulle's Prime Minister, Georges Pompidou.

## Climbing down

This part deals with the synthesis of his political career during the second, and descendent phase of his government (1963–69). During those last five years, the thesis of France's 'grandeur', so proudly proclaimed in the years of opposition, and which had been toned down during the first and ascendant phase of government, dominated as it was by the Algerian tragedy with its antithetical overtones of *fin d'Empire*, came back, almost literally with a vengeance. In many respects it seemed as if the septuagenarian leader now tried to fulfil, with dramatic haste, some of the great promises he had made to France during the years of opposition. Hence the mixture of continuation of the progress made during the first five years, with some ultimately counter-productive interpretations of negativism.

There are two complementary interpretations of his haste after 1963 to assert France's independence in all directions and at the same time. One most justifiable in reality is that advanced by him namely that then and only then, once the Algerian tragedy was concluded, France had become a nuclear power and the internal regime had been consolidated, could he begin to unfold his 'great design' . . . The other interpretation suggests a possible feverishness, accentuated by his age, due to his own feeling, or 'instinct' as he liked to call it in Bergsonian terms – that both from within and from without his country, interdependence was closing in on him.

From within the country, he was dissatisfied by the result of the elections of 1962 which made his parliamentary majority dependent on a coalition with the sister UDT party; the beginnings of a financial malaise due in part to the costs of the Algerian war and of nuclear equipment made him personally impose on Pompidou and his Minister of Finance, Giscard d'Estaing, a plan of 'economic stabilization' which entailed fixed retail prices and a limitation of increases in wages both in industry and especially in agriculture, measures unlikely to be popular. Indeed, French society, already discontented, made itself heard again with increasing force in constant demonstrations of agricultural workers and farmers and even in revolts. And a massive miners' strike in March 1963 (the first since de Gaulle had come to power, because, in the meantime, the trade unions had constantly backed him against the Algerian insurgents) made a considerable impression on him; while at the other end, the industrialists, already in full transnational swing, were growing impatient with his King Canute-like resistance to the penetration of the multinationals into France and the transnational mergers. This accumulation of symptoms gave him an 'instinctive' feeling of the ingratitude of society. As he described this particular moment in his *Mémoires*: 'Because there is no danger in sight, many of our people are soon inclined to go back to an easy life. Some find it particularly difficult to bear the power of the state' (*le pouvoir* in French).[75]

From without, nothing had yet been decided in the matter of the disengagement from NATO, or in that of the transformation of the European *Economic* Community into a *political* confederation of states, or with regard to a new policy towards Eastern Europe. Because of his own inclination, but also because of the classic prescription of national leaders, who when in difficulties at home try to compensate with successes abroad, de Gaulle started a new series of assertions of French prestige in the international arena. Already, his ultimative memorandum of 17 September 1959 (see p. 131) had aroused suspicions in Britain, and especially in the United States with regard to the future of the Atlantic Alliance. On 21 June 1963 France withdrew its fleet from NATO, a preliminary step in the direction of the long threatened complete withdrawal. On 27 January 1964 France recognized Communist China, the first Western power to do so. This was a gesture which indisposed both the USSR and the USA (where on 27 November John F. Kennedy had been assassinated, to de Gaulle's sincere regret.) In March of the same year, he made a triumphal journey to Mexico, but without real positive relevance and in October an exhaustive tour of almost all the Latin American countries which, although France had little to offer them to alleviate their 'dependencia', still saw in him a symbol of 'Liberation'. This journey too, while undoubtedly irritating to American opinion, made a good television impression in France. However, when he came back home at the end of 1964, the peasant agitations had taken on new proportions and the French economy was in no position to cure the chronic illness of that over-producing and still unmodernized sector.

Then, again, at the beginning of 1965, de Gaulle again made use of interdependence in France's favour, and in two ways.

The first was to denounce, with some prophetic justice, as described in the chapter on Reagan in this volume, the pernicious effect of the ill-adjusted exchange-rate of the dollar on the French and European and ultimately also on the American economy. This he did in an historic press conference on 4 February 1965, in which he denounced the fact that in reality the dollar – the international currency – was no longer sufficiently covered by the gold in American possession to be worth its real value.

The fact that many states principally accept dollars as if they were gold, when they endeavour to compensate, in given cases, the deficits in their favour of the American balance of payments, leads the United States to indebt themselves unnecessarily (for nothing) to foreign countries. For, in fact, what they owe to those countries, they pay back to them, at least in part, with dollars which the US can emit as it wishes, instead of paying integrally in gold, whose value is real.

This judicious denunciation had great positive resonance in the world in general, but negative in the United States, where the entire nation smarted under the attack on the dollar, the symbol of US power. Moreover, the more under Lyndon Johnston the United States became bogged down in the Vietnam war, against which de Gaulle had warned Kennedy, the more de Gaulle denounced the inevitable growth of the unnecessary indebtedness of the United States to the states which traded with it. These warnings did not help directly or indirectly French monetary difficulties or Franco-American relations, apart from putting part of the blame for them on this international cause. But they served to give world opinion a lecture on interdependence.

The second opportunity to use interdependence for national purposes was found by de Gaulle in the delayed obligation assumed by the EEC to help in financing the agricultural policies of its member-countries. France had, as already mentioned, a difficult situation in the EEC from this point of view. Although during the Fourth Republic, French agriculture had been actively modernized and, demographically, the rural population had been, to a certain extent, absorbed into the towns, there was still need of a supplementary effort. The peasant agitations were a convincing symptom of this need. In his *Mémoires* de Gaulle described the agricultural problem in a deliberately melodramatic style:

But there is the other side of the coin. Our industrial development ineluctably reduces the relative importance of our agriculture. How, being who I am, could I not be moved and worried, seeing our rural society falling away . . . In this country of permanent villages, of old churches, of solid families . . . this land of legends, songs and ancestral dances, this millenary France . . . etc.

But interdependence offered him a supplementary remedy for this chronic national illness. 'Besides' he continued 'the problem goes beyond national limits.' Explaining that French agriculture produces more than the country can consume he concluded 'we must be able to export'. Upon which he recalled that

I must say that if, when I came to power, I at once accepted the Common Market, it was because of our situation as an agricultural country, as well as because of the progress to be imposed on our industry. Of course, I am fully aware that in order effectively to introduce agriculture in the Community, we shall have to act vigorously on our partners whose interests in this matter are different from ours. But I maintain that this is, for France, a *sine qua non* condition of her participation. We shall have, therefore, to make relentless efforts, leading sometimes even to the threat of rupture. But we shall succeed.[76]

More generally speaking, the conflict between the Gaullist idea of a 'Europe of states' and that of the European Commission which saw the European Community as a supranational organization, had only been aggravated in the intervening years of ill-defined work together. Everyone knew that one day the crisis would explode.

It did so on 30 June 1965, when the Council of Ministers, held in Brussels under the chairmanship of Maurice Couve de Murville, de Gaulle's Foreign Minister, was told by him that before beginning the discussion of other items on the agenda, among which was that of the new powers to be given to the European Parliament, they should first decide on the financing of the Common Agricultural Policy. In so far as after midnight there was still no way of reaching a decision on that single issue, the President declared the session closed.

The crisis thus opened, allegedly on the agricultural problem, revealed almost at once its fundamental cause: the opposition of the national and of the supranational institutions, principles and motivations.

· Although the agenda of that historic Council of Ministers contained the apparently unrelated principal items of the financing of the Common Agricultural Policy (or, on a point of fact, of the last payments to be made to France) and of other new powers to be given to the European Parliament in budgetary matters, the whole conflict was centred on the growing suspicion of the de Gaulle government that the Commission, and through it, the Community as a whole, was reaching a point, or trying to reach a point, from whence the supranational procedures of policy-making would dominate the national or intergovernmental ones. Indeed, in a document submitted to the Council of Ministers on 2 October 1964 (but made public by the President of the Commission in a press conference under the title 'Initiative 1964'), the Commission proposed that the financing of the CAP should be made thenceforward through the budget of the Community itself; that, secondly, and in consequence, the 'own resources of the EEC' should be provided by the direct payment of the custom-tariffs on industrial products into the budget of the Community; and, thirdly, that the European Community should be given a more direct control of the Community budget, thus passing over the national parliaments' sovereign rights in such matters. The 'Initiative 1964' document, soon approved by the European Parliament, increased de Gaulle's apprehensions that the supranational Commission wanted to curb the national states. Moreover, its President, Walter Hallstein, Adenauer's chief European adviser, was personally disliked by de Gaulle, who described him strangely and unfairly in his *Mémoires* as follows: 'I think that if Walter Hallstein is, in his own way, a sincere European, it is because he is first a German, full of ambition for his country.'[77]

Behind all this lay also the particularly nettling question of the interpretation of Article 148 of the Treaty of Rome, according to which at 'the third stage' (very reminiscent of the 'stages' of the Delors Plan so widely discussed now by the Community), i.e. as from 'January 1969, the Council would make its decisions by majority vote procedure, which de Gaulle and the French government of the time considered inadmissible. De Gaulle himself stressed that 'there is no way in which, for the time being, a foreign majority could restrain recalcitrant nations'.[78]

In consequence of which de Gaulle decided then to give a '*coup de barre*' to the progress of supranationality in the EEC and to 'break' the power of the Community. As a result, he decided that France would not return to the Community until these problems had been solved and they practised the policy of '*la chaise vide*' (the empty chair), whereby no French representative attended any kind of meeting of the Community and of its related organizations.

But six and a half months later, the 'Luxemburg agreements' of 30 January 1966 brought the crisis to an end. They consisted of an agreement on the majority vote which could not be applied in the case in which one state had very important interest, the French delegation insisting that in such cases the final decision should be taken by unanimity, and of an agreement between Council and Commission, the latter thenceforward being better informed on the reaction of the member-states through the new organ of a Committee of Permanent Representatives (delegates of the member-states) COREPER, which serves as an intermediary between member-states and the Community, or more precisely between the Council and the Commission. It is an institution unforeseen by the Treaty of Rome.

De Gaulle had, as he had predicted, succeeded. But was this result positive and lasting, or like most of the 'apparent successes' he recorded in the descendent period of his government, ultimately negative and ephemeral? For, with hindsight, it can be seen that the Luxembourg agreements greatly impeded the work of the Community by the 'unanimity vote', and that later, with the open support of the then French government, that clause was rediscussed and amended by the European Single Act of 1988.

But in the meantime, the inability of the European Economic Community to assert itself effectively had disappointed the new generation of Europeans. Even worse was the direct result. For soon the consequences of the combination of the two French imposed Luxemburg agreements and the implementation of the CAP as a particularly active policy of European integration had a cumulatively lethal effect. Left by itself, i.e. without being complemented by the more important financial, industrial, or monetary European policies, the CAP which had been effective in modernizing European agriculture soon grew into the sore thumb of the unbalanced budget and structure of the EEC. If one adds to this negative balance-sheet the protracted negotiations with Great Britain, mostly due to de Gaulle's formal opposition, one can, if sadly, say that although it was true that the European Community as an organization had really started to function after he had come to power, the 'Gaullist' way in which it had functioned during those years had the practical effect of negating in theory and stifling in practice its supranational character and mission, if it had a mission.

Thenceforward, de Gaulle's magnificent qualities of faith, courage and the pursuit of grandeur started to become dysfunctional. His faith in France alone, reinforced by that in the Franco-German alliance, made him constantly and explicitly reject the implicit and ineluctable European and Atlantic interdependence and co-operation.

For instance, the transformation of his rational objectives into a systematic effort to humiliate Great Britain was unwarranted. It is true that Great Britain's entry into the Community seemed difficult to realize, two reasons for this being her links with the Commonwealth and the 'special relation' with the United States – the US–UK Polaris agreement of Nassau of December 1967 had increased de Gaulle's suspicion that Macmillan and Britain harboured the perfidious intention of being America's' Trojan horse' in the EEC. But that did not warrant a permanent veto of principle. For he himself knew and predicted that one day Britain would enter the EEC so that postponement of Britain's entry was also ephemeral. Similarly, he had been right in predicting the disastrous end of the Vietnam war; and in the preparation of the Armistice in which he had actually played a useful role in helping to prepare the US–Vietnam Paris Conference of May 1968. The testimonies of Nixon and Kissinger confirm his important contribution to this end. Similarly, his campaign against the false position of the dollar in the international market was soon confirmed by Nixon's 'floating' of the dollar in 1970.

But these confirmations of his political acumen did not necessarily require the constant provocations of North America such as, to quote one of the most salient, his 1967 trip to Canada culminating in his public slogan '*Vive le Québec libre*' – another splash of irrelevant publicity giving rise to British, Canadian and American antipathy. Moreover his differences of view from within the Atlantic interdependence produced in the end, on 7 March 1966 the 'final withdrawal' of France from NATO, which removed from Paris to Brussels. This was soon followed by the reconfirmation of the Atlantic Alliance in spite of his own personal confidence that France would leave it for good, which he authorized on 4 April 1969.

Even more nettling first for his allies and finally for France was his Quixotic 'opening to the East' starting with his visit in June 1966 to the Soviet Union, which although it led to nothing and could not have led to anything of importance in the relations between the two countries, irritated and disquieted his Atlantic partners. For it gave a misleading impression to world opinion, which he did not deny, that France placed herself now 'between the two blocs'. Ironically, too, that French initiative led finally to the much more serious new German Ostpolitik which was of greater interest to the USSR.

But after his visit to the USSR, de Gaulle went to Poland in September 1967 where, when he expressed his wish that Poland should one day be free, Gomulka arrogantly replied that he preferred a 'protected' Poland. Finally, to add to the discomfiture created by his East-European bravado, the USSR invaded Czechoslovakia in May 1968 as he himself had predicted when he said in confidence that he thought that, alas, the 'Czechs were going too far' and that in the end 'night will fall again over Prague'.

Moreover, in November 1967 he also antagonized Israel and its diaspora by warning of the dangers of a prolonged occupation of the conquered territories. And, finally, on 13 May 1968, he embarked on a trip to Romania to encourage Ceausescu's anti-Soviet stance although his Minister of Internal Affairs, Fouchet, begged him not to leave Paris just then, because between January and March 1968 an insignificant conflict between the students and the rector of the new, and claustrophobic University of Nanterre had laid a powder trail to Paris. Later, on 3 May 1968, the Sorbonne was occupied. Nevertheless, de Gaulle left for Romania, so incapable did he prove to be, probably because of a combination of his age and his education, of understanding the new problems of society. He could not assess the 'students' revolt in its proper light, that is, as a symptom of global change in the minds of the new generation of the advanced societies all over the world.

When de Gaulle returned on 18 May, the situation had changed out of all recognition. On 28 May de Gaulle considered putting an end to his 'contract' and resigning. (Mitterrand announced his candidature in case of a power vacuum.) But on 29 May, he undertook his mysterious visit to Baden-Baden, the headquarters of the French army in Germany. As a matter of symbolic coincidence again, the chief of that army was General Massu who had been the officer who had begun in an unfortunate interview with a German journalist the resistance of the army in Algeria. But Massu and the other generals assured de Gaulle of the loyal backing of the army should he need it, asking only that after the end of the revolt, he should hold new national elections.

The students' revolt was quickly brought to an end; it had been an unprecedented demonstration of 500,000 people in the streets of Paris chanting '*de Gaulle n'est pas seul*' (de Gaulle is not alone). Replacing for reasons which do not belong to the scope of this essay, Pompidou by Couve de Murville as Prime Minister, de Gaulle having witnessed the entry into action of the Brezhnev doctrine in Czechoslovakia in May 1968 renewed the Atlantic Alliance pact in 1969. He then called a referendum in France on a new organization of the state on a more 'participatory' basis, as if he needed a new personal confirmation of his 'contract'. Whereupon, placed in a minority, he resigned on 27 April 1969 and died leaving his *Mémoires* unfinished, on 9 November 1970.

No words can provide a better and more concise description of the synthesis, that is of the third phase of de Gaulle's statesmanship, 1963–69, than a note of 1967 in the diary of Hervé Alphand, his long-serving Ambassador in Washington of 1967:[79]

The popularity of the General seems to suffer from the counter-effect of all these events. His enemies hold against him his solitary aloofness, his rapprochement with the Russians and the Arabs, his suspicion of the Anglo-Saxons; he befriends the poor and quarrels with the rich; he shocks the *idées reçues* and the conventions. The fury of his opponents finds him made of rock and ice. He is certain to be right. He will have to live a sufficiently long time for circumstances to prove that, alone in an ocean of protests and rancours, his view was right.

Alas, he did not live long enough to see how in many respects his view of the future was right, but also in retrospect how wrong he often was in the contradictory actions he undertook in Europe and in the West, during those last negative and unnecessarily bitter years.

## CONCLUSIONS

In the first part of this essay I quoted Georges Pompidou's remark that the essence of Gaullism was Péguyism. I mentioned then, that this life-long and privileged witness had made a surprising observation about de Gaulle's historical significance. He compared him with Philipomenon.

Philipomenon of Megapolis had earned a reputation in the first century BC as the last important military leader in Greek history. Until his final encounter with the Roman legions, he never lost a battle. But he had also shown high leadership qualities and was moved by political ambition. He led the Achaean League, the last bastion of Greek civilization before it was swamped by the inevitable advance of the legions of the Roman republic. He convinced even Sparta, Athens's perennial rival and enemy, equally threatened by Rome, to join the League, and he equipped it with an army as strong as possible at the time. But the League was not strong enough to withstand the Romans, and he lost his final battle and his life.

There is no resemblance between the parts of the life of this obscure Greek military leader, whom Pompidou compared with his erstwhile master, and the situation and events of de Gaulle's life, apart from their common profession of arms, and political ambitions. Any analogy we attempt to draw between Sparta as Germany and the Achaean League as the European Community, or even the aborted European Confederation, leads us straight to the question of which power in the twentieth century played the part of the Roman Republic and defeated de Gaulle. For France was not defeated under him, or after him, as were the states of the Achaean League after the death of Philipomenon. France had been rehabilitated morally by de Gaulle during the war; and he had greatly helped to re-establish France as a European power after the war and Europe as a more self-contained and self-confident unit of the world.

It is true that his dream of *grandeur* was not realized and that in the last five years of his life, he tried the patience of the western world as well as that of the French people. But this cannot be represented as a defeat by somebody else, by another victor. If the Philipomenon allegory makes any sense, it is only in the much more general historical context, in which de Gaulle (like Philipomenon), wanted and thought that he could safeguard the civilization of Athens and Greece (France and Europe) from the domination of another power. Polybius tells us that because Philipomenon believed that Greek civilization had reached unsurpassed heights, which indeed it had in many respects, he also believed that it was invincible. His moving lament at Philipomenon's heroic death deplores the latter's inability to understand the laws of the growth of history. (Polybius himself, later, thought that the advent of the Pax Romana was, to borrow Fukuyama's expression, 'the end of history'!)

Therefore, if from a military point of view, the classical exercise in comparison of the two heroes by Pompidou and Malraux is inadequate because France and her allies had won the war and de Gaulle was basking in that triumph, when it comes to the growth, indeed 'globalization' of human customs, it does make sense. The universal spread of the modern, in great part American-inspired, civilization swept over the advanced industrial democracies, including, of course France. Its new values and style of life were in many respects different from those dear to de Gaulle's heart. Today young French people wear T-shirts (mostly with American slogans) and jeans, sing and dance to 'rock music' at 'discotheques', see 'Dallas' on television, drink Coca-Cola rather than wine, and are as precociously exposed to drugs and sexual diseases as all others. And today's French citizens, like all citizens of advanced industrial democracies, are more interested in the modernization of their domestic life than in the, by now, disideologized politics, or even in the proud ambitions of *grandeur*. This de Gaulle could not accept. Nor would he have been happy to see how Western Europe came a poor third in the competitive electronic revolution; or how a 'unified' Germany had taken the lead in the European Community. His memory seems to haunt now more frequently the otherwise contented French people.

## NOTES AND REFERENCES

1.  Charles de Gaulle, *Mémoires de Guerre*, Plon, 1954, vol. 1, p. 263.

2.  Charles de Gaulle, *Lettres, notes et carnets*, 8 vols, Paris, 1986, *passim*.

3.  Jean Lacouture, *Charles de Gaulle*, 3 vols, Paris, 1984–86.

4.  General de Gaulle, *Mémoires de Guerre* (henceforward MdG), vol. 1, *L'Appel*, p. 5.

5.  André Malraux, *Les Chênes qu'on abat*, Paris, 1971, p. 183.

6.  MdG, p. 326.

7.  Charles de Gaulle, *Mémoires d'Espoir*, vol. 1 *Le Renouveau* (Henceforward MdE), 1970, p. 314.

8.  Malraux, op. cit. pp. 76–77.

9.  MdG, vol. 1, p. 106.

10. Jean Monnet, *Mémoires*, Paris 1976, p. 92.

11. MdG, vol. 1. p. 107.

12. Monnet, op. cit. p. 173.

13. Ibid, op. 174.

14. Ibid, pp. 172–3.

15. Ibid, p. 261.

16. Lacouture, vol. 1, *Le Rebelle*, 1984, p. 78.

17. All quotations here are taken from the English translation of the book *Le Fil de l'Épée, The Edge of the Sword* by Gerald Hopkins, London, 1960, pp. 95, 96–7 and 100.

18. Lacouture, vol. 1, p. 67.

19. MdG, vol. 1, p. 372.

20. MdE, vol. 1, p. 78.

21. Ibid, pp. 498–9.

22. MdG, vol. 3, p. 279.

23. Claude Mauriac: *Un autre de Gaulle*, Paris, 1970, p. 156.

24. Philip Cerny: *The Politics of Grandeur: Ideological Aspects of de Gaulle's Foreign Policy*, London, 1968, p. 22. I must however declare my partiality towards this book as I was one of the supervisors of P. Cerny's dissertation at Manchester University since published as a book.

25. Ibid, p. 79.

26. A. Malraux, op. cit. p. 111.

27. Ibid, pp. 23–4.

28. Quoted in Lacouture, vol. 3, p. 519.

29. Lacouture, vol. 1, pp. 210 and 273.

30. MdG, vol. 1, p. 243.

31. Ibid, p. 246.

32. Lacouture, vol. 3, p. 254.

33. *The Memoirs of Cordell Hull*, New York, 1948, vol. 2, pp. 1163–4.

34. Walter Isaacson and Evan Thomas: *The Wise Men*, p. 202.

35. Lacouture, vol. 3, p. 545.

36. Raymond Aron: *Mémoires*, Paris, 1983, p. 435.

37. Quoted in Lacouture, vol. 3, p. 285.

38. Malraux, op. cit. p. 27.

39. Jean Charlot: *Le Gaullisme d'Opposition, 1946–1958*, Paris, 1983; Jean Charlot: *Gaullism*, London, 1985.

40. de Gaulle: *Lettres, notes et carnets, 1957–8* p. 27.

41. 'It is true that Jacques Soustelle, one of my closest companions during the war and then in the "rassemblement" had been Governor General of Algeria, appointed by Mendès France, and recalled by Guy Mollet. But never, either during

his mission, or after his return, did he send me any kind of communication.'
*Mémoires d'Espoir*, I, p. 21 (author's translation).

42. Ibid, p. 34.

43. See Jack Hayward: *The One & Indivisible French Republic*, London, 1973.

44. William Safran: *The French Polity*, New York, 1977, p. 146.

45. S. E. Finer: *Five Constitutions*, London, 1979, p. 27.

46. Michael Crozier: *La société bloquée*, Paris, 1970.

47. MdE, vol. 1, p. 291.

48. Ibid, vol. 2, p. 120.

49. Ibid, p. 83.

50. Jean-Marie Cottaret and René Moreau: *Recherches sur le vocabulaire du général de Gaulle. Analyse statistique des allocutions radiodiffusées. 1958–1966* Armand Colin, Paris, 1969.

51. Crozier, op. cit. p. 230.

52. Pompidou: *Le noeud Gordien*, Paris, 1974 pp. 140 and 171.

53. Charlot, *Le Gaullisme d'opposition*, p. 27.

54. Ibid, p. 19.

55. Ibid, p. 32.

56. Aron: *Mémoires* p. 434.

57. Ibid, p. 436.

58. E. Jouve, *Le Général de Gaulle et la reconstruction de l'Europe, (1940-1966*, Paris, 1967, p. 93.

59. MdG, vol. 3, p. 57.

60. Monnet: *Mémoires* p. 508.

61. Monnet, *Mémoires*, op. cit.

62. Quoted in Jouve, p. 14.

63. MdE, vol. 1, p. 184.

64. Ibid, p. 191.

65. Ibid, p. 186.

66. Ibid, p. 188.

67. Ibid, p. 189.

68. Ibid, pp. 214–15.

69. Ibid, p. 182.

70. Henry Kissinger: *Memoirs* New York.

71. Émile Noël: *Les rouages de l'Europe*, Paris, 1976.

72. See especially Jouve, op. cit. pp. 316 ff.
73. MdE, vol. 1, p. 207.
74. Jouve, op. cit. pp. 348–50.
75. MdE, vol. 2, p. 14.
76. MdE, I, pp. 164–8.
77. Ibid, p. 195.
78. Jouve, p. 436.
79. Maurice Alphand: *L'étonnement d'être*, Paris, 1977, p. 493.

# CHAPTER THREE
## *Margaret Thatcher*

The fact that the essay on Mrs Thatcher is placed in this volume after the essays on Adenauer and de Gaulle and is followed by the essays on Reagan and Gorbachev, is correct both chronologically and logically. For, once situated between its two gigantic predecessors and the two contemporary leaders of super powers, Mrs Thatcher's statesmanship is seen in its historical context. Like Adenauer and de Gaulle, Mrs Thatcher saw her mission as that of 'reconstructing' a country. But for Germany and France which had both been ravaged by the war, 'reconstructing' meant what it said, the rebuilding of a state which had been shattered by the war. Whereas Britain, whose state and institutions had remained intact, only realized gradually, and when the dust of glory had settled after the Second World War, that it had been toppled from its rank of great power, that its exhausted economy was ill-adjusted to the requirements of modernization and that the morale of its people had also been lowered and corroded by the, to them, unjust consequences of war. Unjust they seemed to the British people because, unlike vanquished Germany and tarnished France, Great Britain had not only been one of the three victorious Powers in the war, but had been the one country which by her lonely resistance to Nazism and Fascism, prevented both these evils from dominating Europe and, through the Axis with Japan, probably also the world. Had Britain made peace with Hitler in 1941 as France had done, while the USA was still neutral and the USSR still bound by treaty to its ally, Nazi Germany, the history of the world would have taken one of its worst turns. Yet so ungrateful are history, and the conditions of interdependence, that the position and status of Great Britain were, after a few years of peace, considerably inferior to those of her wartime Ally, the United States and after a few more years of peace she was falling behind Japan and Germany as well. Like, therefore, Adenauer and de Gaulle, Mrs Thatcher's historical mission, as she saw it long after the end of the war, was to arouse the people of her country to unite in an effort to restore Britain's self-confidence within and her power and prestige abroad. The experience of the last two Labour governments, with their apotheosis in the 'winter of discontent' and mounting external debt, had shown to every Briton how rapid the decline of their country had been. Nevertheless, while the historical task of Adenauer, and to a lesser extent of de Gaulle, had been to build up a new state, Mrs Thatcher's task was to cure from within what she considered to be the causes of the sclerosis of the old state. The historical dimensions of their efforts were different.

In common with Reagan and with Gorbachev, Mrs Thatcher had the experience of living through the 'mutations' of the 1970s. Reagan was already well aware of the limitations of the power of the USA, as evidenced by the Vietnam war and the ensuing dollar and budget crises. Gorbachev, who had lived through the terminal crisis of Marxism-Leninism, was convinced of the need to change its structures in his country. And the three of them had lived through the generational crisis and were aware that the young of their respective countries were psychologically different from their elders, and also but for different reasons that new ecological and technological dangers threatened the developed society. But in the 1970s Mrs Thatcher had only begun to learn, even if by way of shocks of recognition, the lessons of interdependence. Her statesmanship was faced with the modern tests of policy-making by internal and external consultation and power-sharing, towards which she was not psychologically predisposed.

Yet the policy-making processes of the Britain which she was going to govern were already conditioned by external and internal linkages of interdependence. The old Britain, as Mrs Thatcher found it in 1979, retained multiple mutual obligations towards the countries forming the Commonwealth; but that organization was gradually losing its coherence and becoming illusory. More realistic was Britain's membership of NATO, in the supreme matter of defence, and in economic and commercial matters her membership of the European Community. When Mrs Thatcher assumed the premiership, these two major links had been fully established by previous conservative governments. Each of these links conditioned the 'sovereignty' and the freedom of action of Great Britain in exchange for the military and economic security they offered. Since April 1949 Britain had been a founding member of the North Atlantic Alliance, known also as 'the nuclear alliance' and a member state of NATO, the organization of that alliance. Britain's nuclear defence, the ultimate defence in modern warfare, is dependent on NATO and on bilateral treaties; and because of its nuclear equipment it is also directly dependent on the United States. When she came to power, Mrs Thatcher found Britain also a member-state of the European Communities, accession to which had finally been brought to a successful conclusion by Mr Heath's government, as well as a member-state of the OECD, the guidance-organization of industrial-technological democracies. Being also a member of the United Nations, and a permanent member of the Security Council of that world organization of sovereign states – apart from being also a member of practically all the innumerable non-governmental organizations in the world, the framework within which Great Britain has had to make its policies greatly limited its sovereignty.

Two more dissimilarities between Mrs Thatcher's statesmanship and that of three of the others discussed here must be mentioned. The first is the much publicized fact that Mrs Thatcher is a woman, of which more later. Secondly, the record of her eleven years, already commented on by the media at the time of writing, in emphatic historical terms, shows the mark which she has left as a leader who has tried to change British societal and political life. As a person there is no doubt even now that she will remain memorable in British history. Whatever the view of the nature of those changes and of their durability in the future, the fact is that some are self-evident. For example, this can be rapidly measured, as in a litmus test, in the considerable reversal of attitudes and principles, from red to blue, made by the Labour Party. The reversal of their policies was not, to be sure, due only, or even principally, to Mrs Thatcher, but to the historical crisis of socialism. But the change in the British Labour Party's previous fundamental policies for Britain in defence, on Europe, in the relation with the trade unions, in the move away from the theories of state-socialism to the theories of market-capitalism ran counter to authentic established Labour Party positions. The new principles and attitudes were traditionally conservative but had been so strongly accentuated (some Conservative critics would say deformed) by Mrs Thatcher that they soon came to be known as 'Thatcherite'. So, by publicly adopting tenets of both domestic and foreign Conservative policy and by finally getting rid of the obsolete Marxist ideology, like all important socialist parties in all developed countries, the British

Labour Party has now succeeded in re-establishing a semblance of the old bi-partisanship of Butskellism.

Turning now to the originality of Mrs Thatcher's personality in history, what retained and still retains public attention is, of course that she is a woman – indeed in the present collection of statesmen she is the only stateswoman. Given the fact that three of the most able European monarchs, Elizabeth I of England, Catherine II of Russia and Maria Theresa of Austria, were women and given the fact that since the war women have occupied the highest positions in the principal branches of societal life, politics being after all, one of the easiest ones, it is not in itself so surprising that Britain, after Israel and India, should happen to have a woman prime minister in the twentieth century. But obviously this was not the popular sentiment nor, more importantly, was it the sentiment of the male politicians with whom Mrs Thatcher had to devise policies, ranging from those in the Cabinet and the House of Commons to those in the all-male European Community summits. While her womanhood was not a cause of popular antipathy, yet it deeply irritated two large groups in public opinion, otherwise totally opposed to each other: what is popularly called the 'male chauvinists' and what is called the 'feminist lobby' – the latter being by ideological predisposition Left-oriented and therefore resenting that Mrs Thatcher was of the Right. How much of the permanent residual resentment against her was due to the fact that she upset the tradition of male leadership in politics, and how far Mrs Thatcher's personality shows feminine psychological traits, the most striking of which may be the ultimate insecurity she conceals under her over-emphatic self-assurance, is still a controversial matter. The general male relief in the cabinet and in parliament when she left was crudely visible.

Also controversial, or at least as far as this inquiry is concerned, is the question whether the theoretical and practical changes effected by Mrs Thatcher in Conservative politics and in British politics in general did or did not amount to a whole doctrinal body known as 'Thatcherism' (an innovation in English political language which has never known Disraelism, Gladstonianism, Churchillism or Attleeism). Here the view is taken that 'Thatcherism' is a pseudo-concept used by three categories of analysts, who for opposing reasons and with differing aims, believe in the existence of an ideology, or a doctrine or a system called 'Thatcherism'. The three are, on the positive side, Mrs Thatcher herself and the zealots of the younger generation of the Conservative Party who believed, or wanted people to believe that Mrs Thatcher's approaches, politics and theories formed a kind of system or ideology, and that although not exportable to other countries, it had actually been imitated by most Western countries, including and especially the US.

On the negative side, there are the Marxist analysts who are mentally 'determined', as they should be, by their ideological formation and can treat political and cultural developments only in an ideological way as constituting other ideologies in action which might shake the foundations of their own ideology. They define 'scientifically', but in different ways, an ideology called 'Thatcherism' as 'authoritarian populism'; or as 'the mobilization of the *petite bourgeoisie*, squeezed between big capital and the trade unions'; or as the 'result of the convergence of the British economic decline, of the advent of the world recession and the collapse of the third Labour government and of the resumption of the cold war'; or also, in Gramscian terms, 'a passive revolution from above or a possible coherent hegemonic system'.

And, thirdly, and more closely intermingled with the more extreme Marxists are all those who, having felt from the beginning that Mrs Thatcher was a particularly strong political personality, with a particularly organized and renovating 'right-wing' programme, adopted 'Thatcherism' as a pejorative noun and as a weapon to use against her in her political leadership. This kind of what I have already called 'character persecution' sprang naturally from the opposition parties, whose personal target she became; and from some Conservative quarters still deeply upset by the usurpation. But, in truth, the subject of 'Thatcherism' did not deserve *ni cet excès d'honneur, ni cette indignité* (neither this excessive honour nor this indignity) as the French verse goes.

The proof is that the most serious books on the subject are either biographies like Kenneth Harris's *Thatcher* or Hugo Young's *One of Us*; or they are studies of Mrs Thatcher's political action, which concentrate on the impact of her personality on her political action, like Peter Jenkins's *Mrs Thatcher's Revolution*, Sir Robert Blake's *The Conservative Party from Peel to Thatcher*; Peter Riddle's *The Thatcher Government* or Kenneth Minogue and Michael Biddiss's *Thatcherism: Personality and Politics* and Dennis Kavanagh's *Thatcherism and British Politics*; or, overall examinations of her policies but which elevate the subject above the person like, from a conservative point of view, Sir Ian Gilmour's *Britain Can Work*, or Francis Pym's *The Politics of Consent*; or from a liberal-democrat point of view, David

Marquand's *The Unprincipled Society*, and from a Marxist–Gramscist angle, Andrew Gamble's *The Free Society and the State.*

# I

## PERSONAL CIRCUMSTANCES AND HISTORICAL ANTECEDENTS

Mrs Thatcher's personality initially impressed the public more by its unusualness, than by its unprecedentedness. Even the anniversary of her unprecedented ten years as Tory Prime Minister was celebrated by the media more in the style of an entry in the *Guinness Book of Records* than in that of a reconsideration. The personal circumstances often seem, in her case to be records. Mrs Thatcher was the first British woman prime minister; she was the first 'shopkeeper's daughter' to become prime minister; she was the first prime minister with two Oxford degrees, etc. And then: she was the healthiest prime minister and the physically strongest prime minister, or to put it differently the prime minister who lost the fewest working days through ill-health; she is the most hard-working prime minister (to Harold Macmillan's chagrin who frequently advised her to take more time off for leisure and reflection); she is the best-dressed British prime minister, with the most impeccable coiffure; by now she is the longest-serving prime minister in British history: she also won the largest number of elections; and, in the field where the competition with her all-male predecessors is fiercest, she is one of the most pugnacious and one of the most courageous prime ministers. The comparison between the ailing and hesitant Eden in the Suez crisis and the inflexible Mrs Thatcher in the Falklands war comes to mind, as does also the comparison between the impact each of these wars made on national and international opinion, and even on the morale of the British people in general. And, for the millions who saw it, her extraordinary appearance, a couple of minutes after the explosion of the bomb in the Grand Hotel at Brighton, impeccably turned out (because again she was working late into the night) and with characteristic firmness in her eyes, remains unforgettable. So does her extraordinary performance in her last speech in defence of her government in the House of Commons, when she had already resigned as Prime Minister.

A distinguishing feature in Mrs Thatcher's persona is indeed the contrast between the innumerable extraordinary (in the sense of prodigious) achievements of her life as a whole, and the ordinary (in the sense of normal) context of that life. Summed up in the style of *Who's Who*, her biography should mention that born on 13 October 1925, she spent an austere childhood in Lincolnshire under the very strong influence of her father, Alfred Roberts, a cultured shopkeeper and alderman, whom she adored. Sent to Oxford University she graduated in two different and contrasting disciplines, requiring different casts of mind and modes of thinking. But also at Oxford she discovered her fervent passion for politics, and Conservative politics to boot, to which she has committed herself ever since. Married quite early to Denis Thatcher, her life-long husband, she bore and raised two children in a most normal family. Elected MP for Finchley in 1959 she made remarkable progress under the leadership of Macmillan, and after 1964, of Edward Heath. She was finally promoted by Heath, after the 1970 election, to Secretary of State for Education and Science, and already then she was singled out by the Left as a dangerous adversary. Ever since she has been the target of vitriolic personal abuse, starting with 'Thatcher the milk snatcher' when she put through a policy which was not in fact hers. In circumstances which will be discussed later in this essay she was elected Leader of the Conservative Party in 1974. She remained Prime Minister until November 1990.

This almost caricatural, but factually exact précis of Mrs Thatcher's biography can begin to make sense only when filled in with the 'personal circumstances' which helped to produce her legendary destiny. And, as already noted, in the long list of personal circumstances, the extraordinary qualities of her voluntaristic statesmanship are inseparable from the robust normality of her intellect – while by the same token, as every quality has its defects, so the defects of Mrs Thatcher's qualities can themselves be extraordinary.

But, first, the notions of extraordinary, in the sense of abnormality – 'the ordinary Briton', she herself has said, 'is neither a political philosopher nor an economist' – and of ordinary as normal need further elucidation. Normality is intrinsically so unnoticeable that it becomes evident only when confronted by abnormality. And abnormality has come to be made into a doctrine, as we have seen for instance in Foucault's doctrine of 'abnormality' outlined in the Introduction of this book in the section on the generational mutation. As explained there what Foucault attacked was the normality of human life. What Foucault and his disciples challenged was the assumed right of society, of all societies, but especially and more categorically of the societies which followed on the eighteenth-century Enlightenment, to describe and prescribe marriage, parental care and authority, procreative sexual relations, teaching, science and its ramifications of disciplines, self-controlled behaviour, legality and the respect of customary rules, and above all any forms of authority, from respect to coercion – as normal. Foucault's work and that of his many followers, was nothing if not an exercise in the deconstruction of whatever was organized and considered normal since the first appearance of communal life. Normality, from the Latin *norma*, rule, became in their dialectic abnormality: society and community were only a prison, and moral rules only prejudices forcibly imposed by a society believing in science and exerting its unauthorized authority on the human beings who exert it by the diabolic combination of power and knowledge.

Now, Mrs Thatcher may not have wasted any of her valuable time in reading Foucault. But instinctively and intellectually, implicitly and explicitly, she reacted against the spirit of indiscipline, the exaltation of abnormality and the contempt for normality so outspokenly formulated by him, and which became so widespread in the beliefs of the American and European students' revolts of 1968. Those beliefs had spread rapidly ever since the 1960s in the developed society, moving from the most rapidly developed one, the USA, to the slower ones in Europe, among which of course, Britain, and separating the modes of thinking of the older from the younger right across that society. Over and above her education in the particularly rigorous Methodist ethics, morality, self-discipline and work were basic to Mrs Thatcher's spirit, and the spreading smell of dissolution hit her early in life. Her horror of the deliberate debasement of human nature in modern society is manifest. Frequently, almost obsessively, she singled out the three worst forms of that debasement: drugs, vices and terrorism. Crimes against oneself, and even more, crimes against others, perpetrated in the name of freedom, were for her the symptoms of ultimate moral degeneration. Violating the laws of the land was bad enough; but it was much worse, indeed unforgivable to violate the natural laws of human normality, the *values*, as they have descended to us from the Greeks, Judaism, and Christianity.

Most of her biographers and commentators, while remarking on the importance role values play in her personality, automatically and almost mechanically stress her admiration of what she herself called 'Victorian values'. As Julius Gould and Digby Anderson remark 'whether (and how far) the values Mrs Thatcher admires were authentically Victorian was to become a matter for solemn as well as frivolous debate'.[1] Victorian values were stricter and more strongly enforced at that time. Since then, their religious foundations have been weakened by scientific rationalism. The perennial ethical values have had to be consolidated on a new ground. Mrs Thatcher's education has had a strong Christian foundation, and there is no reason why her values should always be qualified as 'Victorian', an adjective which she used in one of her most widely quoted speeches but which she does not always add, as for instance when she said: 'Experience has shown that socialism corrodes the *moral values* which form part of a free society. *Traditional values* are also threatened' (Zürich, 1977), or 'we accept the moral commitments of a free society' (Rome, 1977) etc.

The consequence of this was that with her highly developed national instinct, Mrs Thatcher was frightened by the decline of Britain as a whole. She was alarmed at the decay of the vital qualities of the British people because of the dissolution of the ideas of 'work' and 'decency' in British society and in British politics. The sweet smell of decline was obviously a stench to her. (In London alone Peter Jenkins reminds us that 'Hackney staged an "open day for Gays and Lesbians". Lambeth banned the use of the word "family" from council literature on the grounds that it was discriminatory. Haringey introduced courses on homosexuality into its schools, including primary and nursery schools. When representatives of Sinn Fein addressed Hackney Council a revolver was fired.')[2]

But she was also critical of the British upper classes because they were losing their sense of duty and responsibility, and of the British working class because it was losing its dedication to work. She felt that her generation should react strongly. Hence the apparent contradiction in her political attitude between what is called her 'populism' and what is called her 'dislike of the workers and of trade unions'. Indeed, in matters of industry specifically, she has been as critical of inefficient managers as of inefficient trade unions (with this difference that under socialist governments, when she was in opposition, it was the trade unions which caused the gravest problems). But it was especially towards British society in general that she oriented her thoughts. Her straightforward ideas of normality and perhaps her housewifely instincts of good domestic order made her concentrate her thoughts on the domestic problem of the chronic illness of the British economy and society.

The young Mrs Thatcher had neither the experience nor the special knowledge of political economy necessary to find in and by herself the answers to these weighty questions. What she felt was that something was wrong, moreover that something had been wrong for a very long time in Britain itself and in the consensus on social and economic policies. Together with other members of the younger generation of

Conservative leaders, she questioned the wisdom of the bi-partisan approach through Keynesianism and the welfare economy, and of some of its basic principles among which was the sacred cow of full employment. Like the angry young men of the Left, to whom they were diametrically opposed politically and morally, angry young Conservatives, such as Keith Joseph and Mrs Thatcher harboured an attitude of reproach. But while this attitude was vehemently expressed by the Left in libertarian diatribes and satires, it was still respectfully muted on the Right.

At heart, the reproach was addressed to the generation of their elders, in charge since the war, for having, by their benign neglect and by paying too much attention to societal comfort, allowed the country to decline so rapidly. Hence also the sense of *restoration* which is particularly characteristic of Mrs Thatcher's activity. Already in 1976 she had stressed that 'one of the most obvious changes in Western societies in recent years has been the great increase in the power of the government', and she asked: 'How much further can we go along this road and still remain a free and democratic society? Is it possible to lose our freedom? If so, oughtn't we to *turn back now* before we reach the brink?' (my italics).

Mrs Thatcher's political and socio–economic programme was above all a programme of restoration, first in the sense of restoration of the morale and of the moral commitments of the British people and consequently of the place of Britain in the ranking order of world powers. Secondly, and in a different way, it was a restoration in the sense of a restitution to British society of rights and concessions confiscated and monopolized by the British state. This accounts for the common sense of those operations of restoration: to bring down inflation by preventing the state from spending money that it was issuing without cover; to pay back the public and the foreign debt; to give back 'their own money' to individuals by reducing the taxes imposed upon them by the state for its own benefit; to denationalize and then to privatize industrial enterprises monopolized by the state; to hand over to citizens houses for which they were paying rent to the state; and to dismantle the control which the welfare state was exerting upon the welfare economy and its enterprises through its second network of command and intervention – the trade unions, and other corporate organizations. All these measures were measures directed at the abolition of statist excrescences which she reproached all post-war governments for having condoned. This was to have two consequences for Mrs Thatcher's future performance as Prime Minister. One was that the attitude of reproach directed to British society as a whole was manifest in her style of government – what Harold Macmillan described sarcastically at the end of his life as her 'governess' style. Her reproach was addressed not only, albeit mainly, to socialism and trade unionism, but also to the managers of industry, to the civil service and the bureaucracy, to the professions and to the universities, and even to the 'whole body of voluntary associations, loyalties and activities which gives society its richness and diversity and hence its real strength', now so much less actively 'voluntary'. That attitude of barely veiled reproach was one of the reasons why she aroused such exceptional antipathy, if not detestation, in return, in a multitude of social groups, which she tried to 'revive'.

The second consequence was that once she had come to power, she was resolved to change not only the theoretical base of the consensus of post-war British political society, but also and especially the idea of consensus itself. Strongly adversarial attitudes were going refreshingly to replace the tepid and 'wet' bi-partisanship. This was due above all to the crisis of socialism which had pushed the Labour Party into a divisive extremism. But this was also due to her character, to her partisan predisposition to classify people into those who were 'one of us' on the one hand and 'enemies' on the other.

It is significant that one of the observations often made in the evaluation of Mrs Thatcher's place in British political history is that her government and that of Attlee are the two governments which have changed the national mode of thinking, and as a result have changed the way British society functions. The political, social, and economic principles enunciated in British public life by the Attlee government of 1945 were thought to express the British national mode of thinking until 1974 when it was suddenly challenged and thrown out upon her coming to power. To be sure, in the intervening period there had been great differences in the interpretation of those principles between Conservative and Labour governments, and at the end even between the right and left wings of the Labour party itself. These differences had given rise to spectacular political battles and hard-fought elections with varying results. But such changes did not and could not alter the post-war consensus on the welfare economy, on the policy of growth and on the Keynesian system which was thought to link both welfare and growth into one single syllogism. The best example of how particularly resistant were the roots of the consensus was the dramatic U-turn of the Heath government in 1972 when after electoral promises of policies of austerity and privatization it fell back again on to the Keynesian policies of growth sustained by public expenditure.

Although the young Mrs Thatcher tenaciously pursued her ambition to make the grade in the hierarchy of the Conservative Party and therefore faithfully approved and supported what the leaders or the prime ministers of her party were doing or saying, she nevertheless felt increasingly that something else was needed. According to most of the books written about her and especially those by Peter Jenkins and Hugo Young, the moment of truth occurred for her and her predecessor and mentor in this conversion, Keith Joseph (as he then was), after the above-mentioned U-turn effected by the Heath government in 1972. It is from that moment on that a new sense of national mission began to give substance to what had been until then simply Mrs Thatcher's personal ambition. So while Keith Joseph was preparing the intellectual revolution of conservatism, but had no political ambitions for himself, she was preparing for the leadership of the new and intellectually revolutionized Conservative Party, and through it for that of the country.

## Her qualities and the defects of her qualities

There could be one concise way to describe Mrs Thatcher's political qualities and that is simply by drawing up a list of her outstanding qualities and of the outstanding defects which they entail. To simplify, we have grouped all these qualities and defects under three headings. The three headings are: energy, Englishness, and her bourgeois ethos. Luck, *fortuna*, is not a personal quality, but as in the case of many statesmen, it was constantly on her side until 1990. But all three qualities can easily become defects, especially in the case of such a strong personality as Mrs Thatcher.

### Energy

Energy or the force of life ought to come first. The force of life of a politician requires physical and moral health (Machiavelli's *virtù di animo e di corpo*) and luck (Machiavelli's *fortuna*). And conversely, in the field of politics, a weakness in physical or mental health can have public consequences of disastrous magnitude. Leaving aside the monsters of folly, like Hitler or Saddam Hussein, the judgement of even normal politicians can be impaired by illness. To take only three contemporary examples: Roosevelt at the end of the Second World War and in the preparation of the ensuing peace; Eden at the time of the Suez crisis; or Andreas Papandreou at the end of his career in

Greece were all what a French author has called '*ces malades qui nous gouvernent*'.

Mrs Thatcher was not only a young prime minister (she was 53 when she came to power), but she has also been given the grace of having what seems to be unfailing health. One of the records which she beats most easily is in the number of days of sick leave from her prime-ministerial work. The complete list of her medical absences in the first ten years of her premiership reads as follows: (1) in 1982 a minor operation for varicose veins, which did not entail a stay in hospital; (2) in 1983 an eye operation with a few days in hospital; (3) in 1986 an operation on her hand, with a stay in hospital of a few days. The high number and percentage of working days in the office pack in also the highest number of working hours in a day of any previous prime minister, from particularly early in the morning to particularly late into the night. Mrs Thatcher has always followed her father's precept that 'You work hard, not because work is everything, but because work is necessary for what you want. There was also the feeling that idleness was a waste. To pursue pleasure for its own sake was wrong.'[3] Thus her energy was generated in great part by her unfailing health.

The qualities of self-confidence, the perseverance in achievement, with their dialectical defects of self-righteousness and obstinacy, are also components of what has been called here the complete quality of energy.

But in turn self-confidence and perseverance are the *sine qua non* conditions of courage, one of Mrs Thatcher's superlative qualities. This is not the place to recount the emotional saga of the Falklands war, but one should stress again the virile confidence which was established at once between the female Prime Minister and the Chiefs of Staff, notably Admiral Sir Henry Leach, the First Sea Lord and Chief of Naval Staff. According to all witnesses, she was at once at greater ease with the decisive military leaders than with the so-phisticated politicians or especially diplomats (although the latter had secured the prompt and unanimous backing of Britain by the Euro-pean Community as a whole and the passing of Resolution 502 of the United Nations calling for the immediate withdrawal of the Argentinian forces. But of this more later in section II of this es-say, 'Mrs Thatcher's policies of interdependence'.) And in return the military understood her in the same way, as explained by Admiral Sir Terence Lewin, the Chief of the Defence Staff, who told Hugo Young, when interviewed for the BBC: 'She was a decisive leader, which is what of course the military want. We don't want somebody who vacillates . . . we want a clear-cut decision. She was magnificent in her support of the military.' No British televiewer of the coverage of the Falklands war can easily forget the tense but imperturbable face, voice and behaviour of the Prime Minister during those uncertain days. Nor can one forget her calm firmness during the miners' strike or the way in which she sometimes gave precise answers and pitched her voice during the uproar and the abuse of the opposition in the House of Commons. Everything testifies to her courage.

But as courage derives from self-confidence, so self-confidence derives as noted in the essays on Adenauer and de Gaulle, from faith, that is religious faith. Does religious faith play in Mrs Thatcher's personality such a fundamental role as it did in those of Adenauer and de Gaulle? In her public stance she defends religion and the virtues which follow from it more overtly than say Harold Wilson or Harold Macmillan who, whatever their own beliefs, seemed to think that agnostic religious and moral attitudes best suit the impartiality of the highest political office. But whether personal religious faith is one of the elements of her affirmation in life, whether she prays or not, it is still difficult to know. Although soon after her marriage she became an Anglican (though still not confirmed) thus deserting her father's Methodism, this move might have been made for personal convenience and social reasons. But the Methodist spirit still seems to be dominant in her faith. Indeed, the preaching style of her rhetoric is another sign of her Methodist formation. Moreover, as Methodism is the least mystical denomination, so Mrs Thatcher's faith seems to be free of mystical bonds. The nearest she came to a declaration of her faith was when she told her friend Sir Laurens van der Post that 'the values of a free society like ours come from religion. They do not come from the state'.[4] And on several occasions, as for instance in a speech in Australia in 1976, she invoked the unwritten moral law: 'ultimately the survival of freedom rests on an unwritten moral law, on our own belief in certain natural human rights and that no one should displace them'. Yet the fact that in her political rhetoric religious themes seldom appear and are often coloured by a distinct touch of utilitarianism seems rather to indicate that, in her case, as in that of modern English culture as a whole, personal religious beliefs are buried deep inside, one could almost say 'privatized' (if that were not a very bad pun). But will it ever be known, even when the documents are published, whether, say, during the anguished days which preceded the Falklands victory, she fell on her knees and prayed for divine help? And if she prayed for help, was it for the divine grace, or for the divine recognition that she was right?

Finally, luck protected and, until her last year in power, increased her energy. Like Adenauer and de Gaulle, personal luck followed her like a guardian angel. Moreover her luck seemed to have accompanied her actions and brought her her victories by the peculiarly determining factor that in most cases the adversaries whom she had to confront seemed to make, almost by predestination, mistakes which greatly helped her to win. She fought them, but they lost more than she won. Or in other words, endowed as she obviously is with the offensive instinct, with the desire always to advance, the people and the circumstances which could have stopped her advance presented her, more often than not, with unexpected opportunities of victory. In turn, although thus favoured by fortune, she seemed to have followed by instinct Machiavelli's advice that one should not trust entirely to luck, but wrest the opportunities, or as he puts it 'because fortune is a woman . . . she is well disposed towards young men (in this case woman) because they are less cautious and more aggressive, and treat her more boldly.'[5]

The following are four important examples of Mrs Thatcher's characteristic luck in benefiting by the mistakes of her opponents:

The first is the conquest, unexpected not least by herself, of the leadership of the Conservative party – in spite of not being at the top of the ladder of the party of hierarchical tradition, in spite of her relative youth and in spite of being, incredibly, a woman. She was by then the Chairman of the newly formed Centre for Political Studies whose avowed purpose was to clarify the mounting feelings of the Keith Joseph–Margaret Thatcher group that the Party, under Heath, and after his two successive electoral defeats, had reached the terminal point of a crisis in which it had been engaged ever since 1945. But their ideas were not as yet sufficiently crystallized to form a coherent critical programme. Moreover, it was Joseph and not Mrs Thatcher who had done most of the intellectual work of preparing a Conservative counter-programme. But the sensitive antennae of classic conservatism led Sir Ian Gilmour to detect quite soon that from within the still united party 'the heart of' the Joseph–Thatcher group, like that of Brutus, 'yearned to think upon' . . . 'that every like is not the same'.

In his book on classical conservatism, *Inside Right*, Gilmour noted that

Sir Keith Joseph is right to prefer the expression 'common ground' to the 'middle ground' . . . And the common ground, which is occupied by moderate voters and which is largely staked out by events, is where the Tories should always be camped. Plainly if the middle ground is taken to be some exact spot equidistant from the extremes of Left and Right, and the Left extreme is then moved further to the Left, the middle point will also be shifted to the Left. (*The same would of course be true if the Right extreme was moved to the Right, but that is scarcely an issue*).[6]

The apparently nonchalant parenthesis was the most portentous part of the warning. And in a later passage Gilmour explains also the doctrinal reasons. 'While encouraging a more entrepreneurial and pioneering approach, the Tory Party must not copy the mistakes Liberals made of thinking that everybody is ready to reform himself by self-denial into a capitalist overnight. Besides the Conservative Party is necessarily restricted by the prevailing tendencies of the time: otherwise Conservatism would be either reactionary or revolutionary which would be ridiculous' (p. 169).

It seemed indeed incredible that a woman without a book to her name, and without even a reputation for spell-binding oratory, could revolutionize conservatism. But so divided was the party on whether to terminate Heath's leadership or not, still so intimidating was Edward Heath's sulky presence in the party, that many members who might have been successful candidates in the struggle to inherit his mantle, did not stand. Because she 'treated Fortune boldly' and remorselessly Mrs Thatcher stood for election and was, surprisingly, elected. But Heath's hesitations as well as those of his potential rivals had done half the work.

Luck appeared once again when Mrs Thatcher was at the helm of the Party and therefore Leader of the Opposition, and the mistakes piled up by the deeply divided Labour Party under the depressing premierships of Wilson and Callaghan not only rendered the election of the Conservative Party inevitable, but also allowed for a radicalization of that party's views on the needs of the nation. Wilson's and Callaghan's miscalculations regarding the role of the trade unions in the Labour government and their disastrous financial policies helped the new Thatcher government when it came to power to look like a saviour bringing with it a completely justified 'revolutionized', Conservative programme. That programme attacked the old Socialist creeds and tenets as much as some of the old Conservative beliefs.

The same combination of mistakes by her adversaries and her own good luck which allowed her to advance more rapidly and easily arose after she came to power in May 1979. The Labour Party then embarked on its gravest crisis since the days of Ramsay MacDonald, with the formal split into a Labour Party and a Social Democratic Party, while the bulk of the Labour Party itself was split between irreconcilable left and right wings. Boldly Mrs Thatcher put her radical 'monetarist' programme into execution without a real opposition able even to unite to combat it. Indeed, as a matter of fact, Mr Callaghan's government had already been forced to present the 1976 budget in monetarist and explicitly anti-Keynesian terms – the beginning of Labour's long pilgrimage of self-punishment.

Again, the way in which luck linked the folly of her adversaries and her own audacity and courage in exploiting their mistakes was even more evident in the dramatic episode of the Falklands war. The discredited Argentinian militarists, who thought that they could save their oppressive dictatorship in 1982 by invading a sovereign British territory, admittedly situated at an almost unbridgeable distance, found a tigress. The Falklands war was and remains Mrs Thatcher's most popular victory. It was also the first revenge of the developed society on the series of humiliations it had suffered at the hands of what are called the 'less developed countries', the last being the humiliation of President Carter at the hands of the Ayatollah Khomeini in Iran. The European Community and the United States, which had backed Britain from the beginning, afterwards shared in this more general significance, and her example encouraged Reagan to undertake the mini-expedition to Grenada. But the Falklands war was no joke – and given the problems of communication the result was touch and go for a long time. The victory was a tribute to the heroism of the British air, sea and land forces engaged in the expedition and to Mrs Thatcher's exceptional courage and tenacity. It is equally true that her reward was to achieve national and international popularity to a degree reminiscent of de Gaulle's in the 1960s (she won the 1983 election almost unopposed).

Fourthly, if the mistakes of the Argentinian leaders enabled Mrs Thatcher to achieve a peak of popularity, so too Arthur Scargill made the mistake of choosing the worst time of year to launch his attempt at revolution by means of a coalminers' strike, and thus enabled Mrs Thatcher to win her courageous battle against him and against the revolutionary trade unions as a whole.

Last, but not least, the North Sea oil which began to gush in large quantities at about the same time as she took office, was an obvious element of luck for her initial economic reforms and for her economic policies as a whole.

The defects of the qualities of boldness, courage, and self-confidence soon began to appear in the form of, on the one hand, obstinacy and irritability when faced with contrary advice or opinions, leading to excessive partisanship and obsessive secrecy, within a surrounding *camarilla*. One of Mrs Thatcher's obvious defects was her incapacity to delegate. Her own political philosophy of free and spontaneous initiative and individual activity here came up against her psychological need to approve and to authorize the actions of her ministers in every department. This of course had the disadvantage that when she pleaded that she had not known what had happened, as in the Westland affair which almost brought her down, she was not believed. Finally, her great qualities of personal energy and strength made it very difficult for her to understand and to accept the reasons why many people, and even groups of people, might be physically or psychologically unable to live up to her standards of human self-sufficiency. This personal sentiment also played a part in the formation of her social philosophy. In Mrs Thatcher's case, social Darwinism, which is more basic to American political psychology than to the European and more particularly the British spirit of fairness, was accentuated by what she considered to be her mission to make Britain and every Briton 'stand on their own feet' and so to arrest their common decline and fall. While, as shown earlier, there were positive reasons for taking such a stance, nevertheless, her personal insistence on, and exaggeration of these principles facilitated the spread of the reputation which the Labour Party and the radical intelligentsia wished to pin on her, as an 'uncaring', 'hard' or 'uncompassionate' leader, particularly unsuited to govern in the harsh living conditions of the industrial technological society.

## Englishness

Mrs Thatcher's father's name, Roberts, may indicate Welsh origin, and her mother's name, Stephenson, may be Scottish. But the one was born in Nottinghamshire and the other in Lincolnshire and they themselves lived there all their lives. They, and their daughters, who hardly left Lincolnshire in their formative years, were the epitome of Englishness, taken in the sense of different from Scottish, Irish or, even more, European characteristics.

It is proposed to argue here that while the energy, ambition and public success described in the previous section were extraordinary for a woman of Mrs Thatcher's generation, the ideas which kindled her extraordinary activity were entirely bounded within the English intellectual parameters and infused with the English concept of common sense. Her ideas on economics, politics and, albeit scarce and discreet, on philosophy and religion, are essentially and almost exclusively English. They appealed to English public opinion by their pragmatic and utilitarian common sense as opposed to the ideological purposefulness, the alleged scientific character and the ethical paradoxes of British socialism since the 1960s. And they appealed also to the English public by the authenticity of their evident traditional common sense.

The idea of common sense transcends in English culture the literal meaning of normal understanding to become something like a philosophy of life. The English mind accepts the mystery of the human condition either with Donne's Christian resignation, or with Montaigne's gentle stoicism, which is supposed to have inspired the young Shakespeare. But Shakespeare himself, who is indeed the most natural genius of English culture, further sublimated that stoicism through his endless capacity to observe and re-create in his works most aspects of the fate of humankind, thus reaching, at least in appearance, that position of supreme calm from which 'all the world's a stage and all the men and women merely players'. But does this spectacular interpretation of the torments of the human soul amount to a Christian philosophy (like Dante's) or to a rationalistic one (like Descartes' or Kant's)? Or was T. S. Eliot right to argue that 'the champions of Shakespeare as a great philosopher have a great deal to say about Shakespeare's power of thought, but they fail to show that he thought to any purpose, that he recommended any procedure to follow – "purpose" and "procedure to follow" being the essence of philosophy.'[7] More generally, Bagehot had also opined that 'of all nations in the world the British are perhaps the least a nation of pure philosophy'. In spite of the vague attenuation of that verdict by playing on the word 'pure', Bagehot's judgment remains unfair. In its ultimate depth, the English mind mutely acknowledges the impossibility of understanding 'that which passeth all understanding' – and all philosophy. This is why it is more inclined to concentrate on the way of living rather than on the meaning of life. Hence also the fact that the very great contribution of the English spirit to philosophy was made in moral philosophy, and not in metaphysics.

The affinity of English political thought for moral philosophy, and Mrs Thatcher's affinity for English commonsensical thought, inevitably oriented her political discourse towards moral philosophy. 'It is the underlying moral code which leads ordinary people to judge what is right and just. It is this code which impels Parliament to use its majority as a trust, and pass laws in accordance with our concepts of fairness and justice. It is this code that maintains the rule of law', she stated as far back as 1976. That Mrs Thatcher at the same time declared that she would practise the politics of conviction, and did indeed practise them almost too much, did not mean, as so many of the interpretations of her political personality have averred, that she was an ideologist, or even a fanatical doctrinaire. She gave that impression especially because she preached her principles with almost excessive fervour. But in reality, while her principles were advocated and then applied with distinct conviction, the principles themselves reflected the characteristic wisdom of the English mind, in which she had been born and almost hermetically bred.

The economic ideas of Mrs Thatcher and her group took precedence when she came to power because of the economic crisis and in general also because of the mixture of idealistic voluntarism and materialistic utilitarianism of her economic theory. ('Economics are the method, the object is to change the heart and soul', she was quoted as saying.) They can also be easily reduced to common sense, albeit translated into fashionable monetarist verbiage. What they almost amounted to was: 'You mustn't spend more money than you earn'; 'a government must not print or mint more money than its wealth can cover, lest it produce inflation, a negative balance of payments and a stifling external debt'; or, 'if people want to earn more, they have to produce more and to work more, and to sell, indeed export more'. Hence also the reaffirmation of the virtues of entrepreneurship, with the 'supply-side' obligation on the government to cut taxes and to readjust the equilibrium in industrial relations between labour and employers, after almost forty years of leaning towards the trade unions. Hence, also, denationalization and its corollary privatization, i.e. taking away from the state which could not and would not make 'profits' and giving back to those who want to make a profit for themselves, the industrial and commercial entrepreneurs, the freedom to do so. Following Adam Smith she asserted, that private wealth making was making the wealth of the nation as a whole. Reduced to their essentials, and in spite of their new names, these ideas were variations on the common-sense English themes of Manchester liberalism, mixed with the utilitarian theories of one of the most influential philosophers in English culture, Jeremy Bentham.

Mrs Thatcher's political ideas also came of good English utilitarian-liberal stock: freedom of the individual, protection of private property, representative government, sovereignty of parliament, and the ultimate authority of the constitutional political institutions. She was criticized for her neglect of Tory principles, of the duty to assume active care and responsibility for the welfare of society as a whole, for forgetting Burke's theory of the 'little platoons' which she replaced with that of voluntary association, with the accent on 'voluntary'. What her policies were first aimed at achieving was 'to liberate' the spirit of individual enterprise and the enterprises themselves from the superimposed burdens placed on them by the state and the state's servant, the bureaucracy, which was extending more widely in the favourable conditions of the ever-expanding welfare state. She found it even more necessary to abolish the collateral controls of the non-constitutional, socio-economic but politically and ideologically minded 'interests' and organizations, such as, for instance, above all that of the trade unions, which, at the time, seemed to be the obvious cause of the British industrial and economic crisis.

Mrs Thatcher was also deeply, indelibly, imbued with the other side of Englishness: English patriotism. It sprang partly from her particularly close relationship with her father, which may have coloured all her beliefs with a tint of paternalism – the authoritarian *pater familias* in government, the love of the fatherland in her very marrow. Hence also the mixture of patriotism and authoritarianism. But more generally speaking, her patriotism is made up of all the ingredients of English psychology. One of the main characteristics of English political psychology is the belief in the uniqueness, one might even say the providential uniqueness of the English people. Again, it is Shakespeare who, in *Henry IV* and *Henry V* has given the most complete expression to this candid belief in the innate 'goodness' of the people, and in consequence in God's protection of it. The mixture of national modesty with this conviction of predestined historical continuity gives to English patriotism a character all its own, very different from the all too common aggressive nationalism, which arises from an inferiority complex. On the contrary, deeply entrenched in the historical memory of the English people there is to be found a calm sense of self-achievement. This is due to two causes. One is the satisfaction of being the longest-lasting kingdom in history, the longest-lasting parliamentary regime and the longest-lasting industrial power of the world. To this, one must add also the unprecedented way in which the English language has spread – not even Latin has been so widespread – first to the Celtic parts of the realm, then to the English colonies and then through several of the former colonies, and especially through what is now the United States, to the whole modern world as its lingua franca.

And the second reason is their insularity. Insularity is as much a geo-political position as it is a psychological condition. The first contradicted to a certain extent the second. The British isles, being isles, needed to have their sea-lanes kept open: and the British fleet had to be able not only to defend the country, but also to provide for its trade and manufacture, and later, especially its industrial production the safest and widest, indeed worldwide expansion. More than the mainland powers, and especially large federations of continental size, Britain had to be a maritime power from the beginning. That gave British psychology an added sense of interdependence.

From another point of view geo-political insularity had the effect on British political psychology of a particularly strong sense of sovereignty. Having never, since the eleventh century, been conquered by a foreign power, the English are the only European people with a memory of uninterrupted sovereignty. Hence the particularly strong, but also self-contained quality of English patriotism, which is reflected in the kind of 'Fog in Channel: Continent cut off' attitude of the people as a whole, as well as in the pursuit of the classic policies of balance of power, which still dominates the foreign policy reflexes of the 'normal' Englishman or woman.

Mrs Thatcher's patriotism led her directly into Conservative politics. The Conservative Party has always been the British national party *par excellence*. Ever since the time of Burke, and especially of Disraeli, the Conservative Party has been defining itself as the national party (although Peter Jenkins rightly remarks that 'when Disraeli first said that the Tory party was a national party, he meant that it was the English party. He was referring to the fact that the Liberals nearly always owed their majorities at Westminster to the Scots, Welsh and Irish. Labour has inherited this Liberal ascendancy.)[8]

Ian Gilmour acknowledged the organic links between Conservatism and British patriotism. 'In the absence of religion', he wrote 'patriotism seems the right and indeed the only possible candidate for Tories. "What's good for General Motors may be good for the USA" Mrs Thatcher has said "but nothing that's bad for Britain can ever be good for Conservatives". The Conservative cause is the national cause. Anything that is good for the country is good for conservatism.' But then the text continues with a reservation which Mrs Thatcher would not have accepted: 'Admittedly', concludes Gilmour in his sceptical way, 'the national interest does not always provide a clear and infallible guide for political action.'

Mrs Thatcher's patriotism had two further connotations. One was the global anti-communist crusading spirit on which she founded British defence policy. Already as Leader of the Opposition, she raised her patriotism to such high-pitched denunciations of the constant danger posed by the Soviet Union and world communism for the free world and, from her special point of view, for Britain that the Soviet press gave her the flattering nick-name of the 'Iron Lady'. From her first electoral address in 1950 to 1990 the refrain of the national duty to be constantly on guard against the military danger represented by the USSR was and has remained one of the hallmarks of her patriotism (in spite of the recognition of the changes made by Mr Gorbachev, whom she personally liked and with whom she agreed on many points during his first visit to Britain in December 1984). Thus, in a typical example of the pre-Gorbachev era, in her speech at the Conservative Party Conference in 1982:

First, I want to come to something that dwarfs party politics – indeed to an issue that dwarfs every other issue of our time . . . The first duty of a British government is the defence of the Realm, and we shall discharge that duty. Ever since the war, the principal threat to our country's safety has come from the Soviet bloc. Twenty-six years ago the Russians marched into Hungary. Twenty-one years ago they built the Berlin wall. Fourteen years ago they conquered Czechoslovakia, etc. etc.

This permanent patriotic reminder of the dangers of Soviet Communism, presented, one can presume, two political interests for Mrs Thatcher. One is the electoral motive: in her constituency of Finchley, with a particularly high percentage of Jewish voters, attacks on the USSR were at that time much appreciated. And, on a much higher and more important plane, those attacks and the entire argument of active military and nuclear defence against the USSR coincided with a re-kindling of anti-Communist and anti-Soviet sentiment in the United States. There, President Reagan, after his election in 1980, had revived the campaign for nuclear armament against the USSR, which he denounced as the 'source of all evils' and as a result, promised to embark on the new project of Strategic Defence Initiative, as we shall see in Chapter 4. Although Mrs Thatcher did not, from a strategic point of view approve of the project, she approved of anything that could 'deter' the enemy, because she firmly shared the President's apprehensions about Soviet military intentions.

The other connotation Mrs Thatcher gave to British patriotism consisted in the reaffirmation, in two different ways, of Britain's pride in herself. While Adenauer had to rebuild the Germans' confidence in themselves against the paralysing sense of guilt and shame which afflicted them after the war, and while de Gaulle tried to blow back into the deflated post-war French national psychology the warming sense of 'grandeur' which had always animated it, Mrs Thatcher had to fight, on obviously less important and dramatic levels, with a nevertheless somewhat comparable malaise of post-war British patriotism.

But, especially after she came to power, Mrs Thatcher's patriotism developed a more aggressive character towards the British people in general, than that of previous Conservative prime ministers, with the natural exception of Churchill during the war. It had a passionate and stimulating purpose and style, sometimes indeed with Gaullist purple patches, in which she blended reproach and encouragement together. Reproach seemed to be addressed to the deliberate anti-nationalism of the decadent 'new Left' and of the post-colonial, or in other terms, 'post-imperialist' radical intelligentsia. (This, as already discussed, was renewed with every 'young generation' of that ilk since the 1950s.) But it was also addressed to the, to her, insufficiently energetic industry and trade, especially the trade unions, but also the managers. It was also addressed, if in more veiled terms, to the administration in general and notably to the Foreign Office, whose diplomatic and therefore conciliatory attitudes she seemed to interpret as a symptom of national weariness. Her appeals for more work, more vigilance and more initiative 'if one wants to compete with other powers and reconquer our leading position in the world', had an urgency and sometimes even a stridency, which denoted a sense of national crisis. The stridency was particularly noticeable in matters in which her al-most fanatic respect for the idea of sovereignty, and instinctive dislike for that of internationalism were concerned regardless of whether in the United Nations or in the context of the European Community which, as we shall see, was a major cause of her fall.

## The bourgeois way of life

The epithet 'bourgeois' has often been used, in a critical way, to describe Mrs Thatcher's mentality and politics. Thus, on the Right, Peregrine Worsthorne deplored the 'bourgeois triumphalism' of Porsche-driving yuppies and champagne-drinking Stock Exchange whiz kids, who had invaded the British social stage since Mrs Thatcher had launched her Guizot-like battle cry: 'Get rich' (*Enrichissez-vous*)! But the critical accent in Worsthorne's column obviously fell on 'triumphalism' rather than on 'bourgeois'. For the Left, and notably the Marxist Left, the term 'bourgeois' itself has all the connotations of moral disgust and social revolt with which those bourgeois paragons, Marx and Engels, tried to link it forever, (though for reasons to be presently explained, they preferred to use the French form rather than the German expression of 'bürgerlich' in their native German language). Thus for Mr Henk Overbeek,[9] who, like all Marxists, relishes using the notion of 'Thatcherism': 'Thatcherism

173

is a reasonably coherent and comprehensive concept of control for the restoration of bourgeois rule and bourgeois hegemony in the new circumstances of the 1980s'. (Should one deduce from the use of the word 'restoration' that the author implies that the 'bourgeois rule and hegemony' had been abolished during and by, say, the Wilson and Callaghan governments?)

Also, thirdly, although 'bourgeois' in the Marxist sense figures among other insults hurled at Mrs Thatcher by the radical intelligentsia and especially by the fierce ladies of that occupational category, it is principally used in the post-Flaubertian sense of mental narrowness, moral hypocrisy and cultural philistinism.

In the discussion which follows here the terms of bourgeois and bourgeoisie – and their extension to bourgeois ethos and bourgeois way of life – will be used in their original historical and conceptual value-free meanings. Only when so cleansed can they be used to examine the significance of their relationship to Mrs Thatcher's programmes and policies. Four propositions will be submitted for discussion, in spite of the fact that they are, or *should be*, mostly reformulations of old truisms.

The first is that both historically and etymologically, the word 'bourgeois' (*Bürger* in German and *burgers* in English) has a further and more complete sense than that of a social class. The wider and exact meaning is that of an ethos and way of life.

The second proposition is that although functionally the bourgeois activities in *society* are motivated by the material interest of profit and private property, below and above that lies the deeper purpose of obtaining what Kant called *sibi sufficientia* or, in the classical English sense, 'independence'. The notion of individual self-sufficiency, or independence, comprises the essence of both economic and political liberalism and Weber's ethical sense of capitalism. Besides, what provides the bourgeois with his *sibi sufficientia*, i.e. what he supplies to others or indeed sells, is the fruit of his trained knowledge: in craftsmanship, in professional skills, mercantile ability, technical inventiveness, etc. The more knowledge advanced in the world, the more individual 'independence' could be achieved.

Thirdly, acquiring on the basis of the services which he or she thus provides, the proper financial rewards and social respect, the self-sufficient individual also acquires, more easily in urban concentrations, like boroughs or towns, the modicum of material comforts[10] needed in the home and for the family. This can lead either to wise frugality, or to intemperate greed, according to the person and to the endlessly ascending levels of the 'middle classes', the English name for 'bourgeoisie'. But, above all, this leads to the establishment of the model of a modern, urban way of life, which is the bourgeois way of life. As the middle classes continue to expand in the modern society because of the incessant transfer from the working class to the middle classes (a transfer which is operated through the technological change in *work* itself, from collective and manual to individual and mental work), the bourgeois way of life has become also the general way of life in urban, technologically developed societies. But of this more later.

The fourth and final proposition is that Mrs Thatcher's governments have aimed at, and succeeded in consolidating the bourgeois way of life in Britain, Mrs Thatcher's own philosophy being based on the bourgeois ethos. Now, to clarify the propositions.

Historically, it is known that there already existed in 1077 a '*bourg franc*' (a free borough) in the vicinity of the Abbey of Beaulieu and that since the sixteenth century, the official Latin expression *burgenses* described the inhabitants of bourgs, burgs, and boroughs who were authorized by charters to fulfil their functions as craftsmen or merchants, or both. As craftsmen: masons, carpenters, shoemakers, like Hans Sachs, smiths, shipwrights, etc., they had to have the skills required by their crafts which they afterwards taught to their apprentices. As merchants, they had to have the geographic and economic knowledge of where to find goods which they brought to the market of their 'bourgs', situated between the castles of the nobles and the peasants' villages, and where both these groups came to make their purchases. (It should never be forgotten that the first newspapers were set up and financed by merchants in need of 'overseas' information.) The market of the bourgs thus became the market (*la place, piazza*) where goods and ideas were exchanged. Thus the 'bourgeoisie' preceded by centuries industrialization, which in turn produced capitalism. When they spoke of '*bürgerliche Gesellschaft*' neither Kant nor even Hegel meant 'capitalist society', but 'civil society'. It was Marx who, once more, caused the confusion. He preferred to use the expression 'bourgeoisie' of despised France, rather than his German '*bürgerliche Gesellschaft*', and Anthony Giddens is right to stress that one of his greatest mistakes was 'to identify bourgeois society with capitalism, two heterogeneous, and historically separated, concepts'.[11]

Etymologically in so far as Marx imposed the French word *bourgeois* we had better turn to the original meanings of the word in the French language, and, through it, in scholarly language. Littré, the classical French dictionary, gives seven disparate meanings of the word, as follows: 1. citizen of a town enjoying the rights belonging to this title; 2. (in the collective singular) The entire body of the citizens of a town; 3. Feudal status. 'Bourgeois of the King', he who was exempted by the King from all feudal dues; 4. Person belonging to the middle class of a town; 5. The employer or the master for whom a worker works; 6. The word is used in contrast with nobleman or military; 7. Pejoratively, a man without distinction.

It is therefore evident that in the multitude of disparate meanings of 'bourgeois', the *social* meaning, as member of a class, appears only once among the other seven. Yet all these disparate meanings, which do not fit Marx's definition, do present a synoptical coherence when seen as the ensemble of customs, beliefs, civic duties and rights, tastes, styles, and manners of self-sufficient individuals and their families living, unlike either the nobles or the peasants, in their properties in urban groupings (boroughs and towns). That ensemble can best be defined as a way of life,[12] given also, and equally important to the definition, the fact that the ultimate bond between them is the ethos of self-sufficiency, and therefore of independence or freedom, freedom of knowledge as well as of civil behaviour. From this last point of view, the degrees of personal inclinations which we have seen in the essential action of profit-making between frugality and greed, are reproduced in the personal choices in mores as between austerity and hedonism, the choice remaining with the self-sufficient citizen. Due to the incessant progress of knowledge, and notably of science and technology, which was reflected in the twin processes of industrialization and urbanization, the bourgeois way of life has not only shown unbroken continuity over a millennium of human civilization but it is also extending, on the one hand, in geographic width, over more and more countries and continents, and in social depths, in so far as further echelons of the former 'working class' have been transferred, through the selectivity of technological specialization, to the middle classes and absorbed into the bourgeois way of life, or as the Marxist lament goes, become *'embourgeoisés'*.

It was Mrs Thatcher's government which gave British society such a decisive push toward the bourgeois way of life.

Her premiership occurred when the bourgeois way of life prevailed over the developed society in North America, Western Europe, Japan, Australia, etc. Her programme and her term in office gave the jolt by which the prevalence of this style of living was consolidated. Moreover, in so far as most features of the bourgeois way of life are akin to those of the traditional English way of life ('the Englishman's home is his castle') her Englishness, bourgeois social origin and innate

Conservative cast of thought were suited to the requirements of the new society. There are indeed several, and not incidental, similarities between the contradictory characteristics of the bourgeois way of life and those of Mrs Thatcher's principles and beliefs.

The first characteristic of the bourgeois way of life is the fact that all those who share in it *earn their own living*. It is this characteristic which, in the modern industrial society, distinguishes the accordion-like pleats of the 'middle classes' (industrialists, merchants, tradesmen, shopkeepers, craftsmen, and the ever increasing range of professional purveyors of skills and services, from lawyers to pilots and from artists to dentists, or from scholars to electricians). To be sure capitalism, ever since the first industrial revolution, has divided the population of the advanced countries into those who employ labour and those who sell their work. But modern technology, coupled with social reforms, has attenuated the previously very sharp contrasts between these groups both in form and in substance. A change in social relations was effected by the new dignity of specialized knowledge in modern industrial work; the domination of the employment market by service industries; the institutionalization of the welfare society; the accessibility of the basic amenities of the bourgeois way of life to the expanding middle classes; and the collapse of the alternative hitherto provided by the communist ideology.

There is no great need to confirm, or great difficulty in confirming, this principle as basic to Mrs Thatcher's philosophy. Indeed, she saw it as her patriotic duty to arouse the British people to live by their own efforts and not by the grace of the state and government. The high noon of 'embourgeoisement' of British society in terms of occupational demography coincided with or to a certain extent was one of the causes of the electoral success of her Conservative government, as increasing numbers of 'skilled workers' and of young people deserted the then extremist Labour Party. The supply side economic programme, i.e. the reduction in taxes and the hard monetarist policy which rapidly reduced inflation in the first years stimulated free enterprise and the market. Conversely, the monetarist programme of her first government inevitably increased the number of unemployed by leaps and bounds. The outcry of a society which since the declaration of the three parties in 1945 considered itself to be living within an ethically framed political consensus, in which full employment was the main article of faith, resounded loudly when it found itself to have become what David Marquand has felicitously called an 'unprincipled society'. For it was not so much that unemployment, already well over one and a half million under Labour, grew to over three million under Mrs Thatcher, as that she could calmly consider this figure as a fact of life, painful and particularly acute for a while, but nevertheless natural.

Mrs Thatcher's stoical attitude, which earned her the widespread reputation of being 'uncaring', had some practical and some theoretical motivations. The practical ones were: the reassuring knowledge that unemployment had come to stay in all the highly developed countries (even prosperous West Germany had two million unemployed in the 1980s), and that the unemployment benefits provided by the 'welfare state' cushioned the most acute material, if not moral, pains of that condition. A further practical motivation was that supply side economics would create jobs by reviving production. But on the theoretical side, Mrs Thatcher's stoicism revealed the depth of her English utilitarianism (already noted above) even if it was more in the socially concerned style of John Stuart Mill than in the unambiguously hedonistic style of Bentham. For, politically, her utilitarian mentality presupposed the idea of satisfying the majority, the greatest happiness of the greatest number, the latter being now the ever-expanding middle classes which had adopted the bourgeois way of life. Ethically, however, it evoked rather the bourgeois principle of earning one's own living, defined by Kant as *sibi-sufficientia* – the ability to depend on oneself for one's choice of life. It is true that Kant admits 'that it is somewhat difficult to define the qualifications of being his own master'. But he affirms that in civil society those who own property, the bourgeois, are such free men or indeed *freeholders*.

This happened to be yet another leitmotiv of Mrs Thatcher's rhetoric, as for instance when she exclaimed in her speech at the 1982 Conservative Conference: 'there is no prouder word in our history than "freeholder"'. She was referring especially to the Conservative Party's campaign to sell council houses to their tenants and she boasted that 'half a million more people will now live and grow up as freeholders with a real stake in the country and with something to pass on to their children'.

Hence also the materialistic/moral stimulation of ownership, enterprise and profit in industry, as announced in the initial document, 'The Right Approach'. 'It is time to back words with deeds in spreading ownership and enterprise in industry . . . A wide understanding of private enterprise and a greater identification with its success, should be accompanied by measures to liberate profits.' So the Conservative text 'liberated' the concept of profit from the moral censure imposed on it by socialist egalitarianism. Yet the concept of profit, like that of utility, can lead either to frugality and austerity or, as in Bentham's utilitarianism, to the pursuit of pleasure and hedonistic greed. The dilemma was, after Bentham and James Mill, deeply embedded in the political philosophy of liberalism, towards the essential inequality of which Mrs Thatcher had made traditional conservatism swerve.

Mrs Thatcher's individualistic ideas and instincts are more inspired by her antipathy to the opposite pole of individualism, namely collectivism. (Actually her indignation against anything 'collective' has caused her once or twice to argue illogically that there is no need for a society to be 'collective'. 'Why not a personal society?' she asked, thus producing the gem of a *contradictio in adjecto*.) The collectivist socialist state policies which need the state to implement and impose them, led her to fear the state as much as collectivism. She has proclaimed that the cardinal mission of her government is to 'roll back the frontiers of the state' (so much so that as we shall see in the second part of this essay, she saw the ghost of statism returning to Britain by way of the European Community). Her purpose was to prevent the state from limiting the freedom of choice of the individual:

Choice is the essence of ethics: if there were no choice there would be no good, no evil; good and evil have meaning only in so far as man is free to choose. In our philosophy, the purpose of the life of the individual is not to be the servant of the state and its objectives, but to make the best of his talent and qualities . . . That is what we mean by a moral society; not a society where the state is responsible for everything, and no one is responsible for the state. [13]

But Mrs Thatcher has also stressed the superior motive of the relations between bourgeois liberalism and the state, as well as between political liberalism and permissiveness. This is the rule of law, to which both individuals and the state ought to submit themselves. 'Law is the collective and historical element that is needed to control the actions of individuals, whether rulers or subjects, living and acting in the present', she quoted from Anthony Quinton in her first Airey Neave memorial lecture.

The relations between the state and the individual are governed by the principle of constitutionalism regardless of whether the given state does or does not have a written constitution, and Mrs Thatcher's respect for the law and the law-givers is absolute. Parliament is publicly placed above everything. 'The British Constitution', the 1983 Conservative Manifesto repeated, 'has outlasted most of the alternatives which have been offered as replacements. It is because we stand firm for the supremacy of Parliament that we are determined to keep its rules and procedures in good repair.'

But with this we come to the final, and logically speaking fundamental, dilemma of liberalism, and even more of conservative liberalism: the conflict between private and public interests. Here Mrs Thatcher's late governments had no hesitation in unravelling the logic which links denationalization – taking back the means of production from the state – and privatization – giving them back to civil society. From the general political and economic point of view, privatization, which in Britain was believed a few years ago to be only a pipe-dream, was not only the most original reform undertaken by her government; above all, it had the clearer significance which she had heralded ever since the early days of the new conservative opposition, of the 'restoration' to the private sector of the functions and goods taken from it by political force by the public sector. But the operation of privatization effected under Mrs Thatcher's governments will be discussed in more detail below.

What still remain unresolved in the liberal dilemma of private versus public interest are the contradictions which so often arise between the private life of the individual and his or her obligation to observe the laws of order and of what Mrs Thatcher calls 'decency'. The bourgeois way of life, in the nineteenth century, under distinct severe moral (Victorian) rules, concealed this contradiction for a long while; indeed it managed even to unite permissiveness and puritanism by means of hypocrisy. Mrs Thatcher herself does not seem to be a puritan: although her private life is irreproachable, she has shown understanding and forgiveness for the human weaknesses of friends, even of official friends. Patrick Middleton, quoted by Gould and Anderson, believes

that the values she admires are the values of the inter-war years. That was a period when 'a publicly uncontested value system' allowed a 'measure of deviances to occur without creating a sense of moral threat'. Crime rates were, by earlier and later standards, 'agreeably' low; and despite all the known hypocrisy and injustice 'Georgian values' cut across and united social classes.[14]

But her revulsion against the three plagues of permissiveness: terrorism, drugs and vice is constantly and violently expressed. It is in this connection that she most frequently invokes values, whether Victorian or general.

The bourgeois way of life, especially as it has evolved in the highly developed society, is materially the most comfortable which has ever been widely achieved in the history of civilization. The universal spread of information, and the equally universal spread of domestic technology have had the effect of standardizing resources for those who have the privilege of sharing in it – which in some respects amounts to an equalization of the way of life of the middle classes. Most individual members of the various layers of the middle classes watch the news, 'Dallas' or the Olympic games, if at different times and in different languages. A large number enjoy the stimulating effects of sea-side or skiing holidays, even if in sharply different conditions; most have motorized vehicles, even if some are Rolls Royces and others are Minis. Most of them live longer than their parents. And so the list continues . . .

Marx's predictions that the discrepancy between riches concentrated in ever fewer hands, and spreading poverty would lead to the 'proletarianization' of all layers of society, were given the total lie as science and technology became capitalism's best allies. Modern technology offered capitalism endless opportunities to make 'the bourgeois way of life' accessible and to ensure the social welfare of the 'greatest number' of the people in the industrial democracies in those continents in which such regimes had been established. Conversely, gradually, then abruptly, the communist regimes, and communist ideology, Marx's children, collapsed in an historically unprecedented twilight of the gods, leaving, according to the excessively optimistic American thinker, Fukuyama, no other alternative. The whole world seemed to be queueing up to be accepted into the bourgeois way of life.

Morally, Mrs Thatcher's bourgeois ethos remained as controversial as it had ever been throughout the century of socialist belief (1845–1945). Not only from outside, that is from less developed or underdeveloped countries and continents, or from 'Communist' China and the USSR, were there expressions of disapproval, not untinged with the flavour of sour grapes, of the cult of inequality, and hence of the inhumanity of the bourgeois ethos. But also from within the marginalized new 'poor' in the capitalist countries themselves and the horrors of starving continents stirred the conscience of Christian and rationalist intellectual members of the club of prosperity. Perhaps what is called Thatcherism, and what is attributed here rather to Mrs Thatcher's qualities of personal strength and sound English utilitarianism, was the openness and loudness with which she expressed her belief that the bourgeois way of life was not only good for the people she governed but that it was the only natural and God-given one, while other leaders sought to mitigate or even to camouflage its harsh truth. Changing only the gender, one might easily apply to her Coleridge's assertion that

All my experience from my first entrance into life to the present hour is in favour of the warning maxim that the man [woman] who opposes *in toto* the political or religious zealots of his [her] age, is safer from their obloquy than he who differs from them but in one or two points, or perhaps only in degree.

## II

## MRS THATCHER'S POLICIES OF INTERDEPENDENCE

Mrs Thatcher had vividly epitomized the idea of the defence of internal and external sovereignty in the eyes of the British and foreign public. Therefore, to discuss, as is so frequently done, the problems of the incompatibilities between sovereignty and interdependence which have become so apparent in world politics during her prime minister-ship, without including her would indeed be enacting Hamlet without the Prince.

'National sovereignty' and even more 'national independence' must figure as frequently in the word count of Mrs Thatcher's political rhetoric as *grandeur* did in that of de Gaulle. But there is obviously a great difference between the relatively Quixotic *grandeur* and the relatively Sancho Panchesque 'national interest'. The latter, like the whole family of utilitarian concepts, has a connotation of material practicality and of *common sense*, which may sometimes be absent in the concept of *grandeur* which is, to use Hirschman's expression, much more 'a passion' than 'an interest'. And, indeed in all the meanings that Mrs Thatcher gives to 'sovereignty', the one which prevails is that of national interest. This is not to say that 'national ambition' or even 'glory' are less important in her concept of patriotism. She basked in them during the Falklands war, and her European vision is dominated by Britain's unique role in the defeat of Nazism. She feels, even if only subconsciously, that the 'partners' in the European Community should continue to feel a certain gratitude to Britain, and to her hero, Churchill.

But the concept of national *interest* comes nearest to Mrs Thatch-er's understanding of sovereignty for at least four reasons. One is personal and has already been examined in the first part of this essay: the display of utilitarianism as the determinant element in her philosophy of life, rooted in her English psychology, in her liberal conservatism and in her mercantilism. From this point of view her conception of national interest must in reality be seen as the promotion of the reflexes of personal interest to the level of the nation as a whole. Daughter of a shopkeeper, she naturally embodies the characteristics of what Napoleon called a 'nation of shopkeepers': she visualizes the governance of that nation in terms of honest, but assiduous profitable competition. Helvetius's idea of self-interest, so completely appropriated in the popular history of ideas by Jeremy Bentham, can easily be transformed into collective, and hence also national self-interest. More than an idea it has the ineluctability of a reflex.

If this might seem grossly to depreciate Mrs Thatcher's political intellect, it must not be forgotten – and this is the second reason – that the concept of national interest was just as instrumental in the making of the foreign policy and foreign trade of all powers in the nineteenth and twentieth centuries, and most visibly in that fatal conflagration which was the First World War. Kaiser Wilhelm II, with the help of his industrial and military elites, made the most deliberately Benthamite 'calculus' of the ultimate advantage and utility for his Reich of the final outcome of war, before embarking on it. And, similarly, the policies of most governments of all pre-First World War powers, of the period when all of them harboured the illusion of their eventual domination in the age of imperialism, were based on utilitarian calculations of national interest. And recently, after her departure, the GATT negotiations in December 1990, which should have produced a fundamental agreement on free trade for the whole world, were killed by the conflict unleashed between national interests of great powers and little countries, of single nations or national communities, alike.

The political economy aspect of national interest especially cor-responds with the foreign policy of a seapower in which commer-cial and political 'interests' are inextricably intertwined. More than ever before, now, in the age of interdependence, Britain's interest as an island is to keep her worldwide commercial and economic lanes as open, as active and as profitable as possible. In that sense Mrs Thatcher's instinctive defence of 'sovereignty' has had to ac-cept the traditional limitations imposed on it by the necessity to reach binding transnational agreements. Mrs Thatcher proved to be a strong supporter of GATT and a permanent opponent of any attempt, in any part of the world, to introduce protectionism. Dur-ing her Conservative premiership she removed exchange controls and all the restrictions on the flow of capital practised by Labour governments, reversing the trend established by Labour in the 1970s toward the ideal type of a 'fortress Britain'. Moreover, not only did she keep the United Kingdom open to direct foreign investment, (particularly to Japanese, but also to American, German, French and Swiss capital) but she also encouraged British investment abroad thus greatly increasing Britain's 'invisible returns'. All these manifestations of 'national interest' run counter to the unadulterated notion of sovereignty and convey rather the impression of interdependence.

Fourthly, and finally, Mrs Thatcher's defence of sovereignty extends just as much to the domestic as to the external face of that double-faced notion. Defence of the realm against foreign intrusion was equalled in her concern by the maintenance of order within the realm. After all, the two most difficult and heroic moments of her premiership were the Falklands war, in defence of a part of the sovereign realm almost indefensible because of its geo-political position; *and* Scargill's miners' strike in which she succeeded, by means of force, in giving the positive answer to Edward Heath's unanswered question regarding internal sovereignty: *Who governs?*

But, at this point, it might prove useful to observe a distinction between de Gaulle's conception of sovereignty and that of Mrs Thatcher. De Gaulle's sovereignty was associated with the idea both of the nation and of the state. These were the two terms of his equation of sovereignty. For the nation to be strong it needed a strong state, and, as we have seen, for him the history of France as a nation was inseparable from that of the French state. Hence his constant efforts to strengthen the state and to give more powers to the state. Mrs Thatcher's conception of sovereignty extending over both the state and the nation is similar to that of de Gaulle. But the two differ with regard to the state and its role. Her liberalism instinctively opposed the growth of the state. She denationalized the possessions of the state and she privatized much of what it had taken over from the assets and functions of the private sector. She also instinctively disliked the 'corps' of the professional servants of the state, the bureaucracy, which in her mind are rightly called *civil servants*. Whereas de Gaulle had a centralistic idea of sovereignty, her idea of sovereignty is in some respects decentralizing; decentralizing in the sense that she is reluctant to accept any kind of central authority, which is not responsible to a nationally elected parliament. Also, as we shall see, she confused the notion of any federal, confederal or proto-federal organization – which are by definition and *a fortiori* inherently decentralized – with yet another form of state, the frontiers of which she always wanted to 'roll back'. Hence also her apprehension about the idea of 'integration', the result of which could, in her opinion, only be an integrated super-state.

## *Economics and sovereignty*

1989 was for Mrs Thatcher a year of contrasts, one of those moments in the destiny of a statesman when, having reached a peak, one can detect from there with a sense of vertigo both the heights one climbed and the abysses into which one can fall. Had that year been her last in power, by retirement or otherwise, the fanfares with which the British and worldwide media saluted her tenth anniversary in office would also have been those with which she would have entered history. Although doubts were beginning to cloud her shining reputation, after the election she was still glorying in it: she herself, and many other people thought that in both absolute and relative terms she was the greatest statesman of the world. The economic situation of Britain was still sound, and the reforms which her governments had effected were still universally admired. Indeed privatization had had a most remarkable success, both at home and abroad. Moreover the very word itself, which in Western parlance means the transfer of given enterprises from the public sector to the private one, acquired a much deeper ideological, counter-revolutionary, significance in the vocabulary of the communist 'bloc', then already in its death throes. In that context it meant simply the end of the communist state which abhorred private property. This was one of the reasons why Mrs Thatcher was inclined to think, when in the autumn of 1989 the Marxist-Leninist-Stalinist states collapsed like houses of cards, that the philosophy of 'Thatcherism' might possibly have influenced the formidable ideological changes which had been taking place. Some of her proselytes magnified this far-fetched conjecture into an electoral slogan.

From the point of view of foreign policy her position in 1989 was also particularly radiant, as she was by then the most respected international statesman: respected by Gorbachev, the author of the Russian and the East European revolutions; by the Americans, who were trying out their new President, George Bush, after her old friend and confidant, Ronald Reagan had departed just in time to avoid another 'gate'; and by the European Community where, after the Fontainebleau agreement, Britain had adopted a much more positive attitude, indeed making a great and uninhibited contribution to the launching of the European Single Market.

But because of her pugnacious nature and the feeling that her fight is never finished, as well as her conviction that only she alone could direct it, she unhesitatingly regarded that anniversary as only the happy end of one stage, and bravely embarked on another. Fate, though, teased her from the outset of that second phase. Suddenly, the effects of some old and new mistakes her government had committed in both economic and foreign policy, exploded in her face. In the first year of the second phase, she had to face unprecedented crises, recriminations and reverses. These were interpreted by her foes as a confirmation of their predictions, indeed diagnoses, that all her policies were built on sand and were bound to crumble sooner or later; and by some of her friends they were viewed with sincere doubts that, perhaps after such long years of leading, fatigue was taking its inevitable toll and making her hit the hurdles increasingly harder, with the obvious danger of falling at the next, if such racing metaphors do not seem too disrespectful in this context.

And indeed, a number of acute problems – inflation, monetary stability, and differences of view between Britain and the European Community – surfaced together in a nightmarish way. The flurry of controversy raised by her new legislative programme especially the already notorious community charge or 'poll-tax' aggravated the situation. Moreover, while Mrs Thatcher's personal popularity remained high abroad and among her close followers, it was gradually being overtaken by her mass-unpopularity, so well orchestrated by the different oppositions which had deliberately concentrated their attack on her alone. Very soon, people everywhere began to take a second look at her credentials. The first electoral defeat of her party under her leadership, significantly in the *European* elections, was followed by serious losses in by-elections and by a feverish reversal of the versatile opinion polls in favour of the Labour Party. The poll tax was particularly resented even while it was still being introduced, and its abolition was soon adopted as a rallying cry for violent public demonstrations. Mrs Thatcher's unpopularity in the European Community also grew as she took increasingly aggressive stances against the new urgency given by the Commission and by the majority of member-states to projects of monetary and even political unification – just when her own Chancellor started to profess his belief that the pound should join the Exchange Rate Mechanism (ERM) and indeed the European Monetary System (EMS). The connection between the economic problems which undermined her from within, and the European problems which besieged her from without, was fully established in the final stages of the drama of her resignation in November 1990. But until then it is still useful to examine how the economic and foreign policies of the last Thatcher government first deteriorated separately, and finally converged in one joint crisis with an unexpectedly dramatic denouement.

## Economic Policy

The Thatcher governments had the aim of reducing and dismantling the instruments of intervention by the state in the functioning of the economy. It was an aim which had been loudly proclaimed since the party was in opposition and clearly expressed in manifestos such as *The Right Approach* of 1976. The theme of *The Right Approach* was that after the war all British governments, regardless of party, had allowed the state to oppress and suffocate enterprise, in both senses of the word, as entrepreneurship and as firms. As a consequence, *The Right Approach* stated, 'We have suffered from low productivity and low profits, and therefore low investment and industrial stagnation. Most recently we have endured a wounding bout of inflation, leading to very high unemployment and we are now heavily in debt'. *Ergo*, the cure prescribed by the new government was the opposite treatment: to 'roll back the frontiers' of the state and to 'liberate' enterprise from the chains in which it had been fettered. Here again, it was the *leitmotif* of the return to normality that was heard, with the Thatcher-accentuated Tory belief that what is British is normal. It was normal and British, because Britain was a nation of traders and sailors, accustomed to buying and selling goods from and to all continents and therefore had a vested interest in encouraging the freedom of foreign trade which was essential to its insular economy. This was the artery through which the blood stream of its economy was running. And it was anti-British and abnormal, so the argument ran, to have recourse to protectionism, not to speak of the suicidal idea of the 'fortress Britain' as proposed by the pre-Kinnock Labour Party. The new Left's ultimate aim, said the new Conservatives, was ideological: to build behind protectionist walls a total socialist or even communist state, cut off from the rest of the capitalist world.

But what the Thatcherite Conservatives did not say, or at least not insistently enough, was that Mrs Thatcher's governments could not have inaugurated a *modern* policy of free market and free trade, had the previous Tory government, headed by Mr Heath, not finally accomplished the historical action of securing Britain's acceptance into the European Community – thus putting an end to all the opportunities missed by the Labour government[16] and by the fumblings of the Macmillan government. In a speech in Rome on 24 June 1977

187

Mrs Thatcher herself said that: 'We are the European party in the British parliament. . . . The Conservative Government of which I was a member in 1961–64 first had to negotiate British entry into the Community under Mr Harold Macmillan. The goal was not achieved until 1972 under Mr Heath'.

Yet it was on this very point that the difference between Mrs Thatcher's conception of collaboration with Europe differed from the more modern conception as accepted by the Tory Heath government. Mrs Thatcher believed that Britain, while remaining of course a member-state of the European Community, could and should combine her European policy with the traditional economic policy of free trade with all other continents in perfect autonomy and sovereignty. Heath's philosophy started from the premiss that once Britain had become a member-state of the EC, because it could no longer 'go it alone' in the modern international political economy, it should direct its efforts, as France and Germany had done earlier in the day towards helping the Community to reach further positions of strength in the world economy and *then* to reassert within the Community the qualities and talents with which Britain had once led the world. But it is a mistake to think of Mrs Thatcher as a 'Little Englander' as has often been stated. What characterized her was a post-imperial, post-Commonwealth British sense of authority in world relations and world trade. With that qualification, she was as liberal in foreign trade policy as she was in the domestic economy.

The Thatcher government acted in such a way as to make the state allow the enterprises to operate freely and all kinds of transactions to pass freely through the British economy from one end of the world to the other. Government controls on wages, prices, dividends, foreign exchange and credit were abolished at a stroke. Instead, the principle of 'supply side', (i.e. of the presumed effect of reduced tax rates on individual initiative of all kinds, and especially in commerce and industry) dominated the philosophy of the government.

But in order to make the initiative spin and transactions run freely, the government had some dismantling to do in the overgrown structure of the state, and to pay some enormous debts the 'state' had contracted in the exercise of its 'power'. The foreign debt was paid, thus saving the honour of the country, humiliated when it had gone begging to the International Monetary Fund; and the Public Sector Borrowing Requirement (PSBR) was drastically reduced: by 1982 it was £2 billion less than had been forecast.

Two principles of economic strategy predominated in Mrs Thatcher's programmes. One was classic, i.e. 'normal', but pronouncedly theoretical or even ideological: *monetarism*. The other was modern, post-socialist, and essentially practical, indeed almost improvised by chance: *privatization*.

## Monetarism

Monetarism was based on the 'normal' principle that no more money could be spent if no more were printed. Inflation, which had been viewed in Britain with greater indulgence than in Germany, where it was the national economic nightmare, now became in Britain too the public enemy Number One. Moreover, 'monetarism' was presented as a new 'Thatcherite' system, in practice and in theory. Yet 'monetarism' had already been practised most successfully by the German government under the federal control of the Bundesbank, as well as by the French Prime Minister Raymond Barre in 1976–8. Moreover, as Ian Gilmour again remarks rather ironically, 'besides, monetary targets were first introduced in Britain when Mr Healey was Chancellor in 1976, and in the same year, Mr Callaghan made his (or his son-in-law's) famous remark that we could no longer spend our way out of recession'.[17] Also it was soon proclaimed in British quarters that 'Thatcherite' monetarism was imitated everywhere, including even, but for a much shorter time and within an entirely different economy, in Reagan's United States, which happened to be the country of its theoretical Guru, Professor Friedman.

But what was really startling in that period of Mrs Thatcher's economic policy was the abrasively innocent way in which some of the sacred cows of the socialist philosophy were sacrificed. The first three were the myth of full employment, the myth of the political power of the trade unions, and the myth of the ever-providing state (in French the 'welfare state' is called *l'état-providence*). This sacrifice was not made without severe struggles. National public opinion was indignant at the escalation of the numbers of unemployed from almost one million and a half under the last Labour government, to more than three million. The curbing of the Trade Unions, through severe legislation and through the preparations for the sanguinary confrontation with the communist-led miners required intense efforts. The dismantling of the network of corporations and quangos, which had proliferated in the shadow of the welfare state, required time. All these entrenched institutions were offended by the disrespect with which the government was now treating them. Yet, at the beginning Mrs Thatcher's economic policy startled the world with its rapid successes; having risen like the disquietingly mounting fever of a patient, inflation went rapidly down from 13 to 5 per cent and the GDP grew modestly. The national budgets began to show surpluses, instead of the chronic deficits, thus allowing income tax to be reduced, and labour productivity in manufacturing increased by an annual average rate of 5 per cent. Finally, and as a consequence of all these developments, the pound grew stronger in the world currency market.

There are obviously two schools of thought about the applicability of a *strict* monetarist regime to Britain, although everyone accepts that inflation should be controlled and kept down. The adversaries of the kind of strict and exclusively market-minded monetarism, uncompensated by industrial and social help from the government, opposed it from the beginning as being unsuitable both socially as it causes unemployment and economically because the effects of the crude, monetarist methods on British manufacturing industry could only be disastrous. Experts who share this opinion now make it clear that the disaster occurred in 1979–81, when 'dis-industrialization' was brought about in Britain by excessively monetarist policies.

The opposite school of thought argues that, on the contrary, monetarism had to be strict in Britain if it were to succeed. Looking back on the decade 1979–89 they argue that most of the predictions of the anti-monetarists were invalidated by the first positive results of the government's strict monetarist policies. According to them, Mrs Thatcher had to apply monetarism more thoroughly than anyone else had ever done as the cure for the ailing economy because of the acute crisis. Though it was very painful, in terms of lost growth in 1980 and 1981, it was successful in bringing down inflation and laying the foundations for growth in the future. Inflation came down to about 5% in 1983 and stayed there for 5 years, falling as low as 3.5% in 1986 and growth resumed in 1982 and averaged over 3% per annum for 1983–8. Table 3.1 is an extract from a table of the OECD Economic Outlook and illustrates the dramatic improvement in Britain's position relative to its competitors.

The positive opinion also stressed the importance of the control of public spending as an essential complement to monetary control, including, above all, the proliferating expenditure of the welfare economy. This growth in expenditure arose in large part because of the expansion of the bureaucratic personnel required by the expanding spheres of welfare obligations as a whole. But, especially with regard to the National Health Service, the principal source of welfare obligations, the expenses were growing far ahead of inflation because of the technical advances in medical treatments and the demographic

| | 1976 | 1978 | 1980 | 1982 | 1984 | 1986 | 1988 |
|---|---|---|---|---|---|---|---|
| United States | 4.9 | 5.3 | −0.2 | −2.5 | 6.8 | 2.7 | 4.4 |
| Japan | 4.8 | 5.2 | 4.3 | 3.1 | 5.1 | 2.5 | 5.7 |
| Germany | 5.6 | 3.3 | 1.5 | −1.0 | 3.3 | 2.3 | 3.6 |
| France | 4.2 | 3.4 | 1.6 | 2.5 | 1.3 | 2.3 | 3.4 |
| Italy | 6.6 | 3.7 | 4.2 | 0.3 | 3.0 | 2.5 | 3.9 |
| United Kingdom | 2.8 | 3.7 | −2.3 | 1.7 | 2.2 | 3.4 | 4.2 |
| Canada | 6.2 | 4.4 | 1.1 | −3.2 | 6.3 | 3.1 | 5.0 |
| OECD Average: | 4.9 | 4.6 | 1.4 | −0.3 | 5.0 | 2.6 | 4.5 |

Table 3.1 Growth in GNP in the OECD, 1976–88. (Source: OECD Economic Outlook, 1989)

factor of an ageing population. Yet the control of public spending in the early years of Mrs Thatcher's government led eventually (though not at once) to substantial budget surpluses and reduced the burden of government debt which had accumulated in the 1970s.

In this connection it is also noteworthy that while the North Sea Oil source of revenue was an unexpected, and obviously welcome, benefit which took the pressure off the balance of payments up to 1985 and made external financial policy much simpler, it also represented some very serious inconveniences. It made the pound unduly strong, making it very difficult for manufacturers to price exports competitively thereby compounding the difficulties of the manufacturing industry, already hard hit by the monetary squeeze of 1979–81.

## Privatization

Privatization deserves special mention here as one of the most successful operations of Mrs Thatcher's entire economic policy. It was an improvisation on the theme of rolling back the state and had not been explicitly announced in the manifestos of what is now called 'Thatcherism'.

Although it was not mentioned in *The Right Approach* or in the seminal *1980 Conservative Manifesto*, (which only mentioned the possible sale of the ship-building and aerospace industries and of the National Freight Corporation) 'privatization' was a purely political artefact. Like 'denationalization' but on a much greater scale, and with a deeper penetration into the functioning of the society, privatization expressed Mrs Thatcher's belief in private ownership and private

191

management as against those of the state bureaucracy and its corporate paraphernalia.

The fact that dozens of privatizations have been successfully effected indicates that the British government developed the techniques as it went along. 'Privatization in Britain was not the end-result of an ideological victory in the world of ideas: it was something which was so successful in practice that the government did more of it', writes Madsen Pirie.[19] The particular success of the operation consisted on the one hand of the government divesting itself of its possible financial obligations toward enterprises and services which could, if privately administered, work by themselves. Moreover the operations contributed large sums to the revenue and the national budgets were generously fed by the results of the sale of the enterprises to shareholders.

Further, the ideal type of privatization, involving the distribution among millions of small private shareholders of the ownership of these enterprises gave some credibility to the symbolic image of 'popular capitalism'. Thus in the case of Rolls Royce, 43,700 people applied for 77.2 million shares and in the case of the British Airport Authority (BAA) about 87 per cent of the total applications were for 1000 shares or less. In general, 'the premium went selectively more to small applicants than to institutions' shows Pirie. The privatization of British Gas and British Telecom were the most popular of all. 'Popular capitalism' began to take shape in the new groups of middle-class shareholders.

Ironically, the most 'popular' of all privatizations launched by Mrs Thatcher occurred immediately after her resignation: the privatisation of British Electricity in December 1990. The issue was oversubscribed, and insofar as all applications had to be scaled down, the small subscribers were given preference. But as long as only 20 per cent of all British shares are in private ownership, while the rest belong to institutions, it is still difficult to speak of 'popular capitalism' as the Conservative Party frequently does.

Perhaps the most convincing of all the proofs of the validity of privatization lay in the evident fact that firms which had been languishing for years in near-bankruptcy while in state-ownership, like British Aerospace, Cable and Wireless and Associated British Ports which were among the first to be privatized, started at once and almost miraculously to make profits once they were 'privatized'.

Undoubtedly here too interdependence played its inevitable part and in the exercise changed the character of the ideal type of privatization. It is true that in several cases the multinational companies and foreign investors had to be prevented from acquiring the whole ownership of the enterprise in question. A contentious case was that of Leyland Trucks in which, after several abortive negotiations with other foreign firms and notably General Motors, the Dutch company DAF acquired 60 per cent of the shares, Leyland remaining with only 40 per cent. Finally the proposed sale of Rover to General Motors caused such an outcry that it was abandoned.

But in the meantime, helped by the technique of privatization other foreign firms actively penetrated British industry. Generally speaking, while the almost symbolic participation of the citizen-shareholder gave some credence to Mrs Thatcher's slogan of 'popular capitalism' on the surface, the deep reality also confirmed the increasing concentration of multinational oligopolies, which transcended all frontiers.

Conversely, the new British-invented and British-launched system of privatization was followed and directly imitated in some one hundred countries, thus making the multinationalization reciprocal. Foreign capital belonging to huge investors but which sometimes included also syndicates of small shareholders was organized by merchant banks such as Morgan Grenfell and N. M. Rothschild specializing in this kind of operation. With the exception of Japan, whose large privatization programme was based almost exclusively on Japanese capital, foreign capital was widely involved in other countries. In France, for instance, Renault sold part of its assets to the US firm of Bendix, to American Motors, and to Volvo and Matra sold its fast developing Robotronics to an American firm; in Turkey, Morgan Grenfell picked out the Turkish Airlines; in Spain SEAT, the national car-industry, was sold to Volkswagen; in Canada de Havilland was sold to the American Boeing Corporation, while in America the Washington National and Dulles airports were cleverly acquired by the British bank, N. M. Rothschilds. These are only a few, and not even the most important, examples of the multinationalization of *private* as against *state* capital all over the world, and the opening of national markets to the floods of interdependence.

Moreover in Britain, the 'Big Bang' effected in the City of London in 1986 enabled high street banks and building societies to enlarge their financial services and sell shares often to the benefit of families and small shareholders. As a result national and foreign, small and large capital was inextricably intermingled in one constant, worldwide, communication of instant and anonymous transactions. But everywhere this was accomplished to the advantage of the rapidly increasing private sector and to the disadvantage of the shrinking and comparatively inefficient state sector, in a way which confirmed the British government's original inspiration.

## MRS THATCHER À LA RECHERCHE DU TEMPS PERDU

The opening of the third Thatcher government in 1989, and of her second decade of continuous premiership, was saluted with renewed pugnacity by the Labour Opposition, by now unburdened of some of the ideological albatrosses which made it 'unelectable': the past tolerance of the 'loonie' and Militant Left, the past domination of the Party's policy-making processes by the trade unions and, especially, its long and almost instinctive distrust of the European Community. Its attacks were concentrated almost exclusively on Mrs Thatcher personally, arguing that after such a long time in power, she and her 'puppet-government' had necessarily run out of ideas and could not adapt themselves to the changes of the new world.

Partly in response to this Labour prediction, but mostly because of her own often-repeated belief that her mission to restore Britain's 'normal' well-being and power could not be completed in only ten years and that only she and the Conservatives could do this, she started her new government full of projects and reforms. Drastic reforms of the National Health Service, of the education system, of the traditional functioning of the judicial system, and of such imposing professional organizations as those of doctors and lawyers; of the Universities and, last but not least, of the rates − all these reforms were thrown together on the agenda of the new legislation.

Changes of heart and routine, and even more so, fundamental reforms proposed from above, are always disliked by institutionalized groups. It was, perhaps, inevitable that each of the groups challenged by Mrs Thatcher would fight against her programme. Not only was it not advisable to have all of them up in arms at the same time, especially when popular antipathy towards Mrs Thatcher was increasing, but because they had been prepared in an unnecessary hurry, most of these reforms were ill-thought out and ill-designed.

For instance the partisan, almost arrogant way in which the Thatcher government presented its community charge legislation, with end-less contradictions and retractions and without proper preliminary public consultation, helped to increase its unpopularity and led to unprecedented hostile demonstrations. Similarly, as in a particularly rapid slalom race, many ministers responsible for some of the other policies (student loans, doctors' contracts, etc.) were hitting all the posts. Yet every time that any of them had to correct or retract, it was

Mrs Thatcher who was made responsible for all these faults and her popularity sank rapidly, personally and electorally. The community charge, an especially badly-presented, confused and heavily patched up type of legislation attracted the antipathy of the Scots first and then of thousands of middle-class and lower-middle-class former Tory voters, causing the Tories to lose nearly 300 seats in the May 1990 local elections.

But earlier, in June 1989, Mrs Thatcher had already lost half of the Conservative seats in the European Parliament, to the not wholly justified advantage of the newly-converted pro-European Labour Party, thus helping it to become the major element in the Socialist group, itself the majority group in the European parliament. For somebody who, like Mrs Thatcher feared that Europe would 'bring socialism in by the back door', this was the best way of helping that prediction to come true.

Moreover, all these unpopular 'reforms' coincided also with a new economic and financial crisis, quite unexpected for a government which, in the first ten years, boasted that it had restored the British economy to solid ground. But here we come to a clear example of the interdependence of policies. For Mrs Thatcher's economic and social policies were closely bound with her foreign policy, to which we now turn.

## Mrs Thatcher and the European Community

Like Fate, interdependence weaves its threads slowly and silently but, at a given historical moment, produces knots of problems which it asks one or more historical actors to unravel or, if they have the courage, to cut. It was with such a knot that Mrs Thatcher was presented in 1988, just one year before the celebration of her triumphal decade. Two different strands were twisted together in a rope of events, and as they pulled in different directions, they tightened the rope dangerously around her.

One of the developments occurred in the field of defence in 1986 when Mr Heseltine, the Defence Secretary, who had recommended the purchase of a European-made helicopter resigned after his recommendation had been rejected in controversial circumstances. But his real motive seemed to be opposition to Mrs Thatcher's way of conducting cabinet government. This 'European' motive appeared more fully in his book, *The Challenge of Europe*, published in 1989. The second development occurred in the field of financial and mon-

195

etary policy. In that field Mrs Thatcher's monetarist policy seemed to have won the long and historical battle against British inflation. However, by 1988–9 the two ogres of British economic mythology, inflation and external deficit, had again raised their ugly heads with a vengeance, threatening the Conservative Thatcher government with some of the problems the Wilson and Callaghan Labour governments had been unable to overcome. Inflation which had been as low as 3.5% in 1986 climbed to 7.5% in 1989, and reached double figures in 1990; real wages grew by almost 20%, but without any comparable growth in productivity; and the deficit in the balance of payments account grew, according to the Treasury, to almost 15 billion for 1991, a depressingly high figure. In consequence interest rates remained unchanged at more than 14% for the second year running, a long and very hard test for a debilitated economy.

What had happened, or indeed who was responsible for this unexpected setback? Many fingers pointed at Nigel Lawson, the former 'wonder' Chancellor, now criticized for having allowed this downturn, because of his monetary laxity, and generally speaking, for his enthusiastic encouragement of liberalization before stabilization. While it is true that unemployment had fallen from its peak of 12% to 5% in 1989, well below the European average, Lawson's lack of firmness, of foresight, led to a degree of free spending provoked by the increase in personal earnings and in wealth, and thus directly to the present troubles. Hence the consequences of Mr Lawson's policies (Mrs Thatcher repeated in Parliament with sardonic monotony the cryptic sentence: 'The Chancellor decides') appeared in full light in 1988–9 as: *inflation pressures* first in the property market and then in the retail price-index, his new monetary policy being too loose when compared with the monetary tightness of the early years; *excessive liberalization of financial markets* in ways not foreseen at the time. This gave people so many new opportunities that they launched a credit-financed consumption boom. This, in turn, sucked in imports and led to a large *balance of payments deficit*. The economy was growing too fast.

Now, one of Mr Lawson's principal arguments in defence of his policy was that precisely because he had long believed that it was salutary for the British economy to proceed quickly, he had thought of the stabilizers which would be required. The principal one was to put sterling into the Exchange Rate Mechanism (ERM) of the European Monetary System (EMS), a measure which would have imposed external monetary discipline. Although the ERM is not, and is not meant to be, a guarantee against inflation or domestic economic troubles, it does provide a common international framework within which a national currency can fluctuate in value within agreed limits without the risk of adverse speculation. How much that 'pegging' of sterling would have responded to Mr Lawson's hope that, with those external constraints, added to the normal domestic financial prescriptions, he could more effectively have controlled the spending spree and the credit boom into which the British economy fell during his last years at the Treasury, is again guesswork which still feeds scholarly and political polemics. However Sir Geoffrey Howe has since stated publicly that Mr Lawson, then Chancellor, and he, then Foreign Secretary, threatened to resign in June 1989, on the eve of the European Community summit in Madrid. It was at the Madrid summit that Mrs Thatcher agreed eventually to join the ERM.

But it is here, in this particular incident that the 'linkage of fates' which, according to Norman Angell, constitutes interdependence, showed up with some cruelty one of the deepest contradictions in Mrs Thatcher's political judgement, that of the choice between British sovereignty and European power-sharing. Of course, as far as the episode of the possible entry of sterling into the ERM in 1989 is concerned, this caused further British and economic crises. For Mrs Thatcher, as is well-known, allegedly advised in that particular instance by Sir Alan Walters, her personal financial adviser, refused in different ways to allow sterling to join the ERM. She argued, first, that inflation had already had negative effects on the conditions of sterling's entry and, second, that she had promised at the Madrid Summit (1989) to join the ERM only when the 'time is right' and when the other countries had completed certain other requirements for joining. France and Italy at any rate had not yet done so at the time. And, thirdly, like Mr Lawson himself, and indeed like Mr Kinnock and the new pro-European Labour Party, she wanted to make it absolutely clear that while sterling would be allowed to enter the EMS, which was the 'first phase' of M. Delors' plan for a European Monetary Union, Britain would refuse to advance further into the next two phases: a European Central Bank and finally a European currency.

The conflict between the Prime Minister and the Chancellor over British entry into the ERM itself caused new economic and political difficulties which, fanned by the Opposition and especially by the media, only worsened the British economic situation. For, on the one hand, Mr Lawson's second best policy – tracking but not joining the ERM by 'shadowing' the Deutsche Mark – gave Britain the worst of both worlds. On the other hand, the by now indisputable conflict over financial and monetary policies between the Prime Minister and the Chancellor affected sterling adversely on the London and foreign Stock Exchanges, which all thrive on speculative rumours of 'policy uncertainties'. This was crowned by Mr Lawson's resignation allegedly because of the incompatibility of his position with that of Mrs Thatcher's financial adviser Sir Alan Walters, who strongly opposed British membership of the ERM. He was followed at the Treasury by Mr John Major who, at least in his first months as Chancellor, could not do anything either to reduce the stiflingly high interest rates or to arrest the external deficit, which grew even worse, in the first half of 1990. Finally, all this, combined with unpopular domestic policies, had a rapid deleterious effect on the Conservative government and party (at the end of 1989 the Labour Party was ahead in the opinion polls); and even led to increasing speculation as to whether Mrs Thatcher had become more of a liability than an asset to the Tory Party.

By the summer of 1990 it became increasingly clear that the 'European question' was the pivot on which the future of the foreign and economic policies of the third Thatcher government hinged. Indeed the probable decision that elections would be postponed until the very end of the five year-term, was made in the hope that, by that time, the disquieting economic symptoms, high inflation, and unfavourable balance of payments, would have reverted to more normal conditions. But economic problems could no longer be separated from issues of foreign policy. The speed at which monetary union was being organized in the Community was bound to have a considerable impact on the British economy. Yet it was on this crucial issue that Mrs Thatcher's statesmanship proved defective. She had lost four cabinet ministers (Heseltine, Brittain, Lawson and Ridley) on questions directly relating to European integration, and she failed to show her usual leadership either in finding a way out of the dilemma, or in preventing a split in the Conservative Party on that very question. Personal and ideological reasons explained the unusual hesitations, tergiversations and indeed contradictions with which she tried to paper over, for as long as possible, the cracks opened by interdependence in her traditional foreign policy and that of her party.

It is known that in her youth as a Conservative undergraduate at Oxford, she was wholly dedicated to the idea of Britain's entry into Europe; that she backed Edward Heath devotedly in his efforts to achieve this goal; and that in the manifesto, *The Right Approach*, the debt to Heath and his European stance was explicitly acknowledged.

But Mrs Thatcher's participation as British Prime Minister in the European Community, toward which she had mixed feelings, benefited from a national opportunity. As she came to power at the end of the transitional period of Britain's entry into the Community she was faced with the task, which she accepted with relish, of demanding that Britain 'should get her money back' (i.e. obtain a reduction in her contribution to its running costs) proudly using 'shopkeeper's' language at the European Council meeting in Dublin in 1979. She aroused the stupor and the irritation of Giscard d'Estaing, Helmut Schmidt, Andreotti and others who expected the new, Conservative Prime Minister to be more malleable than the Labour premiers who had preceded her. But she repeated her placid materialistic demand with a monotonous stridency until the 1984 Fontainebleau Summit when, with some compromises on both sides, the budget problem was cleared up. Moreover, by 'persuading', as Helen Wallace has argued[19], some other member states that the 'budget problem' required not only the solution of the British debt, but an entire restructuring by which expenditure on the Common Agricultural Policy (CAP) would be cut down to size so as to facilitate the financing of other policies, Mrs Thatcher emerged from this battle with the enhanced stature of a realistic statesman; while the United Kingdom emerged with a positive, but realistic approach toward European integration. This was summarized in the document 'Europe – The Future' which Mrs Thatcher presented to the meeting of the European Council in Fontainebleau in 1984. But in the exercise she had also helped to delay by some five years the moment when the Community embarked again on its plans for further economic and political integration.

For, in the meantime the Community itself had advanced rapidly on its functionally inevitable trend towards integration. The European Parliament, elected directly for the first time in 1979, soon manifested its overwhelming dedication to integrationism (only the French Gaullist, the Communist and the British Labour MEPs maintained a chauvinistic attitude in the first Parliament). After the second elections, in June 1984, the European Parliament proved to have matured rapidly as the popular institution which could hold its own between the Commission (which it could sack) and the Council (which it cannot overthrow, but whose decisions it can oppose when acting in unison with the Commission). It was actually in the Parliament, under the leadership of Altiero Spinelli, that the institutional movement towards a 'European Union' originated, which produced the 'Single European Act'.

Also, great progress had been made by the European Political Cooperation (EPC), the system by which the member-states, through their Foreign Offices, and with a secretariat in the EC building in

Brussels, are in constant consultation over international problems. British officials, public opinion and the Prime Minister all consider the EPC as one of the most rewarding functions of the European Community. It is both rapid and effective, and yet consultative and voluntary. It is also true that the EPC functioned particularly well during the Falkland crisis. The member-states were, first, unanimous in taking sides promptly with Britain against Argentina, a gesture of European solidarity which surprised the USA and encouraged the British government to take action. Similarly, through the agency of EPC, the Community immediately condemned the United States invasion of Grenada which was a territory under British sovereignty.

Moreover the EPC has also led to decisions in which Britain has had either to convince her partners to accept and support the United States in several international crises, or to dissassociate itself, as a member of the European Community, from some policies or measures taken by the United States. The best known examples of such departures from the US–UK 'special relationship' were the Community's declaration on the Middle East, in Venice, 1980, by which the Community recognized the rights of the Palestinians and not only those of Israel as in traditional American Middle East policy – a difference of view which persists to this day. Also Britain, together with the rest of the European Community, protested against the American decision to ban European firms which undertook to work on the installation of the Soviet gas pipe-line to Europe, and Mrs Thatcher herself had to intervene with President Reagan on this question. She did so again following the US–USSR summit at Reykjavik, when the Community feared that the two super-powers might have taken decisions affecting Western Europe, without the United States first consulting it. On this occasion, Mrs Thatcher flew to Washington in order to find out from President Reagan what had actually happened.

However, in spite of all those signs of intensified collaboration, and in spite of the apparent consensus established by the Fontainebleau meeting about the great advantages of the single market for all the member-states, differences of view on how to organize the market soon emerged. Mrs Thatcher and, at the beginning, a few other heads of government, ministers of finance and governors of central banks seemed to think that all efforts should be directed toward the completion of the lifting of all remaining trade and financial restrictions. But the European Commission (now headed by the more doctrinaire Jacques Delors), the European Parliament, (which was preparing a new treaty for European Union), the governments of France, Italy and, to a more circumspect degree, Germany, all agreed that such important changes could not be made in the Community's commercial policy without simultaneous changes in the monetary, economic and even social policies, let alone in the political procedures of the Community.

After a shrewd victory of the pro-integrationists who, at the Milan conference of June 1985,[20] obtained a concession particularly important in retrospect, a compromise was embodied in the Single European Act, which came into effect in June 1987. This reintroduced decision-making by majority vote and gave the European Parliament new and significant powers. Well advised, Mrs Thatcher acted in a relaxed and European spirit, and succeeded, by asserting her personal authority, in reducing the social and political measures of the Act to the minimum. However, whether she fully realized at the time all the implications and consequences both of the Single European Act and of the opening of the Single European Market in 1992, seems now, in retrospect, to be a moot point. For, what she certainly did not expect was that almost at once after majority voting was established, new proposals would be put forward by the European Commission and Parliament, backed by France, Italy and Germany, and most other states, to complete monetary integration and to enable all European currencies to join the EMS; while it was also announced that the functional development of the system required a complete European monetary union, to be effected in two 'Delors phases'; the setting up of a Central European Bank, and then a single European currency.

It was at this juncture, when both Chancellor Nigel Lawson (and some of his colleagues) insisted on joining the Exchange Rate Mechanism (ERM) and Delors (and the rest of the European Community) proclaimed their intention to proceed rapidly toward a European economic and political union that Mrs Thatcher deliberately attempted to make clear that neither she herself, nor Britain would follow the others along what she called a 'utopian' road. Irritated by the pressures put on her by her Chancellor to join the ERM, and even more so by M. Delors' ostentatiously integrative speeches delivered, among other places, to Mrs Thatcher's horror, at the Congress of the British Trade Unions, she prepared herself to sound and to act in an anti-Communitarian way. Her speech at Bruges on 20 September 1988 was both a back-handed retort to Delors, and a very untimely re-definition of British sovereignty as though it were menaced by a federalist and socialist conspiracy.

The sombre Bruges speech was lit up only twice. The first time was when Mrs Thatcher spoke with a certain candid rudeness of the debt Europe owed to Britain, for having saved her from Hitler's tyranny by her year-long lonely stand in the war. Without it, she said in so many words, 'Europe *would* have been united long before now, but not in liberty, not in justice' (italics in the text). And secondly, when seemingly out of context in September 1988, she suddenly mentioned the other parts of Europe: Warsaw, Prague, Budapest. This passage has proved in retrospect to be more pregnant than it sounded at the time. But otherwise the speech gave the ideal pretext for Mrs Thatcher's new reputation as an 'enemy of the community'.

Indeed, some passages of that speech, which was not one of her best, were counter-productive. The assertion that 'the Community is not an end in itself' is inexact: the Community has an institutional purpose in itself as heralded by the Treaty of Rome. Similarly, it is simply not true to say that 'the Treaty of Rome itself was intended as a Charter for Economic Liberty'. The Treaty of Rome foresaw the reciprocal organization of a 'common' market for six member-states at first – the proof being that Britain, having refused to join it at the beginning, had then to wait six years to be allowed to benefit from that 'Charter of Economic Liberty'. And the peroration of the Bruges speech against the coming of a 'European super-state exercising a new dominance from Brussels' and against the 'corporatism' and 'collectivism' emanating from the same place simply overlooked the fact that the Community has three institutions: the Commission, composed of commissioners *appointed by their respective states*; the Parliament, directly elected *in each of those states* from among national competitive parties; and the Council of Ministers, which is the decision-making organ of the Community, and which is formed by *ministers of the governments of the member-states, responsible to their own national parliaments*.

Finally, after the long investigations undertaken by politicians and journalists as to why Mrs Thatcher's statements about the Madrid Summit and especially about the Single European Act have seemed to be so confused and contradictory, there still remains a doubt as to whether she felt that she had not been given sufficient warning by her ministers of the consequences of the Single European Act, to which Britain had been committed since the Milan Conference in 1985. Be that as it may, it was after the embarrassing public controversies on how far and why the Single European Act committed Britain to take further steps towards 'union' that Mrs Thatcher decided to replace both her Chancellor and her Foreign Secretary.

Obliged in many ways to follow rather than dictate the economic policy of Mr John Major and the foreign policy of Mr Douglas Hurd, a genuine pro-European British politician, Mrs Thatcher seemed in

1990 to have returned to what were her own, and in her view, Britain's permanent views about the European Community, both from a positive and a negative point of view. From a positive point of view, she had adamantly stressed that Britain had come to stay in the Community as it was when she joined it, and that not only would sterling join the ERM 'when the time is ripe' but, according to the Single European Act, she had accepted the principle of majority voting, which might sometimes clash with the principles of national sovereignty. She had also accepted the bigger role for the European Parliament as forecast in the Single European Act (although here again one can foresee future conflicts of attributions between the European and British parliaments). However, she would not agree to go further than the Single European Act and would not accept more institutional changes and more Treaty amendments. (In this respect she shares the view of the newly-converted, pro-European Labour Party and – probably – of the majority of the British electorate.)

From a negative point of view, what was definitely missing in Mrs Thatcher's European approaches, unlike in those of her principal French, German, Italian or Spanish colleagues, was the dynamic sentiment that the whole enterprise was moving forward towards something new, which in its supranationality would be beneficial to all the twelve nation states. The idea that in order to attain this new and stronger status some of the symbolic traditions of self-contained British sovereignty might be altered or adjusted, went beyond her political imagination. It is probable that the same resistance to changes from afar exists in most British people of all generations. But it is equally true that if the British political parties and British governments felt it to be their duty to educate British public opinion in a new, more European and more transnational spirit, that opinion, and particularly in the younger generation, could be more favourably inclined towards the experiences of the future. But, instead of that, Mrs Thatcher sharpened the popular and populist British sentiments of isolationism by frightening the public, suggesting, for example, that a European political union would imply the sacrifice of the British monarchy. The fact that counting in the Duchy of Luxemburg, the Community numbers six constitutional monarchies out of twelve member-states counted for little in such scare-mongering!

The Bruges speech will probably be seen by future historians and biographers as the moment when Mrs Thatcher's mental fatigue began to show up the cracks in her political genius. This is not surprising after nearly twenty years during which day and night she had led from the front, and during which she had conceived of her leadership as a constant race in which she, her party and her country must not be overtaken by anyone else. This should have been the moment for her to pause for reflection, and think of possible accommodations and modifications in those of her policies and attitudes which had proved to be highly controversial. But fatigue prevented her from seeing the possible errors in her own judgement, and from envisaging new solutions different from those in her old repertoire.

Mrs Thatcher preferred to oversimplify problems and to heighten controversy. The vulnerable community charge became the 'flagship' of her government's policy. And she interpreted the fact that most of the member-states of the European Community were in favour of further unification as a conspiracy 'to bring the state back by the back door'. Finally her authority over an increasingly submissive cabinet became increasingly strident. With an opposition which found it much easier to oppose everything Mrs Thatcher said, rather than to explain what they themselves were thinking, British politics and to a lesser extent European politics, became a kind of match opposing 'Thatcher against the rest'. Her fatigue and her courtiers led her to believe that this was the apogee of her glory.

For the last eighteen months of her premiership, no contrary advice was taken as well meant, no clearly given signal stopped the impending collision, no alarm bell was loud enough to be heard. Yet the extraordinary electoral advantage given by the opinion polls to the Labour Party over her own party and over her personal leadership could not constantly be set aside as irrelevant. The figures were soon confirmed in by-elections, culminating in the shocking loss on 18 October 1990 of the murdered Ian Gow's seat at Eastbourne, one of the safest Tory seats on Britain's electoral map. The constant public disorder provoked by the poll tax (which reached its peak in the bloody riot of 31 March 1990 and required a large police presence to put it down) increased the tension. Worse still there had been muted if irreconcilable differences of view within the Cabinet, between the Prime Minister and the Deputy Prime Minister, Sir Geoffrey Howe.

The case of Sir Geoffrey Howe was significant in many ways, which were all made manifest when his resignation led to that of Mrs Thatcher herself. With his departure, Mrs Thatcher lost the only remaining member of her initial cabinet except herself. This is a very characteristic sign of faulty leadership. Any 'boss' who changes his or her executives all the time, and preserves no single member of the 'Old Guard', is likely to be viewed by customers as either too dominating, or too capricious or both. Mrs Thatcher's imperial female predecessors, Elizabeth I of England, Catherine II of Russia and especially the wise Maria Theresa of Austria, preserved their appointed ministers as long as possible. Whereas Mrs Thatcher allowed them to go, or sacked them, but stuck tenaciously to her private advisers.

Another aspect of the significance of Mrs Thatcher's separation from Sir Geoffrey Howe throws a clearer light on the mistakes of her European policy in her last years. When she exclaimed, after his resignation, that there were no great differences between them, she spoke more truth than she was given credit for. If one takes for instance, Sir Geoffrey's celebrated article in *International Affairs* of October 1990, which gave the first premonitory rumble of the thunderstorm to come, the author clearly states that,

'the EC is still very far from resembling the brink of transformation into a single state or "union of states" as experienced in "nation-building" in Europe. It is not a federal system; nor can or will its members be coerced into being one by internal or external force. It is a voluntary association of states based on the common evolution of joint policies recognised in and sustained by law'.

This description by Sir Geoffrey of what the EC *is now* is almost identical with Mrs Thatcher's vision of what the EC *should* always be. The great theoretical difference between the Prime Minister and Sir Geoffrey was that he believed that in the present situation Britain could profit more from the sway of interdependence by handling it from within the European Community, whereas she believed that Britain, although a member-state of the EC, could still ignore the EC when her own interest demanded it.

The *personal* difference between Mrs Thatcher and Sir Geoffrey was that ever since she had signed the Single European Act, she, and her 'Bruges group' thought that she had been caught in a trap, possibly posed at the Milano Conference. From then on she engaged in a vain search for times past, trying to recover the lost portion of Britain's inviolable sovereignty. Her scare-mongering arguments such as the suggestion of a threat to Britain's constitutional monarchy, illustrated how much her political judgement had deteriorated. Moreover, because she reduced the argument to an emotional, populist, defence of British sovereignty at any cost, she also lowered the level of discussion to subjective feelings, instead of raising it to the higher objective level. From that level she could have asked whether in modern conditions of global interdependence the new sovereignty of the European Community or Region – if it ever came to that – would hamper the real, free flow of communication and exchanges by its own short-sighted protectionism.

But no, for Mrs Thatcher it was too late. Although the writing was already on the wall, in the opinion polls and the by-election results , she made her position as Prime Minister of a power belonging to the Community even more controversial by her speech on foreign policy on 30 October 1990 – and notably by the impromptu part of the speech, in which she departed from her brief, and launched out again on a denunciation of M. Delors' plans to bring in federalism by the back door, assisted from within by the British Trojan horse, a tirade which ended in the cry of 'No! No! No!' conspicuously out of place on such an occasion. On 1 November Sir Geoffrey Howe resigned, and on 13 November he very deliberately stabbed the Prime Minister in the back in a speech which could not be answered. Next day, Mr Heseltine, another victim of her anti-Community feelings, put himself forward as a candidate for the leadership of the Conservative Party. The result of the first ballot reflected the surprising new distrust of the party, and after a further expression of her determination to fight and win, Mrs Thatcher finally resigned on 22 November 1990. But when she actually went, Mrs Thatcher still astounded the party, parliament and the public with a dazzling and dramatic performance in the House of Commons.

## CONCLUSIONS

The Queen conferred the Order of Merit on Mrs Thatcher soon after her resignation, the highest honour she can bestow, for it is not awarded on the recommendation of the government but by the sovereign in person in recognition of exceptional services rendered to society.

If I were asked, in conclusion to this essay, to state what Mrs Thatcher's principal 'merits' were, I would point to her constant efforts to roll back the bureaucratic state, and thus to liberate civil society in Britain (though ironically enough Mrs Thatcher has made her dislike of the word and of the concept of 'society' notorious).

But the fact that she did liberate society in Britain, a task on which all industrial countries from, say, Australia to Sweden to the USSR are now engaged, does not imply that she followed these policies for the same reasons and in the same spirit as the rest of the interdependent world.

The difference in motivation was of two kinds. First, Mrs Thatcher's motivation was not limited only to the reform of political, social and economic institutions. In her view, the restoration of the domination of British society over the state required a moral crusade. She attacked head on the ideologies which had spread 'revolutionary', anti-patriotic and 'decadent' sentiments. In her view, the British needed a rude awakening from their consensual habits.

But qualities and defects are so intertwined in an intense personality such as Mrs Thatcher's that her crusade showed concomitantly its counter-productive sides. In the field of the economy, the starving of the manufacturing industry during the anti-inflationary years seemed in retrospect most regrettable, when, largely because of miscalculations, the see-saw between inflation and recession had returned with a vengeance. In the social field, Mrs Thatcher's justified concentration on the constantly expanding middle classes led her to treat with benign neglect the growing number of those who were marginalized as a result. The 'uncaring' image projected by those who from the outset pursued her character assassination found new arguments. Some of her own prime ministerial measures and attitudes surprised the public by their clinical sharpness . Moreover the severity of some of her more maladroit ministers, and the verbal crudeness of some of the early exponents of her ideology who gravitated around Downing Street were quickly attributed to her. They have remained ever since indelibly attached to her (spitting) image. And though in politics she proved to be a most zealous parliamentarian, yet her manner of exercising her leadership, like 'a tigress among hamsters' in John Biffen's striking phrase, was bound in the long run to make her vulnerable to the fate of Julius Caesar.

The other difference between the worldwide phenomenon of 'rolling back the state' and the British variety launched by Mrs Thatcher in Britain, consisted in the latter's refusal to see her endeavours as *part* of a much larger and irresistible world development toward discipline and mutual sacrifices by all states.

Yet by a strange historical irony, it was her initial collaboration with, and presumed influence on, President Bush, which led to the implementation by force of arms of the resolutions of the United Nations condemning the Iraqi invasion of Kuwait. Driven from power, she was reduced to watching from the back benches the developments of a war in which she had earlier exerted so much influence.

It must be recorded here that if most of this essay was written in the past tense, it is because it was concerned with Mrs Thatcher's eleven and a half years in the premiership. It is however not at all impossible that given such an extraordinary and challenging personality, postscripts may be required.

# NOTES AND REFERENCES

1. J. Gould and D. Anderson in M. Biddiss and K. Minogue (eds), *Thatcherism*, London, 1987, p. 29.

2. In Biddiss and Minogue, *op. cit.*, p. 42.

3. Hugo Young, *One of Us*, London, 1989, p. 46.

4. Hugo Young, *op cit*, p. 419.

5. Machiavelli: *The Prince*, edited by Quentin Skinner and Russell Price, Cambridge, 1988, p. 87.

6. Ian Gilmour, *Inside Right. A Study of Conservatism*, London, 1977, pp. 40. My italics, Ibid., p. 169.

7. T. S. Eliot: *Collected Essays*, London, 1948, pp. 125–46.

8. P. Jenkins, *Mrs Thatcher's Revolution*, London, 1987, p. 94.

9. In Bob Jessop *et al. Thatcherism*, London, 1988, p. 3.

10. That modicum consists, for instance, in Britain now, according to recent statistics, of the ownership (63 per cent of households) or use of living accommodation, with central heating (72.7 per cent) and electricity; savings or credit, medical care, education, sound clothing, food and drink, and some, or all, of such commodities as: cooker, refrigerator, washing machine (83.1 per cent), radio, television, (black and white and colour together, 98.1 per cent) video (45.5 per cent), record-player, telephone (83.2 per cent) and private car (63.9 per cent), motor bicycle, holidays abroad, 'time out', etc.

11. Anthony Giddens, *The Class Structure of the Advanced Societies*, London, p. 271 (italics in the text).

12. In one sentence in his book *The Bourgeois*, Werner Sombart recognizes that 'for me the bourgeois is more a human type than the representative of a social class'. And indeed his study does concentrate mainly on the values, character and mores of the human specimen who can be called a 'bourgeois'. He found those values incarnated above all in three personalities and their works, namely the Florentine Quattrocento merchant, L. B. Alberti, who had written a famous book, *I libri de la famiglia*; and afterwards in Daniel Defoe and in Benjamin Franklin. But then the purpose of Sombart's book is to describe the 'modern economic man'. By putting the accent on the economic aspect, i.e. capitalism, his analysis blurs the two distinct notions and falls inconclusively between Marx and Weber.

13. Speech at the Zürich Economic Society, 14 March 1977, in M. Thatcher *In Defence of Freedom*, London, 1986, pp 21–33.

14. Gould and Anderson, *op cit*, p. 43.

15. Albert O. Hirschmann: *The Passions and the Interests*, Princeton U.P., 1977, p. 27.

16. The Labour government's policies toward Western Europe 'add up to nothing more than a catalogue of missed opportunities' wrote Alan Bullock in his authoritative biography of Ernest Bevin.

17. Gilmour, *Britain Can Work*, London, 1983.

18. Madsen Pirie *Privatization, Theory, Practice and Choice*, 1988, London, pp. 9–10.

19. Helen Wallace, 'The British Presidency of the Council: the Opportunity to Persuade', *International Affairs*, 1986, No. 4.

20. See especially, Emile Noel, 'The Single European Act', in *Government and Opposition*, vol. 24, No 1, pp. 3–14.

# CHAPTER FOUR

# Ronald Reagan

Ronald Reagan's historical renown rests on both his personal achievement and his political achievement. His personal achievement is that he was the first actor or, as he himself called it sarcastically, 'ham',[1] in history to have become not only the leader of a state, but of the most powerful state at the time. Reagan's political achievement is that during his two-term presidency of the United States, the world entered into what can be called, in the terminology of this inquiry, the era of complete, openly acknowledged and therefore peaceful interdependence.

Indeed, our inquiry into the concept of interdependence reaches in this chapter a new and more complete explanation. For it is only when one can see the world's political economy from the comparatively high perspectives of the White House that one can grasp the intrinsic significance in terms of mutuality of that concept. Until now, that is to say in the case of Adenauer's Germany, de Gaulle's France, and even Thatcher's Britain, the view of the world's politics was necessarily asymmetric, because the 'independence', or sovereignty of these countries was overshadowed by one particular outside factor. This was the multilateral and bilateral *dependence* of each of these three countries on the United States for ultimate reasons of security, even if de Gaulle denied it, as well as for economic collaboration between states, and through the multinationals.

But the American view of interdependence is obtained from the exact median point from which all dependencies and interdependencies are linked into one global continuum. Once the obsolescence of the Monroe doctrine had been exposed by the progress of communication, the view from the White House on to its own continent, and on to the Latin American backyard, expanded, first with Presidents

Wilson, Roosevelt (and Senator Vandenberg) to Western Europe, then with Presidents Truman, Eisenhower and Kennedy to Eastern Europe, or as it was then called, the Soviet bloc; then with President Nixon (and Secretary of State Kissinger) to China, and eventually with President Carter, to Africa and especially to the Middle East.

To be sure, this expansion of interdependence was not achieved in a continuous progression. There were ups and downs, victories and defeats. Most historians agree that American interest in world politics followed, from 1914 to the 1960s, an ascending line, which culminated after the Second World War in the Pax Americana, with its dialectical antithesis of the cold war; but that since the 1960s it has followed a line of abrupt descent, dramatized by the first setbacks and humiliations on the military, economic and technological planes. This has inspired the overall 'declinist' interpretation of American history by a small group of American historians (one of the prime movers among whom is a British historian who lives in the USA). According to this interpretation in the style of Gibbon, Marx and Toynbee, the American crisis now presents all the incurable symptoms of the 'decline and fall' of empires which 'overstretched' themselves, beyond their capacities, from the Roman empire to the Spanish empire, and more especially the much more similar British empire. All the symptoms point to the same diagnosis of the disintegration of a hegemony which can no longer be sustained. According to the declinist theory the conversion of America, once the richest creditor nation of the world, into the greatest debtor, is blatant proof of its irreversible decline.

The 'declinist' theory, which rightly detected the new limitations on the power, influence and prestige of the USA since the mutations of the 1970s, fails nevertheless to distinguish between the absolute and the relative decline of American power. The Vietnam war was the epicentre of the earthquake which shook some of the USA's erstwhile positions and beliefs. Its impact on the reputation of the country, both in the eyes of the world at large and of its own citizens, was damaging. American loss of reputation in the eyes of its own citizens continues until the present day (between 1960 and 1972 less than 40 per cent of the American population trusted the government 'to do what is right', while since that time, the Reagan administration has succeeded in raising the number again to a majority[2]). This was due not only to the shock of the military defeat of a country which had never lost a war at the hands of a small and peripheral communist state. It corresponded also to a particularly depressing period in the constitutional history of America.

Two presidents, Lyndon Johnson and Nixon, were forced to abandon the presidency because of abuse of power, manipulations, lies, and in Nixon's case criminal complicities. A third president, Carter, provided an almost legendary case of psychological indecisiveness, leading to episodes which brought new traumas of 'national humiliation' at the hands of an eastern dictatorship. Reagan succeeded, by ways and means to be discussed presently, in redressing the morale of the country to a certain extent. But among these means, the decision to continue, indeed to aggravate, a budgetary policy already unhealthy since the 1960s, which turned the country into the greatest world debtor, allowing foreign capital to conquer important positions in the national economy, and the loss of some of the American world lead in science and technology to Japan, Germany and other countries, confirmed the pessimistic predictions. Where the 'declinist' theory falls short is that it fails to distinguish the *absolute* decline of the USA from the *relative* decline in national power and sovereignty of all states, of all categories and dimensions, because of the levelling factor of interdependence.

Had the United States declined *alone*, or had it declined only *absolutely*, other symptoms would have fully confirmed the declinist theory. First among these symptoms one would have noted the evident transfer of America's lost 'hegemony' to the rival power with which it had been wrestling for 'hegemony' for half a century. But the stature of the United States should not be measured against powers which are still, at least as long as Europe is not unified in one way or another, strategically dependent on the United States. They are, therefore still, to all intents and purposes, part and parcel of the American system. The 'twin-track' aspect of those intra-bloc relations affects all possible calculations of the comparative growth or decline of the powers of the Western alliance.

A valid measurement of the stature of the USA in terms of hegemony should only be made by comparing its strength proportionately to that of the USSR. Only the USSR has enjoyed since the Second World War a status of sovereignty, at least from the standpoint of nuclear security and potential economic self-sufficiency (if well-administered), comparable to that of the US over the same period – the period in which between them they have transformed the world into their two rival 'blocs'. By virtue of the physical principle of communicating vessels, or of what Soviet doctrine calls 'the correlation of forces', had the USA declined absolutely so sharply as proponents of the declinist theory want us to believe, its loss of power would have been reflected in the power accruing to the rival with which it was wrestling in the cold war. And indeed, for a time, immediately after the defeat in Vietnam, and especially during the Carter presidency, this seemed indeed to be happening. But the iron law of interdependence, which acts everywhere and simultaneously, was being applied with even more stringency to the USSR and the Soviet bloc, forcing them to beg for admittance into the circuit of the world economy, known formerly as 'capitalist' in their terminology.

As will be seen in this and the next chapter (on Gorbachev), what really happened is that the reality of interdependence – in security, on earth as in the stratosphere, in economy, finance, trade, and last but not least technology – dawned upon all reasonable leaders of the political world. The USA saw former units of its 'bloc' competing with it in a sovereign way, in technology and trade; the USSR saw elements of its world abandoning the Marxist-Leninist system of its 'bloc', and the bloc itself. But while the USA was already the principal link in the chain of interdependence, and had only to conform thenceforward with its rule, the Soviet entry into the world of interdependence requires a complete restructuring (*perestroika*) of the Soviet system and empire. Moreover, just as it sought peace with the USA and 'the West' so as to proceed with that formidable restructuring, the USA, under Reagan, found, or claimed to have found, a new military technology of a kind to convince Gorbachev of the hopelessness of continuing the cold war.

# I

# PERSONAL CIRCUMSTANCES AND HISTORICAL ANTECEDENTS

It is said[3] that Ronald Reagan, when asked on completing his degree in economics at the Eureka College, to which career he intended to devote his many gifts, answered unhesitatingly: 'show business'. Of course he had good personal reasons for this unexpected and, at the time, rather unusual choice. He had already won a personal award for his own performance in a play for which his college had won a distinction in an academic competition. He was attractive to look at and had a warm, deep voice. He was already aware that he was a born communicator. In spite of the fact that in order to pay his tuition fees he had to earn money by doing menial domestic work in the College, thus carrying a double burden, he was very popular with the other students. He led various student teams in sports and drama, and became president of the students' union.

But it is hardly probable that Reagan had the slightest intuition that by following his vocation he was going to make history in two senses. In a personal sense, because he was to be the first, and still remains the only, show business man, ex-professional actor and announcer, ever to accede to this highest of political positions. And in a more general sense because it was in his time that politics and teledemocracy fused, for technological reasons into the area of show business, and he himself became the symbol of that fusion of public activities.

The formal similarities between theatrical and political performances have been evident to philosophers at least since the days of the city republic of Athens. Both performances take place in public, more often than not in a public place: arena, forum, amphitheatre, and for a public audience, in short for 'the public'. The success of both depends on the ability of the performer, orator or actor, to *persuade* the public to believe in the propositions he advances, on his own behalf in the case of a politician, on behalf of the character he impersonates in the case of an actor, and in the sincerity of their feelings and emotions in both cases.

Both are *acting*, but here the word divides into a pun. The political actor produces an action – or indeed determines other people to take an action or decision. He is an actor in the sense that Hobbes gave to the word. The dramatic actor imitates an action, true, or imaginary, and his intention is to carry the public with him into the illusion. Essentially, both perform an act of make-belief, but whereas the political actors use that belief to commit 'the public' to the reality of the decision they propose, the dramatic actors offer 'the public' the possibility to escape reality for a while, and take them into the orbit of illusion. Here again, the words no longer suffice – for does not the political actor, when he promises a glorious future to the public he wants to lead, also practise illusionism? To be sure, both use *words, communicate* with the public by means of words. Thus the two professions are linked by their use of rhetoric. But whereas the orator speaks his own words, the actor speaks those written by another. This explains the ultimate tinge of contempt for the politician who behaves like an actor, so clearly described by Aristotle in his *Rhetoric* (II, 2), when he says that: 'the influence of the declaimers or actors is greater nowadays than that of the poet [who writes his own verses] . . . so it is also in political competitions owing to the depraved character of our politics . . . Political oratory is more difficult for the sufficient reason that it relates to the future.'

In his essay, 'Masks and Actors',[4] Maurice Cranston delves into Rousseau's celebrated contempt for actors and his admiration for political orators. 'Why does Rousseau insist so much on the moral distinction between the two? The explanation may be connected with the strong feeling Rousseau had about the disjunction between appearance and reality . . . The theatre was bad, because it was an admitted temple of illusions.' Indeed, in his *Lettre à Monsieur d'Alembert*, Rousseau insults the art of the actor as 'an art of counterfeit the art of assuming a personality other than his own', or of 'simulating passion while his feelings are cold'. This last reproach was afterwards amplified by another Academician, not d'Alembert, this time, but Diderot, in his *Paradoxe sur le Comédien*, translated into English as *The Paradox of Acting*.[5] According to Diderot the paradox lies in the fact that the best actor is he who does not feel any emotion, who is constantly lucid and in control of himself, for only so can he convey to the audience the emotion and sensibilities of the part he is playing. 'One is one's self by nature; the heart one is supposed to have is not the heart one has . . . What then is a great actor? A man who, having learnt the words set down for him by the author, fools you thoroughly, whether in tragedy or in comedy.' Diderot's accusation that the actor is inherently hypocritical or untrustworthy was turned upside down by Stanislavsky, who considered the so-called hypocrisy to be the fundamental condition of the quality of acting. His influential school is centred around the capacity of the actor always to remain in control of his cool rationality, which alone enables him to express the emotions of the character he is representing. But while theatrical methodology is far from our present concerns, what matters in the case of Reagan's unique reconciliation of two careers, until then so opposed, is the general feeling in society that actors are irresponsible.

There are many reasons for this feeling. One is the general belief that actors, and even more so actresses, display a personal indifference towards morality. Diderot goes so far as to suspect the very motivations of the vocation. 'What makes them slip on the sock or the buskin?' he exclaims. 'Want of education, poverty, a libertine spirit. The stage is a resource, never a choice. Never did an actor become so from any of the honourable motives which might incline a right mind, a feeling heart, a sensitive soul to so fine a profession!' While Diderot obviously exaggerates, it is nevertheless true that society in general used to relegate actors to a social world of their own – in Reagan's America, in the golden cage of Hollywood. This made Reagan's transition from that world of irresponsibility to the essentially responsible world of politics all the more remarkable.

Another cause of the suspicion that actors are irresponsible is the distrust instinctively felt towards those whose talent and profession is that of simulation. The basic words which express the essence of the profession, 'playing' and 'part', run counter to the full commitment implied in responsibility. And yet another reason for distrust is the ability to impersonate other human beings. When and where does the real person, Stanislavsky's lucid actor, end, and the illusory character, which he represents, begin? Here we enter the realm of Pirandello. One of his many plays, which are all variations on the theme of the inseparability of illusion and reality, is particularly significant as a portrayal of the incompatibility between acting in politics and dramatic acting. This is *Enrico IV*. The setting and the performance of the actors are all aimed at confirming the hero in his belief, after a brain injury, that he is the Emperor Henry IV of the Holy Roman Empire. But in fact he knows that he is no such person, but enjoys playing up to their play – only to fall back in the end into the same dilemma. 'He becomes permanently the person he had been representing', writes Pirandello. Where does Henry IV begin and the madman end? Jean Cocteau's witty remark that 'Victor Hugo was a madman who believed that he was Victor Hugo' takes the tragic dilemma even further.

Enlarged and intensified by the dimension of politics and the responsibilities politics bears, the dilemma of illusion and reality takes on quite different proportions. Nero, Ludwig II of Bavaria, are known cases of mad rulers. If, therefore, the boundary between reality and unreality, responsibility and irresponsibility, is so imperceptible, in circumstances at least apparently normal, how much more difficult is it to find it in people whose second nature is to impersonate, to be able to play at being someone else?

This distrust of impersonation is aggravated in politics by the distrust of manipulation. The technical basis of acting is the memorizing and reproducing of words written by others. 'Speak the speech, I pray you, as I pronounced it to you' says Hamlet sarcastically to the actor, and just as sarcastically Shakespeare the actor speaks through Hamlet. While Diderot writes: 'A man who having learnt the words set down to him by the author, fools you thoroughly.' The actor is manipulated by the author – but in politics, the question of who does the manipulating is primordial. Reagan himself for years directed and acted in a most successful programme for General Electric. In his political activities, he switched from the Democratic to the Republican Party. Was he only acting a number of parts, or worse still, reciting parts written for him in the political interests of these organizations, just as he had recited parts written for him in the commercial interests of General Electric and many other lesser companies? Where did the lucid actor Reagan end, who had played scenes of dramatic intensity on the screen, expressing the emotions of characters whom he was impersonating, and where did the fervent Republican politician and ideologist begin? Who produced the parts he played, and who held the strings of what Diderot stigmatized as the 'puppet'?

It was this distrust of the profession of the actor which led to an often quite intense revulsion when the news that Reagan might stand for the governorship of California began to spread. 'An actor!', exclaimed the *New York Times* contemptuously. And Brown, the Democratic governor of California whom he was going to dislodge, most successfully used the slogan: 'A *man* against an *actor!*' In 1966, when Nixon asked William Buckley Jr., a staunch Republican ideologist, why he thought it inconceivable for Reagan to be considered a candidate for the presidency, Buckley replied, as he tells himself: 'Because, I said, people won't get used to the notion of a former actor being President.'

For two reasons Reagan was able to bridge, for the first time, the 'inconceivable' gap between a dramatic and a political role, the latter being taken in a functional sense. ('In a role one is a person of a certain kind put in a certain kind of relationship, and thus detached from purely personal idiosyncrasy', writes Dorothy Emmett.[6]) The first has to do with his person, and is therefore incidental. The second, however, has to do with the developed society and its ways and means of cognition, and is therefore of universal significance.

To take the first first. Reagan was from the beginning a man of multiple interests, and accordingly of talents and of ambitions too. His intellect is a matter of controversy. His intimate friend, former chief domestic and economic policy adviser, and now his hagiographer, Martin Anderson, examines this point as follows:[7]

Some of his more left-wing enemies are convinced that he is rather stupid . . . Others simply see him as . . . someone who really doesn't understand much of what is going on . . . All these views are wrong . . . As Donald Regan observed, 'the President has a unique talent: he is serene internally. When he has made a decision, he lives with it. He doesn't fret over it. And most of all, he doesn't change his mind.'

But his mind had a positive propensity to simplify, a sharp discernment of the order of priorities, and a determination for what is called in Washington 'going to the mat' which, according to Anderson, means that 'if you start something you will finish it!'[8] Ever since his youth he displayed this versatility by taking a degree in economics, by showing a distinct dramatic and rhetoric talent, and by being an obviously natural leader of teams, whether student, sports, or political teams. All these aptitudes accorded with a sound ambition, which was oriented, as he said himself, towards that mixed area called show business.

That he started off as a radio football commentator was a matter of chance as in so many cases of first jobs. But even the somewhat casual way in which he was hired, provisionally, and for $5.00 a week, reflects the favourable way two of his qualities struck the manager of a local radio-station – qualities which were to be manifested in his statesmanship. These were his voice, full of inflexions, which remained one of the assets of his rhetoric, and more specifically the ability to persuade those able to listen to him of the reality of his illusions. Oddly enough, the test he was made to take by the employer's recruiting agent was to 'make him see' a football match which had taken place some time previously.[9] But even while he made constant progress in his job as a sports commentator on radio, he followed his father's work as a local administrator in Roosevelt's 'New Deal' in 1932, and acquired his first impressions of the work of the federal government. After less than five years of successful broadcasting, he inevitably progressed to Hollywood, where he easily passed the film tests, given his pleasant appearance and his overwhelming Irish charm. (But he had to conceal the fact that he wore spectacles; the introduction of contact lenses soon after saved him from that handicap. In his memoirs, significantly entitled *Where's the Rest of Me?*[10] he notes with typical humour, 'without the glasses I couldn't see him at all – but the important thing was he'd see me'.) Hired by Warner Brothers, he soon became, in his own words, 'the Errol Flynn of the Bs. I was as brave as Errol but in a low budget fashion!' . . . 'Like Flynn, Reagan did many of his own stunts, fighting, jumping, diving and the like. He was encouraged to do so: it enabled the director to cut his schedule in half by shooting over the villain's shoulder on Ron's face for most of the fight.'[11]

Though he was unable to take part in active service during the Second World War (unlike Eisenhower, Nixon, Kennedy or Bush) owing to his bad eyesight, Lt. Reagan was however assigned to various film studios to make films for military purposes, ending up at the Roach Studios, nicknamed 'Fort Roach', because of their military purposes. His technical knowledge and his power of imagination enabled him to produce films, for instance of Tokyo as seen from the height at which pilots flew, which surprised military experts by their accuracy.

But already before the outbreak of war the transition had taken place in Reagan's character between the two dangerously interrelated ways of *acting*, in the sense of producing an action or of simply being an actor who simulates. He had already achieved success in his career as a film actor, passing finally from B films to A films. But for personal and political motives he felt that he should get out of the world of make-believe in which he had excelled and into that of reality, if the two can ever be completely separated. His personal reasons are well known, especially as Reagan used the operative phrase as the title of the Memoirs published in 1966: 'Where is the Rest of Me?' This was a line in one of his best known films, *King's Row*, in which the character he played wakes up in a hospital, having had both his legs amputated, and exclaims: 'Where's the rest of me?' This line symbolized for him his own psychological problems. With lucid sincerity he described his condition of being an actor as that of a 'semi-automaton, *"creating" a character another had written, doing what still another person told me to do on the set* . . . Possibly this was the reason I decided to find the rest of me . . . I came out of the monastery of movies into the world'. (My italics, for the further purpose of wondering how authentic can a character be in the make-believe society, and also because the word 'creating', which Reagan himself put in quotation marks was to reappear in his slogan of a 'creative society'.)

The political reasons emerged from two sides. Reagan's real, if intermittent, interest in state administration had convinced him that the growth of social attributions and therefore of the political power of the federal government ran counter to the individualist, pluralist, and federalist philosophy of the Founding Fathers, of the 'elitist' Maddison as much as of the 'populist' Jefferson. But his increasing obligations first as a member, then director, and finally president of the Screen Actors Guild (SAG) during the period of particularly active communist-led strikes and communist political agitation in Hollywood gave a new dimension to his politics. Reagan, having seen with his own eyes the systematic infiltration of the capital of make-believe by the Communists, was by now convinced that their purpose was to use the film industry as a 'world wide propaganda base. In those days, before television and massive foreign film production, American films dominated 95 per cent of the world's movie screens. We had a weekly audience of about 500,000,000 souls.' His own understanding of how effective ideological indoctrination can be with the help of the instruments of make-believe in the era of world communication enabled him to assess adequately the cohintern plans and techniques.

Both his anti-statist and his anti-communist stances, the logic of which sometimes combine in the anti-totalitarian sentiment, estranged him from the Democratic Party, his father's party, and until then his own. That party had already begun to suffer from the internecine feud between its moderate and its radical wings. After a time Reagan joined the Republican Party and dedicated his theatrical talents and techniques to the Republican electoral campaigns, culminating in the campaign for Goldwater's presidency. In the meantime he was also the 'creator' of the 'General Electric Theatre', the most successful commercial programme ever sponsored by a giant corporation, and which ran for years. As a result Reagan became a public personality in his own right. Indeed he was the first of a new type of politician, much better prepared and armed for the politics of the age of information, i.e. a politician whose primary expertise lay in the new techniques of the 'media'. His original links with the media helped him to enjoy a new form of popularity, the popularity of *image*, while his technical knowledge of how to mount a 'show', and his personal friendships among the high administrators of 'show business', made it much easier for him than for professional politicians to adapt and use, for his personal purposes, the new instruments of mass politics. It was then that for the first time he had the opportunity to 'create his own character', and to impersonate it: the common-sense, confident, religious, traditional, robustly American, beguiling and jovial character called Ronald Reagan.

This public Ronald Reagan was to be president of the United States for two terms in the last decades of the twentieth century. The actor Reagan played himself with all the talent and using all the techniques and skills he had learnt when playing other roles. Yet the impression of naturalness which Reagan the actor gave to Reagan the statesman was not obtained without difficulty. Who for instance would have guessed that the easy way in which he spoke was made possible by scribbled notes done beforehand, in a system of personal hieroglyphs, in which he had condensed his thoroughly rehearsed phrases (later to be replaced by teleprompters)? Or that on the eve of his famous debate on television with Jimmy Carter, thanks to friends from the media, he had held a full dress rehearsal in the very hall which was to be used the next day, with dummy Carters posing questions, giving Reagan time to find the best answers?

## The coming of media politics

Far more important, and with a more general significance was the technological and social trend whereby, given the increasing impact made on society by the new media of communication and entertainment, politics itself was becoming a kind of 'show business'. This happened first in the United States and then in all industrial democracies. Reagan was the outstanding example of the new symbiosis between these two arts. The problem is well known and has been and is still most attentively studied. But a brief recapitulation of the main ways in which the techniques of media show-business became indispensable to political activities is still needed here.

Nothing could be more promising for the development of democracy than the increase in the quantity and the perfecting of the quality (in the sense of adequate information and consequently sound political judgement) of 'the people', the ultimate sovereign in representative political regimes. 'Participationist' political philosophers see this technical improvement of communications between political elites and 'citizens' as the long expected bridging of the gap between the two sides of the policy-making processes and as the coming of a 'strong democracy',[12] as Benjamin Barber describes the future political dialogue. The expression 'teledemocracy' is born from the hopeful future vision of the participation of the people at large in decisions and policies, as for instance by means of the increasingly fashionable method of 'phone-ins' in which citizens can question and argue directly with the opinion-makers, politicians, journalists, as well as media (especially TV) personalities. Thus each side can get a more complete picture of the other's feelings and intentions and seek to conciliate possible initial differences of view. But this would work to the advantage of democracy only if the exchanges were mutually influencing and a balance could be fairly drawn between the 'activism' of the opinion-makers and the passivity of the public. If a fair proportion could be established between the mass-penetration and the consequent mass-influence by the media and, on the other side, the open accessibility of the media to the genuine response of the millions of individuals to the questions which the media offer to raise in public discussion, then evidently political participation, that quantitative condition of democracy could be more of a consultation. But how to obtain a fair balance in such an inherently disproportionate equation is another matter.

Another obvious advantage for democracy, indeed a necessary condition for the proper functioning of the media in politics, is their independence from the state and/or the government in power. In most advanced industrial democracies, the media are either entrusted to independent public boards, or their existence is assured by commercial means or private ownership. As a result they escape the frightening fate of the media subjected in dictatorships to the total control and direction of the state. Moreover, modern dictatorships are also one-party states. Thus the lack of preference shown by the media towards one or another political grouping or party would constitute the first proof of the existence of 'free' media. The granting to all political parties or groups of access to the media so that they could publicize their ideas and opinions, equally, or at least in proportion to their electoral weight, is already a *fait accompli* of modern elections.

The fact that in most of the countries of the developed society great 'corporations' form all too visible oligopolies in the press, and especially in television, is said to be alleviated by the editorial independence of the managerial staff. It is true that each of these publicly or privately controlled corporations develop what is called their own 'spirit'. But in so far as programmes of collective discussion between representatives of opposing views prove to be particularly popular and effective, they establish a more direct, participatory contact between the elites and the public of modern society.

While, therefore, from a *quantitative* point of view, both the output and the input of political material by the media is of undeniable advantage to the democratic process – the assessment of the intrinsic *quality* of the presentation by the media is more controversial. What is meant here by quality, in relation to politics, is the fair combination of those essential ingredients of objective representation: accuracy, complete information, just discernment of the order of priority of the subjects, and last but not least, the elimination of bias in presentation. Because of the limitations of their own *format*, the media, and especially television, cannot always fulfil these conditions. Generally speaking, no private or public corporation of information diffusion can be expected to provide fully all four elements of objective communication. The limitations of their own format, i.e. the total volume possible, on the one hand, and the balance between advertising and civic and political interest, on the other, constrains them to be selective, and selectivity runs counter to objectivity.

At least subliminally, but more often than not explicitly, what was called the 'spirit' of press, radio or television corporations does influence the political coverage. Of course the reader or listener can neutralize the preconceived approach of each individual newspaper or radio-station, of different nationality or language, by getting a fair sample of all of them – but this is an obviously excessively time-consuming exercise for a normal citizen. In television, especially, which brings us back to Reagan's political success, for it was the guardian angel of his extraordinary career, even such an effort would prove to be in vain, given the reduced number of stations, the relatively small apportionment of daily programmes to politics and news as against 'entertainment', and the pursuit of localism which prevails in the media. Accessibility to other sources is precluded by the distance between the viewer and the non-local, and especially the non-national sources. But, however this will be remedied, at least in part, by the new methods of worldwide transmission by means of 'cable' and 'dish'.

But television's own permanent *attachment* is to the 'image', the fact that it is an image-conditioned medium of communication leads to another technical form of bias. The insoluble 'chicken and egg' relationship between television and its maker/product, 'image', affects television's contribution to modern political information in three ways. First, it makes it give priority to items and subjects more suitable for 'image' coverage, than for narrative or explanatory coverage. The effects of this technical bias on political information are too well known to be repeated here. I would only volunteer one less well-known example. The summit meeting of the European Council, held at the European Parliament in Luxemburg in 1985 was particularly significant as it ended in a dramatic fiasco. Its aborted agenda covered several subjects of great importance for all the member countries and for the world. During that session there was also a minor incident: from a passing motorcycle someone threw a minuscule bomb on to the grass verge of the precincts of the European Parliament. After the session a study was undertaken, under the auspices of the European Commission, in order to monitor the reporting of the important political events of the session by all media channels in all twelve member-countries. The result was that some did not cover it at all; some allotted a fair time – on average 2.20 minutes, out of which 70 seconds were allotted to the political events, including the ritual picture of the twelve leaders on the steps of the building, and 1.50 minutes to the unrecorded explosion, the grass verges, the police dogs running hither and thither, and the Luxemburg ambulances hastening unnecessarily to the spot. The 'image' reigned.

Walter Cronkite, the well-known American TV commentator, once argued that image journalism at least cannot lie, and that pictures speak for themselves. But Giovanni Sartori has rejected his argument and pointed out that

pictures can lie with infinitely greater effectiveness than has hitherto been the case with written journalism. For one thing, it is much easier: the lying

222

is left to the scissors. You select one image out of a hundred, and you have a much better alibi for discarding the remaining ninety-nine than the journalist whose lines are not so scarce as TV seconds.[13]

Secondly, the primacy of image has the same consequence as films of making faces appearing on the box into stars in their own right. More telegenic politicians and interviewees of all kinds profit too from this conditioned popularity of all kinds. Ronald Reagan's career provides the definitive example of this process. But it also leads to the indisputable control by the staff of the television station of the content of the programmes produced in their establishment, because of their technological know-how, and often also because they choose whom to 'invite'. In his careful inquiry into 'Teledemocracy',[14] Atterton stresses that even in cases of non-commercial educational political programmes, the TV producer dictates how to 'organize' the programme, decides on its component lengths, and chooses the most TV-relevant questions. Besides, in the end this creates the well-known 'narcissism' from which TV professionals, producers and presenters, are known to be suffering.

Thirdly, the image-dominated TV political productions, consciously or unconsciously, introduce the competitive element which belongs more properly to theatrical or sporting performances. A political discussion on television, more especially a confrontation between two candidates, must have a gladiatorial slant: who wins (who is better looking, cleverer, wittier, etc. of the two) is much more important than the force of the ideas they have respectively attempted to put forward. Malcolm Muggeridge once remarked that people always said: 'I *saw* you on television, never I *heard* you.' And Sartori notes that 'the man who reads, the Gutenberg man, is forced to be a mental animal: the man who only watches is only an ocular animal. The impoverishment promises to be of devastating proportions!'

Finally, of late, a new kind of programme has increased even more the element of make-believe, namely political science fiction. They are, as Walter B. Wriston stresses, 'The so-called TV docudramas, part fact, part fiction', which 'attempt to change the record of past events'. Fiction and reality are then cooked together by the TV chefs and their aids (advisers, consultants, researchers) into an inseparable TV omelette, in which the viewers can no longer separate truth from imagination. More recently, a great scandal was caused in the United States when it was reported that a CBS programme had been shown about Afghanistan, in which Mr Dan Rather, one of the best-known TV personalities, was involved, and which was allegedly faked. In

London, it was discovered that London Weekend Television had produced a faked interview with a member of its staff presented to the public as a 'man in the street'. And the Czechoslovak Legal Commission appointed by President Havel as well as the book published by the head of Agence France Presse on Romania have proved how the KGB manipulated television in the recent events in those two countries.

It was thus from this world of make-believe, of the inseparable mixture of information and illusionism, that Ronald Reagan emerged in to political life, and easily climbed to the top. Moreover, what is more significant is that both in his own personality, as in the characteristically 'more direct links' he established between leader and people, illusion and reality remained inseparable. To be sure, he was not the 'puppet' manipulated from Wall Street and Maddison Avenue, as many critics believed; nor was he a simple actor expecting to be given a part to play and a text to recite. He was a true 'persona' in himself and a leader on his own, even if his leadership was reduced, as it could be, to the essentials – and he had his own, simple, established order of priorities. Moreover, as discussed later, the mixture of illusion and reality in his own personality was characteristic and also reproduced some of his major ideas, like the celebrated Strategic Defence Initiative, which when he announced it after a couple of years of preparation, so strangely coincided with the release of the very successful film, *Star Wars*. But of this more later. Here we conclude these reflections on how Reagan was the first personality in history in whom were combined subjectively the talent of the actor and of the statesman, while technically these were mixed with the media show business and the telepolitics or political show business. But there remains the nagging question of how far he had accomplished this change by his own belief, or by his power of make-believe? When one remembers the host of artificial means which he personally used, assisted by the technical fraternity of the media, to prepare in detail the 'image' which had to be projected, one may well wonder how much room was left in that 'image' for the authentic character to come through. In a rather critically one-sided book, Garry Wills put forward the thesis that there was between the President and the people 'a complicity of make belief',[15] an interpretation continued in depth by C. Fred Alford[16] according to whom 'Reagan's appeal stems in good measure from his perceived ability to govern . . . by the way in which he soothes American "anxieties" about a decline in national capabilities.'

There was nothing exceptional about the fact that the 'anxieties' from which the American people had suffered of late were, to use a medical metaphor, psychosomatic. What was new and strange was that the American public could not know until the end of Reagan's presidency whether their recovery had been promoted more by his gift for carrying an audience into easy illusions, or whether 'the rest of him', that is the statesmanship which he manifested, first as governor of California, and later as President of the United States, had the solidity of reality. These are the problems to be examined in the next two sections. But what is evident is that with his presidency modern democracy had already entered the age of media politics.

## Governor to President

The period of Reagan's official political activity stretches from 1 January 1967, when he was elected governor of California for two consecutive terms, to 1 January 1989, when he concluded his two-term presidency of the United States. In the interval between 1974 and 1981, when he campaigned for other Republican candidates and lost one campaign for himself, he perfected and finalized his political *persona*. As a conservative reply to Lyndon Johnson's slogan of a future 'great society', he found the slogan of the 'future creative society'. And he polished the endless variations of 'the speech' originally called 'A Time to Choose', which he had first delivered on 27 October 1964, when campaigning for Goldwater. In that most brilliant 'Speech' he revealed for the first time the 'practical dream' which he continued thereafter to offer to the Americans. The 'Speech' was such a public success that the respected journalist David Broder described it as 'the most successful national political debut since W. Jennings Bryan electrified the 1896 Democratic Convention'.

The campaign for the governorship of California then confirmed the salient features of his statesmanship: an exceptional ability to communicate with the people, a clear, even if somewhat simplistic public philosophy, an apparently genuine determination to apply it, a permanent and stimulating sense of optimism and confidence, as well as the indispensable qualities of good health and good luck. The element of luck played its part in the election to the governorship of California, when the self-appointed 'youth' leader, Stokely Carmichael, made a particularly violent speech, cheered by 20,000 students on the Berkeley campus of the University of California, driving them to shout in unison 'To hell with the draft' (for the Vietnam war). This proved to be the last nail in the coffin of Governor

Brown's chances of being elected on the Democratic ticket. Indeed, the whole issue of the rapidly deteriorating reputation of the campus at Berkeley since 1964 had proved to be a constant advantage for the Republican–Conservative candidate, as against the Democratic–Progressive candidate. (In the campaign against Carter, Reagan's luck held again. The Iranian hostage issue became the most important, so important indeed, that ill-advised as he often was, Carter decided not to campaign in order to concentrate exclusively on the question of the hostages, and lost in both fields as a result. Soon Fate was going to take its revenge on Reagan in a similar case.)

Reagan's campaign for governorship was naturally based on the slogan of the states against Washington. Although federalism is at the core of the American pluralistic, and therefore democratic, conception of politics, it was evident that Article 4 of the Constitution, which sets out the decentralized relations between the governments of the 'united states' and the central government of the United States, was increasingly being interpreted in a way which leant towards the latter. The growth of welfare economics since Roosevelt's New Deal, and the economic, industrial and political compression of responsibilities caused by the Second World War, are the main reasons for this concentration of power in the federal institutions in Washington. According to Reagan's campaign message the increasing cost of the welfare state was the main cause of the increasing budget deficit of the United States as a whole. Lyndon Johnson's plans for a 'great society' raised the level of federal expenditure to a critical extent. This was aggravated by the fact that because some, indeed many of the states were reluctant to commit themselves to the costly social services implied in that plan, the federal grants and subsidies bypassed them and were delivered straight to the local authorities in charge of these services.

This double reduction of the power of the states gave the Republican opposition the opportunity for a two-pronged attack, against inflationary state policies and in favour of federal decentralization. Nixon had already launched the slogan of 'new federalism'. But in 1966, it became Reagan's principal campaign theme. 'Instead of harassing business and industry with regressive taxes, let's adopt a creative approach. We have a leadership gap in Sacramento. They abdicated their responsibility and they continue to seek the answer to every California problem in Washington', he claimed again and again. His other principal themes were the freedom of the individual, the restoration of moral values, notably a campaign against obscenity, and of national values, the latter directed specifically against the campus of the University of Berkeley. The theme of the 'creative society', in which the initiative of the free individual and of local institutions would win back the command now usurped by the egg-head forces of Washington and the Ivy League intelligentsia, crowned it all.

But once elected, Reagan's governorship of eight years proved a considerable success. This is how Lee Edwards sums up very partially his record:[17] *Spending*: when Reagan took office, California was spending a million dollars more each day than it was taking in. When he left he turned over to his successor 554 million dollars. *Taxes*: He was the biggest tax-cutter in the state's history, enacting over $5.7 billion in tax relief. The passage of Proposition 13, in June 1978, which reduced property taxes [rates] to 1 per cent of their 1975 value, can be considered as the birth of the tax limitation movement in America. *Welfare reform*: Many of the measures proposed by the Welfare Reform Task Force and adopted, as for instance: stiffer penalties for welfare fraud, obligation for financially able parents to support minor children who left home and went on welfare, and vice-versa, the obligation of adult children to support their aged parents if able to do so, had obvious positive results. *Crime*: Reagan created the first ever Inter-Agency Council on Drug Abuse and re-introduced capital punishment for most serious crimes. *Education*: He re-introduced order, with some severity, in Berkeley, so that when in 1969–70, Columbia, Harvard, Cornell, Kent, had to close, Berkeley remained open. But at the same time he increased the aid to the state university from 240 million to some 500 million dollars. *Consumer Affairs*: In 1970 Reagan consolidated all the various state consumer protection bureaucracies into one single Department of Consumer Affairs, the first such agency in the nation. *Environment*: Under Reagan, California adopted the severest anti-smog laws in the country and the strongest water pollution law in US history.

While Lee Edwards is obviously inclined to see mainly the good points of Reagan's governorship, Reagan's critics stressed his indifference toward the problems of employment, of the ethnic minorities and of poverty, indeed of the poverty of the welfare policies in California. Moreover, the problem of welfare allocations, centralized in Washington had created a new inter-governmental relation, which served to open Reagan's eyes towards the interdependence in modern politics. The age of welfare had brought with it new constraints upon the federal system, observable only under the angle of interdependence. The social obligations contracted, under the orders of the central government, by each of the states towards their populations, in matters of health, pensions, and education rendered skilful co-ordination necessary between them and between each of them and the central government.

The necessity of contributing to, and allocating the funds needed for the implementation of even a limited national welfare programme (the expression welfare state is even more illogical in the context of American society than it is in general) showed up the inadequacy, in these new circumstances, of the system of intergovernmental relations, complacently described until the 1960s as 'cooperative federalism', with its political corollary of 'consensus'. The obligation to provide increasingly large grants and subsidies weighed heavily on the budgets of the individual states, and even more on that of the federal government. To this had to be added the spiralling costs of defence exacted by the cold war – yet another national constraint. Seen from the point of view of a local governor, in this case that of the important state of California, the problem of financing these national policies seemed to resemble very much what the American economist Lester Thurow[18] had illuminatingly called 'the zero-sum society' in which the advantage obtained by one partner must be a loss for others.

If that description was somewhat metaphoric, in reality from this point of view too, America had entered the age of interdependence. The American states were no longer united by a 'cooperative federalism', but constrained to co-exist in an atmosphere of interdependence. David MacKay is right when he states: 'The 1960s and 1970s were quite different. Consensus on the nature and extent of government intervention largely broke down; jurisdictions were in competition with one another for federal or state aid, and above all governments became economically and politically *interdependent*' [19] and further defines this change as 'competitive interdependence'. The 'competition' in the Federal budget between the increasing welfare and the increasing military expenditure was, for instance, a direct proof of the national–international interdependence. This idea seems to have occurred also to Governor Reagan of California – and led him to think at the end of his successful governorship that the local problems of California and the national problems of the United States were part and parcel of wider developments. Although the Californian problems required the local and national treatment which he thought could be supplied by the 'creativity' of their own society and resources, he also realized that there were other, much vaster and higher causes affecting all of them.

So that while Reagan, with undeniable sincerity denounced as governor the interference of Washington in what was and ought to remain 'a dual sovereignty', and while he preached restraint and economy at home, his eyes were already fixed on the situation of the United States in the developed society as a whole. Seen from Los Angeles Washington might have been a 'harassing' bureaucracy, dictating its commands to the other 'states'. But Washington itself, as capital of the United States, was acting under the constraint of internal and external obligations and pressures. What Reagan now wanted was to gain access to the conning-tower from which one gets the whole view, and from which he could detect how and whether the vessel of the United States could be made to chart another course. His ideas, too, sprang from the new sentiment of *limitation* which had begun to prevail in contemporary American political thought since the Vietnam war. But while some inclined towards the theory of decline (which he instinctively abhorred) and some inclined towards neo-isolationism (which he instinctively shared, but found no longer practicable rationally), he imagined that there was a third way: his 'practical dream'. Soon he presented himself, on behalf of his 'practical dream' as a candidate for the presidency, which he won in 1981.

## II
## REAGAN'S POLICIES OF INTERDEPENDENCE

Reagan's success as governor of California and his popular victory in the presidential campaign proved that he possessed at least three of the most important political qualities. The first two were his ability to persuade people that his policies were the right ones and secondly, his ability to have his policies implemented. Thenceforward the two qualities were combined into one simple talent of leadership, and the two previous personalities, the actor and the administrator, merged into one politician particularly gifted for the task of President of the United States in the media age: 'the great communicator' as he has been called ever since. The third political quality Reagan possessed was, once again, the indispensable providence, which was going to pay a greater part in his presidency than in many previous ones, notably in the three which preceded his.

But, as has been argued at length in these pages, there is a difference of substance between a politician and a statesman, just as there is, for different reasons a considerable difference between knowing how to handle the problems of persuasive communication, and how to handle the problems of policy-making – particularly for the leader of the major super-power in the age of interdependence. Did Reagan ever prove to possess this latter ability too, which is the accolade of modern statesmanship? The answer, which contains a grain of ambiguity, is that he incontestably presented both an overall strategic vision and an overall economic vision – partly deriving from his long acceptance of Republican Party tenets, but partly his own. In some respects his ideological liberalism fitted in with the strategic and economic conditions of the USA in the age of interdependence. But, first a brief analysis of Reagan's policies of strategic and economic interdependence. Though considered separately, they form a single whole.

## Strategic interdependence

There were two personal reasons why President Reagan was able to embrace and keep within one perspective the disorderly, more often than not seemingly incongruous events and developments which buffeted the vessel of his state. One reason was that, according to his nearest and most intimate counsellors and aides, he had an innate capacity to 'simplify' the problems put to him and to his administration. Or to put it differently, Reagan could not even be bothered to examine problems unless they were reduced to their essentials. Much has been written about his endless propensity to 'delegate' the cluster of problems submitted to the White House for decision to members of his team or, especially, to 'task forces', until they had been properly distilled. Only then was the essence presented to him for his consideration. Even then, he preferred the presentation to be as brief as possible, often in the form of the 'one page memo'. His critics have attributed this method of work to his reputed laziness. His collaborators vehemently deny that he was lazy, some argue on the contrary that he was a 'workaholic'. The fact is however that this method of work has been proved in the past to be more conducive to statesmanship than the agitated curiosity of those leaders who think that they must know everything and be personally consulted about everything.

The second reason why Reagan was able to embrace the whole field of vision within one unifying perspective was that he had a political vision of his own. This political vision simplified matters by giving them an order of priority which, even if based on national aspirations rather than on international realities, achieved a coherence of its own. Martin Anderson,[20] for instance, tells us that from the very beginning of his presidency, Reagan established strategic priorities, and that he topped them with the clear commandment: *'National*

*Security was number one and economic policy was number two.'* This might have surprised some of his team, because the great merit of his governorship lay in its economic policies, the famous 'Reaganomics'. He had successfully experimented with them in California, and he had promised to apply them now to the ailing American economy. Indeed, the first eighteen months of his presidency were devoted to the new fiscal and financial policies, and provided him with a brilliant, if somewhat short-lived success.

But in reality a closer reading of the 1980–81 budget, so hotly disputed between the Republican President and the Democratic Congress, discloses that the other purpose of the compression inflicted by 'Reaganomics' on domestic non-defence expenditures was to increase massively the expenditure on defence. Spending on defence rose by seven billion dollars, compared with Carter's last budget, while non-defence domestic expenditure was 41 billion dollars lower. From then on, military expenditure continued to escalate rapidly, reaching heights unprecedented since the Vietnam war, indeed higher in real dollar terms. And the real defence spending went up by 17 per cent in the first budget. As David Stockman shows,[21] it was also much easier to increase the military budget at the very beginning of the presidency, while the Democrats were still afflicted by the succession of defeats ranging from Johnson's Vietnam to Carter's Iran. This was accompanied by a big political campaign designed to reawaken American pride, and to present the new 'unified' strategy. The first three years of Reagan's first presidency (1981–84) were marked in matters of foreign policy by a particularly critical, strident and alarmist style, constantly denouncing the communist danger. Left-wing commentators, in America as well as in Western Europe, at once called it 'the end of *détente*' or 'the new cold war', and maintained that it was deliberately instigated by the new Administration, and above all by its president, with his inflammatory rhetoric.

The USSR and the Soviet bloc were described in that rhetoric as a universal conspiracy, preparing single-mindedly for the conquest and eternal domination of the free world and above all of the United States, the principal power and main defender of that world. Already Carter, in the last phase of his unhappy presidency, had seen in the occupation of Afghanistan by Russian troops a new omen of the permanently aggressive intentions of the USSR. But for Reagan, as far as can be ascertained from his rhetoric, the USSR was the 'evil empire' and the cause of all the external dangers threatening the USA and, as a result, of the internal dangers as well. This conception rejected the perpetuation of the possible 'co-existence' of a free world and of a communist world. Whereas, ever since 1945, the 'Truman doctrine' had assessed the Stalinist policies as a constant danger of a military offensive against the free world, it had also devised the policy of 'containment' in its two versions. For George Kennan, who was the main theoretician, both of the expression and of the interpretation of containment, it signified the West's ability and obligation to defend itself against Soviet aggression, thus 'containing' the fundamentally precarious USSR and the Soviet bloc within its own contradictions until it 'mellowed' by itself. For Truman, and Dean Acheson, especially at the beginning, it meant opposing 'communist' aggression in principle.

But, helped by the increasingly aggressive Stalinist policy of the USSR, 'containment' was replaced in the political vocabulary of the Eisenhower presidency by the expression 'liberation', with such slogans as 'roll back the Soviet armies from Europe'. Under John Foster Dulles, American foreign policy became a doctrine of active confrontation with a somewhat more offensive character than the defensive character typical of containment. But already in the North Korean 'confrontation', and especially in the Vietnam war, the 'communists' proved to be formidable adversaries.

With his 'simplifying' mentality, Reagan declared that the Vietnam war had been unjustly and unnecessarily lost because of weak American political leadership; and that only total American superiority in armament could satisfy a responsible American government. Moreover, with strange intonations of true pacifism, and in accordance with his usual populist electoral style, he expressed his revulsion against the logic of deterrence, implied in the strategy of Mutual Assured Destruction (MAD!); and still on the grounds of populist pacifism, he expressed his disbelief in the SALT treaties as negotiated by Nixon and Ford and signed by Carter with L. I. Brezhnev, because in his view they allowed both sides to keep enough nuclear weapons to ensure mutual destruction. Anderson describes how surprised he was one day in 1976 when, during the electoral campaign, he was flying with Reagan, to hear him intervening in a discussion on nuclear policy: 'You know, I've always liked the idea of START instead of SALT. What we should be trying to do is to reduce the number of nuclear weapons not just limit their growth. Instead of talks to limit the growth of nuclear weapons we should be having *St*rategic *A*rms *R*eduction *T*alks – Start.' Meanwhile, by a further process of simplification, the duel between the USA and the USSR was carried on over the whole world. America's aim was to win as many positions as possible from which to combat 'the source of all evil'. Some, though by no means all, authors even spoke of a 'Reagan doctrine'. This is for instance how Robert W. Tucker describes it:

What came to be known as the Reagan doctrine provides an instructive example of this ability to balance two quite different worlds, The Reagan Doctrine, *qua* doctrine, proclaims a new international order in which the legitimacy of the governments will no longer rest simply on their effectiveness, but on conformity with the democratic process. Governments that have come to power without fulfilling the requirements of that process are to be regarded as illegitimate. Against such illegitimate governments, and particularly against Marxist-Leninist governments, there is a right of intervention. The Reagan Doctrine asserts America's 'moral responsibility' for aiding popular insurgencies against communist domination. Such support is also considered to express the vital security interests of the nation. Since freedom and democracy are, in Mr. Reagan's words, 'the best guarantors of peace', support for popular insurgencies is no more than self defense.

The obvious criticism to be made of the Reagan Doctrine is not unlike that made of its famous predecessor, the Truman Doctrine. Both doctrines proclaim an apparently unlimited and indiscriminate commitment while holding out the messianic hope of redeeming history. But, in its pretensions the Reagan Doctrine goes even further. The Truman Doctrine set forth a policy of containing the Soviet Union and other communist governments, not of overthrowing them. The great postwar pronouncement was directed to the defense of the status quo against certain kinds of change, not to overturning that part of the status quo regarded as illegitimate. By contrast, the inspiration of the Reagan Doctrine is offensive. Its intent is to show that Communist revolutions are indeed reversible, thereby exploding a crucial myth!'[22]

The 'Reagan Doctrine' was therefore, *in its public intentions*, an accentuation of the Truman Doctrine. Like the Truman Doctrine, it saw two sides of the world, two blocs wrestling over the rest of it. What is best called *hostile* interdependence was thus at the basis of American foreign policy ever since 1945. Keohane and Nye explained it in 1977 as follows: 'The United States and the Soviet Union have been . . . interdependent throughout the post war period. Not only are the two countries sensitive to each other's security decisions. Exactly the high level of interdependence in one area – military security – coupled with mutual antagonism has been at the heart of traditional analysis of world politics.'[23] But world politics, in the literal sense of the word, have existed only since the second half of the twentieth century. Since then, until very recently, the makers of US foreign policy have been aware of hostile interdependence. Reagan however, simplified it into a duel between the USA and the USSR, fought out in the whole world, a kind of chess-game (but with jokers). He saw this 'linkage' operating in all directions and modifying all other connections. Developing countries and continents

had, in this perspective, widely adopted a balancing attitude, waiting
to see with which of the two blocs to align themselves for economic
or ideological reasons, indeed switching from one to the other by
means of sudden internal *coups d'état* or revolutions. American foreign policy was particularly concerned with this problem in Latin
America.

In order to preserve the remnants of the Monroe Doctrine which
regarded Latin America as the North American backyard, even the
Truman Doctrine, which had not yet been affected by the installation
of a communist government in Cuba, was formulated in terms of
a universal defence of free peoples against communist subversion.
North Korea and Vietnam were to be considered in this perspective
as threatened by the same danger as Cuba, Chile or Nicaragua; or
to put it in other words, as geo-political pawns in the same game
of chess. For Reagan, of course, the advance of the Sandinistas in
Nicaragua was of more direct interest. Unrepentant as regards the
Vietnam war, indeed believing on the contrary that it had been lost
owing to the weakness of the Democratic Administration, he wanted
above all to stop the communist rot from spreading into yet another
country in the American hemisphere.

He wanted to be free to act, by using any means to put a quick
end to that new Soviet-directed offensive in Latin America. But the
fact is that he was faced with the opposition of Congress, and of a
public opinion which clamoured for 'no more Vietnam'. Thus, while
publicly – in the media – his doctrine of foreign policy went further
than that of any previous president (with the possible exception of
John Foster Dulles's doctrine of 'liberation' during Eisenhower's
presidency), it was restrained in fact not only by his own ultimate
shrewd caution but also by his conviction that a global solution to
the America–Soviet duel, which lay at the root of all the conflicts,
was required. In the case of Nicaragua, he insisted on military aid
to the Contras even if not with official US forces.

## The SDI

For several dissimilar reasons Reagan concentrated on the USA—
USSR confrontation. He knew that the USA had to achieve military
superiority again, and he quickly succeeded by pouring billions of dollars into American re-equipment. He also sensed that the USSR had
entered a phase of 'immobilism', counting more on military than on
revolutionary advances, or as Lawrence Freedman puts it: 'Certainly
the Reagan Administration's combative instincts were tempered by

the lack of enthusiasm in Moscow for a fight. With the leadership so-bered by frustrating experiences in Afghanistan there were no Soviet adventures in the 1980s comparable to those of the previous decade'.[24]

Reagan's faith in the ultimate American military and technical su-periority was one premiss of this reasoning. 'The only way the Soviets will stop their drive for military superiority is when they realize that we are willing to go all out in an arms race. Right now people say there is an arms race, but the Soviets are the only ones racing. If we release the forces of the economy to produce the weapons we need the Soviets will never be able to keep up. And then, and only then, will they become reasonable and willing to seriously consider reductions in nuclear weapons', he is quoted by Anderson as saying in private to his policy advisers, even during the first presidential campaign.[25] Finally, his main reason was, perhaps, his 'practical dream' of a total and absolute defensive weapon.

This derived from Reagan's original populist longing for peace. As mentioned above, 'treaties' on limitation of growth, and even of numbers of nuclear weapons, seemed to him to be useless as long as the arsenals retained by the powers were still sufficient to cause irreparable damage, indeed to 'assure mutual destruction' (MAD); besides, he also had no great confidence in treaties – bits of paper which could be torn up and thrown away at any time. But, at the same time, if one were to accept that, on the one hand there is a natural propensity in artists of all kinds towards fantasy and imagination, and on the other hand, that the young Reagan manifested clear populist political sentiments, one can believe that deep in him there lay a great longing for peace, and that his imagination might have made him 'dream' of future peace on earth.

Perhaps the nearest he came to the spontaneous public expression of this vision of the future occurred for the first time when he had lost the candidature for the Republican presidential nomination in 1976, and was unexpectedly called to speak to the Convention. He was forced to improvise, and in those circumstances, he suddenly referred to a letter he might write now, but which would only be read in a hundred years, and to what people then might think of the achievements of his generation: 'Will they look back with appreciation and say "Thank God, for those people in 1976 who headed off that loss of freedom, who kept our world from nuclear destruction?" And if we fail, they probably won't get to read our letter at all . . .'

Reagan's 'practical dream' was to find a new defence technology which would protect the American territory from any kind of nuclear attack – and which could not be produced, for financial and technical reasons, by the USSR. Its realization started in great secret, and was known to only a few of Reagan's advisers. According to Anderson, who claims to have been one of the few, he was himself responsible for the inclusion in August 1979 of a new section in the Policy Memorandum No 3 for the Republican Party campaign. This new section demanded that a new ABM (Anti-Ballistic Missile) system should be devised – which should

> concentrate on defense, upon making sure that enemy missiles never strike US soil . . . If it could be done, it would be a major step towards redressing the military balance of power, and it would be a purely defensive step . . . Reagan embraced the principle of missile defense wholeheartedly. The only real question he raised was: 'Can we do it? Is the technology available?' And later, 'How soon can we do it? How much will it cost?'[26]

But already, in spite of the fact that nothing had as yet been undertaken, the Republican platform for the 1980 election contained a cryptic sentence: 'We will proceed with vigorous research and development of an effective anti-ballistic missile system, such as is already at hand in the Soviet Union, as well as modern ABM technologies.' What lay behind this unnoticed but pregnant sentence was Reagan's 'practical dream', or rather the transition between the Utopia of the film, *Star Wars*, (in which the forces of good succeed in defeating the forces of evil) and Reagan's political pursuit of what he was going later to call his 'Strategic Defense Initiative'.

We shall follow Anderson's description of the early stages of the development for a few more steps not only because he is the 'witness' who volunteers to give the most complete details about the 'making' of SDI, but also because, in the exercise, he also gives very piquant descriptions of how important policies could be prepared in the White House without the knowledge and behind the back of the government of the day. Thus Stephen Hess[27] reminds us that 'because existing federal agencies have sometimes failed to do an adequate job, presidents have tried to fill the void by creating new White House offices'. Anderson's blunt description of the relation between the White House and the Defense Department on this supreme military project still surprises the student of politics:

> The normal way to proceed would have been to talk to the Defense Department, have them study the project, and give the president their recommendations. That option was never suggested, perhaps because we all knew it would not work . . . Moreover the Defense Department, being the largest bureaucracy in the United States, is the perfect example of the worst of bureaucracy . . . So we did something that, by the book, we should not have done. Without ever formally acknowledging it even to ourselves, a

small informal group on strategic missile defense was formed within the White House.'[28]

It was a 'quadriad', composed of Ed. Meese, as chairman, Richard V. Allen, Anderson himself, all advisers of the president, and the scientist, George Keyworth. Their object was to find 'a policy that relied on *both* offense and defense nuclear war'.

From then on, the preparation of the new defence policy proceeded very fast. Helped by such important outside advisers as Edward Teller, Karl Bendetsen, Jaqueline Hume, William Wilson, and Joseph Coors, the 'quadriad' were able on 8 January 1982 to present their report on the feasibility of the missile defence to the president. In December 1982, the Joint Chiefs of Staff met privately with the president. On 1 February 1983, the Joint Chiefs of Staff recommended to the president that the United States should abandon the MAD system of defence and move ahead with the research and development of a new missile defence system – which President Reagan named Strategic Defense Initiative (SDI). His new deputy national security adviser, Robert McFarlane[29] typed the text of a strategic missile defence statement on his own typewriter, which was edited by the scientist Keyworth and was to become afterwards the text of Reagan's historic speech on television on 23 March 1983. It was then that he announced that he was totally committed to the course of building a 'strategic missile defense' and was ready to sign an agreement with the Soviet Union concerning future mutual *reductions* of nuclear weapons.[30] The speech caused a sensation in the USSR, some anxiety in the rest of NATO, and vehement protests in the Democratic Party opposition. Senator Edward Kennedy at once baptised the new policy ironically as 'Star Wars'. In 1984 an experiment with a Minuteman equipped with sensors of the new system twice proved successful in hitting a target at the height of 4000 miles, and in destroying both vehicles in the atmosphere, without showering the earth with debris. In 1986 a new interceptor missile called ERIS (for Exoatmospheric Reentry Vehicle Interceptor Subsystem) and the high endoatmospheric defense interceptor called HEDI were reported to be most satisfactorily accurate. But many scientists of renown still reiterated their disbelief in the feasibility of the whole project. From a political and strategic point of view open sceptical criticisms were directed at the project in an article published in *Foreign Affairs* by four leading experts in American foreign policy: McGeorge Bundy, George Kennan, Robert McNamara and Gerard Smith. The article underlined the technical unfeasibility, the ultimate inconclusiveness and the counter-productive effects the new strategy might have on

Gorbachev's tentatively positive approaches to a change in the relations between the USA and the USSR.

Robert C. McFarlane, Reagan's national security adviser who, as has been said above, himself drafted and typed on his own typewriter the text of Reagan's television speech in March 1983 in which SDI was first mentioned, explained in retrospect the strategic purpose of the SDI-project. 'Those of us in the White House who proposed the Strategic Defense Initiative', he writes[31]

believed that a re-orientation of our investment strategy to emphasize an area of our comparative advantage – excellence in high technology – could persuade the Soviets that we could outstrip an entire generation of Soviet military investment. If we could do so, we could remove their only claim to super-power status and perhaps lead them to deal more constructively with our concerns about their forces.

And even more firmly he maintained that SDI – as evaluated by the Soviets – seems to have played an important role in leading the USSR to engage seriously in an effort to meet American concerns over the counterforce imbalance. In addition, the prospect of SDI may have been an important influence in encouraging Kremlin leaders to reassess their economic system's fundamental ability to compete, and leading them to the ultimate conclusion that it could not, thus bringing about their acceptance of the need for *perestroika*. That assumption seems now to have been fully confirmed.

But because of the iron law of interdependence things were moving rapidly in the USSR as well, as will be shown in the next chapter. Here let it merely be said that after Gorbachev came to power in 1985, official admissions about some aspects of real conditions in the USSR and the Soviet bloc as a whole abounded. At the same time the new regime made explicit the wish to establish international relations with the 'capitalist' West, and especially with the United States, on a new base. Peace with the West – the *peredyshka* (breathing space) – was the pre-condition of the internal re-structuring, the *perestroika*, sought by Gorbachev.

How decisive a part the SDI played in Gorbachev's policy remains conjectural. Did he believe as Andropov did and, in consequence set the leitmotif of the Soviet argument soon after Reagan's speech, that the main purpose of the new weaponry was offensive and not defensive, as Reagan presented it? In so far as the entire Soviet strategy is itself based on a pre-emptive offensive plan, the advantage obtained by the US by an entirely different 'first strike' strategy cast a dark doubt on the Soviet strategy as a whole. The whole shifting of the armament race on to an entirely new field, much less accessible to backward Soviet technology, raised the spectre of economic and financial means. Did Gorbachev believe that, more as an offensive than a defensive system, SDI would bring about final and fatal domination by US military technology? Did he make a shrewd attempt to convince his colleagues that competition in this new arms race would put *perestroika* out of the question? Or both? Or did he believe that because of internal opposition in the Congress and American political opinion and of the frequently confirmed lack of continuity in American military planning, the SDI project would fade away, too, or might be only a 'bargaining counter' in future negotiations? The Soviet military and civilian leadership were less optimistic in this direction than some sectors of American and Western opinion. The proof is to be strangely found in the perseverance with which the Soviet negotiators demanded that America should put an end to it.

The first and most startling evidence of this concern appeared at the meeting between Reagan and Gorbachev in Reykjavik in October 1986. Though this meeting was a failure, it throws more light on the real relations of interdependence than many other 'meetings', 'summits', or 'conferences' which end in more or less enthusiastic communiqués, but in reality are carpets under which the real disagreements have been swept. As is well known, the final disagreement occurred only at the end of an intoxicating mood of reconciliation and mutual understanding – but as in a flash of lightning, that same final disagreement illuminated very clearly several strategic contradictions. What had happened was that Reagan had been extraordinarily surprised by Gorbachev's readiness to accept the zero-option, i.e. the elimination of all intermediate nuclear forces, the so-called INF Treaty, as prepared by Richard Perle, the Assistant Secretary of Defense publicly associated with the preparation of the re-establishment of US military domination. He himself was also prepared to accept a general agreement of which Perle's tantalizing formula of 'zero-option' had now come, during the talks in Reykjavik, to be the basis. Reagan's unexpected and indeed unforeseen enthusiasm, surprised and irritated important sectors among the makers of Western strategy as a whole, to mention only the most important and closest, the American Chiefs of Staff and the Western Allies (notably the United Kingdom and Mrs Thatcher). To put it another way, Reagan antagonized those sectors most interested in the NATO strategy, now seemingly debilitated by the imminent US–USSR agreement.

NATO – by which is meant here that part of the American and

239

the Western Allies defence system which was still working on the assumption of a Western strategy of *deterrence* – was surprised and alarmed when it learned how near Reagan had come at Reykjavik to put at risk the entire system of deterrence, which had kept the peace for forty years, in favour of a US unilateral system of *defence* of which they knew nothing. Logically they had strong reasons to be alarmed both by START and SDI.

The fact is that from a budgetary and from a technological point of view the orientation towards an INF treaty, not to speak of SDI, cast a serious doubt on the continuity of the NATO system of the 'balance of terror'. The definition given by Reagan himself of SDI as being a 'comprehensive and intensive effort to achieve our ultimate goal of eliminating the threat posed by strategic nuclear missiles', was a denial of defence by nuclear deterrence. The clearest alarm bell was sounded in this respect by the American General Bernard Rodgers, who was then Supreme Commander of NATO. Speaking in his official capacity, he explained that the INF agreement went logically and financially against the strategy of flexible response.

Mrs Thatcher used her 'special relation' with Reagan to see him as soon as possible, and presumably to check again that the earlier re-assurance he had given to her in December 1984 that the aim of SDI was 'to enhance not to undercut deterrence' still held. She was obviously concerned, as were most Western leaders, with the implicitly cynical indifference of a *defence* system allegedly able to cover the American skies with a ceiling of invulnerability, while leaving the European skies wide open to attack. She was also concerned because a US–USSR nuclear agreement raised immediate problems concerning the independent British and French nuclear forces. All these operations, which might have the effect of 'decoupling' the American NATO partner from its European partners, seemed rather alarming to the latter who required more complete information. How much President Reagan re-assured Mrs Thatcher when she visited him in December 1986, soon after his return from Reykjavik, is of course a matter of speculation.

Much more reassuring was the fact that for the time being, Gorbachev himself had refused to sign the projected agreement. Moreover, in a speech to the Royal United Services Institute in March 1985, which was violently attacked by Mr Richard Perle, the then Foreign Secretary Sir Geoffrey Howe had confirmed again the British belief in nuclear deterrence. 'This government', he said, 'is not committed to destruction. It is committed to preserving peace,

by ensuring that potential aggressors are deterred from threatening it.'
But as Ian Davidson puts it.

the Reagan Gorbachev mini-summit at Reykjavik in October 1986 ostensibly
came close to agreement on a major arms control package which would
certainly imply . . . bigger change in the nature of the European security
dilemma . . . European governments can no longer rule out the possibility
of an international regime characterized by a sharp reduction in America's
nuclear commitment to the defence of Europe.'[32]

While the Reykjavik episode stunned the whole world, and especially the Western world, by the rapidity with which both leaders ran
towards the other with what seemed to be the same aim, even more
stunning was the final development which brought the whole negotia-
tion to an abrupt end. The first development was particularly strange
as it revealed that what started out like a joint quest for peace ended by
giving the impression that Reagan and Gorbachev each thought that
the other had tried to hoodwink him. To everybody's amazement it
was revealed in the lightning end of the meeting in Iceland that what
Gorbachev wanted above all was to 'kill' SDI, and that what Reagan
wanted above all was to keep and to develop SDI beyond *research*, as
Gorbachev had suggested, into full *deployment*. When, at the end of the
meeting, Gorbachev demanded that the experiments in SDI should be
limited only to laboratory research, Reagan replied that he intended to
proceed to the state of deployment as soon as possible. On that, the
conversation, and START, broke down.

Of course Reagan had many other reasons not to sign any agreement
there and then. He had to consider the reaction of the Western Allies,
of the Senate's Armed Services Committee, chaired by the powerful
Democratic senator, Sam Nunn, as well as the request of the American
forces, and especially of the US navy, that the sea-launched Cruise
missile should not be included in the nuclear reduction treaty. All
these prerequisites would probably have prevented him from signing
any agreement straight away. But the fact that Gorbachev himself
refused to sign any treaty that did not 'kill' SDI woke him up more
than anything else both to his old impression of the real nature of
Soviet intentions, as well as to the credibility and importance of his
pet project.

The negotiations then lingered on for some time as Reagan had
become much more cautious. It was Gorbachev who was now in a
greater hurry and much more prepared to make concessions, promises
and new offers, for reasons to be discussed below. But on SDI the
differences remained like rocks standing up under the tide. Gorbachev
insisted that the project violated all existing agreements. For instance,

after Gorbachev's successful visit to Reagan in Washington in 1987, the final communiqué still made it very clear that the two sides would 'observe the ABM treaty as signed in 1972, when conducting their research, development and testing as required, which are permitted by the ABM treaty, and not to withdraw from the ABM treaty for a specified period of time'. As S. Talbot remarks about the text: 'The commas and subordinate clauses left deliberately vague what level of testing would be permissible during the period of non-withdrawal.'[33] Indeed, even in 1989, when the INF treaty had been finally signed, after Gorbachev made innumerable new concessions, and events in the USSR itself, in the former Baltic States and the former Bessarabia, let alone in Poland, Hungary and East Germany, exerted growing pressure on him, he still maintained that if SDI were to be deployed the USSR would withdraw from the ABM treaty. It is also the case that in the meantime SDI had changed its technological aspect several times – among other possibilities it was turning now into different technical formulae, as for instance, lasers, battle-management computers, particle beam weapons and tracking radars, the latest at the time of writing poetically called the *shining pebbles*, a galaxy of sensors over American skies.

The American SDI project acted as a kind of final straw in bringing about the massive change in East–West relations which had been taking place since the end of the 1980s. But, as will be argued later, the ultimate and fundamental cause of that change was the terminal illness of Marxism-Leninism and its political manifestations. That illness, in turn, had been speeded up by the information revolution and by the increased effects of interdependence. The unnatural structures of the Marxist-Leninist regimes would have crumbled in any case by themselves, but shattering blows from outside inevitably hastened their decomposition. The SDI, Reagan's invention, was one of these aggravating factors, and it continued to be an obvious bone of contention between the Soviet Union and the USA until the Soviet Union collapsed into chaos.

Yet, regarded on its own, the episode of SDI has some elements of comedy. The fact that the whole idea of an atmospheric shield acting as a military defence and visualized by the public as something out of a science-fiction film had been brought into the real political arena by a statesman who had in the past been an actor was perhaps just a coincidence. But it does also raise the question of the different kinds of political imagination. The element of fantasy in the initial project might well have prevented, did indeed prevent many reputable scientists and politicians from according it any credit. But Reagan's political imagination was not limited by the boundaries of formal reality; he knew, from the formative phases of his personality, that illusion can be transformed into reality as easily as reality can be transformed by individual or collective illusion.

He also knew, from his formation as an actor, that action or acting (difficult to separate in semantics) is in itself determining, that 'the play is the thing'. Tricks have helped to bring about great strategic victories in the past, from the Trojan horse, to Bismarck's Ems telegram. This is not to say that either Reagan personally, or the American administration were 'bluffing' Gorbachev and his team, and that the bluff succeeded. But it can be said that both imagination and acting combined most felicitously in a gamble of statesmanship. Reagan believed so profoundly in his unconstitutionally born project, by science out of science-fiction, that he gambled on having it accepted as a real element in a new military strategy of the number one super-power. The French general, L. Poivier, one of the great Western strategists, put it in a nutshell when, speaking about SDI, he said: 'Now we have military strategies based on make-believe . . . it is as though a dominant player could achieve certain current political ends, while being spared the effort of providing proof of his power with real forces.'[34] And Reagan gambled again, this time with Gorbachev, by refusing to abandon that particular project, although he was offered, for the first time, what no other American president had ever been offered by the leader of the USSR, namely negotiations to begin the reduction of all nuclear armaments. Such a reduction would in turn greatly reduce the risks of the cold war being transformed, deliberately or by accident, into a nuclear catastrophe.

Only further revelations in memoirs and documents will reveal how far Reagan's gamble with Gorbachev on the refusal to demur on SDI was inspired by a feeling that, once engaged, for overwhelming internal reasons on a descending spiral, the Soviet Union would later accept further conditions; or how far his own stubborn belief in SDI determined his trenchant attitude at the end of the Reykjavik meeting. The fact remains that the last day of the Reykjavik conference, marked as it was by alternating dark clouds and blue skies like an equinoctial storm, had suffered a change in historical perspective. The strategic improvization and the cumulation of mistakes and counter-mistakes, resulted in a step forward for the West. Or, in other words, it was a comedy of errors in which, to continue in the Shakespearean mode, all is well that ends well.

If the SDI project was the enigma at the centre of Reagan's overall strategy of interdependence, the same cannot be said of Reagan's determination to reconquer by all means, old and new, at least the American strategic parity with the USSR, lost during the presidencies of Nixon and especially of Carter. He represented the feeling of the majority of the American population, which agreed by 56 to 38 per cent with his basic judgement that 'whenever there is trouble around the world – in the Middle East, Central America or anywhere else – chances are that the Soviets are behind it'; and by 66 to one that as long as the situation continued there should be no reduction in military spending.[35] As a result he invested enormous sums in the old and new military programmes, regardless of costs and payments in the belief that only in this way could American superiority be reconquered. As I. M. Destler puts it in his article on 'Reagan and the World: an Awesome Stubbornness':

> yet on the positive side, with the INF pact concluded and US Soviet agreement already reached on many features of a strategic arms accord, the Reagan record on arms control stood a real chance of proving historic. If it did, who but quibblers would dwell on the administration's erratic route to getting there? And might not Ronald Reagan's policy stubborness be judged as partly responsible for the impressive result?[36]

It is probably for the same reason that American public opinion allowed Reagan to achieve his second term as president in peace in spite of two startling mistakes which he made in the domain of interdependence which, however, did not besmirch it in the way other presidencies had suffered since that of Lyndon Johnson.

The first of these mistakes originated in Reagan's attitude towards the communist infiltration of Latin America, notably through the Marxist-Leninist Sandinista government in Nicaragua. This issue combined in a strange way with the problem of the Americans held hostage in the Lebanon. Or, rather, it was combined in a strange way by some higher and some lower officials, with, or without Reagan's knowledge. The second mistake, although less scandal-prone was far more disquieting. It was the enormous military expenditure which destabilized the budget, already debilitated by the generosity of Reaganomics towards the American tax-payers with their high standard of living. This led to a rapidly escalating national and international debt, which lowered America's position in the world.

To turn briefly here to the 'Iran–Contra affair' as the whole episode has now come to be known. Altogether, the relations of the USA with Central and Latin America, considered as the US sphere of influence in the Monroe Doctrine, are of constant concern to Americans. The sensitivity of the American government and of American public opinion is immediately alerted when these relations come to the fore. The mixture of ideological and economic issues involved in these relationships, since Castro's successful communist revolution in Cuba, has accentuated the anti-communist sentiment of the nation and affected its assessment of Soviet intentions. The extent to which American intervention in Vietnam was undertaken as a result of the American policy of fighting communism everywhere, remains a moot point. But it was their main preoccupation in Latin America. Reagan was particularly vulnerable to this kind of simplified, telescoped interpretation, and as we have seen, he had reduced all strategic problems to 'the source of all evils', the USSR. Reagan's fixation obscured the difference in perception and interpretation in his own mind between a major and a minor event, and between a local and a global trend. All effects flowed from the same cause. Now it is true that the sensitivity of the USA towards the penetration of Latin American countries was vividly sharpened especially after the 1963 Cuba crisis; and that Nicaragua could be visualized as a future basis of Soviet attack directed against the USA. But Reagan's ideological obsession and the offensive character he gave to his 'Doctrine' led him to demand an immediate counter-offensive action against the danger he detected. As M. Anderson faithfully expresses Reagan's simplified view,

down in Latin America, the United States had a very troublesome foreign policy with Nicaragua. A communist regime forcibly took power and was rapidly developing strong and friendly ties with the Soviet Union. Worse, Nicaragua was arming itself with billions of dollar weapons, and was rapidly becoming a source of all kinds of trouble very close to our own shores and borders. We already had one Soviet semi-satellite – Cuba – armed to the teeth just 90 miles off the coast of Florida, President Reagan did not want to let another Soviet semi-satellite develop on his own patch. The one hopeful sign in Nicaragua was a group of rebels who went into the hills and launched a guerrilla war against the new communist dictatorship.

These were known as the Contras. But, continues Anderson, 'Reagan and most of the Republicans in Congress wanted to send them economic and military aid. Others weren't so sure. They weren't sure of the guerrillas . . . They weren't even sure that the new Communist government was all that bad'.[37]

Like Lyndon Johnson, who sharpened the stand taken by Kennedy in Vietnam, Reagan gave an offensive character to the suspicious attitude already taken by Carter towards the Sandinistas. Carter had first hoped that their guerrilla victory over the dictatorship of Antonio Somoza in 1979 would solve the problem of 'human rights' (Carter's obsessive concern) in Nicaragua. But once convinced that the new regime was openly Marxist-Leninist, and therefore pro-Cuban and pro-Soviet, Carter's attitude to the Sandinistas changed. Reagan, who had no illusions about the regime, even in opposition, decided once in power that the USA should openly oppose it by offensive means. He decided that the Contras should be assisted with money and arms in their fight against the communists. This was in harmony with the Reagan doctrine as a whole. Thus, for instance, in 1983, without even consulting the government of the United Kingdom, which exercised sovereignty over Grenada as a Commonwealth country (and according to some authors, without even consulting the State Department) eight thousand US troops in three days liquidated a communist regime installed with the direct assistance of Cuba and then quickly withdrew, leaving the islanders free to proceed to a democratic election. This quick and successful operation, compared by the US media with the British campaign in the Falkland Islands, delighted the majority of American public opinion. Seldom did Reagan's popularity reach such heights as then.

But the long and inconclusive intervention in Nicaragua soon lost popularity both with public opinion and with the majority in Congress, particularly when it turned out that the Contras themselves had little respect for human rights. Americans were largely opposed to the idea of getting involved in long overseas military commitments, and in particular in the complex relationships of the Central American states directly involved. In August 1987 the President of the Republic of Costa Rica, Oscar Arias Sanchez, put forward a plan for the pacification of the area which was endorsed by the five Central American presidents. At a later meeting of the five presidents in 1988 together with an international advisory team which had been set up to monitor progress, the results proved to be very disappointing. But at least at that meeting the Sandinistas agreed for the first time to negotiate directly with the Contras.[38] On 3 February 1988, the House of Representatives rejected by a majority of eight Reagan's request for a smallish grant (36 million dollars) for the Contras. Since then official help was only granted on humanitarian grounds.

It was from that moment that the operation was continued from the White House. This eventually led to the Iran–Contra scandal, and compromised, indeed endangered, Reagan's presidency. Here again Anderson's surprisingly candid description of the events must be quoted:[39] 'The essentials of the Iran–Contra affair were simple and straightforward. The United States agreed to sell military weapons to Iran', he wrote, and explained afterwards that the enormous sums Iran was paying were transmitted through unofficial channels to finance the Contra operations. And Anderson continues:

we capped the whole sorry episode by misleading our own Congress and attempting to get around a law passed by Congress and signed by President Reagan. The law expressly forbids our intelligences agencies from providing military aid to guerrillas intent on overthrowing the new communist dictatorship in Nicaragua. Through trickery and deceit a small band of people in the White House and the CIA managed to take some of the profits made on the sale of US arms to Iran and use them to purchase weapons for the freedom fighters in Nicaragua.

Anderson then concludes that during this period of time President Reagan was deeply affected. For the first time in his life his personal credibility was challenged, and soon the majority of the American people were convinced that he had lied to them.

That may have been the effect on the Americans. The main significance of the Iran–Contra affair was that the President, or people working for him, had deceitfully circumvented the ban imposed by Congress on aid for the Contras. But for Reagan's European allies, the serious danger was that the Americans were supplying arms to the Iranians as part of a deal to free hostages held by Iranian sponsored terrorists. This was revealed late in 1986, after the Americans had strained the tolerance of their allies in seeking support for their bombing raid on Libya; and after they had insisted that the Tokyo summit in May should reach clear conclusions against helping or doing deals with the terrorists. The revelation that the Americans had been dealing with the Iranians all along was a very severe blow to European confidence in Reagan.

Sadly, when it seemed that the old actor was going to enjoy resting on the laurels of his popular presidency, he was forced by the logical development of the Iran-Contra affair to appear once more on the screen, once the main instrument of his popularity. But this time the role he was to play was tragically different or, as others would put it, he had no role, no prompter and no stage setting. As a result of the increasingly direct, embarrassed, and embarrassing references of Colonel North, and especially of Admiral Poindexter, during their trials, to the direct or indirect approval the President had given to the whole plan, the judges asked Reagan to testify. He was allowed to do so by television, through which he would answer, as though in court, the questions put to him by the lawyers. There were not a few who believed that re-situated thus in the 'medium', which suited him so well, and in which and by which he had made his whole extraordinary career, the 'great communicator' would once again show his mastery.

But either because he had been advised to play the role of an old man answering monotonously to most questions with 'I can't remember', or 'I don't know', accompanied by a meaningless smile, or because this was indeed the first time since his presidency when he had not been provided with theatrical props, not even a prompter, the performance caused general dismay.

## The economic interdependence

Reagan's second mistake, or defiance of the laws of interdependence, arose in connection with this determination to gamble with the public finances and the national budget and to maintain both civilian and military expenditure with borrowed money. The three principles of the economic policy which went by the name of Reaganomics were: the 'anti-government' nationalism, the supply side economics and later, as an inevitable but also a deliberate consequence, national indebtedness. The first two were set in motion at once and with great gusto in 1980, in order to benefit from the disorder in the Democrat camp at the end of the Carter presidency. 'Early victories were necessary in order to cow the opposition and stampede as many members of Congress as possible onto the winning bandwagon', wrote the meteoric David Stockman, the first director of the Office of Management and Budget in his book, significantly entitled *The Triumph of Politics*,[40] written after his mission to keep the budget balanced had also been 'stampeded' by Reagan's 'political' decision to spend more both on defence and on non-defence items than the country could possibly afford.

It was, if I am not mistaken, Hugh Heclo, Professor of Government at Harvard who coined the expression 'anti-government national-ism'.[41] It sounds deliberately self-contradictory, yet the expression encapsulates in one single concept the two aims of Reaganomics which were bound to clash with each other, and were only eventually to be reconciled and continued by the extraordinary means of national and international indebtedness.

Nationalism, as we have already seen, was not only the first premiss of the Reaganite political syllogism. It also contained an obvious element of mysticism which inspired the prophetic leader's irrefu-table arguments – indeed the more irrefutable, the higher pitched the rhetoric. Since Shakespeare's *Henry V*, no leader – neither the Founding Fathers nor Lincoln in their supreme moments – has used such lyrically nationalist incantations as for instance this passage from Reagan's state of the nation address in 1984:

How can we not believe in the greatness of America? How can we not do what is right and needed to preserve this last best hope of man on earth? After all our struggles to restore America, to revive confidence in our country, hope for our future, after all our hard-won victories earned through the patience and courage of every citizen, we cannot, must not, and will not turn back. We finish our job. How could we do less? We're Americans!

And this theory of absolute nationalism, of 'priority number one is National Security', was effectively put into practice in the new and unprecedentedly successful military and diplomatic strategy in relation to the USSR.

But already, even in this brief quotation, the two contradictory propositions are juxtaposed. America is the best hope of man on earth, but it is not the American state which deserves that accolade. It is the patience and the courage of her citizens. In de Gaulle's conception, France is great because of the historical greatness of the French state. In Reagan's definition of nationalism the state is passed over, and replaced by the 'citizens'. Now we know of course that as the governor of a state in the American federation, Reagan was animated by the antipathy of the periphery against the central federal state, that he had come to Washington to 'cleanse it' (a typically populist expression) of the sins which were destroying America. And we also know that as a Republican he was dedicated to the principle of what Nozick was to call in a different context 'the minimal state'.

But Reagan had a third, politically significant, reason to be critical of the allegedly dominant and interventionist federal government. This was his belief that, under cover of the particularly flamboyant title of 'The Great Society' which Lyndon Johnson had given to his general welfare policy, it was the society which lost. He denounced the whole policy as a farce in which the state, and the state bureaucracy postured as the protectors of society, and were in reality stifling it under the weight of their controls, monopolies and levelling trends. Behind 'The Great Society' there lurked the conspiratorial welfare state. 'Government is not the solution to our problem. Government is the problem', was one of Reagan's favourite phrases.

'The Reagan Revolution required a full frontal assault on the American welfare state' writes David Stockman. And he continues: 'Accordingly, forty years' worth of promises, subventions, entitlements and safety nets issued by the federal government would have to be scrapped or drastically modified.'[42] It was the extravagance of the federal welfare state which was responsible for the creeping inflation. Already at the end of the Carter presidency, when inflation was climbing to double digit levels, a feverish anti-inflationary economic policy was embarked on, which reversed many of the policies introduced to keep down unemployment, support agricultural prices, raise money for social security by taxation and introduce a minimum wage. As a result the phrase which won Reagan the 1980 election, 'Are you better off now than you were four years ago?' expressed the overall feeling of the middle class across the entire federation. Generally speaking, American citizens had not harboured an ideological predisposition towards social justice, leading on towards the welfare state, typical of the citizens of the Western European industrial democracies. Indeed, from an ideological point of view, as Richard Hofstaedter (the importance of whose work in American political philosophy has been posthumously confirmed by the Reagan experience) said, it had been America's fate as a nation 'not to have ideologies but to be one'. And he further explained that within that one American ideology, the predominant movements and trends had more often than not a populist character. This oscillated between the enjoyment of the freedom and comfort of the private individual and the permanent fear that obscure 'forces of privilege' dominated and manipulated the whole societal complex.

From a practical point of view, the American 'citizens' have had neither the tradition nor the possibility to become addicted to the dispensations of the welfare society. American economists and political scientists often remind us of a supplementary practical cause of the fundamental difference in social psychology between Americans and Western Europeans. This is made particularly explicit by David Calleo when he asks

Why are European countries able to raise so much more in taxes, proportionately, than the United States? Judging from Europe's experience, America's fiscal problem may be that it spends too little on civilian benefits rather than too much. It seems difficult to separate the greater tolerance for higher taxes among French and German citizens from the substantially higher level of benefits those citizens – particularly middle-class tax payers – receive from the state. Higher pensions . . . free medical care . . . better police protection and superior public amenities in general . . . make Europeans' willingness to pay higher taxes not so difficult to understand. But to expect Americans to pay a European level of taxes in return for an American level of civil expenditures is politically unrealistic.[43]

Thus the two-pronged attack of Reagan's policy, one directed at the confirmation of the superiority of American power in the new, interdependent world, the other directed at cutting the 'welfare budget' so as to be able to reduce taxes, was bound to meet with the approval of the (silent) majority of the United States, already disturbed by Soviet military superiority and domestic inflation. The first twelve or eighteen months of the Reagan presidency were a success. The new military policy took some time to reveal its efficacity, for obvious reasons, but the financial and fiscal measures achieved immediate results. Inflation was reduced from 12 per cent in 1980 to some 4 per cent in 1984; the budget deficit forecasts improved from a deficit of $44 billion for 1981 to $15 billion for 1982, and a surplus of $37 billion by 1983, although military expenditure went up from $152 billion in 1981 to $214 billion in 1985, and taxes were cut to an unprecedented degree. Even unemployment, which had spiralled up dramatically as the inevitable consequence of the reduction of inflation, fell considerably afterwards. The rapidity and the success of this Reaganomic operation stunned the nation and the world. The official theory of the supply-side economics had an element of reality in it; but people could not help thinking, after the initial success, that there was an element of wizardry in it.

To take the reality first. The very name 'supply-side economic policy'[44] indicates that it stands at the opposite pole from Keynesian 'demand-management' economic policy. Supply-side economics is the transformation of the rather simple belief – that if people and companies were to pay less in taxes they would be able to save and invest more – into an economic and political philosophy. Yet what should generally speaking be a matter of the technique of fiscal policy must have fundamental implications on the economic policy in general. The idea was therefore bound to amount to a revolution when it was introduced just at the time of the dominance of the welfare state and demand-management. Even if the welfare state did not openly assume its ultimate role as an instrument of distributive justice in the USA, it was still a mechanism whereby the state collected increasingly higher taxes in order to be able to subsidize the many, and increasingly expensive, public programmes of a modern industrial society. Taking as their examples the crises of the American economy, and above all the crisis of the British economy, the supply-side theorists argued that their main cause was the welfare state. Or, to put it differently, they argued that the cause of these crises was the unnatural way in which the state paralysed the essential productive functions of the private sector in order to feed the all-consuming needs of the public sector. For reasons of public psychology already noted above, American public opinion was more predisposed to welcome 'the return to private initiative' and to 'creative freedom' than was public opinion in the European democracies. It rejoiced especially in the cuts in the growing public expenditures.

The 1981 budget was the turning point towards the overall 'supply-side' and 'anti-government nationalism' Reagan policy. It provided for an increase of $7 billion in defence expenditure, and cuts of $35 billion in non-defence expenditure. But the cuts did not change the structure of the budget, in which *grosso modo* the two major items were 28 per cent for defence and 47 per cent for social welfare programmes: social security, 'medicare' which became a federal budget charge, and especially pensions. The latter is a constantly rising item in the budget, both because of the evidently increasing average longevity of American citizens, and because American public opinion and the president himself are particularly inclined to favour this category of citizens. As a result, social security taxes, instead of decreasing, were increased from 31 per cent of federal revenues to 36 per cent in 1987. Also, although David Stockman believed, and believes to this day, that 'the worst nonsense of all in the budget of course was farm subsidies', he recognizes that 'politics triumphed' in that formidably strong pressure group, or as they call it in the USA, 'iron triangle': interest, Congress and media. Because of this pressure, and because of the poor export performance of agriculture since the 1970s, those subsidies have remained almost intact. The main cuts were made in the public transport, energy, housing, police, and scientific research programmes – from 24 per cent of the federal expenditure in 1980 to 15 per cent in 1988. Finally, as had been promised, the Economic Tax Recovery Act of 1981 cut personal income taxes by 23 per cent or $162 billion. This continued almost unchanged throughout Reagan's presidency, in spite of a shift towards higher taxes in 1986. The shift arose in part as result of increasing pressure from Congress, now openly hostile to Reaganomics, but also in part because of the sad evidence that tax cuts had not had the immediate effect of stimulating and reviving the economy, which had been prophesied. The 'supply-side' theory was obviously not going to be the expected panacea.

But then what kind of wizardry was hidden behind Reagan's success in increasing defence expenditure, bringing down inflation, reducing unemployment, cutting income tax, all at the same time – measures which logically, in practice, cannot go together? His aggressive spirit, and his national confidence were of course part of Reagan's policy. Only John Kennedy had shown the same impulses at the beginning of his dramatic presidency. He too had sought to 'revive' the energy of the nation by a double frontal attack, by an intensive re-armament in the sphere of foreign policy, and by cutting taxes in the sphere of domestic policy – in both cases much more modestly than Reagan did. But Kennedy was young, with a progressive mentality, and he brought young people with him to the helm. Moreover America was then still undefeated, the most advanced and the wealthiest power in the world. All the indicators of what Susan Strange rightly calls the structures which form the power of the United States (security, production, financial and knowledge structures) were still pointing upwards. ('Still' was the operative word, as the circumambience of interdependence was spreading even then over the 'commanding heights' of the USA; and as Kennedy himself had presided over the ominous defeat of the Bay of Pigs, and embarked on the Vietnam expedition, which was to become, after his death, the most shattering event in modern American history.)

Although Reagan was exceptionally dynamic by nature, he was nevertheless over seventy years old when he embarked on his frontal attack on traditional internal and external policies; and America was already submerged in commercial, financial, monetary and technological difficulties. Moreover its economic reputation had suffered from the misadventures of the dollar, just as its military reputation had suffered from the Vietnam war, and its political reputation from a series of unlucky presidencies. What kind of tricks could the great conjuror now perform in order to launch policies, in themselves contradictory, into the relatively and absolutely weakened structures of the USA? How could he overfinance national security while reducing taxes? How could he keep both inflation and unemployment down at the same time?

The answer had Reagan's supreme quality of simplicity: by running deficit budgets. And the answer to the question how to cover those deficits was also marvellously simple: by enormously increasing the national and the foreign debt.

American political and economic literature is unanimous in recognizing this fact. It ranges from candid apologias to objective explanations, to more or less severe or pessimistic criticisms. One example of lesser severity is provided by Anderson, in the double role of one of Reagan's economic advisers at the time, and apologist now of Reagan's 'Revolution'. He writes:

From 1980 through the end of 1987, President Reagan borrowed $7.00 for every $3.00 he spent. The United States was one of the best credit risks in the world, people poured money on us, and we obliged, borrowing easily, quickly and almost guiltlessly. But credit carries with it danger and risk. Borrowing the trillion plus dollars may have been the smartest thing we ever did, but we soon had to cut back our lust for borrowing. There are still many problems. The federal deficit is too large. Our international deficit is too high. The huge debt overhanging the third world is a financial threat. The irresponsible call for protectionism is growing.[45]

In the second category of scholarly objectivity, Robert Gilpin explains:

the United States was able to finance its massive government budget and keep interest rates from rising through heavy borrowing in world financial markets . . . In effect, what the United States and foreign exporters experienced under the banner of Reaganomics and 'supply-side' economics was a debt financed recovery driven by a powerful Keynesian stimulus. The 'economic success' of the Reagan administration was largely dependant upon the pyramiding of massive debt and the siphoning of capital from the rest of the world.[46]

A sample of the third category of comment comes from the pen of Professor Benjamin (note, not Milton) Friedman.[47] Writing just before the election of Reagan's successor to the presidency, Friedman insists especially on the consequences of American indebtedness. With some exaggeration, and some omissions which will be discussed later, he denounces the fact that

the United States is now the world's largest debtor nation, dependent on the goodwill of the countries that lend the money to keep the party going. The nation is surrendering the ownership of its productive assets, not in exchange for assets it will own abroad, or new plants and other facilities at home, but merely to finance higher and higher personal consumption.

Insisting that future generations of Americans will suffer from the consequences and that America's role will inevitably be compromised by Reagan's imprudence, he adds that: 'In the meanwhile, jobs are plentiful and profits are high, because Americans are spending amply . . . The average American has enjoyed such a high standard of living because since January 1981 our government has simply borrowed more than $20,000 on behalf of each family of four.' He argues that the Reagan presidency was a period in which 'US investment in new business plant and equipment has fallen to a smaller share of national income than in any previous sustained effort since World War II' (but here Friedman leaves out military investment); and he also argues that the gap in foreign trade between US exports and US imports had risen almost eight times from the $25 billion under Carter in 1980 to $161 billion in 1987. He concludes that as America paid for this growing excess of imports over exports, she sent more and more dollars abroad. Foreigners then invested these funds in US financial markets. Meanwhile, the Japanese and Germans still appeared to think of themselves as debtors. 'But attitudes toward world leadership will change soon enough as America's financial problems circumscribe its scope for maneuver in world affairs while the new creditors' financial strength does the opposite.'

This last and somewhat cryptic sentence quoted from Friedman's very long article directs the discussion towards quite different perspectives, some of which were overlooked by him. One perspective which he has not examined sufficiently in his incisive analysis is the historical one. While it is true that Reagan deliberately aggravated the problems of American dependence on foreign markets, Friedman does not indicate that this dependence had begun long before. As we have shown earlier (see Introduction), the American 'liquidity deficit' started in 1970, when the whole world was so inundated with overvalued inflationary dollars that President Nixon had no other option than to abolish the Bretton Woods agreement by putting an end to the convertibility of the dollar into gold. Since that time, the American economy has been conditioned by the usage made by foreign countries of the floating dollars, especially by Germany and Japan which accumulated most of them. American indebtedness therefore had started long before Reagan, who in one sense was already operating in pre-set conditions. That he did not try, by internal measures, to remedy the situation he inherited, but instead worsened it by basing his expansive military and economic policy on 'borrowed money' can be seen in retrospect as a deliberate political choice with controversial results.

Another perspective from which Reagan's policies must be viewed is that of the ever more accentuated transnationalism of credit which developed as a sequel to the transnationalization of the economy of the industrial democracies. To criticize the indebtedness, and especially the foreign indebtedness caused by his financial extravagance is of course fully justified. But the argument is less apposite if it isolates these kinds of transactions from the transnational and interdependent context in which they operate as against the international and state centred. The relations between the USA, the imprudent debtor, and Japan and the Federal Republic of Germany, the calculating creditors, has necessarily to be seen on at least two levels. So should the American economy now also be seen, or to use a current expression, 'the two American economies'. Beneath, or perhaps to put it more clearly, parallel to the state-to-state relations ('the US Federal Bank owes to Japanese and German central banks large sums of accumulated dollars'), there is a more dynamic circulation, indeed bloodstream, of transnational transfers of technology, services and capital. In these incessant mutual transfers the multinational corporations of course play a major role. One can even speak now of the multinationalization of the previous technological, financial and monetary relations at all levels. Multinationalization creates such an intensive and general financial and monetary mutuality, helped by the lightning speed of communications, that in the end it is difficult to be sure at given moments who owes what to whom, and who owns what.

Now it is evident that at present American public opinion, alerted by such pessimistic analyses, has developed a new sensitivity to the danger of 'foreign penetration' of the American economy, to its 'loss of sovereignty'. Japanese take-overs are particularly watched – and indeed are more frequent as Japan is the principal creditor. In this connection it is significant that one of the most important Japanese purchases, that of the entire Columbia complex of Hollywood, one of the cradles of the American film industry, was concluded only after President Reagan's departure. Maybe, for Reagan, who since his youth had been very much aware of the worldwide influence the cinema and the media can exert, and had fought against their infiltration by communists, this foreign take-over might have been, if only symbolically, particularly painful. But, in reality, on the one hand, as the *Financial Times* put it in simpler terms: 'foreign groups still own only some 5 per cent of the total US assets . . . and only 16 percent of all direct investments in the US . . .' Japanese investment 'is little more than a tenth of US investment in the UK'.[48] On the other hand, although Japan is indeed the most difficult market for foreign capital to penetrate, old, indirect linkages between American and Japanese industries compensate at least in part for the new Japanese thrusts. Nevertheless, it is also clear that within the G7 group of important industrial democracies, often shrunk for more important questions to G5, the US, Germany and Japan form a special G3, and indeed in view of their future technological collaboration, the USA and Japan are already symbiotically linked in a G2.

But this brings us to yet another perspective from which Reaganomics should be observed. This is the defence relation which reveals the paradoxical situation that the two greatest creditors in US dollars are the two major countries defeated in the Second World War, both of which were subsequently reconstructed (especially Japan) with American help and under American supervision. Moreover, neither Germany nor Japan is permitted to have nuclear armament of its own, and Japan has been freed from the enormous burden of military expenditure which the USA, the UK, and in a different way France, have had to bear for the defence of industrial democracies against communist aggression. Thus the principal relation between the USA and the two debtors is that between defender and defended. And yet the USA, who bore the main costs of the war (with the UK) and of the cold war and reconstruction, and whose fiscal deficit and monetary instability is in part caused by its efforts in the war and during the post-war period, is now in their debt. It is not surprising that American public opinion should feel a certain impatience with what seems to Americans the excessive reliance of its allies, and especially the two defeated countries, on American military spending, which is double the proportion of the national income spent on defence in the Federal Republic of Germany.[49] But this impatience is not entirely justified either. For Americans, as argued above, should pay higher taxes to balance their budget and reduce the 'middle-class entitlements' if they want their country to keep the leading geo-political role it has taken on since the Second World War.

Moreover the fact that these two countries have accumulated the highest debt in floating dollars has not only a symbolic, but a real meaning. For Germany and Japan, involuntarily and indirectly, and sometimes directly, have contributed to Reagan's military re-armament policy. By 'lending' money to the USA, these non-nuclear powers were contributing to the American attempt to recover military, and especially nuclear, superiority over the USSR, so that it could continue to shelter all its allies under the nuclear umbrella. And, moreover, the USA remained, until the end of Reagan's presidency, the only industrial democracy which possessed *together* all four elements of power: security, production, financial power and knowledge, or in more current terms, military, economic, monetary and technological superiority all *together*. In some of these four directions the USA may have lost its lead, but no other power possessed them all at once. Of course if the Soviet Empire continues to disintegrate at the same pace, and the prospects of a longer peace, not based on the negative arguments of deterrence, become more credible, the one absolute superiority which the USA enjoys over its allies, namely military superiority, might lose importance. Such an event, associated with the regional groupings formed in Europe and in the Pacific might change America's geo-political position for good. But while this is pure speculation, what is real is that at the end of Reagan's presidency that position was still intact.

Last but not least, another perspective in which Reagan's policy of creating indebtedness must be viewed is the specific constitutional and political system of the USA. The relations between the executive (the president) and the legislature (Congress), and the relations between both of them and the interest groups which play such a determining role in the policy-making processes of the USA, must be taken into consideration. Reagan's principal quality was always considered to be his talent as the 'great communicator'. And indeed, as has already been noted, never has a politician combined personal talent, the technique of using the media, and simple but strong personal convictions, so well as Reagan. He was liked and loved by American public opinion, 'silent' and 'media' alike. Yet that did not imply that he had been able to convince either Congress or the interest groups behind it or the general public to adjust their family budgets and their standards of living so as to be able to pay higher taxes in the public interest.

This is not the place to discuss the well-known problem of American democratic processes of policy-making, and of democracy in general. The particularly awkward circumstance that there was a Republican president and a Democrat congress has also added ideological and therefore demagogic complications to Reagan's administration. But in any event it is fair to think that had Reagan changed his views about taxes, and national interest and discipline, and had he campaigned for austerity and national sacrifice, he would not have been elected, let alone re-elected. He therefore preferred, as many authors show, not to choose between guns and butter, but by going behind the open political stage – which he filled with his personal charm and his contagious confidence – he decided to go forward with both guns and butter. What remains to be discussed is whether his calculated gamble had positive or negative results, or both, and what the results of the gamble look like in retrospect.

## CONCLUSIONS

Because of a mixture of the instinctive adaptability of his political judgement to the new rules of interdependence Reagan's presidency will probably be considered in history as a successful one, and at least from one important point of view as one of historical significance. But history is always slow to give its final verdict, and thrives on 'revisionism'. It may thus still be some time before one can conclude that the happy combination of those two qualities of his statesmanship amply compensated for its many drawbacks.

Adaptability to the political rules of interdependence may seem to be merely a polite way to describe a political performance which was particularly buffeted by these rules. The pervasiveness of interdependence is as clearly illustrated in Reagan's historical record as the moral of a fable. For, what could better prove the immanence of interdependence than the story of a president who, in order to extricate his country from strategic dependencies, ties it up in economic dependencies – thus proving that when interdependence is expelled through the front door it returns through the back door? Or who, trying to close the 'window of vulnerability' of his country's sovereignty against intrusion from the stratosphere by a foreign power, abandons such elements of sovereignty on earth as the currency, foreign trade, and technological advance to other, foreign, powers?

Obviously it can be argued, and later proved, that Reagan was aware of the essential complexity of interdependence, and notably of the linkage between strategic and economic dependency. Having fixed a simple order of priorities, he then made a political choice, a gamble. As we have seen, 'security, number one, economics number two' was his order of priorities, and his order of the day. In the light of that argument, he can be credited with having considered that if the strategic conflict with the USSR could be won, whatever the cost, the ensuing peace, tranquillity and normality which that victory would bestow upon the free world would allow all the debts incurred in making the effort to be settled afterwards. This was the basic use which Reagan made of the logic of interdependence. Thus instead of drowning in the waves of interdependence, he may actually have been sailing upon them.

Furthermore, it can be seen in retrospect that this crucial decision was buttressed by two other examples of interdependence. Both have already been mentioned and need only to be recalled here – especially as the first will have to be examined from within in more detail in the next chapter. The first of these is that Reagan was aware, instinctively, and from the unfolding of events, that the communist world was disintegrating. He sensed that a further challenge to the colossus with the feet of clay might bring it down.

But – it must be added – for Reagan personally this was a lucky accident: it so happened that his leadership of the United States coincided with the break-up of the Soviet empire. The break-up was not of his making, nor can he be given credit for the Western policy of 'containment' which had confined communist imperialism within its own internal contradictions. Indeed, Reagan's past rhetoric abounded in Republican-style demands for 'intervention' and 'liberation' and could have given the Soviet military-industrial complex all the motives they needed to develop rigorous internal and external security methods, and in the end to embark on an offensive military strategy. But the wise and firm policy of 'containment', denounced by the Right wing the world over as too timid, had blocked most

Soviet attempts at expansion by revolutionary or military means.

The second reasonable calculation to base policy on interdependence in the 'security number one, economics number two' order of the day concerned the economic problem itself. The first premiss of Reagan's syllogism was that if the major cause of instability in the world economy, the cold war, could be brought to an end, a greater degree of stability could be restored to the world economy. Therefore, for the sake of the economy itself, economic considerations should be subordinated to strategic considerations. The second premiss was that since the United States was the leader of the defence of all industrial democracies especially in strategic matters, and notably of the two ex-enemy powers, Germany and Japan, precluded from possessing nuclear weapons, it was natural, and moral that the latter should contribute financially and in other ways to put an end to the costly and destabilizing 'cold war'. That this effort took the form of a fantastical and egoistic new technical 'defence' of the American skies, and that the financial contribution of Germany and Japan was extracted from them by the dubious method of paying for dollars with dollars, thus increasing the American foreign debt to unprecedented proportions, did not prevent Reagan from drawing the conclusion of the syllogism. This conclusion was that the general benefits of the end of the cold war, including the economic benefits, were so obvious that all methods, of all kinds which helped to attain that goal, and which would avoid a direct confrontation with the media-pampered American electorate could and should be used.

The priority given by Reagan to strategic over economic objectives was continued although in totally different conditions and with different motivations by his successor, President George Bush. The end of the cold war was not the 'end of history'. It was, in the case of Iraq's invasion of Kuwait, the possible beginning of the beginning of a new order. But of this later.

# NOTES AND REFERENCES

1. In the OED the expression 'ham' is given as (*slang*), meaning 'amateur, inexpert performer, inexperienced acting or actor, one who rants or over acts'. Reagan's adversaries in electoral campaigns have so described him.

2. In Gabriel A. Almond and G. Bingham Powell, *Comparative Politics Today: A World View*, London, 1988.

3. Lee Edwards, *Ronald Reagan. A Political Biography*, New York, 1980, p. 23.

4. Maurice Cranston, *Masks and Actors*, London, 1977, p. 4.

5. D. Diderot, *The Paradox of Acting*, New York, 1957, p. 33.

6. Dorothy Emmett, *Rules, Roles and Relations*, London, 1967, p. 158.

7. Martin Anderson, *Revolution*, New York, 1989, pp. 285–6.

8. Ibid., p. 39.

9. 'The red lights flashed "On" and Ron began describing from memory the fourth quarter of a game played between Western State University and Eureka College the previous fall. Twenty minutes later, wringing wet from tension and determination, he wound up his "broadcast" with the traditional "we return you now to our main studio". MacArthur entered the studio. "You did great! Ye be here from Saturday and I'll give ye five dollars and bus fare"'. Lee Edwards, op. cit., p. 28.

10. Ronald Reagan with Richard G. Hubler, *Where's the Rest of Me?*, New York, 1961.

11. Lee Edwards, op. cit., p. 37.

12. Benjamin Barber, *Strong Democracy*, California University Press, 1984.

13. G. Sartori, 'Video-power', *Government and Opposition*, 24, No. 1, 1989, pp. 35–53.

14. F. Christopher Atterton: *Teledemocracy. Can technology protect democracy?*', London, 1987, pp. 91–2.

15. Garry Wills, *Reagan's America* New York, 1987.

16. C. Fred Alford, 'Mastery and Retreat: Psychological Sources of Appeal of Ronald Reagan', *Political Psychology*, vol. 9, No. 4, p. 582.

17. Lee Edwards, op. cit., pp. 211–14.

18. Lester Thurow, *The Zero-Sum*, London, 1981.

19. David Mackay, *American Politics and Society*, London, 1989, p. 64. Italics in the text.

20. M. Anderson, op. cit., pp. 283 ff. One of Reagan's intimate personal advisers offers in his book a very detailed account of the making of the national security policy of the Reagan presidency, and stresses his personal role in the preparation of the Strategic Defence Initiative (SDI). In so far as, until the publication of the memoirs of Reagan, Schulz or Weinberger, he is the the only 'witness to the creation' of the SDI his testimony will be used here quite extensively. However, although *grosso modo* his account can be collated with the actual events of the development of SDI, the reader must be warned that his is a highly personal account. In addition it is also particularly interesting because it throws a surprising light on the 'kitchen-cabinet' procedure of high policy-making in the White House during Reagan's presidency, from the SDI to the Iran-Contra affair. Even if taken with a large pinch of salt, this testimony should be of great use to the student of American politics.

21. David Stockman, *Triumph of Politics*, New York, 1988.

22. Robert W. Tucker, 'Reagan's Foreign Policy' in *Foreign Affairs*, 68, No. 1, 1989.

23. Robert O. Keohane and J. Nye, *Power and Interdependence*, London, 1977, p. 42.

24. Lawrence Freedman, *The Evolution of Nuclear Strategy*, London, 1989, p. 397.

25. Anderson, op. cit., p. 76.

26. Ibid, pp. 86–7.

27. Stephen Hess, *Organizing the Presidency*, Brookings Institution, 2nd edn., New York, 1988, p. 225.

28. Ibid., pp. 93–4.

29. Robert V. Allen had to resign because of the accusation that he had been bribed by a Japanese acquaintance.

30. Of interest also to political scientists is Anderson's statement that Shultz, the Secretary of State, and Weinberger, the Defense Secretary, were told of the speech only two days beforehand, and Paul Nitze, the top arms control adviser, only a few hours before, Anderson, op. cit., p. 98.

31. Robert C. McFarlane, 'Effective Strategic Policy' in *Foreign Affairs*, 67, No. 1, 1088, pp. 33–48.

32. In Roger Lellouche and John Roper, (eds.), *Franco-British Détente Cooperation. A New Entente Cordiale?*, Royal Institute of International Affairs, London 1989, p. 154.

33. S. Talbot, 'When START Stopped', *Foreign Affairs*, 67, No. 1, 1988, p. 54.

34. Quoted in Lellouche *et al.* op. cit. p. 24.

35. Public Agenda Foundation Poll, May 1984.

36. In Charles Jones, ed. *The Reagan Legacy, Promise and Performance*, New Jersey, 1988, p. 253.

37. Anderson, op. cit., pp. 391–2.

38. Oscar Arias Sanchez, 'A Time for Peace', *Government and Opposition*, 22, No. 4, Autumn, 1987, pp. 452–6.

39. Anderson, op. cit., pp. 303.

40. David Stockman, *The Triumph of Politics*, Brookings Institution, Washington, 1987, p. 162.

41. See his 'Reaganomics and the Search for a Public Philosophy' in John L. Palmer, *Perspectives of the Reagan Years*, Washington, 1986, pp. 31–58.

42. Stockman, op. cit., p. 9.

43. David Calleo *et al.*, 'The Dollar and the Defense of the West' in *Foreign Affairs*, 66, No. 4, 1988, pp. 846–62.

44. The American economist Herbert Stern is credited with having coined this expression, which benefits from its neo-classical resonance, in the 1970s.

45. Anderson, op. cit., pp. 179–80.

46. Robert Gilpin, *The Political Economy of International Relations*, Princeton, 1987, p. 362.

47. Benjamin Friedman, 'The Campaign's Hidden Issue', *New York Review of Books*, 13 October 1988.

48. *The Financial Times*, 10 October 1989.

49. Calleo *et al*. op. cit., p. 853. Within NATO alone the per capita proportion of military costs in the national income is $1209 in the USA, $561 in the FRG, $544 in the UK, $632 in Norway and $294 in Italy.

# CHAPTER FIVE
# *Mikhail Gorbachev*

To assess Gorbachev's statesmanship presents the difficulty that he is still in power. His career is still therefore fraught with unpredictability. Moreover, compared to the other statesmen Mr Gorbachev's period in power, as we begin to examine it, is much shorter and his proclaimed task much more complex. His purpose was to 'restructure' the whole country, to 'reform' the petrified structures of a formerly totalitarian state, indeed an empire, now suffocating not only the 'revolution' it claimed to bring into the world, but even its own existence. Inevitably, therefore, given the limited and provisional record of his startling action, this chapter will be more tentative in its conclusions than the previous ones.

Conversely, for this book, concerned with the impact made by the overall phenomenon of interdependence on modern statesmanship, and politics in general, the advantage of examining Mr Gorbachev's case is that he himself sees his own and world politics through a similar perspective. Indeed, the most complete definition one can give of his political goal is that he is trying to reintroduce the Soviet Union into the circuit of technological and political interdependence of the modern world from which her previous leaders had removed her on grounds of ideological incompatibility with 'the capitalist world'. This self-isolation condemned the USSR to the acute and progressive backwardness, decay, and 'immobilism' from which it so evidently now suffers.

The expression 'interdependence' is frequently and appositely used by Mr Gorbachev, not only in his theoretical discourse on the modern world but also in his popular rhetoric. Even in the first pages of the introduction to his book *Perestroika*[1] he states very clearly that 'all countries are more interdependent than ever before'; that 'we are all passengers aboard the ship Earth'; and that, discarding any ideological commitment 'we have no universal solutions but we are prepared to cooperate'. Later this leitmotiv reappears even more clearly and frequently:

'The global problems, affecting all humanity cannot be resolved by one state or a group of states. This calls for cooperation on a world wide scale . . . We are perfectly well aware that not everything by far is within our power and that much will depend on the West, on its leaders' ability to see things in sober perspective at important crossroads of history . . . the controversial but interdependent and in many ways integral world is taking shape'.[2]

Or: 'Now allow me to deal with another major reality of our time. It also requires a new way of thinking. I mean the unprecedented diversity and increasing interconnection and integrity of the world.' Or finally, 'having seen our interdependence, the integrity of the world . . . having adopted at the 27th Congress the concept of a contradictory but interconnected, interdependent world, we began to build our foreign policy.'

To be sure, one can legitimately argue that Mr Gorbachev's concept of 'interdependence', a word he adopted from the vocabulary of modern social science, is germane also to Marxist theory. The Marxist root of Gorbachev's idea of interdependence can be said to be the explicitly proclaimed internationalism of Marxism as a whole. Its first political organization, and its anthem were both after all called 'the International'. But, in reality in Marx's theory of internationalism there was – like everywhere in Marx's work – a hidden ambivalence, indeed duplicity. While it is true that his internationalism is an element of his *Weltanschauung*: the world must be seen in its historical globality, it is also true that in his ideology, internationalism is a revolutionary postulate: the world will be unified only by the Communist Revolution.

But once this theory was applied in practice, i.e. once Marxism became Marxism-Leninism, only the postulate remained. In practice, the USSR became an empire and 'socialist internationalism' was transformed by Lenin, and after him especially by Stalin, into the slogan of submission of all Communist parties and individuals all over the world to the national interests of the USSR. After he had invented in 1919 the contradictory formula of a Soviet-state (i.e. a commune-state, which is a contradiction in terms) it took all Lenin's opportunism and intellectual cynicism to proclaim in 1920 the idea of 'socialism in one country'. Stalinism was bound to flourish in these conditions. According to Stalin, the world was to be divided into one 'socialist country', later turned into a 'bloc', and one 'bloc' of imperialist market states, which were doomed to be 'overthrown', thus bringing about the Communist world revolution. The objective condition of interdependence was explicitly rejected, and explicit Stalinist aggressiveness, based on military, more than revolutionary, grounds replaced it. But Gorbachev and his generation had had time to see clearly that this was wrong in both respects. The USSR could not win either the cold war or the hot war. Nor was interdependence something to be afraid of. But of this more later.

The second way in which Marxist theory contains the concept of interdependence, even if not under that name, is its basic recognition of the 'structural' effects of technology, which in turn might be said, with obvious simplification, to be the motor of the deterministic Marxist theory of modes of production, and of the class-war it engenders. But here too, the rationale proved to be inadequate. Marx's principal contention that the capitalist mode of production, as it advanced through the technological progression, must inexorably lead to the climax of the class-war – which was in his view the law of causality of history – was proved wrong. Rapid technological progress not only led to an abatement of the class war in advanced industrial democracies, putting an end to the myth of the irreversible proletarization of the working class; this progress proved to flourish only in the conditions of market economy and bourgeois society. And still worse, by inexorable logic it was stifled in the arch-centralistic Marxist-Leninist-Stalinist state, hermetically closed against any 'capitalist contagion'.

By the 1960s the elites of all the apparats of the USSR, the party, the army, the intelligentsia and the MVD, were stunned by the extraordinary speed of the scientific and technological developments in the West because these developments did not confirm the Soviet view of the corresponding deterioration of the capitalist system. Even Khrushchev and Brezhnev, successive leaders of the Communist Party of the Soviet Union (CPSU), proclaimed that the *nauchno tekhnologicheskaya revolyutsiya* (scientific technological revolution, or NTR) had to be fostered in the USSR and that it was deterministically bound to be led by the 'truly progressive' and also 'revolutionary' intelligentsia of the USSR. What with the early success of the *sputnik*, the effective technological modernization of the Armed Forces, and with the intensive nuclear equipment of the USSR, its leaders, from Khrushchev to Chernenko, with the possible exception of Andropov, claimed that the NTR was obviously working in favour of the Marxist-Leninist-Stalinist revolutionary state. And they also claimed that the NTR could be accommodated within the totalitarian structure. Yet already under Brezhnev, a *détente* with the capitalist world was sought in order to procure from it the discoveries and specifications of its evidently far more advanced scientific revolution.

It was at that point in history that all the Soviet elites began to doubt whether this could be achieved in the suffocating political, economic and social conditions of their system of government. Or as Gorbachev himself put it: 'At some stage this became particularly clear in the latter half of the 1970s. Something happened that was at first sight inexplicable. The country began to lose momentum. Economic failures became more frequent. Difficulties began to accumulate and deteriorate . . . stagnation began to appear in the life of society . . . And all this happened at a time when scientific and technological revolution opened up new prospects for economic and social progress.'[3] The gap between the gerontocrats and the younger generation grew increasingly. The young generation saw clearly how science and technology favoured 'capitalism' because of its openness, and were prevented from revitalizing 'socialism' because of its own seclusion behind its impenetrable monolithic structures. Interdependence was knocking at the door.

## Chernobyl and other events

Gorbachev was and is the exponent of the idea that these conditions should be drastically restructured (*perestroika*) and that what was needed first, in view of the information revolution, was freedom of information (*glasnost*). After the last decade of 'immobilism', he was finally given the political leadership to initiate and carry through these 'reforms' required by the age of interdependence.

To be sure the sense in which Gorbachev used the notion of 'interdependence' was also ambiguous, notably before Chernobyl. For instance he still claimed that the decisive criterion in the relations between the socialist and the capitalist countries, the USSR and the US, should be 'the *correlation of forces* on the world scene, the growth and activity of the peace potential',[4] a formula which, in its transparency was not far distant from the perennial Soviet vision of the increasing rallying of Western *peoples* to the USSR's peace campaign, and against their warmongering governments. Before Chernobyl, his exaltation of the superiority of the communist system over the capitalist system, and his disparagement of the latter, and especially of American imperialism, was far more striking than it became later.

Chernobyl brought real interdependence back to the centre of affairs, literally with a bang, and not only for Gorbachev. As an example of negative interdependence, i.e. of the interdependence of the damage that man can inflict on man, it could not have been more real and at the same time symbolic. All the frontiers of sovereignty, 'borders', 'nations', which hinder positive interdependence, were contemptuously ignored by the poisonous gases passing uncontrollably from the Ukraine to Scandinavia, through Poland to Italy, Germany and France, to Scotland and Wales. For Gorbachev it was a national disaster. But it was also an international opportunity. Nationally, Chernobyl was the jewel in the crown of the Soviet nuclear industry. Gorbachev's own national reputation was badly shaken for he himself caused disappointment by speaking about the accident in public only two weeks afterwards. Even then he presented a very confused and embarrassing report, aggravating the bad impression by introducing, in a crude propagandist way, an invitation to Reagan to meet him at Hiroshima in order to sign a treaty banning all nuclear armament!

But in spite of that, internationally, the effect of the true, non-ideological law of interdependence, even if in the terrible form of the Chernobyl explosion and its disastrous results, offered great advantages to Gorbachev in his difficult position. One can even speak of a pre- and a post-Chernobyl Gorbachev policy and style. The disaster brought forward the two major themes which have marked Gorbachev's discourse ever since.

One theme is that of truly positive external relations with the West. Here as we have already seen in the chapter on Reagan, and as we shall see from the opposite angle in this present chapter, Gorbachev has gone further than was expected. The meeting at Reykjavik which had followed Chernobyl by six months, was arranged in great haste at Gorbachev's insistence. Moreover his instant acceptance of the 'zero-option', as proposed by Reagan ever since the start of their exchanges and although it was still linked at Reykjavik with the hope of inducing the Americans to abandon SDI, surprised everybody. Just as surprising, later on, was the impression he gave that Soviet domination in Poland, Hungary, and even in the German Democratic Republic could be replaced by other forms of collaboration within the Warsaw Treaty Organization. Obviously, with this new realism Gorbachev hoped to achieve two aims. The first was to be assured that while undertaking his domestic reforms he would not be faced with attack from the Western powers, and therefore could, in all safety, slow down the rate of military expenditure (not to speak of expenditure on ABMs if the USSR had to compete with SDI). Secondly, Gorbachev hoped to discover how a non-market economy, with planned industry and agriculture, and state-controlled foreign trade, could possibly 'co-operate' with the interdependent market economy and free trade of the developed society. The most dramatic confirmation of this dilemma was later the pathetic appeal he issued to the G–7 nations assembled on 15 July 1989 in which he asked how the USSR could join in the work of that informal financial and monetary crisis management institution of the developed society. This happened at a time when, because of its own constitutional definitions and monolithic structures, the USSR was still unacceptable either to GATT or to the International Monetary Fund, or to OECD or even to the Council of Europe, which are the statutory gates of the minimal conditions for participation in the free world circuit of interdependence.

From an internal point of view, Gorbachev wanted to use this new relation with the 'capitalist-imperialist' world to be able to promise peace to the Soviet people. Peace, it should be recalled, had also been the first slogan of Lenin. This time, however, peace had another, supplementary meaning, not that of communism on earth, as promised by Lenin, but of relaxation of the political and economic asperities endured for seventy years by the Soviet people, because of Lenin's promise. The argument that in a world of peace, the USSR would not have to sacrifice so much for the military 'defence of socialism', the simple hope that for once butter would come before guns, and openness would put an end to terror, was sufficient to win him popular sympathy in the USSR and in the Soviet bloc. But, conversely, this implied both the dismantling of the massive structures of the totalitarian Marxist-Leninist-Stalinist state, *and*, if he were really sincere and determined, a wrestling match with the millions of parasitical Stalinist bureaucrats who still exerted the power of the state, and who would not accept its destruction. In real terms, this meant a fight with the Party, Lenin's omnipotent organization, later Stalin's cowed 'bureaucracy'.

In its first part, this chapter will deal, as in previous cases, with Gorbachev's personal circumstances and antecedents, and the extent to which his reforms were from the beginning and are still now meant to liquidate the Marxist-Leninist-Stalinist state, party and, last but not least, ideology, as the peoples of Poland, Hungary, the GDR, and some of the component Soviet republics have already been doing. The second part, entitled 'Gorbachev's policies of interdependence', attempts to assess how successful Gorbachev's policies can be internally, i.e. how much the intrinsic pluralism of interdependence can

replace the essential monolithism of the Marxist–Leninist–Stalinist
structures, and externally, i.e. how could the internal reforms help
the USSR to catch up with the scientific and technological revolution
of the Western world?

# I

# PERSONAL CIRCUMSTANCES AND HISTORICAL ANTECEDENTS

In the four previous essays, we tried to discover the extent to which
the personalities of the respective statesmen were moulded, from
their formative years to their appearance in public, by their personal,
i.e. hereditary, family, societal, cultural and religious features and
circumstances. In all four cases the biographical records were there
and had been fully utilized by biographers and journalists, who then
explained how the seeds of the personality could be discovered with
hindsight once that personality had grown to historic proportions.
This is not the case with Gorbachev. Try as you will, and indefatigable
researchers like Dev Muravka, Sewerin Bialer and especially Zhores
Medvedev, have done so most conscientiously,[5] still the biographical
record remains very unrevealing. We do not have a fully satisfactory
biography of the personality of the most daring leader of the USSR
since Stalin. He just appeared in the driving seat of General Secretary,
and was soon to be transformed into the head of state of the USSR,
without any early public signs of such a predestination.

He was born, according to official biographies, on 2 March 1931
in the village of Privol'noye in the Stavropol region – an agricultural
region north of the Caucasus, with a population ethnically Russian,
and where his mother still lives. On the occasion of his visit to the
Pope in December 1989, it was learned, *urbi et orbi*, that he had been
christened as an infant. There was nothing surprising in that. In spite
of the atheistic stance and campaigns of the Marxist–Leninist–Stalinist
regime, orthodox Russians in villages and even in towns have continued to observe the rituals of the faith, and especially the baptism of
children. Yet, according to Medvedev,[6] his father was the oldest party
member in the village, and was awarded an Order of Lenin. He died
in 1976. Mikhail Gorbachev went to school there, and according to
the brief but somewhat official biography by Mark Jones,[7] he worked
on the land during school vacations. At the age of eighteen he was

awarded the coveted order of the Red Banner of Labour. He went on then to Moscow University and as a student joined the Communist Party. After graduating in law he went on to postgraduate studies in agricultural economics. He returned to the Stavropol region and, according to the same biographer, 'from March 1962 he was engaged full time on party work. He became First Secretary of a City Party Committee, Second Secretary of a Territorial Committee, and from April 1970, First Secretary of the Stavropol Territory. He was elected to the Central Committee at the 24th Party Congress in March 1971.' From that time it took him fourteen years to find his way up, like a mole, through the tunnels of power of the Soviet career structure. He finally emerged fully fledged in 1984 as the First Secretary of that formidable machine.

In the underground workings of the party machine, promotions and demotions are the result of clashes of obscure influences, or of accidents, sometimes real, sometimes arising from causes different from those alleged by the controlled information media. Gorbachev's rapid ascent was favoured both by influence and by accident. As Medvedev shows, in his careful biography, 'although Gorbachev's rise had been noteworthy in provincial terms, on an All-Union scale he was well behind many others. When he became a member of the Central Committee in 1971, no one outside Stavropol *krai* had ever heard of him . . .Gorbachev's neighbours seemed, in the Soviet scale of evaluating political potential, to be party cadres of a higher calibre than Gorbachev. It is very important to keep this in mind, because it is not general public perception or foreign perception of Gorbachev as a leader that will determine his political success. It is the attitude of his close colleagues in the Party apparatus and in the government. And if they do not accept him as a natural leader, with superior talent, skill and knowledge, he will be unable to make much impact on Soviet policy.[8]

Now, of course, that the national and the world public, have had the opportunity to assess Gorbachev's personality directly it is beyond doubt that his talent, skill and intelligence are above the usual. The combination of courage, wisdom, natural power, and personal and diplomatic subtlety, of calculation and farsightedness, of exceptional public charm and of introspective gravity, make of him one of the most brilliant political figures of the post-war world and certainly of the Soviet Union.

These qualities doubtless helped his ascent from the depths of the CPSU. But how he achieved this without any public recognition is still difficult to understand. This is where personal relations and accident play their part. For how can a man whose initial jobs were all in agriculture, one of the least rewarding tasks in Soviet politics, even if as first secretary of the fertile Stavropol region, acquire not only the reputation but also the ambition to become one day the boss? How can a man devoting his time to the organization of better harvesting methods (for which he was congratulated by the Central Committee in *Pravda*) raise his sights from the level of tractors and kolkhozes to general visions of the future? According to most biographers, and to Medvedev in particular, two personal relationships 'modernized' him. One was the relationship with his wife, Raisa, whom he had known since his childhood. While she was taking a doctorate of philosophy at Moscow University, she had become deeply involved in the intellectual life of the capital. From everything that is known of her and indeed now seen or heard of her, she seems to have a particularly inquisitive and penetrating mind, and a great aptitude to follow and understand the trends of the modern society. She also seems to be very ambitious, for herself and for her husband and she may have injected into his earlier, more modest and parochial personality a dose of confidence in his own future and in his 'star', as de Gaulle would have put it.

The second influence was that of Zdenek Mlynar, a former leader of the reformist wing of the Czechoslovak Communist Party, now in exile. Mlynar studied at Moscow University at the same time as Gorbachev, and they even shared a room. Mlynar's developed sense of European culture and his awareness of the pitfalls of Soviet Marxism might have helped the young Russian communist to acquire more critical attitudes towards the real situation of his country and party. But relationships, in the terminology of the Kremlin, also mean the patronage of some junior members of the hierarchy by their seniors. Gorbachev's patrons were his immediate chief, the Central Committee secretary for agricultural affairs, Kulakov, who came from the same region, and who was considered to be a rival of Brezhnev's and one of his possible successors. Kulakov died in somewhat mysterious circumstances, leaving his post vacant. The official communiqué stated only, in most unusual terms, that 'his heart stopped beating', and there were rumours of suicide or worse. Gorbachev's other patrons were first M. Suslov, the aged and austere ideological chief of the CPSU, one of the longest-serving members of the Politburo; and Andropov who had only recently been promoted to the Politburo but who, because of his long connection with the apparat of the KGB, carried a particularly great weight in the constellation of power, as was proved by his own accession to leadership after the death of Brezhnev. Suslov and Andropov had different horizons, but sufficient acumen to discern the original qualities of Gorbachev's mind in the monotonous mediocrity of the apparatchiks who surrounded them.

His friendship with Andropov proved to be particularly important for Gorbachev. As in the case of Kulakov, fate, in the shape of the scythe of Death, put a very rapid end to Andropov's career. There followed the tragi-comic episode of the 'election' of the ancient and moribund Chernenko, who himself had devolved a lot of his tasks on Gorbachev, thus bringing him into the very centre of affairs. After fate, again wearing the mask of Death, removed Chernenko from his path, Gorbachev was elected First Secretary of the Party, which by then badly needed a shake-up. The passage from Secretary General to head of state seemed almost inevitable, after Gorbachev had succeeded in surprising the USSR and the world with the entirely new slogans of *glasnost* and *perestroika*.

In the guise of a conclusion to this necessarily brief and enigmatic biography, one can only try to use the few facts available in order to attempt to answer one of the essential questions about Gorbachev's ultimate political orientation. Is he instinctively orientated towards saving and reviving the system in which he was born, and are his reforms similarly motivated? Or, is he, because of his formative experiences, in reality fundamentally opposed to the principles of that system and does his determination to restructure it therefore go much further than 'reform'? Does he indeed aim at replacement with opposing structures: the market instead of total planning; pluralism instead of monolithism; constitutional freedoms instead of coercive absolutism? Did he realize, in short, with his friends Yakovlev and Shevardnadze that the system was exhausted? The known facts of his past justify either of these interpretations.

Evidently his undeniable intelligence and inborn qualities of states-manship will help him to make many 'qualitative jumps', as for instance that which transferred him from General Secretary of the Party to head of state, with all the great differences which these two positions imply. For as head of state he could open up his own views and aims and advance from Marxist-Leninist 'reform' to anti-Marxist-Leninist market system 'restructuring'. In his 1988 Reith lectures, Geoffrey Hosking rightly distinguishes between a Gorbachev Mark I, and Gorbachev Mark II. Will a Gorbachev Mark III appear in 1991, with an entirely different philosophy from that with which he hedged his bets until now? Will he be able to face all the contradictions and incompatibilities between the official ideology and the reality?

This question can be examined better against the background of 'historical antecedents'.

In contrast with the little we know about Gorbachev's personal circumstances, the policies of *glasnost* and *perestroika*, for which Gorbachev asked for and obtained the leadership of the USSR, have been expounded at great length and in great detail. They represent the recognition, which could no longer be delayed, that if the Soviet state was to survive, it would have to be subjected to a surgical operation, carried out in the full light of day. This is why the name *perestroika* (restructuring) was so well-chosen, for it was the structures of the state itself which had to be changed. The Marxist-Leninist-Stalinist state had been structurally malformed as a monolithic state from the beginning. Now it needed to be totally dismantled and recast, if still possible, in a normal pluralistic mould. So, while in order to understand Gorbachev's rescue mission one need only examine the last phases of the Brezhnev era of stagnation and corruption, in order to understand the Brezhnevite period one has to go back in history to Stalinism (of which Brezhnevism was the last convulsion) and beyond Stalinism to Leninism, and beyond Leninism to Marxism. It is only then that one can uncover the original and fatal flaw in the state structures, and examine if and how they can be restructured.

This kind of diagnosis of the present ills by scrutinizing the formation of the Marxist-Leninist-Stalinist state from its very beginning and finding the initial congenital malformation is practised by Gorbachev himself. He too accuses the past of having overburdened and deformed the present and, even more so, the future of the USSR with misleading ideological prescriptions and with its practical misdeeds. But it is noticeable how much more seldom he mentions the Marxist foundations either because in a typical Russian way, he now considers Marx's German western ideas alien to Russian realities and/or because he thinks that what was relevant in them was fully incorporated into Leninism. And he reserves all his wrath and indignation for Stalinism and its final degeneration: Brezhnevism. Leninism is not only therefore silently absolved, but still presented as the model to follow and as what would have led to pure and successful 'socialism' had Stalinism not corrupted it and stifled it with such perversity.

Gorbachev's book *Perestroika* is full of references to Lenin and Leninist inspiration – even if sometimes the quotations are inserted into the text without much consideration for their relevance. But strangely, and indeed very significantly, the first reference to Lenin's ideas in the book has a double connotation. On the one hand, Lenin's remarks on the 'evolution' of the state are highly, almost damningly critical of the ways it was taking. And, on the other hand, Gorbachev insistently draws attention to the fact that those most relevant remarks belong to the *late* period of Lenin's work (the distinction between late and early Lenin being reminiscent of Lukacz's desperate attempt to distinguish between the 'young' and the 'mature' Marx). The quotation analysed below is significantly the first in the book. And, significantly, it draws attention to the difference between the *late* writings of Lenin, and the rest of his works and the Leninist ideology.

So indirectly, that is by allusions and using the 'party-code', Gorbachev says a lot when he presents his thoughts on Lenin with the following introductory message:

*Turning to Lenin* has greatly stimulated *the Party and society* in their search to find explorations and answers to the questions that have arisen. *Lenin's works in the last years of his life* have drawn particular attention. . .Today we have a better understanding of Lenin's *last works* which were in essence *his political bequest,* and we more clearly understand why these works appeared. *Gravely ill, Lenin was deeply concerned for the future of socialism.* He perceived the lurking dangers for the new system. We too must understand his concern.[9]

Decoding this text, and notably the sentences I have italicized, *Turning to Lenin* means repudiating Stalinism, turning from Stalinism to Lenin. But it is not to the whole Lenin that Gorbachev suggests one ought to turn, to find the answers. Gorbachev makes it clear that it is only in 'Lenin's works, written in the last years of his life', that the relevant answers can be found and he openly stresses that when 'gravely ill Lenin was deeply concerned with the future of socialism'.

Now considering that Lenin was 'gravely ill' from 1922 to 1924 (his last public appearance, after his first stroke, was at the Congress of Soviets in Moscow on 22 November 1922), this reference has two meanings. One is the reminder that official policy at this time was the New Economic Policy (NEP). The NEP was Lenin's policy of neo-capitalist compromise, allowing the private ownership of land by peasants and some freedom of manufacture. And the other is that Stalin had already been appointed General Secretary in 1922 – the period 1922-24 being just the time when Lenin realized how dangerous that appointment was. (This was the period when he wrote to Kamenev, asking him to ask Stalin to apologize to his wife, Krupskaya, to whom Stalin had been rude; and in his 'testament', later confiscated by Stalin, Lenin warned the party against him.)

But there is something even more directly relevant. At that period all Lenin's writings dealt with the New Economic Policy, and during his serious illness, Lenin wrote, or rather dictated, only a few messages and addresses, and only one 'work' (in the sense that it has always been considered sufficiently important to be included in Lenin's *Collected Works*.[10] This was *Better Fewer but Better*, dated 3 March 1923,[11] which is a clear denunciation of the frightening growth in the power of the bureaucratic state, indeed of the state-apparatus (or, according to my basic theory, of the Apparat-State).[12]

Starting with the sentence 'In the matter of improving our state apparatus', Lenin continues 'we have so far been able to devote so little thought and efficiency to our state apparatus. Our state apparatus is so deplorable, not to say wretched, that we must first think very carefully now how to combat its defects, bearing in mind that these defects are rooted in our past.' This drastic condemnation leads, according to Lenin, to the dilemma he clearly, if dramatically stated: 'Either we prove now that we have really learned something about state-organization (we ought to have learned something in five years) or we prove that we are not sufficiently mature for it. If the latter is the case, we had better not tackle the task.'[13]

These are very striking judgements and admissions. Although in form they refer to the recruitment of officials in the ever-growing state apparatus, in reality they have a deliberately profound resonance – which is also the resonance to which Gorbachev attaches so much importance, otherwise why should he draw attention now to what could be only an occasional piece?

Gorbachev is right in that respect. Lenin's remarks have all the significance and the importance of a physically and politically impotent man seeing, like the sorcerer's apprentice, how the evil genie of the totalitarian state he had uncorked is invading the whole territory of 'socialism in one country', infesting its whole atmosphere with its poisonous ideological fumes and flattening everything under its pressure. And Gorbachev makes clear its intention in quoting especially that final cry of despair out of Lenin's whole opus, in which he admits that 'we had better not tackle the task'.

Lenin's historical task had been to link Marx's incomplete political theory with the 'praxis' of leading the revolution to its logical and constructive end. Both Marx and Lenin were revolutionaries. Their aim was to overthrow capitalism and smash (*zerbrechen*) the bourgeois state, Marx's principal revolutionary target. And so absolute, so irresistible was their aim to destroy something unjust – in essence private property and its consequence, capitalism (although Tsarist Russia was scarcely a good example of a capitalist regime) that they believed that once the injustice was removed, normal life, a life of natural justice, would re-establish itself in all its spontaneous harmony. Neither Lenin, nor Marx, let alone Engels, ever described how, and by what form of human organization the state would be succeeded once it was 'smashed' (*zerbrochen*) by the revolution. Although Marx was taunted by the anarchists in the First International to answer this question, to which he gave only evasive and contradictory replies, the subject was not of such importance for him. The Paris Commune of 1871 was the nearest Marx ever came, in his confused visions, to what he wrongly believed to be a communist revolution, and it came to an end too soon to prove anything in terms of post-revolutionary organization.

But for Lenin, it was entirely different. The Russian revolution of February 1917 caught him off balance, just when he was trying to give some hasty answers to the question of the relation between the state and the revolution. *State and Revolution* was the title of a book which he was working on but which he finished only after he had carried the Bolshevik revolution of October 1917 to a successful conclusion, and when the immediate problem of what to put in the place of the 'smashed' state hit him in the face. His pathetic exclamation, scribbled in his personal 'blue notebook' reveals the depths of his confusion, and of Marx's confusion too. 'But further on', wrote Lenin, 'Marx speaks of "the future state of communist society". Thus even in *communist* society the state will exist! Is there not a contradiction in this?' was Lenin's entry in his notebook.[14] Yet in *State and Revolution*, and during the first year of the revolution, he managed to paper over the cracks of this confusion, arguing, on the one hand, that the revolution, having smashed the previous state, then finds its own natural organization in the spontaneous action of the communes or, in Russian, soviets, to be taken in both the territorial and corporate functional sense of that expression, in both languages. In communes, self-management prevails, and 'every cook governs'. But at the same time Lenin insisted with due caution that what was also needed was a 'state of the dictatorship of the proletariat', essentially transitional (only five years he once asserted) whose single aim was to be the state to put an end to all states in history.

But Lenin suffered two direct disappointments, two evident refutations of Marx's and his own early utopianism by reality. One, the most important of all, was the total failure to abolish private property and to establish 'social property' which he and Marx believed would instantaneously and *ipso facto* bring about the self-managed society (i.e. without a state) by means of the simple act of the prohibition and expropriation of all private property. If Lenin had ever believed in this enormous qualitative leap, 1917-19 were the years in which he recognized that this was a misleading illusion. Here again, Gorbachev and his followers throw a direct light on the problem. Thus Leonid Abalkin, the then deputy prime minister (economic) and the architect of the 'economic reform' to come, dotted the 'i's and crossed the 't's, very early on when he wrote:

Life has shown that social property in itself is no guarantee of success and that obstacles to the development of the productive forces, to scientific and technical progress may arise even under such property . . .In the socialist society where there is only one master, the emergence of disproportion contradicts (except in extreme conditions, as in wartime) the very nature of social property.[15]

So, once it was confirmed that the abolition of private property was not the Open Sesame Marx had predicted, which would enable society to function automatically and harmoniously, the Russian Bolsheviks, had to take revolution back under the control of the oppressive state.

As is well known, Lenin first re-founded the Russian state on 19 July 1918. It took over all the 'branches of industry', then transformed the revolutionary party into the new bureaucracy (apparat) of the state, and the state into an apparat state. Then, no longer believing in a European, let alone a world revolution, he accepted *de facto* what Stalin was to proclaim *de jure*, the reality of 'socialism in one country'; which on 6 July 1923, when he was already 'gravely ill', was expanded from a 'country' to the whole of the former Russian empire in the guise of the Union of the Soviet Socialist Republics. In all this he had the full support and collaboration of Stalin, and of Trotsky. For Trotsky had the double honour of re-creating the army – an institution which, together with the police is, according to Marx, incompatible with a Communist, as distinct from a 'Jacobin' political organization – and of using that army to crush the last 'soviet' which still opposed the 'state', the Kronstadt Soviet (commune) in 1921. Finally, when Lenin was already mortally ill, he had the terrible privilege of seeing how Stalin carried off the package he, Lenin, had so well prepared.[16] Stalin then transformed it during and after industrialization into a totalitarian apparat-state, and during and after the war into an imperialist state, pursuing territorial expansion, first with the help of Hitler, and then with the help of the Western allies.

The Marxist-Leninist-Stalinist state was therefore from the beginning a constitutional misfit, a living lie, which was doomed to disintegrate because of its congenital malformation. This malformation became increasingly perceptible with the advance of the industrial technological revolution, and with the passage of the USSR itself from the phase of primary industrialization, in which some forms of political mobilization can be of help, to the phase of industrial technological production for which participation is ineluctably required. For participation requires political, cultural and social freedom as well as transnational co-operation of free exchanges in an interdependent world. The Marxist-Leninist-Stalinist state could not, because of its very nature and origin, fulfil any of these conditions. The USSR, as a monolithic state, ruled by a progressively more corrupt party bureaucracy, and as a multinational empire, ruling over territories either annexed or occupied, was bound, given the basic flaws in its structure, to flounder under the weight of these burdens.

After the Brezhnev decade of 'painful and shameful immobilism and corruption' (Gorbachev's expressions) the country was in a hazardous situation. The Marxist-Leninist-Stalinist apparat state was visibly incapable of coping with the technological advance and with the interdependence, internal and external, which that advance was imposing on all states. Its main apparat, formerly the revolutionary party, had been transformed into a corrupt and inefficient bureaucracy. Its ideology, which until the 1950s provided it with official spiritual authority, had been shattered after all the sacrifices Stalin had asked it to make – first through its subservience to the state, then through the great betrayal of the temporary alliance with fascism; and finally by being transformed into an instrument of Soviet imperialism. And since the Marxist-Leninist-Stalinist state was by definition (by Lenin's own definition) an *oppositionless* state it stifled its society to the point of making it the most backward of all the societies of the industrial powers in the modern technological age. Only one other apparat made any progress in the USSR during that time, the apparat of the Armed Forces, but this could be a rival to the Party. Lenin's terrible warning now acquired dramatic significance : 'Either we prove now that we have really learned something about state organization or we prove that we are not sufficiently mature for it. If the latter is the case, we had better not tackle the task.'

Gorbachev's reform was aimed at both the Party and Soviet society, with the latter gradually acquiring predominance. Hence the demand for more light (*glasnost*) on these particularly sombre problems, and a rapid restructuring (*perestroika*) of structures ill-adjusted from the beginning. For only by making these hasty but indispensable adjustments could the Soviet Union, in Gorbachev's view, enter the circuit of interdependence which linked all the modern industrial technological states. Thus:

Having adopted at the 27th Congress the concept of a contradictory but interconnected and interdependent and essentially integral world we began to build our foreign policy on this foundation . . .To be sure, distinctions will remain. But should we duel because of them? Would it not be more correct to step over the things that divide us for the sake of the interests of all mankind, for the sake of life on earth?[17]

The only optimistic, if not Utopian part of Gorbachev's otherwise realistic discourse was his idea that 'distinctions will remain'. In reality if the USSR succeeded in entering the interdependent world, it meant that it should abandon all its previous differences, or in other words its incompatibilities with the scientific-technological revolution. All these incompatibilities, of which only the principal will be mentioned here derive from the initial incompatibility between the monolithic revolutionary will and the pluralistic evolutionary society. *Voluntarism*, which in theory was Marx's contribution and in practice that of Lenin, Trotsky and Stalin to the making of revolution, is motivated by the belief that revolutionary *will* can transform the perennial human condition. Hence also, in the case of the French Revolution and especially the Russian Revolution, the militant atheism.

Now, all revolutions are manifestations of human will, as all are supposed to 'smash' unjust situations so that natural justice can re-establish itself in its abode; but, first, in all revolutions, including the French Revolution, it is difficult to distinguish between the part played by the voluntary action of their leaders and the even more chain-reaction-like involuntary consequences of the actions of the impulsive people, masses or crowds, escalating with the reactions of those attacked. And, secondly, all revolutions have a local or national self-limitation, in spite of the universality of the aim of the pursuit of human justice.

But the Russian Revolution of November 1917 was different in both respects. It was the first in which a pre-established 'organization', the party, set in motion, directed and constantly controlled the actions of the herd-like 'people' – thus establishing the new pattern of party-revolutions, from the Fascist and Nazi revolutions to the present-day Sandinista revolution. And its declared principle was as Marx, Trotsky and Mao knew so well, and Lenin too but to a more limited extent, that a communist revolution could make sense, and be viable, only if it was worldwide. But, because, historically the Russian Revolution took place in a backward country the initial and general incompatibility so created between 'world communist revolution' as against 'socialism in one country', engendered many other incompatibilities such as :

- essentially decentralized communist self-management versus mono-lithic totalitarian statism;
- federalization of different peoples versus domination by the Rus-sian people;
- social and political equality versus party-dictatorship and cor-ruption;
- pursuit of scientific-technological advance versus ideological cen-sorship and obscurantism;
- pursuit of personal initiative and responsibility in conditions of police control and bureaucratic oppression;
- participation in the information revolution under state control of all communications;
- pursuit of intensive, as against extensive production in inefficaci-ous planning conditions;
- increase of distribution and sales of products without market and market prices.

All these and many other incompatibilities evident for at least the last forty years, but predictable for the last seventy years, indeed ever since 1919, exploded like a time-bomb in Gorbachev's hands as he seized the helm of the decrepit empire.


## II

## GORBACHEV'S POLICIES OF INTERDEPENDENCE

To start with a metaphor, Gorbachev's self-assigned mission was to keep the heavy ship of the USSR floating on the waves of the information revolution washing over it, and to continue to sail, al-though very late and in difficult conditions, towards the open seas of interdependence. The metaphor is appropriate insofar as in reality the alternative for the Marxist-Leninist-Stalinist system is either to sail with the wind or to sink. Hence the common point of the two initial policies of interdependence Gorbachev proposed: to catch the fast wind of the freedom of information in the old sails: *glasnost*; and to throw out as much of the ballast of the old system as he could, in the attempt to restructure the ship of state into a new model, slimmer, lighter and more adaptable to modern techniques: *perestroika*.

It was, however, very clear from the outset that although the two policies were presented as inseparable, *glasnost* has had an immediate success and has made a direct impact, while *perestroika* faces grave problems of practical applicability, indeed of feasibility.

The first advantage of *glasnost* was that being in essence a freeing of communication and information, it was inherently consonant with the revolution of the same name. *Ipso facto*, the USSR and most European communist countries have become yet another link in the chain of communication-information which now surrounds the whole world, instead of continuing with their powerless Canute-like struggle against the waves, now literally the electronic waves, with such ridiculous devices as jamming and censorship, or such degrading ones as spying, jailing and torturing people who sought information.

The second advantage of *glasnost* was that, as the similarity of names itself indicates, it was opposed to and had to replace the preponderant obligation of the individual Party member and of the Marxist-Leninist-Stalinist party, to observe and obey *partiinost* (partyness). *Partiinost* is the compulsory rule whereby the Party member puts the interests of the Party, as defined by his superiors in the Party, above his own judgement, consciousness and interest. Koestler's *Darkness at Noon* is the classic description of the tragedy of the mind caught up in *partiinost*, which is the blindfold every Party member must wear. It separates the communist mind from the evident reality and, worse, from elementary human ethics. Compared with this supreme exercise in obscurantism, *glasnost* enlightens and opens the personal judgement of the erstwhile censored and brain-washed Party member. Once he can bask in the freedom of information, all the lies and chicaneries of the Party are revealed in the new transparency. *Glasnost* sweeps away *partiinost* by forcing the individual and collective communist mind to use its own judgement in the light of truth and objectivity. It acts as a disintoxicant and chases away the spells of the Party agit-prop, the very important mission of which is to keep human judgement in a state of constant intoxication. Indeed, as we shall see later, Gorbachev tried to situate himself and his judgement *above* the Party by becoming head of the *state*, an entirely different perspective.

This was also the cause of the third advantage: the instant popularity of the abrogation of the existing measures prohibiting freedom of information. Regardless of Marx's materialistic dogma of economic determinism, human beings tend by their idealism towards knowledge and truth. By granting the citizens of his state access to universal knowledge and the pursuit of truth, Gorbachev not only gave them the direct satisfaction of using this new freedom of information but he also restored in them a sense of human dignity which had been so deeply humiliated by the Marxist-Leninist-Stalinist despotism. What remained problematic, but in many senses different, was the disjunction operated by the government between freedom of information and expression on the one hand and freedom of association, on the other, with which it is always constitutionally and logically linked. This problem, however, insofar as it derives from the fundamental condition put forward and insistently repeated by Gorbachev, that all freedom of information must be comprehended within the 'restructured' one-party system, can be more appropriately discussed with the general problems of the restructuring, of *perestroika*.

Because *glasnost*, as a politico-administrative measure, which consisted only in abolishing interdictions and lifting prohibitions, was so easy and so immediate in its effects, its requirements were from the beginning and remained different, indeed opposed to the requirements of *perestroika*. In *glasnost*, once the rules and the agencies of censorship, control and spying had been abolished 'at a stroke', by decree, free speech and writing, free reading and listening came back as natural functions, as normality always wins over abnormality.

But the restructuring of the Marxist-Leninist-Stalinist system, so as to change it from a more sophisticated one-party state into a market-democracy freely communicating with the world market requires the taking of very serious measures. First of all, many state institutions and political habits which had hitherto been considered essential for that system had to be uprooted; and, afterwards an even more difficult task had to be undertaken: the elimination, destruction if possible, of at least some of the more insuperable obstacles to a market economy installed by the old system, and the presentation of a plan of what should be constructed in their stead. In this field, the Gorbachev administration has most dramatically failed, after five years of practising *perestroika*. Indeed, on 24 November 1989 in an article in *Pravda* of two and a half pages, Gorbachev deliberately wrote:

Some people reproach us that we have no clear-cut detailed plan to realize the concept of *perestroika*. I believe that we would have made a serious theoretical error if we had tried to impose ready-made schemes upon society, or to force contemporary realities into a procrustean bed. This was the characteristic failure of Stalinism with which we have parted ways. [18]

And, moreover, he did not hesitate to add that 'unfortunately so far *perestroika* in the party is slower than in society as a whole, which creates certain difficulties in securing its vanguard role'.

These were poignant confessions, which still reflected the incapacity of the Gorbachev government to obtain popular support for the operation of restructuring both what was not working before it came to power and what it had destroyed since then. And this was indeed also the great difference already described, between *perestroika* and *glasnost*, which needed no action apart from the official gesture to open the doors, remove the obstacles and take off the gags. The rest is done by the people, liberated at last in that respect and running in myriads of centrifugal ways. But *perestroika*, the operation of restructuring, must bring them back to a centripetal purpose. Their common effort is the *sine qua non* of the gigantic constructive action which is, implicitly and explicitly, required in the great change so loudly heralded. But, in turn, that effort could not be achieved without presenting to those who are meant to produce it, a design clear and acceptable, at least to the majority of the people, of what they should construct. Even the generations of workers who died building the great cathedrals of the Middle Ages knew what they would look like when they were finally built.

Considering the peculiar lack of directions and indications from Gorbachev on how the policy of *perestroika* could help the USSR to re-enter, as he evidently wishes, the circuit of interdependence of the developed society, the best way to assess its chances is by examining two questions:

- how should and could the obsolescent Stalinist empire which had until now blocked the current of world interdependence, be opened up to it and participate in it?
- how should and could a non-market, even an anti-market state, indeed power, participate in the world market without itself becoming a pluralistic market-state?

## Transforming the empire

The three-pronged action by which Gorbachev hoped to arrest the visible decline, and possible fall of what had been the mightiest revolutionary power in history, was in itself an exercise in interdependence. The military problem, and notably that of military expenditure, was as dependent on the state of the economy as the latter was on the shift from defence and heavy industry to consumer goods and technology expenses and investments; the reduction in military preparations was as dependent on the disarmament and peace agreements with the West, as those agreements were on the military and political liberalization effected or to be effected by the leadership of the USSR, both within its own state system and in that of the states of the 'socialist commonwealth'; the political reforms were as dependent on the promises of the communist leadership as their implementation was dependent on the reactions of the social and national groups now enabled by *glasnost* to manifest their opinions; those popular reactions were as dependent on the effectiveness of the economic reforms as the latter were on the political and societal reforms, which in turn were dependent on the external situation and on the USSR's chances of forging new and lasting links of peace and collaboration with the West; which in turn, etc. . . .

It is to the credit of Gorbachev to have realized from the very beginning that he had to advance on the three fronts simultaneously, because each one conditioned the other. To use Geoffrey Hosking's perspicacious distinction, there was a Gorbachev Mark I, who hoped that once *glasnost* had begun to liberate people's feelings and once *perestroika* had been announced, most problems would be instantly solved, and a Gorbachev Mark II, who during and after the first four years of internal failures and external successes concentrated mainly on the latter.

Thus as from September 1989, when he made the resounding speech on multilateral disarmament at the United Nations and also added categorically that 'the new phase requires the de-ideologizing of relations among states', Gorbachev surprised everybody by seeming, on the one hand, to look on with benign neglect, if not approval, while Poland, Hungary, the GDR and Czechoslovakia abolished the one-party communist system; and on the other hand by the much more real and much more significant announcement of the unilateral reduction of Soviet armaments and forces. To take first the military strategic overtures which Gorbachev made, in order to impress both the Western leaders and Western opinion with the genuineness of his intentions concerning disarmament, and, at the same time, to arouse in the Soviet peoples the hope that at least they could be sure of peace in the world. The new reduction and withdrawal of forces amounted, according to NATO calculations[19] to a balance in which the conventional land-based forces in Eastern Europe would amount to:

| Forces | NATO | Soviet forces after cuts |
|---|---|---|
| Main battle tanks | 22,000 | 27,000 |
| Artillery | 14,458 | 24,500 |
| Personnel | 2.21m | 2.2m[20] |
| Combat aircraft | 3,977 | 5,250 |

This, of course, hardly corresponded to NATO's proposals – as for instance with respect to the essential question of tanks, where

NATO had proposed that neither the Warsaw Treaty Organization, nor NATO should have more than 12,000 tanks in Europe,
while Gorbachev proposed reducing Soviet tanks by 10,000, leaving
27,000. But three other circumstances gave a different significance
this time to the Soviet proposals. One is that the cuts would according to American quasi-official estimates[21] 'reduce the aggregate
combat power of the Warsaw Treaty Organization by some 20–25%',
which considering the basic superiority in quality and effectiveness
of NATO-equipment would render future offensive actions of the
Warsaw Treaty forces very improbable. The second circumstance
was that, for once, it was clear that those cuts had been made without
and against the general assent of the Soviet military, but, conversely,
they were bound to have a favourable effect on the overall Soviet budget expenditures. And thirdly, it was clear that once it had
been announced that Soviet troops would be withdrawn from the
four countries the anti-communist opposition in those states, now
'de-ideologized', would be strongly encouraged to overthrow their
respective Marxist-Leninist-Stalinist regimes.

This happened with a speed and a violence which probably surprised even such well-informed observers as Shevardnadze and Baker
after their particularly discreet fishing tête-à-tête in September 1989.
In all four countries public demonstrations and mass demonstrations between September and November 1989 defeated the forces
of reaction which until then had mastered them with their batons,
water-tanks, tear gas, machine guns and tanks, but which now either
refused, or were not even asked, to carry out their local Tienanmen
Square performances. The people in action in all four countries, plus
to a lesser extent Bulgaria, rejected the old Marxist-Leninist-Stalinist
leaders like Honecker or Zhivkov. They were rapidly replaced in the
parties, in an understandable mood of panic, by younger accomplices
like Egon Krenz and Adamec who were readier to 'do a Gorbachev'
as the saying goes, than the previous ossified leadership. The people
filled the streets, responded unanimously to calls for general strikes
and physically demolished walls, even the great Berlin wall, that most
appropriate symbol of Marxist-Leninist-Stalinist evil.

They also imposed their constitutional demands which the new
'leaders' of the Party accepted with hypocritical enthusiasm, as if those
demands were just what Marx, Lenin and Stalin had heralded and
prescribed. Above all, the reformists obtained at a stroke freedom of
information and of association, and the unretractable promise of free
multi-party elections, leading to parliamentary constitutional regimes.
What kind of parties and regimes these were going to be depended on

the different historical, social and political background of each of these countries.[22]

In Poland, the opposition had been visible ever since 1956. The spontaneous alliance between the workers, notably the dockers and steelworkers from Gdansk, farmers and intellectuals, formed a powerful resistance, under the aegis of the Catholic Church backed by a powerful diaspora in the West. The Catholic Church plays the median role in this alliance, as it influences on the one side the opposition both of the trade unions and of the intellectuals, and on the other, parts of the government and state-apparat, notably the army. Indeed, when on 13 December 1981, it became clear that the Communist Party was too incompetent, obsolete and corrupt to 'govern' the country or to stop, by its own means, the general revolt of the people, General Jaruzelski, the head of the army, formed a Military Council of national salvation and imposed martial law. Short of Soviet intervention, this was the only possible solution and although the Catholic Church opposed it openly, behind the scenes it helped to keep some bridges with the government open and to advise *Solidarnosc* not to carry its formidable opposition into the streets. The argument was particularly reasonable as the endemically bad economic situation of Poland was aggravated by the refusal of the USA (but not of the European Community) to continue its economic collaboration with a regime under martial law. The real opportunity occurred in September 1989 when Gorbachev announced the 'dis-ideologization' of relations between states and the Soviet decision not to intervene militarily – the explicit renunciation of the Brezhnev doctrine – in the affairs of other 'socialist' states; the opposition then rapidly organized elections and won them, putting the Communist Party in a minority. A new government was formed, headed by a Catholic Prime Minister, Tadeusz Mazowiecki, whose first and almost sole duty was to save the country from bankruptcy, for bad economic organization is Poland's Achilles's heel.

In Hungary, which in 1956 gave the most heroic proof of a total revolt against Soviet Communism, and demanded to be allowed to hold free elections and to become neutral (i.e. to leave the Warsaw Treaty Organization) Janos Kadar, the president imposed by the Soviet tanks which crushed the revolt (in the midst of the Suez crisis) sensed that plain Marxist-Leninist-Stalinist methods were no longer enough. In a country which, in contrast with Poland, has a particular talent for running its economy, a 'new economic mechanism' was allowed to operate after 1968, and later on, private enterprises were allowed to function. The party was restricting itself to 'macro-economic co-ordination', and intervening less and less in the management of industry and commerce: and the progress of small forms of co-operatives and of joint ventures with foreign capital, particularly needed by a country dependent on foreign trade, proved most successful. Soon accepted, like Poland and Romania, as a member of GATT, of the IMF and of the World Bank, the Hungarian regime succeeded in managing its economy, although with great difficulties. But the economic liberalization it was thus striving to achieve could not make progress without political liberalization. Again, as in the case of Poland, once sure that at least under Gorbachev the USSR would not repeat its murderous military intervention, the Hungarian people easily re-enacted its magnificent conduct of 1956 and forced the government, this time, to throw out Kadar, to achieve complete *glasnost*, and to call multi-party elections for 1990.

The events developed in East Germany even more rapidly than anywhere else and than anyone, with the possible exception of Mr Gorbachev who had come to embrace Herr Honecker just ten days before, could have thought. The events were also more spectacular than anywhere else because first tens of thousand of professional people, experts and academics voted with their feet, passing through Hungary and Czechoslovakia to the Federal Republic of Germany; and, secondly, because once Egon Krenz had lifted the travel restrictions, millions of East Germans crossed the frontier sweeping aside the wall of infamy in a torrential march. Here again the demonstrations were enough to transform the ferocious East German police (there were four kinds of police) into jovial customs officials overnight; and here again the Churches, and especially the Evangelical Church played a predominant part, providing the population with refuges where they could meet and associate together.[23] Soon after, however, between the autumn of 1989 and that of 1990, the East German rising led to the reunification of Germany. Obviously, in present-day conditions of interdependence, this fundamental change led to an overall geopolitical reconsideration of Europe and the whole western world. So the history of East Germany could no longer be synchronized with the much slower and more parochial history of, say, Czechoslovakia.

For, in Czechoslovakia, Mr Adamec too tried, though with less talent, to 'do a Gorbachev'. But here again the developments, although very similar in style and rhythm to those in the other countries, differed in two respects. One was the general strike in September 1989 which proved above any doubt that all social classes, ethnic, cultural and religious groups were ready to a man to put an end to the Marxist-Leninist-Stalinist regime. And the second, which greatly influenced the first, was the fact that the 'Prague spring' of 1968 had lasted long enough before it was crushed by the forces of the Warsaw Treaty Organization (with the exception of Romania) to produce a complete philosophy of a modern 'socialism with a human face', which needed only further updating of its basic logic to unite the entire population behind its programme under the personnel already trained in democratic government and indeed even behind its own former leader, Alexander Dubcek, who was still alive. It is true that in Czechoslovakia, unlike in Poland or in Hungary, there will always lurk the problem of the not always harmonious relations between Czechs and Slovaks. But, whereas an inherently arch-centralistic communist regime can only aggravate the ethnic anomalies in a given state (as is clearly the case in the other two communist federal states: the USSR and Yugoslavia), a really constitutional pluralistic regime is almost congenitally favourable to federal collaboration (as is proved by the case of Switzerland, the United States and the Federal Republic of Germany). Soon in Czechoslovakia, with the writer Havel as the new President of the Republic and Dubcek as President of the Parliament, real democracy was on its way.

A more complicated situation developed in Romania. Here Ceauşescu, and his wife, both evidently pathologically mad, had transformed, as the popular joke went, 'socialism in one country' into 'socialism in one family'. A form of oriental despotism and nepotism, comparable in cruelty and tyranny with the worst African or Central American dictatorships had so oppressed the population, through one of the most systematic secret police networks (*Securitate*), that for a long while nothing seemed to happen. However, when it happened, on 19 December, first in Timisoara, a town on the frontier with Hungary, Ceauşescu, who was in Iran on that day, ordered the army on his return to suppress the revolt by any means. This the *Securitate*, troops and tanks proceeded to do, killing hundreds. Then on 21 December 1989 in Bucharest itself, Ceauşescu, for the first time in his life, was howled down by a crowd which he had assembled to show his popularity. In Bucharest, however, the situation changed entirely, when the Army, whose Minister had 'committed suicide' on the previous day on the orders of Ceauşescu, refused to shoot the demonstrators. Ceauşescu and his wife realized that all was lost. On 22 December they fled in a helicopter from the roof of one of the munificent palaces he had built in Bucharest. He was arrested the same day; mysteriously kept somewhere for another two days; and 'judged' and 'executed' with his wife on 25 December.

A Front of National Salvation, composed of high members of the Romanian Communist Party, who had recently been dismissed by

Ceauşescu because he doubted their loyalty, improvised a government. They announced democratic reforms, rapid elections and other forms of *glasnost*, and asked for help from abroad. This came rapidly and in great quantities, thus gradually improving the conditions of the literally starving and frozen Romanian population.

In Romania, however, the people showed no confidence whatsoever in the post-communist and allegedly democratic government which, in order to convince the people, declared the Communist Party 'illegal' and 'dissolved'. But the old Romanian political parties, like the National Peasant Party and the Liberal Party, met with great difficulties in reorganizing their cadres and their activities.

The heavily manipulated parliamentary elections of May 1990 resulted in overwhelming majorities for the Front of National Salvation. The genuine, extra-parliamentary opposition demonstrated in increasing numbers throughout the country and in Bucharest against the usurpation of the government. The latter preferred the violent techniques of the Chinese in Tiananmen Square to the *glasnost* practised by Gorbachev, and organized the beating up of the demonstrators by *Securitate* agents and so-called miners. Since then, a gulf has opened between the stagnant regime and the people as a whole, who still await in the words of the popular slogan they chanted in the streets 'the second revolution'.

Thus Gorbachev Mark II had allowed the world to see that he would not, and more probably could not, stop the former satellites of Stalin's empire from repudiating and liberating themselves from the Marxist-Leninist-Stalinist model of political and economic organization. 'Provided they remain within the Warsaw Treaty', Gorbachev repeated openly, 'the "sovereign states" members of the pact can choose whatever political regime they want'.

While it is true that the three Baltic republics have the very unhappy geographic position of being an enclave within the Russian territory, it is even truer that they are maritime states near an open sea; that they had been free sovereign states; and that they were acquired by Stalin through his dirty bargain with Hitler. For these considerations, and especially the latter one, Gorbachev could have been expected to show greater flexibility. Nevertheless, the old Stalinist imperialist mentality soon came to the fore. Among the reasons why Gorbachev took such a stance, the most obvious one is that if he did not reject Baltic separatism, he would also have to reconsider Bessarabia and Bukovina, the two Romanian provinces, and Karelia, the Finnish province acquired in the same way. (Even Ceauşescu had asked for an annulment of all changes made through the Nazi–Soviet Pact in his speech at the Congress of the Romanian Communist Party in November 1989.) But the real reason is the fear of the Russian leaders that the ambitions of the Bielo–Russian and Ukrainian republics, which for voting reasons the USSR declared to be 'sovereign states' in the organization of the United Nations, might be aroused. Lithuania is contiguous with Bielo–Russia and West Ukrainians are Catholics like the Lithuanians but with this difference that until very recently the Ukrainian Catholic Church was prohibited. As Geoffrey Hosking reminds us: 'Ukraine is thus the key to the Soviet Union's national problem. That's why Soviet leaders tend to be nervous and rigid in their treatment of it. Life would be much easier for them if the Ukrainians would just quickly allow themselves to be assimilated in the Russian nation.'[24] Thus Gorbachev himself was forced to declare that the national emancipation of the East European states of the Soviet bloc would not be extended to the three Baltic republics.

But here we come to the most serious aspect of the structural disintegration of what was called the 'Union of Soviet Socialist Republics': the demand of the Russian Federal Republic (RSFSR) itself to leave the Union. The departure of the Russians is tantamount to the collapse of the entire centralistic scaffolding erected by Lenin and Stalin in 1923. Given also the rise of Boris Yeltsin to the key position of President of the RSFSR, of which more in the next section, the conflict of views and interests between the Russian Republic and the Soviet Union was bound to be intensified both in theory and in practice.

Yeltsin had succeeded Sakharov, the most luminous figure in Soviet political life, as leader of the Democratic Platform, the opposition in the Congress and in the country as a whole. In theory Yeltsin not only fully maintained the principle of decentralization of the Platform, in federal matters, if need be even of the secession of all the Republics – but added to it a strong element of Russian chauvinism, which was consonant also with his populism. Basing himself on the undeniable fact that the Russian Republic comprises 90 percent of the territory, 72 percent of the population and the major part of the industry of the Soviet Union, Yeltsin argued that the independence of all the Republics, by freeing them from the control of the USSR and the CPSU, should be pursued by the RSFSR not only on grounds of democratic self-determination but in Russia's own interests. Freed from the economically disadvantageous and politically conflictual links with the subjugated minor republics – whether Baltic or Muslim – Russia, cleansed of the stains of past imperialism, could concentrate on herself and her homogeneous democratization. Obviously, if the minor and peripheral republics would prefer to continue their association with the RSFSR, endless variations on the theme of sovereignty could be devised to accommodate them in new forms of collaboration. The only point less clear in Yeltsin's otherwise nationally stimulating and internationally daring theory was whether, in its slavophile enthusiasm, it took too much for granted that the Ukrainian Republic was also committed not to dissociate itself from its traditional links with Russia.

In practice, as the political situation within the leadership of the USSR changed so rapidly, it became less easy to predict whether Yeltsin, who was proposing a radically federal and democratic '*perestroika*' from his new position of strength as President of the RSFSR, and as a former member of the CPSU, from which he had ostentatiously resigned, would find means of collaborating with Gorbachev, the President of the USSR and leader of the CPSU; or whether he would openly oppose him. But it is necessary first to examine whether and how the Marxist-Leninist-Stalinist state could be transformed peacefully into a modern democracy.

## The Marxist-Leninist-Stalinist State.

The other way in which *perestroika* could indeed 'restructure' the Marxist-Leninist-Stalinist state itself, and not only the federation, is by means of a change in the role of the Party in state affairs, and indeed a change in the relations between Party and state. But this, the most important point in any form of the Marxist-Leninist-Stalinist system, as has been seen in the reforms in all four East European countries, where voluntarily or involuntarily, the Party has lost its monopoly of power, is also the point on which Gorbachev's attitude is the most inscrutable. In his long and important article in *Pravda* of 20 November 1989 he firmly reiterated the view that the Communist Party must maintain its monolithic rule in the USSR, regardless of the fact that all other Communist states have started their respective *perestroiki* by abolishing it. And in the very first day of the December 1989 Congress of Deputies he used his authority to postpone the discussion on Article 6 of the Constitution which made mandatory the monopoly of power of the Communist Party of the Soviet Union (CPSU), although with only two thirds of the vote.

But it was at the 28th Party Congress of July 1990 that, given the personal and ideological struggle within the leadership, Gorbachev's position on this issue, and indeed his personal position too, was really shaken. Until then, Gorbachev's position was (or at least he believed it was) *above* internal party strife, as head of state, and *central* because he thought that in the end he could reconcile the attitudes of the left and right oppositions to *perestroika*. The radical left wing opposition or Democratic Platform led by Yeltsin enjoyed great popularity with the masses. Apart from the creation of an independent Russian state, Yeltsin's programme demanded that the state should be pluralist in all respects: a market state with free internal and external trade and a competitive economy, a liberal state with a constitution based on the separation of powers, and a multiparty state in which the CPSU would either become merely one of the competing parties, or disappear for good.

The right wing opposition led by Ligachev took an overall 'traditionalist' position, claiming that the whole idea was too ambitiously utopian, too vast and premature, and that the time schedule proposed for its implementation was foolishly short. The 'traditionalist' opposition was only the tip of the iceberg of the massive resistance of the all-powerful apparats to reform: the party apparat, the administrative and economic apparats and, last but not least, the armed forces apparats. These apparats not only held that *perestroika* could not be achieved, but by their silent, and very active sabotage of the reforms they could easily obstruct their implementation. In the middle stood the government, headed by the Prime Minister, Nikolay Ryzhkov. Though he approved wholeheartedly of the idea of *perestroika*, he was, as we shall see below, taken aback by the period of 500 days allotted to the implementation of the economic programme. In any event, Ryzhkov and the government were attacked from both sides, and his resignation explicitly called for. *Above* all this Gorbachev stood for a while.

Yeltsin drew the consequences from Gorbachev's hesitation to put an end to the monolithic rule of the CPSU and resigned from the Party at the Congress itself. Gorbachev then evidently realized that the Party, with all the might of the silent apparats behind it, would fall into the hands of the 'traditionalists', and would oppose not only the feeble Ryzhkov and his government, but *perestroika* as a whole and himself as its creator. With his talent for party intrigue, he succeeded in winning approval for his 500 day economic plan, and blocked Ligachev's advance, but only at the price of having himself confirmed as head of the otherwise untouched CPSU. At the time this move was very shrewd. But it may yet cost him a lot, for he had boxed himself into the corner of the 'traditionalists', whose main demand was that the Party and party rule should be maintained as before, with all the political, social and economic consequences deriving from this continuation. As there was now a second party, the Democratic Platform which had split off from the CPSU, and as the head of this party was himself the elected head of another state, the RSFSR, which claimed autonomy, a potential duality of power was established, and Gorbachev's personal role in the internal politics of the USSR was reduced to that of defender of the obsolescent Leninist–Stalinist structures.

Of course it can fairly be argued that when he kept control of that old but still so dangerously powerful machine, Gorbachev intended in reality to adapt it to the new demands of the plan for a rapid modernization, and therefore to reduce its old totalitarian powers to very little, perhaps eventually even to nothing.

While it is impossible, especially in the characteristic *chiaroscuro* of communist politics, to guess what will be the outcome of these tortuous manoeuvres and counter manoeuvres, one can still attempt to follow one red thread in order to predict the future of the Marxist–Leninist *state* of the USSR, and therefore of Gorbachev himself. One must watch carefully the extent to which, under the pressure of the colossal social and economic changes now in train, the new political life will accept the separation of powers, the *sine qua non* condition of democracy, and the abolition of which had been the *sine qua non* condition of the setting up of the Marxist–Leninist state.

The separation of powers, first of the judiciary from the other two powers and then between the executive and the legislature, is the very foundation of the Western democracies. It is the overall and original constitutional mechanism of a truly representative government. But to speak of separation of powers in connection with the Marxist–Leninist–Stalinist system is a contradiction in terms. For the key political principle of that system is the explicit negation of the separation of powers. The foundation of Marx's conception of the politics of communism was the concentration of all powers in the working-class self-administration and therefore the abolition of the bourgeois myth of the separation of powers. 'The Commune was to be a working, not a parliamentary body, executive and legislative at the same time', wrote Marx in *The Civil War in France*. And he added hastily, with regard to the judiciary, that 'the judicial functionaries were to be divested of that sham independence which had but served to mask their abject subservience to all succeeding governments', thus making of the judiciary an arm of the administration. Lenin stressed emphatically the necessity in theory for the 'soviet government' to abolish the separation of powers as a fragmentation of the 'people's power'. In his book, *Perestroika*, Gorbachev does not mince his words about Stalinist illegality. Thus:

the emphasis on strict centralization, administration by injunction and the existence of a great number of administrative instructions and restrictions belittled the role of law. At some stage this led to arbitrary rule and the reign of lawlessness . . . Stalin and his close associates are responsible for those methods of governing the country. Any attempts to justify that lawlessness by political needs, international tension or alleged exacerbation of the class struggle in the country are wrong.

And as far as the judiciary is concerned he adds specifically: 'Courts, procurators, offices and other bodies called upon to protect public order and combat abuses were often ruled by circumstances and found themselves in a dependent position.'[25]

But when Gorbachev speaks of law, he seems to be giving to that supreme concept a transcendence which contradicts the deterministic idea shared by Marx, Lenin and Stalin, that laws are a by-product of the class-war and that constitutionalism was invented and used by bourgeois society in order to protect its social dominance. Gorbachev's assertion that: 'democracy cannot exist and develop without the rule of law, because law is designed to protect society from abuses of power and guarantees citizens and their organizations'[26] is nearer in spirit to the classic idea of the law as the supreme arbiter everyone has to obey than to the parody, of a 'class instrument of repression' proposed by Marx, Lenin and Stalin.

It is possible to conjecture that Gorbachev reconciles in his mind the obvious contradiction between the idea of an immanent and universal rule of law with the idea of a Soviet Union still in need of a monolithic system of government, in a kind of new model of a *Rechtsstaat* of socialist legality. But this will be resisted tooth and nail by a bureaucracy petrified in illegality and arbitrariness and in a country which has never known a true constitutional regime except for the brief experiment of the years 1906–17. Therefore, if genuine, his intention to restore the rule of law can have only two possible solutions: either, it will be eroded and finally defeated by the boycott of the communist apparat state; or, regardless of whether it is genuine or not, the idea will be carried to its rightful conclusion by the Russian people themselves, as it has been by the Polish, Hungarian, and Czechoslovak peoples. The second outcome is the most probable. But is greatly dependent on how effective the economic restructuring will be. This is the third element of 'restructuring' to which we now turn.

## Becoming a market state

The question posed here is whether it will be possible to integrate the USSR in the interdependent circuit of the developed society, created and sustained by market states, if it does not itself first become a market state. Of course a great industrial socialist state, with enormous riches and resources in raw materials can *trade* and especially *counter-trade* with market states in the world market. 'Counter-trade' is an umbrella term for several sorts of trade, including barter, which Eastern countries used because 'they were desperately short of hard currency and they lacked convertible currency of their own.'[27] The most usual forms of current East–West counter-trade are called 'counter-purchase', 'offset', 'buy-back', 'barter' and 'switch trading'. Among many other examples of each of these variations the most quoted one is the 'sophisticated' agreement whereby 'the Soviet Union and three Western partners, including America's Pepsico signed a $1.5 billion deal that involves exchanging ships built under contract in Soviet shipyards by a Soviet-Norwegian joint venture for Pepsi.'

But if this kind of operation was good enough for Stalin, and to a lesser degree even for Brezhnev (although the latter was aware of the increasing backwardness of the USSR in the scientific technological revolution), this is not what Gorbachev was trying to achieve. What he was trying to do was to open the very structures of the particularly centralized state to the confluent currents of interdependence of the developed society: monetary, financial, industrial, technological, scientific and cultural interdependence. Such an aim cannot be achieved by barter or trade between states; it requires the interpenetration of societies, i.e. the unquantifiable and uncontrollable multitude of operations in which free companies, firms, centres of research, universities of a developed *national* society do not only exchange goods, credit, currencies and technical and scientific discoveries with other, or all other, similar societies, by means of the electronic information network of the modern markets, but they also interpenetrate each other and their countries. If Gorbachev wants to situate the Soviet Union in the web of interdependence, which is the world market, the only way open to him is to turn it too into a market state. And in order to turn it into a market state, he must first change it politically into a constitutional-pluralistic state based on the separation of powers.

A 'socialist market', or 'market socialism' is held to be the easy and natural answer to that, and it is with this compromise in mind that

Gorbachev might hope to reconcile the contradictions and avoid falling into the sin of capitalism. But there are two formidable difficulties in the way of that solution where the Soviet Union is concerned, for it is after all an exclusively command and planning communist system. The two fundamental changes it must make are the restoration of the private economy and the opening of the free domestic and international market.

As far as the first condition is concerned the initial encouragement given by Gorbachev to co-operatives and the ambivalent idea of 'leasing' land to the *kolkhozniki* (collective farmers) were only timid beginnings which, as we shall see, remained even more timid, in the programme of government presented at the December 1989 Congress of Deputies.

As far as the second condition is concerned, the experiences of Hungary, Yugoslavia and with less effectiveness, Poland, have clearly shown that the moment the market was opened – and worse still, the moment the national market tried to work with the world market – the operations were increasingly of a capitalist nature, and increasingly incompatible with the residual forms of socialism. W. Brus in Oxford and K. Laski in Vienna, who have both published seminal studies on market socialism in East European countries, draw the following conclusions at the end of a recent very complete and detailed study of this problem:

A cruel East European wisecrack defines socialism as 'the painful road to capitalism'. It may be too much, or at least premature, to see in market socialism simply a stage on this road (or slide as many would say) but there is little doubt in our minds that the distinction between capitalist and socialist economic systems, as hitherto perceived, becomes under market socialism thoroughly blurred. If therefore marketization is accepted as the cure for economic ills of 'real socialism' not only the original Marxist promise has to be cast aside, but also the very concept of transition from capitalism to socialism.[28]

Just as clear are the 'six principles for business with Eastern Europe', as enunciated from the other end of the telescope by Robert A. Mosbacher, the current US Secretary for Commerce:

Growth of East–West trade must be founded on sound commercial decision . . . it is up to the governments to create an attractive and profitable business environment.

After remarking also that 'Political freedom and economic freedom go hand in hand', and that some security export controls must remain, Mr Mosbacher concludes that 'within this framework, we will be helping Eastern Europe develop a competitive free enterprise system, the key to integration into the global economy'.[29]

Yet the USSR has not even embarked on the preparations for the changeover from a command economy to market socialism. The first coherent programme put forward in 1989 was that of Dr Leonid Abalkin, the deputy prime minister in charge of economic reform and who is one of Mr Gorbachev's authorized spokesmen in such matters. But this was not and is not always the case. Dr Abalkin's most consistent views and his direct criticism of the economic and political system, indeed his idea that multiparty democracy would be more suitable, were at first brushed aside by Mr Gorbachev as being too radical. As long ago as 1984, Dr Abalkin, then director of the Moscow Institute of Economics, became known as one of the few Soviet economists who was not encumbered by the sacred cows of the Marxist theory of socialism. Thus, on the subject of the crucial principle of the abolition of private property, and the dedication to social property, he was quoted in an interview in 1986 as saying that 'social property in itself is no guarantee of success and obstacles to the development of productive forces, and scientific and technical progress may arise even under such property . . .' He constantly stressed the importance of cost benefit as against growth rate. 'An industry's performance should be judged on the extent to which it fulfils its customers' orders . . . It is up to you to decide whether to produce more or less . . . Your performance is judged by the final result.' He also stressed the direct importance of the work force and its participation in the success of enterprises. 'The workers should be made fully responsible for the results of their collective work. They should be rewarded for successful final results . . . so that the successes and failures should affect the income of each member of the collective.' Moreover, the turnover tax 'should be collected when the products are ultimately sold to the population [this] will put pressure on the enterprises to produce goods which are in demand.'[30]

The views which were considered too radical four years ago were considered with greater interest after the recognition that during those four years *perestroika* had made no progress and that the people, in a national as well as a social sense (miners, students), stimulated by *glasnost* as well as by developments in other 'socialist states', were becoming dangerously restive. As a result, during a conference of 1400 economists, managers and officials held in Moscow between 15 and 18 November 1989, Dr Abalkin, then economic deputy vice-premier, opened a discussion on the 'timetable' to be submitted to the next (December) Congress of Peoples' Deputies. The following diagram of the timetable – to be implemented in only five years – is described in the comments of Quentin Pell[31] on Dr Abalkin's eight broad steps:

- denationalization of property;
- financial overhaul through a unified tax system, use of credit leverage through the banking system and drastic stabilization of the money supply;
- an active structural policy to boost the consumer sector, export growth and cut wastage of natural resources;
- the gradual creation of a market, with output produced in excess of state orders to be sold at free price;
- a gradual rapprochement between controlled state prices and free prices, and adjustment to world market levels;
- the creation of a financial market, stock exchanges and a state controlled trade in securities;
- intensive development of foreign economic ties;
- development of a currency market through actions and regular trade, to introduce partial convertibility of the rouble.

And so as to underscore the real meaning of the *perestroika* as finally brought about, Dr Abalkin insisted that:

we have become convinced on the basis of our own experience that there is no worthy alternative to the market mechanism as the method of co-ordinating the activities and interests of economic subjects. It is also the most democratic form of regulating economic activity. The financial market is the most important component of the market mechanism . . .It is necessary to admit the existence of the labour market under socialism . . . The desire to regulate by fiat the movement of labour resources, and the level and degree of differentiation of incomes only led to the curtailment of personal freedoms . . .

But the ever accelerating succession of transnational events and the ever more divisive, and therefore more procrastinating, Soviet politics completely upset the projects of Gorbachev and Abalkin. The Congress of Soviet deputies in December 1989 was the most lamentable fiasco. It demonstrated on the one hand, that there were now three clear attitudes toward the realization of *perestroika*: one completely opposed to it, led by Ligachev; one asking to 'catch up with the wasted years' by compressing Abalkin's timetable into an heroic crash programme of 500 days which was going to be presented later by Professor Stanislav Shatalin and favoured by Boris Yeltsin, and one, in the centre, of Prime Minister Ryzhkov, genuinely pro-*perestroika*, but pessimistically realistic about its feasibility in any foreseeable future. On the other hand, it was clear that a new duality of power had been established between the USSR and the RSFSR, and between their two Presidents. Both Yeltsin and, more cautiously, Gorbachev were in favour of as complete and as rapid a transition to the market economy as possible; but otherwise the rivalry and differences of view between the two men were as irreconcilable as ever.

Seeing himself so assailed by time and dangers, Gorbachev decided to proceed to a rapid double clarification. He asked for, and immediately obtained, a 'Summit' encounter with President Bush in Malta, which was so successful that it was followed in June 1990 by his triumphal visit to Washington. These two encounters brought about the change from the bipolar hostile interdependence, into the multilateral peaceful interdependence of countries or, more popularly, 'the end of the cold war'. But Gorbachev also brought forward the date of the 28th Congress of the CPSU, announced for the autumn of 1991, to midsummer 1990. It was in these two crucial decisions that what can be called Gorbachev's 'statesmanship of interdependence' was so clearly revealed. That statesmanship consisted in his exceptional gift for trying to advance in internal politics by promising successes in foreign policy, and to advance in external relations by promising structural changes in internal politics.

Of course, modern political history abounds in examples of statesmen like Metternich, Palmerston or Briand who, having first been crowned with glory in foreign affairs, were then entrusted with the leadership of their countries. But in the 'statesmanship of interdependence' the gift for interlocking domestic and foreign policy-making is much more significant because by now the two processes of policy-making are themselves so interdependent. And in the case of Gorbachev it was even more important as his 'domestic politics' amounted to no less than a formidable counter-revolution against the Marxist-Leninist regime and his 'foreign politics' to the end of the cold war. This kind of balancing act entails the risk for the statesman of falling into one or other of the sides which he is interplaying. More than President Bush, of whom it was said jokingly that as President he was an excellent Secretary of State, Gorbachev was obviously much more effective abroad than at home.

Indeed, at the point from which we continue our narrative, that is after his triumphal return from Malta and Washington to Moscow and to the 28th Congress of the CPSU Gorbachev's internal position had already been shaken by the lethal splits in the Party and by the duality of power between his state of the USSR and Yeltsin's Republic of the RSFSR which the latter now demanded should be recognized as a sovereign state. But these political and constitutional problems were in reality the reflections of the great economic dilemma which is the subject of this section, i.e. of whether and if so how, the transformation of the command economy of the USSR into a market economy could be achieved? It was on this fundamental question that all the other questions depended, and that the contradictory political attitudes were based.

The right wing or Conservative opposition denied the possibility of that transformation of the USSR and Ligachev, its main spokesman, asked outright for the resignation of the Prime Minister Ryzhkov, 'because of his thoughtless radicalism, improvisation and lurching from side to side'.[32] The left wing radicals or Democratic Platform (a quarter of the 4000 delegates) argued that the 'cause of the economic disaster lay in the excessive budget on military expenditure 'which has ruined our country', [33] and also demanded the resignation of Ryzhkov. Gorbachev still seemed to be at the centre of, and also above the Party quarrels. Indeed, before the Congress there had been much speculation whether he might leave his position as head of the Party, and conduct all his policies from the Presidency of the state. But the problems thrown up for the party during the Congress were so violent that he was forced to remain.

The problems were difficult in theory because of their immensity and in practice because of the vested interests and mental inertia of those who, for the last five years at least, had been urged to try out some of the solutions proposed.

According to American economists, the great changes in policy comprised at least the following: the acceptance of private property, as the basis of the market economy; an agragrian reform which would reintroduce private ownership of the land; the legalization of private property allowing the development of private industry and above all small enterprises; monetary reform whereby, first, the rouble should be devalued to its real international value and secondly, the billions of inflationary roubles issued by the government should be withdrawn from the market; a new fiscal policy, the main aim of which would be to reduce the governmental deficit, which in the command economy of the USSR included all the deficits of the heavily indebted and frequently bankrupt monopolistic state-enterprises; a wholesale reform of price control. And so on . . .

Now, between 1985 when the implementation of *perestroika* was first attempted and 1989 when it became evident that no progress had been made, and that, on the contrary, because of the chaos created by half-measures the Soviet economy had gravely deteriorated, Gorbachev and his advisers had made two great mistakes of assessment. The first great mistake was to think that all these interrelated reforms could be effected piecemeal. Having embarked on a few of them, one after the other, the Gorbachev-Ryzhkov (Abalkin) leadership was soon forced to recognize that they were the concentric circles of the major reform or *perestroika* as a whole. This was also the explanation of why the policy, put forward under the name of Stanislav Shatalin, professor of economics, stressed first of all the inevitable linkage between all these reforms, and also the urgency of the measures to be taken for their implementation. The new global programme was also compressed in time, into a crash-programme of 500 days starting from 1991.

Gorbachev's second mistake was his underestimation of the obdurate opposition of the apparats and their staff to any reform which might affect their vested interests. Although it is more probable that 'the piece-meal reforms' would not have been achieved even if they had met with general enthusiasm (which Gorbachev seemed to have thought would emanate from *glasnost*), the resistance they encountered at the hands of those who should have implemented them would have jeopardized them in any event. For instance, the legalization of private enterprise, at first especially of small enterprises, was, according to the often quoted American economist, Ed. Hewet, systematically sabotaged by the 'authorities'. The would-be owners had to get licences from the appropriate ministry. The ministries balked or extracted bribes and the few enterprises that got licences had little access to credit or raw materials. For all those reasons, the new owners had high costs and little competition. So they charged exorbitant prices, creating bitter resentment toward 'markets'.[34] The majority of the new Central Committee (that is of the Central Committee elected at the 28th Congress of the CPSU) opposed the legalization of private ownership of land. Gorbachev achieved a hard-fought compromise by which the admissibility of such an anti-Marxist-Leninist-Stalinist measure would be submitted to a national referendum, in which Gorbachev optimistically hoped for a favourable answer. Insofar, however, as the organization of the referendum at the republican and Soviet levels would still be controlled by the present generation of apparatchiks, Gorbachev may suffer another serious disappointment – if the referendum is ever held.

Exasperated by such dismal results and by the waste of five years, frightened by the deterioration of the entire economy (according to American official data, 1989 saw the Soviet economy deteriorate to the lowest points of economic statistics since the proclamation of *perestroika* in 1985), propelled from behind by the bold programmes announced by the President and the Parliament of the RSFSR for their own 'state', and encouraged by better promises of more active financial collaboration with the US and Western Europe, notably by Germany, Gorbachev asked for a new programme which should be both fundamentally comprehensive and rapid. Hence the 500-day crash programme proposed by Professor Stanislav Shatalin. Both Gorbachev and Yeltsin approved the programme. Yeltsin was particularly favourable because the very intensive schedule for the USSR as a whole suited his own presidential programme of rapid and, if need be, exclusive modernization of the RSFSR. Ligachev and the 'conservatives' (who in the meantime had lost important positions in the Central Committee) denounced the Shatalin plan as at once utopian and 'adventurist'. Ryzhkov (who was still protected by Gorbachev as his Prime Minister, although both right wing and left wing oppositions insistently demanded his resignation) and Abalkin also disapproved of the plan, arguing that if even the initial, moderate and piecemeal implementation of *perestroika* had failed so badly, what chance could such a radicalized programme have?

Moreover, Stanislav Shatalin himself, in an exceptionally frank interview in *The Financial Times* declared that 'the 500-day plan, already adopted by the Russian Parliament under Mr Boris Yeltsin requires a draconian credit squeeze from the very start to bring the country's excess liquidity under control, and an immediate start to mass privatization to break the powers of the central state apparatchiks'.[35] In the same interview, Shatalin made it clear that the planned monetary stabilization would be extremely brutal, ('We need three to four months of a very cruel policy.') and that some social programmes and pension increases would have to be frozen. He sympathized with the foreign banking circles which said that they would not grant massive loans to the USSR unless and until it 'closed unprofitable enterprises and liquidated the budget deficit'. 'Charity is all very well,' added Shatalin, 'but we do not want to be beggars.'

Squeezed in the middle, rather than, as he possibly still thought, presiding over the debate from the height of his presidential chair, Gorbachev soon had to realize that the Shatalin '500-days' plan was impracticable, but insofar as Yeltsin's Russia still held to its principles he promised to present in October 1990 a more realistic programme which would reconcile the maximalist and the minimalist theses. If even in theory this was a difficult task, in practice it was much too late to do anything of the kind. For, in practice, the ugly results of inflation, and of inflationary policy, had already progressed so rapidly, that any attempt to adopt the necessary remedy, that is drastically to reduce and firmly to stabilize the excess money supply, was now out of the question. Indeed, in the meantime, the government itself had taken measures whose only result could be a huge escalation of inflation. It had raised the wholesale price of meat and grain by 50 and 90 percent respectively; it had allowed state enterprises to use official, and therefore high, prices instead of market prices and it had allowed for a 100 percent compensation in wages. All these measures being the best, or worst, recipes for hyperinflation. Whatever improvements could follow from Gorbachev's intermediary programme of October 1990 could only be too little and, especially, too late. Given also the anarchic situation in the Federation, and notably in his relations with Yeltsin's Russia, Gorbachev's internal position seemed to become increasingly precarious. But his unique external prestige and excellent foreign relations, and his reputation both at home and abroad as 'the man of peace', recognized by the award of the Nobel peace prize in October 1990, compensated in this age of interdependence for domestic inefficiency. For a country like the USSR which needed above all peace and good foreign relations, Gorbachev still seemed the best leader.

## The end of the Cold War: the beginning of peace?

It has already been mentioned that before facing the dramatic 28th Party Congress, which he was bringing forward by one year, Gorbachev wanted fully to consolidate his new friendship and that of the USSR with the Western democracies, and notably with the USA. He therefore asked for a new 'summit' with Bush, which took place in Malta in December 1989, and was completed by his visit to Washington in July 1990. There followed his encounters with Mrs Thatcher, Mitterand and the European Commission and Parliament, and, last but not least, Kohl's visit to Moscow, also in July 1990. On this occasion the USSR surprisingly put an end to its opposition to German reunification, in an obvious exchange for solid economic assistance which only Germany could or wished to offer the Soviet Union. But, generally speaking, ever since the Malta conference, Gorbachev's talks with the West were carried on in a different way. Gone were the panache, the bluffs and the ruses and traps of Rejkavik and before. Gone also the reluctance to speak of 'aid', 'help' or 'loans', terms which the USSR had never used in its conversations with the West. Now Gorbachev was going to tell his friends, who knew the facts as well as he did, that *perestroika*, the democratization of the USSR, had brought the country to a crisis point, and that indeed the Soviet Union itself was in real danger of dissolution. All those who had an interest in the birth of the new democracy in the USSR, and therefore of a lasting peace and interdependent cooperation should 'help'. In his style of statesmanship of interdependence, indeed in his balancing act between domestic and foreign policy, he needed successes in the latter, before the confrontation he was preparing at home. And, indeed, his foreign negotiations were more successful than ever before.

Future historians who will enjoy the privilege of examining the documents of this period will probably consider the importance of the statement by Mr James Baker, the American Secretary of State after his meeting on 29 July 1989 in Paris with his Soviet opposite number, E. Shevardnadze, in which he affirmed that 'they [the Soviets] have been very, very firm with us. They would not use force in Eastern Europe. To do so would mean that *perestroika* has failed'. The *New York Herald Tribune* of 15 August 1989 which published the statement commented that 'Mr Baker's account dates Moscow's explicit statements to Washington about its shift in East European policy to the period before the most dramatic changes took place in Poland or Hungary, and before East Germans began to emigrate to the West in substantial numbers.[36] The long fishing holiday week-end in August 1989 enjoyed by the two colleagues, seems in retrospect to have been at the root of more detailed cooperation, both over the coming elections in Nicaragua, where the Russians ceased providing assistance to the Sandinistas, and over the imminent, and up to a point foreseeable, upheavals in Eastern and Central Europe. What President Bush felicitously called 'the adherence of the Soviet Union to the obligation which it undertook at the end of World War II to permit self-determination for the countries of East-Central Europe' was then discussed in practical and positive terms between the USSR and the West.

It is now clear that the basis of the agreement was that the USSR agreed to cooperate in the democratization of the East and Central European countries if they remained, even if somewhat formally, in the Warsaw Treaty Organization, and even more formally in the Comecon. This decision had been taken not only to facilitate the overall negotiations with the West. It was taken, as both Shevardnadze and Gorbachev publicly confirmed in their speeches at the 28th Party Congress in July 1990, because in any event the USSR could no longer resist the pressure of those countries and peoples for their liberation. Thus Shevardnadze declared at the Congress: 'Did we, the diplomats, the ministers and the top political leadership know what was going to happen in Eastern Europe? . . . Yes we foresaw everything, we felt everything. We felt that unless serious changes were made, tragic events would follow . . . The totalitarian regimes which had been imposed upon them were doomed.' And Gorbachev, in response to the frequent question from the floor on 'why did we lose Eastern Europe?' sarcastically ridiculed the idea that the USSR could again send military forces into those countries 'to teach them how to live'.

So Gorbachev ostensibly went to visit the East German President, Erich Honecker in Berlin in September 1989, but in reality to give instructions to Egon Krenz (a member of the Central Committee with special responsibility for security who was widely considered to be Honecker's most likely successor) to help people to demonstrate freely against the Honecker regime in the streets of Leipzig and Berlin. Krenz, thinking that he would be the 'East German Gorbachev', gladly obliged, and had Honecker arrested in the process. But the Soviet authorities also hoped that developments would stop at what I have called the 'Krenz threshold'. That threshold was rapidly crossed by the German people once released from restraint. Once the Berlin wall was destroyed, unification had to follow – and that changed the entire geo-political situation of Europe, convulsing both Eastern and Western Europe.

Also in Czechoslovakia, according to the official investigation set up by President Havel, it was discovered that two KGB generals were sent from Moscow to 'stir' the people up. Together with their colleagues in the Czechoslovak secret police, they simulated the shooting of a 'student' by Czech armed police, a student who was in reality a young security officer and whose 'body' was quickly spirited away unhurt but whose rumoured death urged the demonstrators to extremes. There too, however, the equivalent of the 'Krenz threshold' was rapidly crossed and true democracy installed. In Romania, the last one to move, given the Ceauşescus' terribly oppressive regime, the execution of the dictator, and the installation of a Krenz-style regime under Ion Iliescu was carried out under the auspices of the KGB. But there the 'Krenz threshold' was not passed. However, in Poland where democratic reform had long been underway under the communist glacis, and where democratic reforms started in earnest, the first non-communist president since the war has been elected.

In all these countries the indispensable imports of oil and gas from the Soviet Union were sharply reduced and their price increased. The importing countries were not only deprived of the preferential price reduction they were entitled to as members of Comecon, but forced to pay prices higher than those of the world market.

Gorbachev's visit to Washington at the beginning of June 1990 was a triumph for the diplomacy of interdependence. Although, or perhaps indeed because, the visit was not so popular as previous ones, when the crowds had chanted 'Gorby, Gorby', in the intimate atmosphere of a tête-à-tête in Camp David the talks were much more positive and went straight to the point in practical matters. The failure of *perestroika* and the growth of ideological and federal oppositions led Gorbachev to speak to Bush in a much more open way than ever before. It was clear that he was now ready to make greater concessions if not sacrifices on the external plane in order to obtain corresponding compensations on the internal front. The unification of Germany was accepted as a *fait accompli* but some modalities, notably whether a united Germany should form part of NATO could not be solved at the time. Nor could the problem of the conventional forces in Europe, be solved yet. They were still under discussion at Vienna and the Western allies considered an agreement to be a prerequisite for embarking on 'the new patterns and structures of cooperation' of the Conference for Security and Cooperation in Europe (CSCE).

This time also Gorbachev showed himself more predisposed to hear from Bush how the USA could 'help' (an expression which otherwise he hated to use) the grave economic problems of the USSR. But Bush, while promising to do everything to 'reintegrate the USSR in the world economy'(i.e. in the capitalist world) such as for instance supporting the Soviet application to become gradually a member of GATT, or to be treated on the basis of most favoured nation by the USA, held back in matters of state to state financial or technological assistance. Moreover he showed himself rather sceptical about the intentions of American private banks and companies to commit themselves to large Russian 'ventures' as long as the USSR had not embarked in earnest on the transition to a market economy.

The reasons why Bush was so reserved in this respect were cumulative. First, like most of the partners in NATO, and especially Mrs Thatcher, he thought that to provide the USSR at once with indiscriminate financial and technological assistance, while her military power remained formidable, and while Gorbachev's own political position was precarious in his own country, amounted to taking risks with Western security. Secondly, the American economic and financial situation was still somewhat critical, because he found himself in the position of having to ask the people to pay more taxes in order to reduce the public, and particularly the external debt. The country was really not in the position it was when, after the war, it had so easily provided massive support for the rehabilitation of Europe, an operation which in any case was entirely different in quantity and quality to the 'restructuring' of the Soviet economy.

But generally speaking, Gorbachev's talks with Bush in June 1990 might be considered by future historians as the concluding act of the 'cold war'. For immediately after that visit, President Bush informed his NATO allies of his opinion that thenceforward the West could be sure that war with what was formerly the Soviet bloc, or indeed with the USSR alone, was now absolutely improbable, especially as long as Gorbachev remained in power. On the contrary, thenceforward the NATO powers should concentrate on how to institutionalize the new *de facto* situation in new structures and procedures of European collaboration. This explains the ringing communiqué issued by the NATO summit on 7 July 1990, in the middle of the 28th Party Congress in Moscow: 'The member-states of the North Atlantic Treaty Organization propose to the member-states of the Warsaw Treaty Organization a joint declaration in which we solemnly state that we are no longer adversaries.'

What, however, Gorbachev did not obtain even after this startling armistice between NATO and the WTO was the financial assistance, the 'bridging loan' he now needed more than ever, for not only was the USSR starved of capital, its people, also were threatened by starvation. Hence his new receptivity towards 'help' which might serve to pave the way towards increased production of consumer goods and lower inflation, through external credits, so as to keep the population (especially the workers) less unhappy and more productive.

This idea of a 'bridging loan' also partly explained the startling reconciliation between Kohl and Gorbachev, during the former's triumphal visit to the USSR at the end of July (in the rural surroundings of Gorbachev's birthplace), when at the reasonable price of accepting that a united Germany would be a member of NATO, whatever NATO might mean in the future, Gorbachev was assured of the massive financial, industrial and commercial shot in the arm which only Germany and the European Community seemed to be prepared to promise immediately. Meantime, in collaboration with the West, the designs for modernization and 'restructuring' of the economy, would be 'phased', to borrow Abalkin's terminology, over a decade, for indeed even the most optimistic economists agreed that *perestroika* would take at least fifteen years to achieve its 'objects'.

In September 1990 a bilateral treaty of cooperation was initialled between the Soviet and German governments providing for an interest free credit of 2bn Deutschmarks over five years, as the first part of a loan from a consortium of German banks, to help fund the cost of keeping Soviet troops stationed in East Germany.[37]

Of course, the German loan, important as it was, was but a drop in the ocean in comparison with the enormous injection of capital the Soviet Union so badly needed. Thousands of transactions were being negotiated with the USA, Canada, Great Britain, France, and Italy and through the European Community as a whole, and last but not least, with Japan. But the negative attitude of the bankers and especially of the Japanese bankers who showed a distinct lack of interest in investing either in the USSR or in Eastern Europe, created a vicious circle. While the bankers argued that if the USSR wanted loans, investments and joint ventures, her government should first bring down inflation and absorb the excess liquidity, Soviet economists answered that in order to fulfil these two conditions they needed financial, commercial and technological help from abroad. The governments of the western democracies, with the exception of Germany, did not entirely share the attitude of their bankers. They recognized that the USSR should at least be accepted in GATT and particularly in the IMF, which required its members to be a market state, with free trade and with a representative system of government. Seeing that the disarmament negotiations seemed to be coming to a satisfactory end, western political circles tried to convince their national bankers to follow the courageous example of the German banks.

From a political point of view it was argued that the final interest of all industrial democracies was that after the end of the cold war, there should follow, naturally, a long and lasting peace. Interdependence, which, as we have seen, had forced the end of the cold war, by its very functioning, now just as clearly demanded that the quiet of peace should allow the peoples of the world to heal their war wounds and to cooperate with each other and benefit from the 'peace dividend'. At the end of the cold war, though not only because of it, most countries were facing serious financial, commercial and industrial problems though they were much less serious than those which faced the USSR whose total counter-revolution exposed her to great risks. Most countries in Latin America, Asia (with the exception of Japan and the three little 'dragons'), and Africa, were in a state of virtual bankruptcy. The western democracies themselves, in North America as well as in Europe (where the newly liberated Eastern European countries were in an evident need of rehabilitation) had obvious budget difficulties. The fight against inflation, budget deficits and negative trade balances was becoming more difficult than ever. (This was true even in prosperous Germany which was faced with the cost of German reunification.) 'Global' solutions were needed. But in any event 'globality' means above all peace, which in turn means the lifting of all obstructions to the free flow of communications. A long and constructive peace, that is a peace lasting long enough to enable the peoples to transform the *de facto* situation of willy-nilly interdependence into a *de jure* order is the *sine qua non* condition.

The first sign of hope of such a transformation of the expiring cold war into a new world peace and of *de facto* interdependence into *de jure* interdependence was the United Nations' unprecedented, unanimous, condemnation of Iraq in September 1990 after it had invaded, occupied and annexed the sovereign state of Kuwait. The firm behaviour of Gorbachev's USSR and of China were the extraordinary symptoms of the new universal need of peace. Moreover, as I have argued elsewhere[38], Iraq's aggression was the last convulsion of totalitarianism − and as such it was doomed. Even if, in October 1990, the Council of the United Nations showed less solidarity, and Israel itself acted as the odd man out in United Nations discipline, yet the worldwide condemnation of Iraqi aggression remained unaltered. But, Gorbachev's greatest contribution to history is that he obeyed the injunction of interdependence by removing in his first six years in power as much as possible of the totalitarian obstructions and walls. This achievement will last long after his own career has come to an end.

## IN GUISE OF CONCLUSIONS

As I was finishing this chapter, with the natural regret at having to leave the subject without expressing a final opinion about the future, or making any final assessment of Gorbachev's statesmanship, I happened to see an article by Allen Lynch in the summer 1990 issue of *Foreign Affairs*, with the rather strong title, 'Does Gorbachev Matter Anymore?'[39] This of course comforted me, because since my book cannot possibly predict the end of Gorbachev's fantastic career in the USSR, and the impact it will ultimately have on the evolution of European and world history, the idea that what he has achieved up to now will necessarily be considered more important than whatever he might or might not achieve in the future would attenuate to some extent the inconclusiveness of this essay.

As it happens, the assertion that Gorbachev's own career may not matter any longer is justified in two senses, the one straightforward, the other paradoxical. In the first, straightforward sense, it is true because what has already happened in these first six years has had such a massive historical significance, that if he himself cannot continue and achieve his aims in the way (or ways) he wanted, it is certain that those who will follow or replace him will not be able to reverse what he has done. Or rather, in the second, paradoxical sense, what he has *undone*. For, as has been said so often in this essay, while the positive effects of Gorbachev's policies for the USSR, the mythical *perestroika*, are still to come, the negative effects, from the point of view of a conservative citizen of the USSR are irreversible. As Allen Lynch puts it:

Events have come to the point where there can no longer be a question of a return to some mythical status quo ante for the Soviet Union. The depth, strength and complexity of the modern Soviet state preclude a return to a neo-Stalinist political and institutional order. Any Soviet leader proposing such a path would have to address the following questions: How could a return to hypercentralized methods of administered economics and politics cure any of the problems now universally recognized as afflicting Soviet society? How could such a course prevent the permanent placement of the USSR on the margins of international economic and political life?[40]

Ergo, if no Soviet leader could rebuild what Gorbachev has brought down, Gorbachev has obviously earned a place in history which, whatever happens to him, or after him, can never be forgotten. In this sense, like Lenin, but against Lenin, he was a revolutionary. Because revolutionaries destroy what stands in the way of the future, without knowing, or even caring much about what the future will bring. Gorbachev's book on *Perestroika* is as weak and utopian as Lenin's *State and Revolution*. But just as Lenin made it impossible for the Tsarist regime ever to return, so Gorbachev has done enough to prevent the Leninist regime from ever returning. Worse might follow – and indeed the initial destruction of Lenin's monolithic one-party state might be followed by the destruction of the USSR as a whole. From this point of view it might be true to say that Gorbachev no longer mattered once the work of destruction had been achieved. But what still mattered was the question whether his political genius was so great that only he could continue to steer the USSR into a less disastrous transition towards the new conditions which interdependence would impose on that ex super-power? For interdependence had to become *global* to be *real* – and one of the greatest obstacles to the globalization of interdependence was the geo-political and ideological obstruction presented first by the Communist world (including China), then the Soviet bloc, and finally the USSR. Now, in order to survive, thanks to Gorbachev, the two latter have successively opened their doors to the invigorating draughts of interdependence.

311

Whatever the vicissitudes they will meet, they will no longer obstruct global interdependence and, if wisely led, they will themselves find it easier to overcome the obstacles in their path than when they were imprisoned in the claustrophobic Marxist-Leninist state structures.

We have often in this essay invoked Geoffrey Hoskins's pertinent question whether, after the successful *glasnost'* of Gorbachev Mark I, and the failed *perestroika* of Gorbachev Mark II, we shall see the emergence of a Gorbachev Mark III. Sadly, at the time of writing, in early 1991, it rather seemed that there was in reality only one Gorbachev, but who was divided within himself from the beginning. He was therefore unable to transform himself into the new man required by the events which he had unleashed. Originally an *apparatchik*, he has seemed to be compelled to remain a prisoner of the *apparat*-state (as formed by the armed forces, the KGB, the bureaucracy, and the weakened Party). Alas, it would not be the first time that revolutions eat those who unleashed them.

Possibly the greatest mistake Gorbachev made was his failure to seek to be popularly elected as President – as Yeltsin did in Russia – thus escaping the control of those who had appointed him and subsequently controlled him. From then on, challenged as he was on the one side by the new, elected Presidents of the emancipated Republics and by the new radical opposition aroused by *glasnost'* and seeing his reforms sabotaged from the other side by the resistance of the *apparat*, he fell again under the latter's influence. Abandoned by his friends and mentors, Yakovlev and Shevardnadze, and by all the *perestroika* economists, from Abalkin to Petrakov to Shatalin, he explicitly allowed the KGB to control the economy and the army to assist the Soviet police to take over the Baltic Republics, thus confirming Shevardnadze's warning of the coming of a dictatorship.

As these events coincided with the outbreak of the Gulf War against Iraq, under President Saddam Hussein (who had been shrewdly encouraged in secret by the rightwingers of the Soviet army in order to destabilize the post cold war peace), the West could not do very much to prevent Gorbachev from adopting old Soviet methods. The serious consequences for him and for Russia, and, given the iron law of interdependence, for the West too, cannot be foreseen.

## NOTES AND REFERENCES

1.  M. Gorbachev. *Perestroika* London, 1987.

2.  M. Gorbachev, *Socialism, Peace and Democracy*, London, 1987.

3.  M. Gorbachev, *Perestroika*, p.59.

4.  M. Gorbachev, *Socialism, Peace and Democracy*, p.9 (my italics).

5.  Zh. Medvedev, *Gorbachev*, Basil Blackwell, Oxford, 1986.

6.  Medvedev, op.cit., p.22.

7.  M. Jones (ed.), *Socialism, Peace & Democracy*, writings, speeches, reports by M. Gorbachev, biographical note, np. London, 1987.

8.  Medvedev, op.cit., p.xx.

9.  M. Gorbachev, *Perestroika*, London, 1987, pp.25–6 (my italics).

10. Fyodor Burlatsky, the political theorist and one of Gorbachev's closer and earlier advisers, underlines only too clearly this bibliographical point. As he points out, 'Lenin's latest works, written when socialist construction had already begun are, of course, especially valuable. This applies above all to the *Report on the Substitution of a Tax in Kind for the Surplus-Grain Appropriation System, The Tax in Kind, The Importance of Gold Now and After the Complete Victory of Socialism, On Cooperation, How we Should Re-organize the Workers and Peasants Inspection* and *Better Fewer but Better*. In these works we find answers to many basic points. Needless to say it would never occur to any of us to mechanically compare the 1980s with the 1920s. But there is one thing where comparison is possible, even necessary. In those days, like today, the country was on the crest of radical change. In those days, it was changed from War Communism to the New Economic Policy. Now it is change from extensive to intensive development based on the latest achievements of science and technology'. (F. Burlatsky, 'Lenin and the Strategy of Radical Change' in *USSR – A Time of Change*, Moscow, 1987, p.26).

11. V. I. Lenin, *Collected Works*, pp.700–12.

12. See my *The Politics of the European Communist States*, London, 1965.

13. Lenin, op.cit., pp.700 and 704.

14. The Blue Notebook, Appendix III to K.Marx, *Critique of the Gotha Programme*, Lawrence and Wishart, London. n.d.

15. Leonid Abalkin, 'The Pivot of Economic Life in USSR' in *USSR: Time of Change*, pp.49 and 57.

16. Lenin and Stalin prepared together, in constitutional theory and in political practice the new *territorial sovereign* state. See G. Ionescu: 'Lenin, the Commune and the State' in *Government and Opposition*, vol. 5. No. 2, Spring 1970.

17. M. Gorbachev, *Perestroika*, p.139.

18. Quoted in *The Financial Times*, November 1989.

19. *The Financial Times*, 9 December 1989.

20. Minus 50,000 troops to be pulled out from the GDR, Hungary and Czechoslovakia.

21. Les Aspin, (Chairman of the House Armed Services Committee) in *Los Angeles Times*, 16 November 1989.

22. See for this G. Ionescu: *The Politics of the European Communist States*, London, 1968.

23. See Karl Cordell, 'The Role of The Church in the GDR', *Government and Opposition*, Vol.25, 1, Winter 1990, pp.48–59.

24. Geoffrey Hosking, The 1988 Reith Lectures 4 'The Flawed Melting Pot' in the *Listener*, 2 December 1988, p.14.

25. M.Gorbachev, *Perestroika*, p.xx.

26. Ibid.

27. 'A necessary evil', *The Economist*, 25 November 1989, p.1157.

28. W. Brus & K. Laski, *From Marx to the Market*, Oxford, 1989, p.151.

29. In the *Washington Post*, 27 November 1989.

30. Leonid Abalkin 'Interview with Eco Magazine', 1986 in *USSR: A Time to Change*, pp.48–62.

31. *The Financial Times*, 30 November 1990.

32. *The Economist*, 7 July 1990, p.47.

33. Ibid.

34. *International Herald Tribune*, 5 April 1990, p.4.

35. *The Financial Times*, 10 October 1990.

36. *The New York Herald Tribune*, 9 December 1989.

37. *The Financial Times*, 12 October 1990 described the arrangements in the following way: 'The credit is lead-managed by West LB, the biggest of the German public sector landesbanks. In the agreement, Bonn said it would pay DM12bn for the repatriation of Soviet troops at the end of the four-year period, with an additional DM3bn interest-free loan for the cash incurred in the interim. The other DM1bn is expected to be paid over next year. As it is an interest-free loan, the banks receive the coupon payments from Bonn, set at 20 basis points over the six-month London interbank offered rate. This represents a considerably more generous margin than they would normally receive on federal government debt.

38. G. Ionescu: 'The Last convulsion of Totalitarianism' *Government and Opposition*, vol. 25, No. 3, pp.497–519.

39. Allen Lynch, 'Does Gorbachev Matter Anymore?', *Foreign Affairs*, Summer 1990, pp.19–29.

40. Ibid pp.20–21.

41. Isaiah Berlin, *The Hedgehog and the Fox*, London, 1953.

42. L. Tolstoy, *War and Peace*, tr. C. Garnett, London, 1915, pp.1505, 1507.

# CHAPTER SIX
# *Conclusions*

> It is only by the study of the interconnexions of all the
> particulars, their resemblances and differences, that we
> are enabled at least to make a general survey and thus
> derive both benefit and pleasure from history.

Polybius (205–125BC) *Histories* W.G. Patton translation, London,
1922

Three things stand out more prominently from our enquiry into the
adequacy of the political judgement of five statesmen. One is already
known as 'the end of the cold war'. The second is the theme of the
adjustments which have had to be made between the concepts of state,
sovereignty and power and the concept of interdependence. And the
third and direct answer to the object of our enquiry is that although
modern statesmen see that connection more clearly than those of the
previous generation, the old mental dichotomy is still cutting through
the processes of policy-making.

## THE END OF THE COLD WAR

The 'end of the cold war', or at least the official proclamation of the
end implicit in the invitation issued by NATO to the WTO in July
1990 to lay down its arms and embark on cooperative relations, took
place as the writing of this book was nearing its end. This was of
course a happy, but not a surprising coincidence. For, because of the
succession of events in the historical canvas, 1945–1990, as recorded in

315

the five, often over-lapping biographical case studies, the book is, even if in a somewhat pointillistic manner, a history of those forty years of the 'cold war', with the hindsight of interdependence. Moreover, as the 'cold war' was rapidly drawing towards the victory of the democracies over totalitarianism, the book implicitly and explicitly followed the story. 'Historical canvas' is in this context an apposite simile, insofar as behind the canvas of the five paintings one could detect the fresco of the agony of Marxism-Leninism, the original, and most obdurate, of totalitarianisms.

Projected on to the phases of the cold war, the record of the western statesmen is impeccable. for they were all four, including the more elusive de Gaulle, dedicated anti-communists, and each of them played a leading part in the capitulation of international communism. In this respect their statesmanship deserves historical recognition. Their basic conviction and almost instinctive assumption was that the normality of human life, in its pains and pleasures, required politically the basic freedoms of democracy, which had been forbidden in abnormal and anti-human totalitarian communism. Thus they applied with firmness, and in spite of many ups and downs, the simple policy of confidence in their own regimes and of 'containment' of the communist regimes within their own irremediable abnormality.

At the same time the western statesmen, during their period in power, had to bow to the new societal forms of welfare, within the structures and functions of their own 'sovereign' states. Internal sovereignty – in democracies, the sovereignty of the constitutional representative government – was closely associated after the second world war with the spontaneous, national and transnational organizations of the welfare society, as represented in the new processes of power-sharing by non-parliamentary 'groups' and organizations of industrial employers, financial institutions, trade unions, farmers' associations, and last but not least, ethnic and cultural centres. Here too, some of the powers of the 'state' were compressed and absorbed by the ever expanding civil society.

The four western statesmen fulfilled the internal and external demands of interdependence in various ways, with different motivations and with more or less success, according to the state of their countries at the time and to their own brand of statesmanship. Although he was the first to introduce a coherent system of constitutional decentralization through federation and through the social market, Adenauer enjoyed two great advantages which the others did not have. In the first place he was not allowed to, and therefore did not, organize the external defence of his country. The defence of the Federal Republic was assumed at great budgetary cost by the three allied powers, while the emerging German government was able to invest its rapidly growing resources in its new social, economic and political structures. Secondly, Adenauer was able to set up these modern structures from scratch, on the *tabula rasa* left by the total destruction of Nazism.

De Gaulle's own inclination, as we have seen, was towards a strong state, sovereign and independent in both internal and external affairs. He found the accommodation with the requirements of interdependence most difficult. Nevertheless France, in his time, i.e. within the hostile interdependence of the pre-Gorbachev era, was a modern Western military power. Although he was totally unwilling to accept any ultimate federalistic objectives in the European Community, he placed France, together with a renascent Germany, at the head of that organization. He did his best to stimulate French foreign trade in all directions and, with the adoption of a neo-corporatist economic plan, he actually offered direct participation in the policy-making processes to the 'groups' in civil society.

Mrs Thatcher and President Reagan both brought back the idea of a free market to the very centre of their economic policies, as manifested later also by the privatizations in Britain. They thus dislodged their respective states even more clearly from the commanding heights of their economies. Though the 'welfare state' was maintained in Britain, the emphatic liberalism of the Thatcher governments and in America of the Reagan governments more often than not ran counter to the principles of the social market.

Finally, without any irony, it can be said that the Gorbachev counter-revolution amounted to a dramatic attempt to transform the monstrously centralized Soviet state into something – anything – which would be more compatible with the modern society and with the requirements of interdependence.

## THE CATEGORIES OF SOVEREIGNTY

> *If the prince can only make law with the consent of a*
> *superior, he is a subject; if of an equal he shares his*
> *sovereignty; if of an inferior, whether it be a council of*
> *magnates or the people, it is not he who is sovereign.*

Jean Bodin *Six Books on the Commonwealth*. (M. J. Tooley translation, Oxford, 1967, p.43)

While the instinctive reactions of the western statesmen responded most aptly to the ambiance of war – hot or cold – created by communist aggression, each of them feeling that he or she was exercising the most important attribute of sovereignty, namely the defence of his or her country against external aggression, it cannot be said that they were so well suited by the subtleties and flexibilities inherent in the new policies of interdependence. The ambiguity of their rhetoric and, presumably, of their actual political judgement led all of them, as we have seen, to practice the inevitable policies of interdependence while explaining, and presumably believing, that they were defending and promoting the sovereignty of their states.

Although Adenauer's policies were firmly integrationist, externally through the European Community, internally through the federation and the social market, yet he claimed that he was above all pursuing Germany's sovereignty. But in reality proclamations of 'German national sovereignty' were more mythical than the *Realpolitik* of interdependence which he handled so well.

If this was the case, one must ask why did his rhetoric refer so frequently to the myth of German sovereignty, why did he continue to feel that it should be kept alive in the minds of his followers? The question is now loaded with further implications, as in the meantime the FRG, having achieved full sovereignty for the 'unified' Germany under Chancellor Kohl, has seemed to neglect the duties of interdependence. In spite of the passage of time and of the difference of situations, it remains very doubtful whether Adenauer in 1991 would have handled Germany's relations with the United States, Great Britain, France, Israel and Turkey in the 'sovereign' way the Kohl-Genscher team handled them during the Gulf War.

With de Gaulle, Mrs Thatcher and Reagan, the problem was different, and less acute than in the case of Adenauer. For them, there was no moral and mental necessity to adapt their political judgement to new vistas: they were not weighed down by remorse or a sense of guilt nor did they have to rebuild their country in a new and different manner. Heirs of great powers, their ambition to continue to be leaders of great powers was justified this time by the fact that their countries had won the war which Germany had lost, and that their democracies had proved their superiority over fascist regimes. In the periods in office of Reagan and Thatcher the superiority of democracies over communist totalitarianism was also fully confirmed. So, even if they were aware of the geo-political and ideological changes brought about by interdependence, they had some grounds for thinking that their own successful upholding of the sovereignty of their countries had played an essential part in those developments.

Yet, all three of them had also a natural and shrewd understanding of interdependence. All of them had felt the universal impact of the technological revolution, not only on the increase of the military power of their country but also on the economic, financial and cultural activities of their nations. All three of them also fully understood, and supported, the multinationalization and transnationalization of the world economy, and acted accordingly in their domestic policies, recognizing that their national economies should be parts of the whole.

What was more difficult to comprehend readily was the association of the concept of the national state with the new concepts used in international parlance such as 'subsidiarity', 'regionalization', and 'integration'.

'Subsidiarity' is a noun not yet recognized by most dictionaries, which still speak mainly of the adjective 'subsidiary', as used in previous centuries in theological and legal language. It was introduced into the terminology of the European Commission in a 1975 Report, during the presidency of the then Mr Roy Jenkins. Since that time it has spread into the language of international relations and into that of interdependence. It describes the situation in which categories of decision-making processes are logically divided between, say, macro-, medium- and lower grades of decisions and policies. According to their differing importance they are referred to the respective competences of supra-national, national and local authorities. 'The supra-national authorities are called on to solve only those problems which the national authorities cannot solve or implement by themselves' is the current communitarian explanation. In a constitutional system these three categories of problems are better solved, according to their competence, by the policy and decision-making processes at local, state or federal, levels. But here the comparison between informal transnational subsidiarity and the federal system stops, precisely because federation is the constitutional structure of a centralized legal co-ordination in which, according to the constitution, the federation decides upon the macro-political problems, while the 'States' in American parlance, or the 'Länder' or the 'Cantons' in the German and Swiss political vocabulary decide 'subsidiarily' on national and local problems.

But situations of subsidiarity caused by interdependence cannot be defined so easily in constitutional terms. The politics of interdependence, geographically global and in perpetual technological change, require a kind of vast *Commedia dell'Arte* of policy-making processes.

Speaking only of modern diplomacy Susan Strange has described perceptively the new processes as follows: 'Henceforwards diplomacy has to be conceived as an activity with not one, but three dimensions. The first familiar dimension is the bargaining and exchange of views and information between representatives of government, the conventional diplomats. The second, newer dimension is the bargaining and exchange of views between representatives of enterprises. And the third is the bargaining and exchange of views between a government representative on one side of the table and a representative of an enterprise, whether based in the same or another state on the other.'[1]

In proper processes of policy making, institutionalized groups (and the subsequent 'group-thinking') consisting of well trained and authoritative government representatives, with experts of functional agencies of various competences, are required to take rapid decisions, on different issues, with different experts, to be implemented afterwards by states or other institutions. The UN, GATT, the IMF, the G-7 and G-5, the summits and, in a more integrative way, the EC, are already well attested examples of the ad hoc institutionalization of interdependent policy-making processes and agencies. It is in relation to them that the sovereign nation-states might find themselves in a position of 'subsidiarity'.

And it is in relation to them that British, French or, say, Danish patriots have sometimes found these processes not only nationally, but democratically offensive. They had already had some difficulty in accepting that in the politics of any modern nation-state there now prevails a form of what Roger Putnam has felicitously called, even if in a slightly different sense, the politics of the 'selectorate'. (As the expression shows the 'selectorate' is the modern combination of the official policy-making power of the popularly 'elected' representatives of the nation with 'selected' national dignitaries such as judges, governors of the Central Banks, corporatively elected or appointed leaders of trade unions and of professional associations, leading scientists, vice-chancellors of universities, heads and personalities of radio and television.) But while these non-elective functions are by now generally accepted in modern states, what the patriots seem to find more difficult to accept is the part played in global processes of policy-making by the cosmopolitan, non-elected experts of organizations such as the IMF, the World Bank, the European Community, GATT, OECD or any of the various UN agencies.

'Regionalization' is another irritating consequence of interdependence for sensitive citizens of sovereign states. 'Region' in this sense means those new aggregated units of power in the world, formed under the impact of interdependence by sovereign states, more often than not bound by vicinity, economic position, and historical background, so as to concentrate their resources and organize the trade and communications between them, and with the rest of the world, in common.

W.W. Rostow described 'the coming of age of regionalism' – the title of a very interesting article[2] – as a 'metaphor of our time'. He writes:

The political structure of the global community would require greatly strengthened regional institutions if we are to deal with the agenda history has set for, say, the next half-century. New technologies have had a kind of domino effect on regional organization. I am inclined to believe that there will be no 'Fortress Europe', no 'Fortress North America' or 'Fortress of the Pacific Basin' – not only because of the globalization of movements of capital and communication, but because of the highly diversified new techniques.

In one of the earliest and inevitably over-simplified descriptions of an interdependent world of regions, or centres of power, in Herbert J. Spiro's chapter: 'National Sovereignty and Supranational Interdependence' in the book *Between Sovereignty and Integration*, this is made graphically clear (see Fig. 6.1 on following page). Spiro proposed the model of a pentagon formed by some of the most salient 'centres' of power. Although forming one constant global unit of interdependence, each of the five 'centres' or 'regions' entertains all the reciprocal relations of dependence of each on the other. Spiro clearly explained that 'the salient facts about a pentagon are simple: 'it contains ten pairs, ten triangles and five quadrilaterals. ... The diagram is not only abstracted from the rest of the real world – lesser centres of power, less developed countries, international organizations, circumscribed regional international systems, supranational corporations or churches, but it also has a symmetry which is wholly absent in the real world'.[3]

By now Herbert Spiro's early representation of the almost automatic interplay between the centres or regions has been much more multipolarized, as a result of the impact of the circumambiance of interdependence. But the attempts to solve the inherent technological and commercial rivalries between Japan and the USA through the Structure Impediment Initiative negotiations; and the difficulties between the EC and the USA on the reformation of the latter's agricultural policy; the constant monetary readjustments and the GATT multi-issue negotiations prove that, in the meantime, Spiro's idea of global inter-relations has now become a premiss of the 'subordination' of national structural policies to prior transnational mutual arrangements.

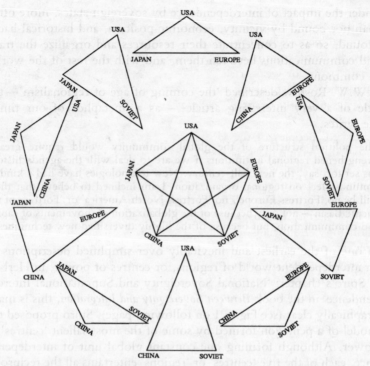

*Source:* G. Ionescu (ed) *Between Sovereignity and Integration,* London, 1976, pp. 180–1.)

Fig, 6.1. *A pentagon of interdependent 'regions'*

But in the past and still today, the idea of the 'regionalization' of European powers in a community still offends the feelings of patriots and even of statesmen in some of the sovereign states. Moreover, even the creation of 'regions', *if undertaken in a spirit of 'hostile interdependence'*, and in a spirit of regional protectionism, might present as many risks as national protectionism brought with it before the Second World War. While the tendency towards geographic grouping and in this sense regionalization is inevitable in conditions of interdependence, it goes against the grain to think that the purpose of the operation would be to obstruct and interrupt interdependence. As W.W. Rostow has underlined, the 'coming age of interdependence' could not lead to the creation of 'Fortress America', 'Fortress Europe' or 'Fortress Pacific', 'not only because of the globalization of movements of capital and communications, but because of the highly diversified new techniques'.

There is no doubt that both in internal and in external politics there are pressing problems of insufficiency of resources to satisfy the demands, or indeed the supplications of all people in a country and of all peoples in the world. The spirit of positive interdependence starts from the premiss of mutual sacrifice made by all states, large or small, strong or weak, rich or poor, as in the end they all depend on each other. Indeed, at the start of the 1990s the international community has urgently to attend to the needs of the rapidly deteriorating underdeveloped countries, as well as to the needs of the suddenly 'liberated' peoples of the USSR and Eastern Europe in their effort to become viable market states.

It is here that Western democracy itself must be seen in the new light. The electoral game on which democracy is based (and there is no better method of conducting a polity) has, in the ambience of *teledemocracy* increasingly taken on a tendency towards greed and demagogy. Politicians *protect* their own voters: American motorists, French and German farmers, Japanese industrialists, British skilled workers, against the inescapable duty of mutually accepted sacrifices. In order to win power and remain in power modern governments promise to increase the social and national privileges, and their oppositions criticise them for not offering more. No democratic government has sufficient courage to ask its voters to accept what may appear in the short term to be sacrifices in order to comply with the need for transnational equalization, or indeed of transnational social justice, required by interdependence, in the interests of longer term prosperity.

Of course equality, or even more so, inequality of power, or of rank, between contemporary states can be and is objectively measured and sometimes internationally acknowledged. But states being nation-states, the nation reacts by subjective assessment. This is a mixture of illusion, and frustrations, of ambition and resentments, and produces an almost instinctive reluctance of the 'sovereign' peoples to be treated, and to behave, as equal to others. The two world wars and the forty-year cold war have sensitivized peoples even more, insofar as equality and inequality were mostly measurable in terms of a nation's power. Hence also the appearance at that time of the concept of 'super-powers' and of the revival of the concept of 'hegemony' – taken here in its classic, Isocratic, sense of the measuring of international relations and not in the modern, social, Gramscian, meaning of class-relations.

The coming of interdependence with its flattening, circumambient effect should facilitate the acceptance by the sovereign people of an implicit 'equalization', once all are submitted to the general rule imposed by interdependence and hence of the regionalization of groups of states. And the end of the cold war, by transferring the criteria of power from the military to the economic, and above all, to knowledge and information, has upset the scales of measurement. But this is to anticipate, insofar as the discussion is still linked with the attitudes which the four western statesmen, and for obvious reasons especially the three European ones, have adopted 'on behalf of their sovereign peoples' toward the new modality of power-sharing in conditions of interdependent equalization.

Finally, for Gorbachev, both subsidiarity and regionalization meant something quite different from what they meant in the western world, particularly in the context of the great changes taking place in the USSR. At the beginning of his 'revolution' his political judgement seemed to be exceptionally well attuned to the new conditions. While it must still be remembered that Gorbachev finds himself at present in such a situation of flux that any attempt to express a final opinion is dangerously premature, it can be said that his decision, at the 28th Congress of the CPSU, to remain leader of the Soviet 'communist' party and through it of the country called the USSR gave rise to new doubts. For now it was his political rivals who advocated competitive pluripartyism and the regrouping of the units of the former Soviet Empire in loose 'regional' structures, based on decentralized contractual links.

Obviously, the solution proposed by Gorbachev's political rivals was more consonant with the principles of interdependence which he had preached. His clinging to the integrity of the USSR itself, i.e. to the arch-centralized monolithic state, kept under the command of the Communist Party, the instrument of that same coercive monolithism went directly against the grain of his initial principles. Whether it was one more delaying tactical move or whether his political judgement had failed to comprehend the particularly heavy requirements made by modern politics on the obsolescent state which he conducted, is still a question for the future.

# THE POLITICS OF INTERDEPENDENCE

We said that after 'subsidiarity' and 'regionalization', the third concept of the international political economy which has been and is disliked bothby patriotic citizens and by leaders of nation states like de Gaulle and Mrs Thatcher, was that of 'integration'. But here there is a semantic difference. For, unlike 'subsidiarity' and 'regionalization', which are newly coined expressions designed for the ad hoc purpose of describing current operations, 'integration' is a well-established and very broad notion, used with many different meanings, not all of which arouse resentment in a patriotic breast.

Generally speaking, integration is the action by which the parts come together and aggregate into a whole (integrum). Hence, politically, it is the action through which separate units of a foreseeable and achievable community, which are complementary, and need to strengthen each other, try to join together, partially or totally. Both in its general meaning, and in its political meaning, integration has been defined as an 'action', as a dynamic factor which regardless of whether it leads or not, to the complete achievement of an integrum, or of a community, is maintained in motion by its own rationale. Such an action is propelled by motives objectively superior and dialectically opposed to the erstwhile autonomy of the component parts. In the present case the motive power is the pressure of interdependence. The success of the 'action' will depend on the farsightedness, determination and talent of those who are convinced of the necessity of the purpose.

But most of the senses in which the concept of integration is used politically do not repel patriotic citizens or leaders of nation states. In particular the concepts of social integration and national integration are highly regarded. The two senses are often coupled together, honourably, as in Disraeli's concept of 'One Nation', dishonourably as in Lenin and Stalin's 'socialism in one country', and most horribly in Hitler's 'National-Socialism'. Of late the process of social, or as it is less ideologically called, 'societal' integration, has been, as so often repeated here, the great achievement of developed democratic states. In most of these states the class struggle, and even the differences between classes, have been greatly attenuated by the expansion of the vast categories of the middle classes. This has been caused by the transformation of much heavy manual labour into technically skilled labour, and by the increasing availability of domestic amenities resulting from the application of technology in the domestic sphere. In spite of the accentuation of the extremes, the fabulously rich and the miserably poor, the expansion of the middle classes has led to greater social homogeneity, and as a consequence to the collapse of the class ideology of revolutionary Marxism-Leninism.

But it is from a societal point of view that this homogeneity is even more evident. The expansion of the middle classes has occurred at the same time as the information revolution which, by keeping everybody everywhere 'in touch' with world developments, has brought about a greater cultural and political integration, a new awareness and participation. Tocqueville had prophesied this new societal integration when he wrote about the nascent American democracy: 'In spite of the differences which wealth and poverty, authority and obedience, create between two human beings, the common mentality based on the acceptance of the normal course of life itself, brings them together at the same level and creates between them a kind of imaginary equality, different from the real inequality of their condition'[4].

Societal integration was both the cause and the effect of the politics of all the developed countries (in the sense that they could not become developed if they did not achieve integration, and they could not achieve integration if they had not pursued that purpose with tenacity). 'Welfare', as a means of societal harmony was and is the sacred cow of democratic politics, even if exaggerated by left-wing, and restrained by right-wing governments. Those governments had before their very eyes two examples of national disasters in countries which did not, or could not, follow the politics of societal integration. One was the example of the *disintegration* of the USSR, in which false ideological politics conducted by a dictatorial party led to an unbridgeable cleavage between the ruling clique and the non-responsive, harassed and persecuted population. The catastrophic fall of the communist states provided the *per a contrario* proof of the rightness of democratic politics.

But there is another disastrous example of the failure to achieve societal integration, which because of interdependence raises grave problems of political responsibility for the present and future generations of the statesmen of the developed countries. This is the difficulty – almost the impossibility – for the governments of the less or underdeveloped countries of Latin America, Asia, not to speak of Africa, to achieve a minimum of societal integration without substantial external financial and technological assistance. All the efforts of the international organizations seem to be directed towards this object, and if true and lasting peace can be established after the end of the cold war, it may yet be achieved, if very slowly. Bilateral *dependencia* has been swept aside by *interdependence*, in which the plight of the dependent countries directly affect the conditions of the countries on which they are dependent. The greatest inequality in the world today is that between the developed countries and the rest of the world – and interdependence abhors inequality. The example of the 'three little dragons' the newly-industrialized countries of south-east Asia, which have effected such a successful transition, with initial foreign help, from underdevelopment to a status of competitiveness with the

highly developed countries, is the first encouraging sign of the advance
of less developed countries.

Now, the particular meaning 'integration', which patriotic citizens
and leaders so dislike is specifically 'transnational integration', i.e.
the absorption of their sovereign state in 'communities', with other
allegedly 'equal' partners, and under new names in which the original
name of their countries will only be 'subsidiary'.

By means of a more modern political education the future generation of European statesmen will find, it is hoped, the way of ac-
commodating the old patriotic sentiments with the new and equally
patriotic necessity of following the clear indications of the spirit of
interdependence and above all of the peace it alone can bring.

Indeed, because of its rapid rhythm, interdependence had already
provoked one negative and one positive proof of its omnipotence, just
as the dust of the demolitions marking the end of the cold war began
to settle. The negative proof was Saddam Hussein's invasion and
annexation of Kuwait, a small, neighbouring Arab state. The positive
proof emerged just as quickly. In spite of the danger of being proved
wrong by future developments, it can be stated with confidence
that the almost unanimous condemnation of Iraq by the 150-odd
members of the United Nations which ordered Saddam Hussein to
evacuate Kuwait immediately, had the historic significance of being
the first *de jure* consecration of the *de facto* world interdependence
and of the need for peace. And so did, implicitly and explicitly, the
reappearance on this first occasion of the United Nations as the legal
forum and possible instance of world interdependence. For what
the United Nations' judgement achieved in this first case was the
reassertion of the *right* of the interdependent world to defend itself by
all possible means against those who, anywhere in the world, threaten
peace. What followed after, or will follow, cannot efface the uniquely
universal character of the resolution of the United Nations.

But the failure in December 1990 of the GATT Uruguay Round,
launched in 1986 was, in the context of this book, a great disappointment to those students of politics who still hoped that world
statesmen have by now grasped the right priorities of modern political
judgement. The test of Iraq's defiance was met with the unanimous
answer: 'No more aggression'. GATT should have followed with the
answer: 'No more protectionism'.

The suitability and profitability of the participation of a given
state in one or another trend of interdependence can no longer be
measured in terms of mercantilist national interest. The assessment
of the true national interest consists rather of an actuarial calculation

327

of the disadvantages caused by the opposing, abstaining or delaying country on the whole transnational trend, and in consequence upon the individual country, directly and indirectly. Hence the intensification of the opposite tendency, i.e. of the competition to get, technologically and politically, at the top of the scale and among the initiators; hence also the aggravation of the contrasts between developed and less- or non-developed countries.[5]

On a more general and abstract plane the task of 'reconciliation' of the logic of the 'inside out' state-centred perspectives with the 'outside-in' society-centred perspectives which now faces political judgement will not be easy. It will not be easy so long as national politicians think that interdependence threatens their states and sovereignties. There is no reason why nation-states should disappear: they are still the best balanced political associations. But there is even less reason why they should make the necessary continuation of their existence more difficult by refusing to share power increasingly with their society at home and through it and with it, with the interdependent society at large. The world of interdependence knows enough about the human condition, about the passage of each human being between the mystery of birth and the mystery of death, to take a more positive, even if somewhat resigned, view of the role of politics. With the new mechanisms of politics, which have been described in preceding sections, with the domination of the decentralizing tendency of society over the state and its propensity to centralize, and with the need to maintain order and justice, without either of which the human individual cannot develop and human associations cannot hold together, the modern statesman, like Aristotle's 'true statesman' must 'have his eyes open not only to what is the absolute best, but also to what is best in the present conditions'.[5]

## NOTES AND REFERENCES

1. Susan Strange, 'The Name of the Game' in N.X. Rizopoulos (ed.) *Sea Changes*, New York, 1990, p.243.

2. In *Encounter*, September 1990.

3. In G.Ionescu (ed.) *Between Sovereignty and Integration*, London, 1974, pp. 160 - 1.

4. A. de Tocqueville, *De la démocratie en Amérique*, Paris, 1961 edn, vol. 2, Ch. 5, p.159.

5. Aristotle, *Politics*, (E. Barker edn) Book IV, 1228 B, §3.

# Index

# Index